798

K23

Ostension

Ostension

Word Learning and the Embodied Mind

Chad Engelland

The MIT Press
Cambridge, Massachusetts
London, England

MIT Press books may be purchased at special quantity discounts for business or sales promotional use. For information, please email special_sales@mitpress.mit.edu.

This book was set in ITC Stone Serif Std by Toppan Best-set Premedia Limited, Hong Kong. Printed and bound in the United States of America.

Library of Congress Cataloging-in-Publication Data is available.
ISBN: 978-0-262-02809-7

10 9 8 7 6 5 4 3 2 1

Each mortal thing does one thing and the same:
Deals out that being indoors each one dwells;
Selves—goes its self; *myself* it speaks and spells,
Crying *Whát I do is me: for that I came.*

—Gerard Manley Hopkins, SJ, *Poems*, 54

How does a gesture differ from some other movement?
In that it expresses something?

—Ludwig Wittgenstein, *Big Typescript*, 154

Contents

Preface

The day my wife showed my infant son how to point, I discovered a new wonder. His pointing opened a new way of our being together. He could point out things for us and we could point out things for him, and this reciprocal ability allowed us to consider the same things together. Sharing the world in this way afforded us the means to teach him words for things.

What's puzzling about pointing? To understand such a gesture is to understand that the movement, which naturally arouses our interest, is not the point. Instead, the movement directs us beyond itself to some item in the world. Learning to point requires something more than simply copying the attention-arousing movement. Pointing contains an ingredient of understanding, and this understanding admits of complementary roles: I can point while you follow, or vice versa. How can a prelinguistic child learn to point?

Children can learn to point because it is something they already understand in virtue of their animate, bodily awareness. Specific acts of pointing, in which people take turns deliberately making their interests manifest in a nonlinguistic manner, presuppose a backdrop in which our bodily actions regularly and without a communicative intention make our interests available to others in a prelinguistic way. In fact, deliberate teaching by pointing is something of an anomaly characteristic of modern, Western societies. In any case, it is not needed, because infants are equipped to learn the meaning of words through accidental teaching or speech overheard as language speakers move about the world. I term the movement that enables such learning *ostension*. Included in this class are gestures, bearing, posture, facial expression, tone, and so on. Even absent-minded movements, such as handling something or moving our eyes toward something, tend to betray our interest. Ostension is bodily movement that manifests our engagement with things, whether we wish it to or not. (For instance, suppose I am looking for my glasses, and I go about the room groping and rummaging through things. I am not trying to advertise my intention, but anyone watching will understand, on the basis of my bodily movement, that I am looking for my glasses. Now let's say you spot them and point them out to me. In that case, you intend for your gesture to disclose the intended item to me. When I follow your gesture and find the glasses, I will spontaneously display looks of recognition and satisfaction. The fact that bodily movement can betray our intentions independent of or even against our will is an Augustinian insight.)

Ostension is philosophically puzzling, because it cuts across domains supposedly unbridgeable: public–private, inner–outer, mind–body. A gesture is public, yet it reveals something heretofore private; it is outer, yet it has an inner dimension; it is corporeal, yet it is essentially mental. In its innocent simplicity, it leads us to reconsider the dichotomies that remain our heritage despite our professed anti-Cartesianism.

I dedicate this book to my wife, Isela, and our children, who renew our wonder before things.

Acknowledgments

This book first saw the light of day as a short paper on Augustine and Wittgenstein delivered in Boston at the December 2010 meeting of the American Philosophical Association. Some of my readers may remember that a terrible winter storm kept many on the program from attending. I am grateful to Gareth B. Matthews, my commentator, for his incisive and generous remarks. A few months later he died of cancer. That he would comment on my paper under such circumstances testifies to his commitment to the profession. Other helpful remarks on that paper came from Madeleine L. Arseneault, Michal Gleitman, and Jared Millson, and, via email, from Paul Bloom, David Meconi, SJ, and Irwin Goldstein. Through the stimulation of that reception, a short paper grew into a long book. For the form of the whole, I am particularly indebted to Alex Levine and several anonymous reviewers solicited by my editor, Philip Laughlin. For helpful remarks on different chapters, I am thankful to Robert Sokolowski, Gretchen Gusich, Molly B. Flynn, Alan Rome, and Kevin Klonowski.

Introduction: Minding Ostension

To the despisers of the body I want to say my words. I do not think they should relearn and teach differently, instead they should bid their own bodies farewell—and thus fall silent.

—Friedrich Nietzsche[1]

Plato marked a turning point in the appreciation of language by philosophers. In the *Cratylus*, he shows that words are thoroughly conventional. Those who coin them do so with only a superficial understanding of the things spoken about. Accordingly, philosophical knowledge comes from inquiring into the natures of things rather than from learning to speak. Despite discovering the conventionality of language, Plato still accords speech a crucial role. Insight into the nature of things occurs by means of a conversation carried out with conventional terms: "For this knowledge is not something that can be put into words like other sciences; but *after long-continued intercourse between teacher and pupil, in joint pursuit of the subject*, suddenly, like light flashing forth when a fire is kindled, it is born in the soul and straightway nourishes itself."[2] Words, though conventional, are nonetheless significant, for philosophy occurs in the midst of a dialogue carried out by means of them. In this way, Plato represents a striking alternative to someone like René Descartes, who happened upon his fundamental insight without conversing with anyone else. In the *Discourse on Method*, he recounts the circumstances: "Finding no conversation to divert me and fortunately having no cares or passions to trouble me, I stayed all day shut up alone in a stove-heated room, where I was completely free to converse with myself about my own thoughts."[3]

Hans-Georg Gadamer and Donald Davidson take Plato's dialogical concern as their point of departure.[4] Rather than understand philosophy in Cartesian fashion as a soliloquy in thought undisturbed by the presence of others, both Gadamer and Davidson envision philosophy as a conversation between interlocutors about things. They testify to a turn intrinsic to philosophy in its last century toward conversation as an explicit theme. Such a turn naturally raises the issue of language acquisition. Ludwig Wittgenstein's *Philosophical Investigations* begins by critically appropriating the account of word acquisition in Saint Augustine's *Confessions*, and the issue of word acquisition can be found in other analytic authors such as Willard Van Orman Quine, Wilfrid Sellars, and Stanley Cavell.[5] Nor is this interest exclusive to the analytic tradition. Prompted by Aristotle's *De interpretatione*, Martin Heidegger observes that words emerge from our joint openness to things, and word acquisition comes up in other continental figures such as Maurice Merleau-Ponty, Jürgen Habermas, and Robert Sokolowski.[6] The dialogue of philosophy, emphasized by Plato, originates from ordinary language acquired by ordinary means.

I.1 Philosophical Questions of Mind and Language

Michael Tomasello, one of the foremost psychologists of first word acquisition, remarks that language acquisition is an empirical problem, not a logical one.[7] In my view, language acquisition involves two sets of problems: one that is empirical and one that is philosophical. I would like to isolate my philosophical problematic by distinguishing the acquisition of first words, which presuppose no prior lexicon, and the acquisition of subsequent words, which can call upon the stock of words already acquired for help. In this book, I focus on some of the philosophical questions that arise in first word acquisition. Table I.1 presents these problems.

Ostensive acts, such as gazing and pointing, figure centrally in philosophical discussions concerning how children learn their first words (P1).

Table I.1
Synopsis of problems.

P1	**The Problem of First Word Acquisition**
	What is the principal prelinguistic means for intentions to be aligned and first words learned?
P2	**The Phenomenological Problem**
	Are embodied intentions manifest or inferred?
P3	**The Intersubjective Problem**
	Which theory of mind allows ostensive cues to be bodily borne?
P4	**The Epistemological Problem**
	How can ostensive cues, notoriously ambiguous, be correctly understood?
P5	**The Metaphysical Problem**
	What is the ultimate status of ostension and language?

Augustine says the prelinguistic infant wishes "to show, manifest, or ostend" (*ostendere*) his hidden desires to others; but lacking dexterity and speech he meets with little success.[8] Instead he pays attention to the way the actions of others manifest their intentions and thereby learns the meaning of their words. Augustine calls the manifestation achieved in bodily movement the "natural vocabulary" of human beings.[9] Wittgenstein, though highly critical of Augustine, nonetheless insists that ostension, not ostensive definition, is necessary for children to get an initial handle on words.[10] Ostension differs from the mere association of sound and percept characteristic of Locke and the empiricist tradition.[11] It affords the child public intentional cues to guide the associative process. Ostension likewise figures prominently in recent psychological accounts of word acquisition. Paul Bloom and Michael Tomasello emphasize that infants learn words only by following the intentions of language speakers, and such intentions are made available through gestures and gazes occurring in the context of everyday shared practices.[12] Bloom thinks he vindicates Augustine's account of word acquisition and Tomasello says he endorses Wittgenstein's.

"Ostensive definition" is a familiar topic among analytic authors. W. E. Johnson coined the term to name the way in which meaning could be assigned to proper names through the perceptual presence of the indicated item.[13] Although Johnson does not discuss its use in first word learning, Bertrand Russell makes ostensive definition the basis of word learning: "'Ostensive definition' may be defined as 'any process by which a person is taught to understand a word otherwise than by the use of other words.'"[14] Ostensive definition likewise figures prominently in the Kripke–Putnam account of reference, according to which rigid designators, principally names and natural kinds, are fixed by ostension rather than description.[15] Philosophers of science such as Thomas Kuhn and David Hull accord ostensive definition a central role in the activity of science.[16] In this text, I follow Augustine and Wittgenstein in thinking that first word learning happens thanks to ostension, rather than ostensive definition. Children learn to speak without being trained or taught simply by following the actions of speakers, and the kinds of actions that manifest our intentions are much wider and more variegated than pointing gestures. Even though I focus on ostension in first word learning, much of what I have to say in the last four chapters is relevant to the contemporary analytical appeal to ostensive definition for subsequent word learning.

Why is ostension necessary? Initial word learning requires that the infant share the speaker's intention so that the right association can take place. Ostension provides the prelinguistic means by which the coordination of focus can occur. Donald Davidson calls this coordination "triangulation,"

John Searle "collective intentionality," and psychologists "joint attention." This book examines the philosophical issues that arise with ostension, the bodily manifestation of intention. The most prominent issue made famous by Wittgenstein and Quine concerns the ambiguity of a given ostensive act (P4). One and the same gesture might ostend *ball*, *round*, *red*, or *bouncing*, and these iterated possibilities are just the tip of the iceberg. Concerning this seemingly overwhelming logical ambiguity, the burning question arises (P4): How is the gesture disambiguated so that language learning can occur? Another issue, which deserves more attention, is the question concerning how ostensive acts are available to each of the parties involved. This is the phenomenological question (P2): Do such acts occasion inferences to hidden intentions, or do they make such intentions manifest? Answering that question in the way that I do leads to a related question in the philosophy of mind (P3): What concept of mind allows for the manifestation of intention in bodily movement? Here it becomes necessary to draw on classical resources and develop a new approach to the so-called problem of other minds. Ostension requires that the prelinguistic infant have not only specifically human powers of understanding but also generically animal powers of perception and movement. It is the interweaving of these two kinds of powers that makes ostension possible. Ostension also raises some metaphysical questions concerning the place of animate movement in nature (P5): How do animate movement and language relate to the world as known by modern science? Making sense of ostension requires combining analytic interest in word learning, phenomenological interest in the embodied mind, and classical interest in animate movement.

There is much more to language acquisition than ostension and its attendant problems. Children must have perceptual experience of the world and the kinds of things to be found within it. Moreover, they need syntax, not just semantics; and syntax seems to need more than ostensive acts to get going. Finally, children need miscellaneous skills, such as parsing streams of speech into words, memory, and motivation. Thus ostension is a necessary but not sufficient condition for first word acquisition.

I.2   Contemporary Resources

This book has three parts. In the first, I call upon contemporary philosophical resources and look to empirical research in psychology and neuroscience relevant to ostension in first word learning. In the second, I appropriate historical resources from philosophers who argue for the importance of ostension. In the final part, I investigate the questions that arise in the course of the first two parts. Table I.2 summarizes the theses I defend in the course of the book.

Recent trends in philosophy and science bear on the topic of ostension. As a matter of convention, I regard a philosophical resource as "contemporary" if it was published in the last sixty or seventy years, and "historical" if it was published more than sixty or seventy years ago.[17] In terms of influence, I consider an analytic author contemporary if his or her chief writings come after Wittgenstein's *Philosophical Investigations* (1953), and I consider a continental author contemporary if his or her writings come after Merleau-Ponty's *Phenomenology of Perception* (1945).

In the opening chapters, I look at the role of ostension in the contemporary discussion concerning the problem of first word acquisition (P1) and defend the primacy of ostension (T1.1–5). In dialogue with philosophers and scientists, I argue that the prelinguistic basis for word learning must be public, not private. Ostension, not mere association of sound and percept, accounts for the possibility of learning linguistic conventions. I distinguish ostension from ostensive definition. Whereas the latter involves a communicative intention and presupposes prior linguistic competence, the former does not. Ostension, not ostensive definition, is at work in first word acquisition. Finally, I argue that for ostension to work, the meaning of the language speaker must be available in a prelinguistic way through bodily action. To make sense of such availability requires action theory and phenomenology.

In chapter 1, I examine philosophers such as Quine and Davidson, who insightfully focus on ostension, and I identify what is promising and yet wanting in their accounts. Davidson rightly desires to move Quine further from private evidence in view of the publicness of language. Davidson also recognizes that ostensive acts need not involve a communicative intention. However, his own account of the public basis of language lacks adequacy, because he cannot specify how intentions are publically available. I argue that his investigation would benefit from a phenomenological reconfiguration. A number of important contemporary movements contribute to this phenomenological project. Specifically, certain analyses of perception, action, and life highlight that the mind is on display in bodily movement. As a consequence, the separation of inner and outer proves problematic, and I follow thinkers who instead prefer to speak in terms of the interplay of presence and absence. I conclude the chapter by discussing Gadamer's suggestive analysis of play, which goes a long way toward addressing the lacunae in Quine and Davidson.

Table I.2

Synopsis of theses.

On the Problem of First Word Acquisition (P1)

T1.1   Public, not private, evidence is relevant for explaining first word acquisition.

T1.2   Ostension, not just association, is essential for first word acquisition.

T1.3   Ostension, unlike ostensive definition, need not involve a communicative intention.

T1.4   Ostension, not ostensive definition, makes the meanings of language users publically available to infants in a prelinguistic way (ostensive definition presupposes linguistic competence).

T1.5   Phenomenology and action theory are needed to account for how ostension makes meaning publically available.

On the Phenomenological Problem (P2)

T2.1   Manifestation, not inference, accounts for ostension.

T2.2   "Joint presence" names what ostension achieves more aptly than "triangulation," "collective intentionality," or "joint attention," which suggest a purely mental alignment.

On the Intersubjective Problem (P3)

T3.1   Prelinguistic joint presence happens thanks to the mirroring of bodily movement or animation.

T3.2   Bodily movement, whether deliberate or not, makes manifest our affective engagement with things.

T3.3   Such manifestation occurs against the background of the reciprocal mirroring of animate self and animate other.

On the Epistemological Problem (P4)

T4.1   Ostension is considerably more ambiguous than ostensive definition, because the learner must identify ostensive acts on her own and disambiguate them for herself.

T4.2   Understanding everyday contexts and routines helps us disambiguate ostensive acts.

T4.3   The inclinations of our joint human natures constrain our desires and highlight certain features of the world over others.

T4.4   Ostension affords the learner the opportunity to identify a thing, and this identification is organically related to further growth in understanding the thing in question.

On the Metaphysical Problem (P5)

T5.1   Ostension as manifestation is a philosophical kind of movement irreducible to the mechanical movement of physics and physiology.

T5.2   Language continues to move in the dimension of joint presence first opened up by ostension.

T5.3   Being human involves appropriating the animal power of manifestation for the sake of making a world jointly present.

T5.4   The publicness of language, rooted in our joint animate natures, cannot meaningfully be denied.

T5.5   Manifestation and joint presence have a substantive and not merely methodological priority.

In chapter 2, I turn an appreciative eye toward scientific findings. Research in psychology, evolutionary anthropology, and neuroscience provide background empirical support to the philosophical analysis of ostension. In addition, I highlight where scientific research may be enhanced by adopting a less mentalistic and more phenomenological vocabulary. For example, recent research underscores the importance of an infant's ability to follow the intentions of language speakers in order to learn the meaning of words. The ability to achieve joint attention is typically taken to be thanks to a theory of mind in which the child infers intentions or reads minds. I think the same empirical results sit more comfortably with a phenomenological understanding. Children can learn words because of ostensive cues, which work because bodily movement makes intentions manifest. I conclude the chapter in 2.6 by making the case for the primacy of ostension in first word learning.

I.3 Historical Resources

This book offers four original studies of relevant philosophers, detailing how each thinker handles word acquisition, ostension, the interpersonal reciprocity of the mind–body relation, disambiguation, and the nature of movement and the public character of language (P1–P5). Influential representatives of ancient, medieval, analytic, and continental philosophy share a "family resemblance" concerning the centrality of ostension with its roots in the animate body. Their analyses, drawing upon diverse schools of thought, offer the possibility of transcending the limits of one or another specific tradition. The historical resources thereby set the stage, as it were, for the investigations in the final four chapters. Each historical figure affords a unique perspective that enriches our understanding of ostension.

In chapter 3, I connect Wittgenstein's rejection of private languages to his belief that bodily ostensive acts are necessary for language. His analysis of bodily expression, operative in ostension, leads him to reject the distinction between inner and outer evidence. This chapter underscores the centrality of word acquisition in his thought, its relatedness to the classical tradition, and its kinship with phenomenology. In chapter 4, I turn to a continental figure, Maurice Merleau-Ponty, who likewise provides an account of word acquisition on the basis of ostension. He struggles to work out the ontology of ostension and the reciprocal interpersonal awareness it entails; the interweaving of the body's two dimensions, inner and outer, makes it possible for the visible body to reveal the invisible intention. In my view, he recovers Aristotelian and Augustinian insights into the aware-ness characteristic of the animate body.

In chapter 5, I turn to these classical sources. Augustine is the first thinker to develop an explicit explanation of first word acquisition; he thinks the key ingredient is the naturally disclosive character of bodily movement. He is also the first to account for the reciprocal awareness needed for osten-sion. Acutely aware of the ambiguity of ostension, he suggests that disam-biguation occurs through everyday routines. His view exploits the classical awareness of both the instituted character of words and the disclosure proper to natural movement. I argue that he regards word acquisition as a problem of phenomenology and not epistemology; in this respect he is not a proto-Cartesian, as is all too commonly supposed. In chapter 6, I find sup-port for Augustine's view in Aristotle. Though Plato demonstrates the con-ventional character of words, Aristotle is the first philosopher to have the resources to handle ostension, because he highlights the disclosive charac-ter of bodily movement and the awareness proper to all animals. Ostension and intersubjectivity figure prominently in his defense of the principle of non-contradiction, which holds that something cannot both be and not be at the same time and in the same respect. Aristotle tells us that the denier, Cratylus, was reduced to a plantlike state, able neither to speak nor to point. Finally, Aristotle's analysis of animal perception provides constraints for interpreting ostension.

Why have I included these four thinkers? Augustine, Wittgenstein, and Merleau-Ponty have a developed theory of first word acquisition in terms of bodily movement. These three are, to my knowledge, the three most influ-ential philosophers to have given sustained attention to the topic. Their inclusion, then, should be noncontroversial. But what about Aristotle, who lacks an explicit account of first word acquisition? I have included Aristotle because he articulates the conceptual resources appropriated by Augustine's account; his analysis of animate movement proves crucial to a viable theory of ostension. Why have I excluded other analytic thinkers whose thoughts on word acquisition might merit extended consideration? Part of my strat-egy is to bring about a conversation among ancient, medieval, continental, and analytic philosophers and demonstrate how mutually enriching such a conversation can be. Among analytic philosophers Wittgenstein seems the best representative for this project, because his reflections unfold with reference to Augustine and complement the other thinkers in question. I also happen to think he has a compelling account of ostension, although I do not find it adequate in every respect.

I.4 Philosophical Investigations

The contemporary and historical resources are, to use a Platonic phrase, "a prelude to the song itself," which is the philosophical analysis of ostension carried out in the final four chapters of the work. In chapter 7, I focus on the phenomenological question concerning the appearance of ostensive acts (P2 and T2.1–2). I argue that Wittgenstein, Merleau-Ponty, and Augustine are right that ostensive acts make intentions manifest rather than motivate inferences to hidden intentions. Accordingly, I advocate that we think of sharing items in the world as *joint presence* rather than joint attention. In joint presence, an item in the world is present to at least one of us as present to both of us together.

In chapter 8, I work out the philosophical theory of mind that supports the phenomenological interpretation (P3 and T3.1–3). Animate perception and action, as embodied activities, reveal our intentions to each other. I defend Augustine's and Aristotle's account of the animate mind on display in its bodily actions, and I appropriate Merleau-Ponty's discussion of flesh. Prelinguistic joint presence is possible because perception is an embodied activity that advertises our attentions to others, and because a certain class of animate movements are purposive and betray our intentions. Whether intentionally communicative or not, our bodily movements reveal our intentions to others. These considerations lead me to revise Russell's appeal to analogy along phenomenological lines; there is indeed a mirroring of self and other, but it is based on perception and presence rather than inference and absence. In this regard, I suggest that Aristotle's hylomorphic account of mind, when phenomenologically developed, offers more support for ostension than dualist or behaviorist accounts of mind.

In chapter 9, I turn to the epistemological question concerning the disambiguation of ostension (P4 and T4.1–4). I distinguish between disambiguating ostensive definitions and disambiguating ostension in first word learning. The latter situation is infected with even more ambiguity than the former. I argue that Wittgenstein's appeal to disambiguation through training cannot apply to first word learning, because disambiguation occurs even in the absence of training. I think Augustine's idea that everyday routines and games disambiguate ostension is a valuable one, and I develop some Aristotelian suggestions concerning the way perception privileges some features of the world over others. Our joint bodily natures constrain the world of relevance by our desires and the logic of our perceiving. In this way, the philosophy of mind worked out in the previous chapter provides suggestions for how the notorious ambiguity of ostensive acts is naturally manageable. In a concluding section, I discuss the interplay of language and understanding with reference to Kripke, Putnam, and Kuhn.

In chapter 10, in a speculative spirit I clarify key terms in my argument: animate movement, language, and mind (P5 and T5.1–5). Regarding movement, I contrast the Cartesian reduction of all movement to physical motion with the Platonic and phenomenological view that the movement of manifestation is distinct from, and not reducible to, physical movement. Animate movement makes ostension possible, and I argue that the Cartesian denial of such movement is unsustainable. I think animate movement, inscribed into our ostensive acts, carries on in the words learned; spoken words make the world manifest to each of us together. I reflect on the unique status of the human being who is that animate being capable of moving in the dimension of joint presence, a dimension that builds on basically animal powers of action and perception by putting them into a new, specifically human service. I defend the publicness of language by showing, in my own way, the impossibility of meaningfully denying it. To institute a private language, a human would have to institute a nonhuman way of life. Finally, I argue for the primacy of manifestation as philosophy's proper point of departure and return. Taking ostension seriously has far-reaching implications for thinking about language and the practice of philosophy.

I.5 Phenomenology

The question of this book is prior to epistemology. Instead of the question "What justification do I have for understanding the intentions of another?" this book asks the prior question about the origin of the meaning of our terms. It is a question of intelligibility, not epistemology; a question of availability, not justification. Wittgenstein opens this possibility in his answer to skepticism. He gives not an epistemological rejoinder but a logical one: skepticism cannot be sensibly stated because it presupposes language ordinarily acquired.

The fact that I use the word "hand" and all the other words in my sentence without a second thought, indeed that I should stand before the abyss if I wanted so much as to try doubting their meanings—shews that absence of doubt belongs to the essence of the language-game, that the question "How do I know ..." drags out the language-game, or else does away with it.[18]

To the epistemologically minded reader, this book may sound like an attempt to develop arguments to justify our ascription of mind to others.

The very formulation of such a program, however, requires that there be sense to our terms, and it is just this sense that I seek to elucidate and defend.[19] In this, I agree with the judgment of John Searle:

Epistemology is of very little interest in the philosophy of mind and in the philosophy of language for the simple reason that where mind and language are concerned, very little of our relationship to the phenomena in question is epistemic. The epistemic stance is a very special attitude that we adopt under certain special circumstances. Normally, it plays very little role in our dealings with people or animals.[20]

Here I am concerned precisely with the phenomena of our everyday dealings. I do, however, wish to go further than Searle's bracketing of epistemology by deploying a method for analyzing the phenomena in question: phenomenology. In chapter 9, I will offer a phenomenologically enriched approach to some related topics of epistemology.

I construe phenomenology quite broadly. In my view, examples of phenomenological analysis can be found in ancient, medieval, modern, and analytic philosophy, even though they especially predominate in the movement bearing the name. Phenomenology, as I understand it, focuses on how something is experienced or made present. Accordingly, it employs the language of presence and absence, manifestation and hiddenness. It understands "presence ... as cancelling an absence."[21] Phenomenology studies how something emerges from hiddenness to manifestation. Wittgenstein gives the basically phenomenological injunction: "Don't think, but look!"[22] Such looking is no easy business, because things are shrouded in familiarity: "The aspects of things that are most important for us are hidden because of their simplicity and familiarity. (One is unable to notice something—because it is always before one's eyes.)"[23] So difficult a task is this that Wittgenstein implores divine aid: "God grant the philosopher insight into what lies in front of everyone's eyes."[24]

Merleau-Ponty also thinks what is closest to us is hidden. Perception gives us objects together with other people who are likewise perceiving the world. However, we tend to overlook this joint activity of perception in favor of the objects it gives us:

Our task will be ... to rediscover phenomena, the layer of living experience through which other people and things are first given to us, the system "Self-others-things" as it comes into being; to reawaken perception and foil its trick of allowing us to forget it as a fact and as perception in the interest of the object which it presents to us and of the rational tradition to which it gives rise.[25]

It is an error to reconstruct perception on the basis of the objects it gives us rather than to return to the logic of perception itself. Phenomenology is the attempt to resist this tendency and to look and see what lies in front of everyone's eyes, hidden by dint of its simplicity, familiarity, and effectiveness. It is not a method of introspection.

In analytic circles, phenomenology is usually taken to mean "the description of things from the first-person point of view," which serves as an occasional complement and corrective to objective investigations. John Searle, arguing that his brand of phenomenology is important for contemporary philosophy, puts it this way:

First of all, we begin with the phenomenology of our ordinary experience when we talk about dealing with money, property, government and marriage, not to mention belief, hope, fear, desire and hunger. But the point is that the phenomenological investigation is only the beginning. You then have to go on and investigate logical structures, most of which are not often accessible to phenomenology. And, of course, in the course of the investigation, phenomenology plays another role: it sets conditions of adequacy. You cannot say anything that is phenomenologically false. You cannot say, for example, that every intentional state is conscious or that every intentional action is consciously intended, because that is phenomenologically false.[26]

In continental circles, phenomenology is taken in a more comprehensive manner, as a systematic investigation of how things appear. Now, an appearance requires someone to whom it appears, but that doesn't make appearance merely subjective or contingent. Phenomenology investigates the necessary or "objective" structures at work in a given kind of appearance. Phenomenology identifies fundamental features of experience, such as intentionality, and distinguishes related phenomena such as perceiving, remembering, and anticipating. Sokolowski comments: "The necessity found in such forms of presentation is more like logical necessity than like psychological generality."[27] Phenomenology also investigates how a given topic appears. There can be a phenomenology of material objects in general or even of particular things, such as smoking or trauma.[28] Appearance belongs intrinsically to what is phenomenologically investigated; consequently, the usual contrast between phenomenological and logical investigation is overstated. The logical approach seeks to grasp the necessary structure of the thing in question, and the phenomenological approach holds that the way something appears is an essential part of this necessary structure.

To analyze ostension, I will need to take phenomenology in a way different from how it is typically understood. Analytic authors such as Searle append phenomenological analyses to their logical analyses for such topics as intentionality. Continental authors such as Husserl or Heidegger deploy phenomenological analyses of intentionality, material objects, intersubjectivity, tools, art, and being. These approaches focus on how we experience things. In the case of intersubjectivity, the form of the question often appears as "how can this appearing thing appear as a fellow subject?" Husserl approaches intersubjectivity through pairing, and Heidegger by giving a phenomenology of moods. But the question of ostension is much more complex than intentionality and intersubjectivity. It asks how the intentionality of the other is intersubjectively available in a prelinguistic way. Rather than trying to get into the consciousness of the other, or trying to share the world in a merely global way, ostension concerns *how specific items in the public world can be mutually manifest as the target of joint attention.* Among phenomenologists, Merleau-Ponty seems to have pursued this project furthest. Among other traditions in philosophy, Augustine, Wittgenstein, and Aristotle make exemplary contributions. Accordingly, in the historical chapters, I identify the family resemblance of the various "phenomenological" approaches of these thinkers. I also think contemporary philosophical and scientific trends, as it were, "grope toward" or stand in need of the phenomenological approach. Triangulation and collective intentionality invite a phenomenological account; the concept of "mindreading," with its untoward suggestion of something magical, asks for a phenomenological clarification. As an ostensive act is a bodily movement that *shows* the target of one's intentions, the proper method for this subject matter is one attentive to grasping the manner of such showing.

I.6   The Publicness of Language Logically Entails a Phenomenology of Ostension

Today, no one doubts Plato's thesis in the *Cratylus*. The sounds of our words, even though constrained by certain phonemic patterns, are arbitrarily conjoined to their sense. There is debate about the conventionality of syntax, not semantics. Granting that words mean what they do by convention, the question arises: how do these conventions first come to be shared when no other conventional terms are available to provide definitions or linguistic context? What's at stake in this question, as Quine realized, is the publicness of language. This book seeks to safeguard the publicness of language by showing just what is required to secure it.

For language to be public, its first conventional terms must be established in reference to a prelinguistic commonality. Augustine identifies two ingredients necessary for the constitution of this prelinguistic commonality: the publicness of the perceived world and the publicness of our affective engagement with things by means of our animate action. Let me say something about each, because in what follows I will be in large measure following his lead. Rather than give a causal account of perception in terms of private stimuli, he offers a phenomenological account in terms of joint presence. Each of us perceives and understands with our own powers, but the object of perception and understanding is available equally to everyone. "Yet each one sees it with his own mind, not with mine or yours, or with anyone else's mind, since what is seen is present to all alike who behold it."[29] He therefore distinguishes what is "common and, so to speak, public" from what is "our own individual or, so to speak, private property."[30] Whatever is not altered when perceived is common. For example, both of us can see the same morsel of cake, but only one of us can taste it. How does the publically available world come to be shared in a focused way? How can we see that each of us is seeing the cake (and not, say, the plate, the table, the balloons, the people, or the party favors)? Without some prelinguistic cue for coordinating attention, how would an infant ever learn the word for cake? This is where Augustine makes an original contribution. The perceived movements of our animate bodies, targeting as they do specific items in the public world, enable us to perceive and understand that we are perceiving the same item as another person: "Their intention was disclosed from the movement of their body, as it were, the natural words of all peoples, occurring in the face and the inclination of the eyes and the movements of other parts of the body, and by the tone of voice which indicates whether the mind's affections are to seek and possess or to reject and avoid."[31] The infant can see someone eyeing the last slice of cake, because his bearing and look make it plain. The perception of the natural expressiveness of the animate body allows language to be what it is—common and public—despite the fact it involves conventions and individual resources.

One way to affirm the publicness of language is to deny inwardness altogether, which is the path taken by Quine in his behaviorism. Yet there is an ineluctably inward dimension to this problematic, which Aristotle terms "*pathēmata*" and Augustine "*affectiones*." I've called it "intention" in this introduction. I will also refer to it as "affections" or "affectivity" in the course of my investigations. Our affective engagement with things is not restricted to our emotional responses; whatever is perceived and understood affects us insofar as it is perceived and understood. This inward dimension does not compromise the essentially public character of language. Experience happens for each of us individually and thereby in common. By means of the inward dimension each of us shares in the one public language. Merleau-Ponty puts it this way: "Language leads us to a thought which is no longer ours alone, to a thought which is presumptively universal, though this is never the universality of a pure concept which would be identical for every mind. It is rather the call which a situated thought addresses to other thoughts, equally situated, and each one responds to the call with its own resources."[32] Where are the meanings children learn? They are inside insofar as they *must* be learned (we cannot literally read the minds of others), but outside in the sense they *can* be learned (ostension advertises our minds to others). Put in phenomenological language, meaning is hidden but able to be manifest through ostension.

This book defends the public nature of language against the theoretical pressures to make it something private. In doing so, it safeguards philosophical discourse and ordinary conversation. Its specific focus is first word acquisition, which introduces infants to the most primitive language games. The publicness of language logically entails a phenomenological account of ostension, and this phenomenological account urges us to review and revise how we think about the mind, human nature, and language. In this way, I aim to develop Robert Sokolowski's suggestion: "Phenomenology shows that the mind is a public thing, that it acts and manifests itself out in the open, not just inside its own confines. Everything is outside."[33]

I Contemporary Resources

1   The Philosophy of Action, Perception, and Play

A child learns his first words and sentences by hearing and using them in the presence of appropriate stimuli. These must be external stimuli, for they must act both on the child and on the speaker from whom he is learning.
—Willard Van Orman Quine[1]

How do children learn the meaning of their first words? Thinkers from every theoretical persuasion admit they must make the right association of sound and sense in order for communication to occur. For example, John Locke writes: "To make words serviceable to the end of communication, it is necessary as has been said that they excite in the hearer exactly the same idea they stand for in the mind of the speaker. Without this men fill one another's heads with noise and sounds; but convey not thereby their thoughts, and lay not before one another their ideas, which is the end of discourse and language."[2] The controversy emerges concerning how this association can occur. On Locke's view, the child is simply habituated to the association in the presence of named objects: "For if we will observe how children learn languages, we shall find, that to make them understand what the names of simple ideas or substances stand for, people ordinarily show them the thing whereof they would have them have the idea, and then repeat to them the name that stands for it, as white, sweet, milk, sugar, cat, dog."[3] Training through showing establishes the association.

Locke's association theory passes over just what is most interesting about the process. In the first place, how does the input to the association occur? How, that is, does the language speaker "show" something to a child, and how does the child understand that showing? Much more is involved than a merely mechanical habituation. In the second place, Locke envisions the Western model in which an adult attempts to teach language to children; but as I will detail in chapter 2, such a practice is not universal, nor can it be responsible even in the West for most of a child's first words. The child, rather, succeeds in making the right associations because more is going on than mere associating: the child is following the intentions of language speakers as they go about the world.

Many contemporary philosophers have come to see that ostension explains how the intentions of language speakers are available to infants in a prelinguistic way. In this chapter, I first review the prominent role Quine and Davidson accord ostension. Then, I follow Davidson in censuring Quine's occasional appeal to private evidence, because it undermines the publicness of language learning. I make my own Davidson's suggestion that ostensive acts need not be deliberate by arguing that they do not need a Gricean communicative intention to work. I then point to a lacuna in Davidson and Searle, both of whom assume the prelinguistic availability of intentions to others without giving an adequate account of how this availability occurs. To remedy this lack, I marshal resources from a variety of quarters: an Aristotelian approach to action, an enactive account of perception, the embodied understanding of mind, and the language of presence and absence. Animate actions, such as turning one's body in order to perceive something, make our intentions prelinguistically available. In the concluding section, I show that these various elements are present in Gadamer in an unsystematic way.

1.1 The Relevance of Ostension

Few contemporary philosophers have given word learning as much attention as Quine. His principal justification for singling out behavior as the bearer of meaning comes from how we learn the meaning of our words. "Language is a social art which we all acquire on the evidence solely of other people's overt behavior under publicly recognizable circumstances."[4]

Table 1.1
Chapters 1–2: The problem of first word acquisition.

T1.1	Public, not private, evidence is relevant for explaining first word acquisition.
T1.2	Ostension, not just association, is essential for first word acquisition.
T1.3	Ostension, unlike ostensive definition, need not involve a communicative intention.
T1.4	Ostension, not ostensive definition, makes the meanings of language users publically available to infants in a prelinguistic way (ostensive definition presupposes linguistic competence).
T1.5	Phenomenology and action theory are needed to account for how ostension makes meaning publically available.

If meaning is learned solely through behavior, he reasons, there is no external criterion for determining correctness of meaning. A single behavior might admit of multiple but undetectable interpretations. So, in the famous case, his Western linguist tries to decipher the native's expression of "Gavagai!" The linguist assesses the behavior and practices of the native and decides the native is saying something about the white furry creature hopping past. But what, exactly? Quine says he could be referring to the item as rabbit, as rabbit part, or as stage of rabbit growth.[5] It is possible, further, that behavior and induction from multiple examples will never determine the native's meaning. Quine calls the fundamental ambiguity of behavior the "ostensive predicament."[6] He thinks the problem is not just the ambiguity of gesturing, which Wittgenstein identifies, for he thinks this can be remedied through repetition in various contexts. For Quine, the problem is that to get "rabbit" as the term of the ostension an observer would have to know already what a rabbit unit is, and "this cannot be mastered by pure ostension, however persistent."[7] Only in light of a system of signs can we decide what "gavagai" means, but that meaning could be quite different in another system.[8] Behavior, being intrinsically ambiguous, gives rise to multiple systems, and there is no way of determining whether or not those systems diverge or converge. Thus, the indeterminacy of translation is the logical result of Quine's behaviorism.

In my view, Quine rightly emphasizes the centrality of ostension. He observes that the language learner has to attend to the speaker to see which object he is considering in order to make the right association of sound and sense.[9] However, his commitment to a purely external account of behavior leads him to construe ostension artificially. In one place, he presents the observer as a geometer, who must extend a line from the extended finger until it hits "the ostended point" on a solid surface.[10] The interpreter can decide the extent of the ostended point only by inducing from multiple cases with indeterminacy as the result. This mathematical characterization misses the fact that ostension achieves a joint presence by bodily disclosing for each participant some item in the world charged with interest. The observer turns with the one who ostends to something ostended, not to a geometrical point; some item from the joint world comes to the fore as the object of attention. Ostension makes something jointly present to each, and presence involves people for whom it is present, people who together experience the world but from different points of view. In this way, there is an ineluctably "inward" dimension to ostension, and there is more to behavior than the behaviorist can see. In fact, Quine's occasional pleonasm, "overt behavior," suggests that behavior itself might carry an inwardness he wishes to suppress.[11] He later speaks somewhat more phenomenologically of gestures in terms of "salience":

Pointing ... contributes by heightening the salience of a portion of the visual field. Primitively this salience is conferred on the pointing finger and its immediate background and neighborhood indiscriminately, through the familiar agency of movement and contrast. Even in this primitive effect there is a gain: most of the irrelevant stretches of the scene are eliminated from attention, and much laborious elimination by induction is thus averted.[12]

But what does it mean to "heighten salience" except to make outwardly manifest something inward, namely one's attention? The ostended item now appears as an item engaging your attention; without the ostension, your attention would remain hidden; with the ostension, it is made plain. Movement and contrast make manifest; they lose this effect when construed behavioristically. Quine is right to emphasize ostension, but he does not see all there is to see in the phenomenon.

Davidson adopts Quine's understanding of ostension and interpretation. He advances the problematic by bringing out the complex relationality at work:

There is a prelinguistic, precognitive situation which seems to me to constitute a necessary condition for thought and language, a condition that can exist independent of thought, and can therefore precede it. Both in the case of nonhuman animals and in the case of small children, it is a condition that can be observed to obtain. The basic situation is one that involves two or more creatures simultaneously in interaction with each other and with the world they share; it is what I call *triangulation*.[13]

Each participant engages an item in the world as engaged by the other participant:

It is the result of a threefold interaction, an interaction which is twofold from the point of view of each of the two agents: each is interacting simultaneously with the world and with the other agent. To put this in a slightly different way, each creature learns to correlate the reactions of other creatures with changes or objects in the world to which it also reacts.[14]

I find this account particularly illuminating, because it clearly points out that the key achievement for triangulation is the ability to "correlate the reactions of other creatures with changes or objects in the world." Elsewhere he suggestively characterizes this correlation as "tuning in" or "reacting in concert" to the responses of others to things.[15] He says triangulation is necessary for the advent of thought because the interaction with another gives rise to the possibility of error and thus objectivity, and because it accounts for the content of our thought in terms of publically available items in our world. For Davidson, language is the specifically human achievement that makes use of the basically animal power of triangulating in order to understand the world.[16]

1.2 The Irrelevance of Inner Evidence

According to Quine, "Ostensive learning is fundamental, and requires observability. The child and the parent must both see red when the child learns 'red', and one of them must see also that the other sees red at the same time."[17] Davidson thinks he is more faithful to Quine's problematic than Quine himself. Davidson agrees with the "triangular arrangement" but notes the problem with the way Quine characterizes the evidence that makes observability possible. Davidson writes, "[Quine] adds that instead of speaking of the joint witnessing of an occasion it would be more precise to speak of witnesses subject to receptually similar impingements—that is, subject to similar patterns of nerve firings."[18] Davidson distinguishes Quine's "proximal" view of evidence from a "distal" view. According to the proximal view, only private nerve stimuli count as evidence. According to the distal view, intersubjectively available objects and events count as evidence. Davidson argues that Quine's proximal view undermines the public character of language and leads in Cartesian fashion to relativism and skepticism.[19] He does not dispute the scientific findings concerning the nervous system cited by advocates of the proximal view, but he does deny the skeptical implications of those findings.[20] For joint meaning, physiology is not enough, because we need to look outside "the skin of the speaker" to understand the meaning of the speaker.[21] Proximal evidence is irrelevant for joint understanding:

The difficulty is that your pattern of stimulations and mine are guaranteed to prompt assent to distally intertranslatable sentences only if those patterns are caused by the same distal events. Such a theory would be a distal theory in transparent disguise, since the basis of translating your sentences into mine (and hence for comparing our sensory stimulations) would depend on the shared external situations that caused both our various stimulations and our verbal responses. All mention of sensory stimulations or other causal intermediaries could be dropped without cost to the theory of meaning, or the account of evidence and knowledge.[22]

Though Davidson does not do so, his line of thought should lead him to invert the referents for distal and proximal. The public items of the world are proximal or most manifest; the private sensations are distal insofar as they are not available as such to ordinary experience. I do not think someone who never triangulated with another (a bizarre possibility to be sure) would for that matter understand the object of his or her thoughts in terms of nerve stimuli. The natural perspective is to think that we perceive things, not nerve stimuli; as Hume points out, it takes a bit of philosophy to coax someone into believing in some kind of mental (or neural) mediation.[23] Dagfinn Føllesdal, it seems to me, gets it exactly right: "In my daily life, where I learn and use language, I cannot observe the sensory stimuli of others. And I have never observed my own."[24] In any event, I endorse Davidson's conclusion that triangulation rules out the "proximal" content of nerve stimuli, which are necessarily private and so not candidates for triangulation, in favor of the "distal" content of items in the public world. He thinks what holds for meaning holds for first language acquisition as well.[25]

Human conversation, opened up by ostension, requires public, not private, evidence. In analyzing ostension, I am methodologically bracketing private evidence. I am not denying its existence; I am just denying its relevance for the topic at hand. This does not amount to a behavioristic rejection of the mental. Rather, I think the mind is on display in animate behavior. The mind of another is genuinely given and thus public in his or her animate activity, even though that mind is given to me in way that differs from the way it is given to him or her. There is a difference in the *manner* of givenness, not in the *fact* of givenness.

1.3   The Irrelevance of Communicative Intentions

According to the usual picture of ostension in first language learning, an adult language speaker gets the attention of an infant non–language speaker and then baptizes a present object with a conventional name: "This is a 'fork.'" Ostension, it seems, trades on just this triangulation of language speaker, infant, and object in the world, a triangulation accomplished principally by the adult. Davidson suggests the teacher need not be teaching for the child to be learning: "Consider the situation that is fundamental in the acquisition of a first language: ostensive learning (which may be intentional on the part of a teacher or parent, or simply a matter of the initiate picking things up from the linguistic environment)."[26] Davidson's point recovers an insight from Augustine, recently confirmed by contemporary psychology: children generally teach themselves the meaning of words adults use. How can children learn words if language speakers are not teaching them? Infants use nonlinguistic cues to figure out what people are doing and thus to figure out what people are speaking about.

Paul Grice thought "M-intentions," later called "communicative intentions," are involved in conversation. To speak is to intend that your listener understand your speaking as being for the sake of motivating an action: "'A meant something by *x*' is (roughly) equivalent to 'A intended the utterance of *x* to produce some effect in an audience by means of the recognition of this intention.'"[27] As we will see in the next chapter, some cognitive scientists and linguists think Grice's communicative intention is necessary for ostension; as I noted above, Quine, too, says that children learn words through "overt behavior," suggesting perhaps that the behavior must be intentionally communicative. Following Augustine and Davidson, I think on the contrary that behavior reveals our intentions just fine even in the absence of a communicative intention. Let's say I see you grimace as you bite into your sandwich. You advertise to me, whether you want to or not, that you dislike the food I made you. Granted you might have grimaced with a specific intention to communicate your displeasure to me, but you need not have. Grimacing is a fairly automatic expression that only good manners and due vigilance can restrain. Consider another scenario. After hearing the novel Basque term, "Gatza," I see a little container with white crystals passed to the speaker. No one was trying to teach me the word (I am the only non–Basque speaker at the table, and, while they are trying to include me in the conversation as much as possible, no one thinks to try to include me on such a mundane feature of meal-taking). The action of passing the salt naturally focuses attention on the salt even if no one specifically intends it to do so. (How can you be sure the word signifies the salt and not the passing? You can't, without repetition in different contexts.) For prelinguistic sharing of attention, a Gricean communicative intention is not necessary.

1.4 The Need for a Phenomenological Approach to Action

What makes possible the prelinguistic triangulation of self-other-thing? Davidson says, "The interaction must be *made available* to the interacting creatures."[28] He accounts for this availability in terms of the similarity of generalization: "All people generalize naturally in much the same ways."[29] He writes, "The sharing of responses to stimuli found similar allows an interpersonal element to emerge: creatures that share responses can correlate each other's presences with what they are responses to."[30] He does not say just how these patterns of generalizations coordinate into triangulation. Is it just a further generalization about the generalizations of others? Repeated exposure to similar stimuli gives me the concept "fire" and the proposition "fire is painfully hot," and I accordingly avoid it in the future; alongside these generalizations, I further generalize that other people respond to fire similarly; and, by applying the above generalizations to those around us, we can share the world of experience.[31] I think something more complex is occurring than layers of generalization. In the first place, it is one thing for me to avoid fire and something else for me to see someone else doing an activity that I take to be avoiding fire; there is a sameness, to be sure, but there is also a reversal of roles. Second, this reversal involves a phenomenological difference: when I pull back my hand from fire, I do not pay any attention to my bodily behavior; however, anyone else perceives the event by means of the behavior. Third, ostension functions even without a causal reaction or even when the causal chain is unknown.[32] For example, someone could simply turn to the fire while speaking of it. To function as the "framework in which thought and language can evolve,"[33] triangulation requires the reciprocity of role playing, attention to the reciprocity of manifestation, and consideration of the way our movements betray our attentions. The associative principle of similarity is not enough. Triangulation calls for an account of just how the triangle is constituted.

What is true of Davidson's triangulation is true of Searle's collective intentionality. Searle's notion presupposes a background awareness of others: "The biologically primitive sense of the other person as a candidate for shared intentionality is a necessary condition of all collective behavior and hence of all conversation."[34] In calling this awareness biologically primitive, he wishes to exclude an epistemological stance that would handle such awareness through inference: "I do not infer that my dog is conscious, any more than, when I come into a room, I infer that the people present are conscious. I simply respond to them as is appropriate to respond to conscious beings. I just treat them as conscious beings and that is that."[35] Instead, he seems to believe that awareness of others is a brute fact that resists further analysis or can be analyzed further only biologically rather than philosophically.[36] I agree that inference is not at work here and that we are not dealing with an epistemological question. Nonetheless, there is more philosophical work to be done to unpack the phenomenological question (rather than epistemological question) concerning just how the others are *available as conscious beings* in a way that differs, say, from the way tables, chairs, and mannequins are available in the surrounding room. Searle is right that biology can help uncover grounds for believing that a certain animal has conscious experience, but it is not clear to me how the science of biology has the resources to answer the question of availability. For instance, evolutionary biology might speculate as to the usefulness for intentions to be available, and neurology might isolate areas of the brain correlated with the perception of others (in fact, we'll look at both these contributions in the next chapter), but such approaches do not answer the philosophical question concerning how the consciousness is mutually manifest. The phenomenological investigation can characterize how the intentions of others are on display. This will in turn invite the discovery of the corresponding logical structure.

With the question of the prelinguistic availability of intention, we arrive at the central question of ostension. I don't think anyone else has broached the question in exactly the way I think it needs to be raised. I do think, however, that a number of contemporary trends contribute in helpful ways to this quest. For mutual availability, the intentions of the other must be put on display in a prelinguistic way, and these intentions must be perceived and understood. Various tributaries converge on the importance of a living being's activities as it is at work in the world, and I think the various voices, largely inspired by Aristotle or phenomenology, furnish the resources for answering the question about ostension: (a) Work on action gives resources for showing how intentions can be available for perception; (b) the enactive account of perception as a kind of action helps make sense of the availability of another's intentions even when he or she is just looking at something; (c) work on the embodied mind provides resources for showing how intentions can be perceived; and (d) the language of presence and absence affords a more public vocabulary than intention and perception for speaking about how minds are together in the world.

(a) Aristotelian Action

How can an action viewed from the outside allow us to see what is "inside" another, namely his or her intentions and affections? This question is ill conceived. Action itself makes plain the intentions of others; action puts the inside on the outside. To understand this claim, we must recapture the interweaving of intention and movement. In *Mind and World*, John McDowell criticizes the naturalistic view of bodily action. According to the naturalistic picture, bodily movements are "mere happenings." Human agency, then, becomes relocated to an inner realm of action that is either understandable in terms of nature or is, in antinaturalistic fashion, not understandable in that way:

Either way, this style of thinking gives spontaneity a role in body action only in the guise of inner items, pictured as imitating bodily goings-on from within, and taken on that ground to be recognizable as intentions or volitions. The bodily goings-on themselves are events in nature; in the context of a disenchanting naturalism, combined with a conviction that the conceptual is *sui generis*, that means that they cannot be imbued with intentionality.[37]

Against naturalistic pressures, McDowell invites us to enrich nature in order to allow for bodily agency: "Intentional bodily actions are actualizations of our active nature in which conceptual capacities are inextricably implicated."[38] He thinks recovering Aristotle's sense of the human as the rational animal whose first nature develops into a second nature gives us the resources for handling this mutual implication.[39] I agree with McDowell's contention that bodily movement is not a mere happening but instead expresses the intentionality of the agent, and I agree that Aristotelian principles are relevant to giving a philosophical account of action today. McDowell's interest, however, consists in getting the mind back into the world. Once it is there, the question becomes: how is one mind manifest to another in a prelinguistic way? His suggestions move us in the right direction.

Michael Thompson's *Life and Action: Elementary Structures of Practice and Practical Thought* is of fundamental significance regarding this complex of issues. Working within Sellars's contrast between the manifest image of Aristotelian or phenomenological philosophy on the one hand and the scientific image on the other, Thompson argues that certain categories central to our self-understanding as living agents can be given a philosophical foundation only on the basis of the manifest image. Among these are the Aristotelian concepts of life-form and action-in-progress.[40] He offers an analytic defense of these concepts in terms of Frege. Another criticism of the naturalistic account of action comes from Alicia Juarrero in *Dynamics in Action: Intentional Behavior as a Complex System*.[41] She argues that action theory remains plagued by a commitment to modern mechanical causality, which in principle cannot account for the intentionality of action and thus for the difference between a wink and a blink. She regards the Aristotelian understanding of context, form, and end as relevant for action, and she finds support for these notions in contemporary biological theory. Both Thompson and Juarrero move us in the same direction as McDowell.

Again, however, my interest is not in action per se but action as revelatory of intention. Coming from an epistemological direction, G. E. M. Anscombe writes in *Intention* that action shows others what our intentions are:

Well, if you want to say at least some true things about a man's intentions, you will have a strong chance of success if you mention what he actually did or is doing. For whatever else he may intend, or whatever may be his intentions in doing what he does, the greater number of the things which you would say straight off a man did or was doing, will be things he intends.[42]

My interest is not in the intended end of an action but in the advertisement of attention that action co-accomplishes. To make my meaning plain, consider the difference between the following descriptions of the same scenario:

(1) I am attempting to pry a Lego piece off of another one. I try various things: I use my fingernail, I try to get a good grip on each piece and pull, and I try to use another piece to dislodge it. In frustration, I give up.

(2) You see me handling some Lego pieces. You see an intent look on my face (a furrowed brow) as I grip the pieces. You see me try to pry a Lego piece off of another one. As I drop them to the floor and let out a sigh, you sense my exasperation.

The first is a description of an activity as it appears to the agent of the activity. The second is a description of an activity as it appears to someone watching. The person watching understands quite a bit even though not a word was spoken and even though the agent was not intending to advertise his engagement and frustration to his companion. This might be clearer if we consider a slight variation that involves a communicative intention:

(3) I want you to see that I am prying a Lego piece off of another one. (You put it there quite inconsiderately, since it is in a hard place to get to.) I grunt a bit and see if you are looking at me as I try various things: I use my fingernail, I try to get a good grip on each piece and pull, and I try to use another piece to dislodge it. In frustration, I give up.

In this case, in addition to doing the action, the agent also wants his companion to pay attention to the action and learn something from it. But the viewer won't, for that reason, learn anything more about the state of affairs than was already available in the second description (with the additional implication of annoyance at the person in question for the state of affairs). The point is that doing an action advertises one's affective engagement to others, and this advertisement need not enter into the intention of the agent at all. In fact, this intention can enter into the intention of the agent, as in the third description, only because it is a feature of all actions that they make affective engagement manifest, as shown in the second description. The original action will be performed although generally with two differences: first, the action might be exaggerated (accompanied, for instance, with groans of annoyance), and second, the agent will look at the viewer to ensure that he is seeing the action. The action, however, is the same.

(b)   Perception as an Action

The account of action as making manifest intention would seem to exclude the manifestation of intention in perception, because perception is a passive process that doesn't change what is perceived. It is here that the value of the enactive or sensorimotor account of perception shows itself. According to the view advocated by the psychologist J. Kevin O'Regan and philosophers Alva Noë and Evan Thompson, we have to do something in order to perceive something.[43] Perception is not a matter of passively modeling the world but of actively exploring it. For example, when we say, "Let me see it," in the presence of a novel object, we want it passed to us, so we can turn it over and get the right angle and perspective on it. Perception is an embodied set of sensorimotor skills that puts us out of our heads among things in the world. I will follow the enactive account of perception in making sense of ostension, not because I am interested in perception per se, but because I am interested in giving an account of how the target of one's perception is available in a nonlinguistic way. It is so available, I argue, because the enactive account of perception is correct: we have to do something to perceive something. Even those who regard perception as more of an internal modeling will surely admit that enactive theorists are right that perception involves a kind of action. When we are walking along the sidewalk and see a cluster of people looking up into the sky, we will naturally look up to see what they are looking at. The reason is that although perception is a passive process—it doesn't change what is perceived—it is an embodied activity and as such advertises the interest of the perceiver. My thesis is not tied to the enactive account, even though it sits better with it than with the internal modeling picture.

(c)   The Enactive, Embodied, or Animate Mind

The enactive account of perception belongs to a larger movement that underscores the mind's animate embodiment. Such thinkers as Francisco Varela, Evan Thompson, Eleanor Rosch, Nicholas Humphrey, Mark Rowlands, Shaun Gallagher, and Dan Zahavi reject the Cartesian separation of mind and body; they take into account recent scientific discoveries while not discounting the first-person point of view.[44] Similarly, Maxine Sheets-Johnstone, drawing on Aristotle and phenomenology, perceptively calls attention to the meaningfulness of animate movement.[45] Thompson's *Mind in Life: Biology, Phenomenology, and the Sciences of Mind* is exemplary, and I will take it as illustrative of the movement.[46] The human mind and its rich experiences is a living, bodily being that enjoys life thanks in part to processes science has discovered and modeled. After working out a philosophy of the organism and embodied sensorimotor subjectivity, Thompson comes, in the final chapter, to the question of intersubjectivity. Following the phenomenologist Edith Stein, he details four stages of empathy or intersubjective understanding:

1. The passive or involuntary coupling or pairing of my living body with your living body in perception and action.
2. The imaginary movement or transposition of myself into your place.
3. The understanding of you as an other to me, and of me as an other to you.
4. The moral perception of you as a person.[47]

For my purposes the first and third are most relevant. Thompson thinks it is the third stage that corresponds with the role of joint attentional scenes in Michael Tomasello's account of word learning.[48] "Through reiterated empathy in joint attentional scenes—the experience of oneself as an other for the other—one can gain a nonegocentric and intersubjective view of one's own lived body as an individual intentional agent in a public world."[49] In chapters 7 and 8, I will offer a similarly motivated account that underscores the sharing of items in that public world. He concludes the work by observing that "the knowing and feeling subject is not the brain in the head, or even the brain plus the body, but the socially and culturally situated person, the enculturated human being."[50] Thompson rightly underscores the embodied, animate mind and points in the direction of cultural learning. My argument picks up where *Mind in Life* leaves off, and it does so by emphasizing the way the second-person perspective, inscribed into our embodied selves, makes items in the world jointly present to each of us together.

(d)   The Language of Presence and Absence

The pre-Socratic philosopher Heraclitus appealed to a common saying when discussing those who did not understand his doctrine: "Not comprehending, they hear like the deaf. The saying is their witness: absent while present."[51] Something can be perceptually present in one way even though it is absent from our understanding and attention. I lean somewhat heavily on the phenomenological language of presence and absence, because I think the term "intentionality" can appear to name something internal and private. "Presence," by contrast, suggests something that is not inside the person but instead in between the person and items in the public world. The selfsame waterfall, for example, can be present to each of us together. To say that we both intend the same waterfall invites needless controversy concerning just what is the target of the intention: the item itself or some kind of private mental representation. In using the language of presence and absence, I am following Heidegger's transformation of Husserl's phenomenology. In *Logical Investigations*, Husserl discussed the interplay of empty and fulfilling intentions: we can simply talk about toasters when none are around, and we can have them perceptually given to us.[52] In *Being and Time*, Heidegger translated this interplay of empty and fulfilling intentions into the language of absence and presence.[53] The toaster can be absent or present to us in different ways; when we go through our morning routine and use the toaster for toasting, it is absent from our explicit consideration (we're thinking about our day, the weather, our sleep, or the child's diaper), but if it starts smoking it comes to conspicuous presence.

I am not the first to find Heidegger's shift in phenomenological terminology valuable. Robert Sokolowski's *Presence and Absence: A Philosophical Investigation of Language and Being* develops Husserlian themes within a Heideggerian vocabulary.[54] Presence and absence enable us to speak of the dynamism at the heart of experience: "When we appreciate the presence of a thing, we appreciate it precisely as not absent: the horizon of its being possibly absent must be there if we are to be aware of the presence. The presence is given as canceling an absence."[55] In *Varieties of Presence*, Noë understands perception in terms of presence:

Instead of thinking of perception as a passage from inside to outside, from in here to out there, I urge ... that we think of perception as a movement from here to there, from this place to that. We ourselves (whole persons) undertake our perceptual consciousness of the world in, with, and in relation to the places where we find ourselves. We are at home in the world.[56]

The emphasis on presence is a valuable one, but its intersubjective possibilities need to be developed. Because we are at home in the world, we can be at home with others among items potentially clothed with words. Because perception does not occur in our heads but in the world, we can come to have items jointly present. It is the movement of our embodied selves that makes items in the world jointly present for prelinguistic participants. I will say more about presence and absence in sections 7.4 and 7.5.

1.5   A Sketch of the Phenomenological Account

Curiously, it is Gadamer who among recent authors comes closest to bringing together action and manifestation. It is curious because, in contrast to Quine and Davidson, Gadamer *disavows* the leading question of this book.

He regards first language learning as "an enigmatic and profoundly veiled process."[57] He writes, "What sort of folly is it to say that a child speaks a 'first' word."[58] Learning is rather a gradual process in which the first steps become what they are only through subsequent developments, and the first evident steps are the result of previous, hidden developments. We do not find in Gadamer an account of first word acquisition, but we do find, scattered here and there, just about all the elements needed to formulate one. Gadamer principally focuses on the truth that comes to presence in the work of art, which he then uses to consider the truth at work in language and human conversation more generally. Central to his analysis of art and conversation is the concept of "play," which encompasses the frolicking of sea otters, the wrestling of grizzlies, the baby's interaction with a ball, the child's pickup game, as well as the adult's sporting event and the theater. In each of these varied activities, the players submit themselves to the movement of the game and thereby participate in something larger than themselves. Gadamer thinks the movement of play is characteristic of nature in general although it admits of a uniquely human modality that underlies communication and deliberate showing.

I would like to focus on two issues he highlights that I find especially relevant to ostension. The first is that play is a kind of movement with a to-and-fro structure endlessly repeated. The ball, for instance, recommends itself for play to the cat and the child because its movement is variable yet regular. Gadamer connects the movement of play to the turn-taking intrinsic to conversations.[59] The second is that this movement in which the players participate involves a presentation to each and potentially to others:

One can say that performing a task successfully "presents it" [*stellt sie dar*]. This phrasing especially suggests itself in the case of a game, for here fulfilling the task does not point to any purposive context. Play is really limited to presenting itself. Thus its mode of being is self-presentation.[60]

Kids playing baseball are not intending to put on a display; they are intending to play the game. However, the play itself is intrinsically a display, and there is much for the spectator to follow. He writes, "Openness toward the spectator is part of the closedness of the play."[61] The reality of play occurs "in between" the players and not in their heads.[62] Appearing belongs essentially to the playing, and, as Gadamer suggests, the same holds true for action and nature more generally. Play, then, involves a reciprocal movement of role-taking, and this movement is made manifest to the players and spectators. "In the end, play is thus the self-representation of its own movement."[63]

Self-presentation is "a universal ontological characteristic of nature."[64] The idea of play entails players capable of self-movement, and Gadamer follows the classical view that living beings exhibit self-movement:

Expressing the thoughts of the Greeks in general, Aristotle had already described self-movement as the most fundamental characteristic of living beings. Whatever is alive has its source of movement within itself and has the form of self-movement. Now play appears as a self-movement that does not pursue any particular end or purpose so much as movement *as* movement, exhibiting so to speak a phenomenon of excess, of living self-representation.[65]

We can perceive such self-expression throughout nature. "And in fact that is just what we perceive in nature—the play of gnats, for example, or all the lively dramatic forms of play we observe in the animal world, especially among their young. All this arises from the basic character of excess striving to express itself in the living being."[66] Animate beings, as self-movers or players, naturally put themselves on display.

Gadamer thinks the self-presenting movement of play takes on a unique quality in the case of human beings, who bring to it purposive rationality: "For the specifically human quality in our play is the self-discipline and order that we impose on our movements when playing, as if particular purposes were involved—just like a child, for example, who counts how often he can bounce the ball on the ground before losing control of it."[67] Rationality lets us take advantage of play's naturally communicative movement. In this bouncing game, for instance, the onlooker could intend the very same thing as the participant: "No one can avoid playing along with the game. Another important aspect of play as a communicative activity, so it seems to me, is that it does not really acknowledge the distance separating the one who plays and the one who watches the play."[68] The viewer is, as it were, drawn into the play. Gadamer gives the example of viewers of a tennis match, who follow each bounce of the ball. What the viewer and player understand is the intention embodied by the movement. In play, he thinks that "something is *intended as something*, even if it not something conceptual, useful, or purposive, but only the pure autonomous regulation of movement."[69]

Gadamer roots showing in the logic of play. In the context of a phenomenology of artistic imitation, he makes some remarks that bear directly on the theme of ostension:

When we show something, we do not intend a relation between the one who shows and the thing shown. Showing points away from itself. We cannot show anything to the person who looks at the act of showing itself, like the dog that looks at the pointing hand. On the contrary, showing something means that the one to whom something is shown sees it correctly for himself.[70]

Showing is a reciprocal act that targets items in the world. It is an invitation to see, and it is satisfied by the other's looking. Still thinking principally of imitation, Gadamer writes about the fulfillment of an act of showing:

What is shown is, so to speak, elicited from the flux of manifold reality. Only what is shown is intended and nothing else. As intended, it is held in view, and thus elevated to a kind of ideality. It is no longer just this or that thing that we can see, but it is now shown and designated as something. An act of identification and, consequently, of recognition occurs whenever we see what it is that we are being shown.[71]

What he says of the showing of art appears equally true of the showing of ostension. Something comes to presence, not just as intended by me, but as intended by another. I recognize the item to be, as it were, bathed in the other's attention.

Gadamer does not mention the role of the body in this connection, but he does recognize its disclosive power. Speaking of the gestures at work in Werner Scholz's pictures, he says, "For what the gesture reveals is the being of meaning rather than the knowledge of meaning."[72] The contrast here seems to be between a phenomenological and an epistemological approach; the one considers the very meaning of gesture, the other the conditions for its certitude. He also points out that the dualistic and behavioristic approaches cannot do justice to the phenomenon: "A gesture is something wholly corporeal and wholly spiritual at one and the same time."[73] Of course, these cryptic remarks call for further analysis.

In Gadamer, the self-presentation characteristic of playful movement provides the foundations for understanding and employing ostensive acts that show items in the world to each other. Though he has many of the elements necessary to give an account of how the intentions are made mutually manifest in a prelinguistic way, he does not put them together. To facilitate the achievement of this end, let me expand on these Gadamerian themes. Playing is obviously quite important in the life of a child, from the infant's first explorations and interactions with things, to ritualized games and routines, to the more elaborate, rule-following behavior opened up by language. The child not only wants to play, she wants to be seen playing, which is an evident cause of delight. If the prelinguistic child can perceive others perceiving her playing, she can perceive others acting. The phenomenological analysis of chapter 7 will renew Gadamer's insight into the public appearance characteristic of play, action, and nature. Gadamer's orientation to art leads him to overlook a characteristic feature of most forms of play that I think is essential for joint presence: the movement of play distinguishes means and ends. The child sees another pick up a ball and throw it and she translates the action into her action space, picking up the ball for herself and throwing it. The interplay of players, the mirroring or interaction of agents, and the world-directness of the play or action prove to be crucial ingredients in the logical account of ostension. I will develop these points at length in chapter 8. Finally, a main issue for ostensive accounts is the problem of disambiguation, which I address in chapter 9. Gadamer's recognition that showing is embedded in play provides important direction on this topic. Ostension takes its place within the playful routines and interactions that fill a child's world.

2 The Science of Prelinguistic Joint Attention

As the cool stream gushed over one hand she spelled into the other the word *water*, first slowly, then rapidly. I stood still, my whole attention fixed upon the motions of her fingers. Suddenly I felt a misty consciousness as of something forgotten—a thrill of returning thought; and somehow the mystery of language was revealed to me. I knew then that "w-a-t-e-r" meant the wonderful cool something that was flowing over my hand.

—Helen Keller[1]

How children learn their first words is a burning issue in contemporary psychology, a topic whose interest is not only ontogenetic but phylogenetic: how children learn their first words might shed light on how humans long ago instituted their first words. This book likewise takes as its point of departure the question of how children learn their first words, but it asks the question in the philosophical, not the psychological voice. That is, it seeks to disclose the prelinguistic resources logically presupposed by first word acquisition, and one of the things logically presupposed is the availability of another's attention through his or her bodily movements. This is a logical remark, not a psychological one. A comment by Wittgenstein might clarify my meaning:

I contemplate a face, and then suddenly notice its likeness to another. I *see* that it has not changed; and yet I see it differently. I call this experience "noticing an aspect."

Its *causes* are of interest to psychologists.

We are interested in the concept and its place among the concepts of experience.[2]

Wittgenstein trains his attention on experience in order to clarify its conceptual structure. The same phenomenon would be of interest to psychologists, but they would look for a causal account, not a philosophical one. How do these two ways of approaching the phenomenon interact? Richly. Merleau-Ponty pioneered a way of doing philosophy in constant dialogue with discoveries of psychology. In doing so, he provided crucial conceptual resources to psychology and related disciplines. In fact, the team that discovered mirror neurons found early encouragement in challenging the traditional compartmentalization of action and perception by reading Merleau-Ponty's groundbreaking phenomenology of intersubjectivity. One of its members, Vittorio Gallese, brought these philosophical analyses to the attention of his colleagues.[3] For this reason, the neuroscientist Marco Iacoboni, who helped research mirror neurons in humans, called the team's method "neurophysiologic phenomenology."[4] Psychologists of first word acquisition regularly find it useful to frame their research programs in terms of the philosophical tradition, and philosophers who turn to the topic would do well to pay heed to the latest psychological research.[5] This book deals with a phenomenon of interest to psychology, but it does so from a philosophical perspective. In this chapter, I want to review some trends in science, especially psychology, relevant to my philosophical topic.

2.1   Word Learning and Joint Attention

The linguist Derek Bickerton usefully distinguishes protolanguage and language. Protolanguage is the sort of communication characteristic of four classes: children from about one to two years of age, trained chimps, feral children, and speakers of pidgin (in which adult language speakers from different languages must resort to an improvised means of communication). All four groups employ words without supervening structure or syntax. They may form sentences but the words are serially ordered without any rules, and these sentences are infected with ambiguity: who gave what to whom can be understood only according to context, not syntax. Protolanguage is necessary for language, though language radically differs in kind because of the introduction of syntax.[6] Sokolowski comments: "Children need a reservoir of protonames before syntax can kick in; the speech of under-two-year-olds is a kind of playful identification of things, still waiting for the rule-governed combinatorics of grammar and syntax."[7] Thus there are two stages of first language acquisition: the acquisition of protolanguage (or words) and the acquisition of syntax.

The means for the second stage of first language acquisition, acquiring syntax, is a matter of some controversy. Tomasello advocates a single process for both word and grammar acquisition, while others, such as Noam Chomsky and Steven Pinker, argue that an innate faculty is at work for formal grammar.[8] The debate concerning the second stage of first word learning is beyond the scope of this book. Instead, I focus on the first stage of first language acquisition in which ostension figures prominently. The role of joint attention for this stage is uncontroversial. As Tomasello writes: "Everyone, of all theoretical persuasions, thus agrees that something like the [joint attention] account given here—with some arguing over details— is necessary for the acquisition of a major part of human linguistic competence."[9] In this section, I would like to highlight just what I take to be in need of clarification regarding the uncontroversial appeal to joint attention. My question is this: how are the attentions of each mutually available for joint attention to take place? I think the usual way of broaching the question treats it one-sidedly as a cognitive problem when it is also a phenomenological one.

Bloom glosses Augustine's account of word acquisition as intention following.[10] In *How Children Learn the Meanings of Words*, he says, "Augustine's proposal is no longer seen as the goofy idea that it once was. Increasing evidence shows that some capacity to understand the minds of others may be present in babies before they begin to speak."[11] Studies show, for instance, that children associate a new word not with what they are looking at but instead with what the speaker is looking at. Moreover, if a speaker is bodily absent and yet a new word is heard in the presence of a new object, children will not learn the word. In one study, researchers had children look at one object while the researcher looked at another one that was hidden from the child. The researcher said, "It's a modi," and the child would look up and try to see the object the researcher was looking at. Later, the child assumed the researcher's object and not the child's was the modi. Another study put children in a room alone playing with a new item. An adult voice from another room said, "Dawnoo! There's a dawnoo!" The children did not learn the word.[12] Bloom speculates that word learning does not begin before twelve months because it "must wait for children to develop enough of an understanding of referential intent to figure out what people are talking about when they use words."[13] He calls this ability a "naïve psychology, or theory of mind," in the sense that it involves an insight that in some cases can be impaired, as with autistic children.

The paradigm of joint attention constitutes a major challenge to a conception of first word learning prominent among many philosophers. Only in modern Western societies do parents spend time trying to teach children words; elsewhere children learn by eavesdropping, and even in Western societies most words are not learned by teaching.[14] Research also shows that beginning at nine months of age infants do have the sophisticated social-cognitive powers necessary to overhear speech with understanding.[15] In that respect, the one-year-old does not simply parrot words; she does role-reversal imitation. Also, children are remarkably good at word acquisition even without feedback, which suggests that word learning happens principally through the infant's own basically reliable understanding of the situation.[16] Many philosophers, such as Locke, Russell, and Wittgenstein, take for granted the modern Western model and hold that children learn language by being taught. The truth of the matter, as Augustine saw, is that children learn language by teaching themselves.

2.2   The Conceptual and Phenomenological Problem of Mind Reading

Tomasello has exploited philosophical resources in his research with humans and chimpanzees. From Wittgenstein, he learned that acquiring speech presupposes a context of practice: "One of the central insights of Wittgenstein's ... trenchant analysis of linguistic communication is that new potential users of a language—for example, children—can break into the code only if they have some other means of communicating with, or at least communing with, mature users."[17] Tomasello thinks that sharing attention through "uncoventualized, uncoded communication," such as pointing in relevant contexts, provides the basis for word acquisition. He adopts John Searle's analysis of collective intentionality, but in contrast to Searle he argues that it is a uniquely human phenomenon that accounts in large measure for uniquely human attributes such as speech.[18] With Rakoczy, he points out that collective intentionality presupposes a mutual availability of intentional agents of action: "Specifically, we-intentionality plausibly builds on, but is not reducible to individual social cognitive abilities to interpret each other. Only if I have some grasp on your acting intentionally, can I enter into a shared we-intentional action with you."[19] I think they are right to push Searle to investigate the phenomenon further, but I think the problem is not just cognitive, not just an issue of "grasping." Rather, the question is phenomenological: How can another's understanding become available for such grasping? It must be embodied and put on display in the world.

In the absence of a phenomenological account of ostension, psychologists are prone to refer to the phenomenal basis of collective intentionality as "mind reading," which suggests it involves something purely cognitive. Bloom, for instance, titles a paper "Mindreading, Communication, and the Learning of the Names for Things," and Tomasello and his colleagues begin a paper with the sentence: "Human beings are the world's experts at mind reading."[20] Prelinguistic joint attention cannot be handled simply by ratcheting up the cognitive powers of the viewer. The intentions themselves must be put on display in order for them to be understood.

At the risk of appearing pedantic, let me further develop the analogy with reading to make my point plain. The reader of a text understands the author's meaning by reading the visible symbols on the page or screen; she does not intuit or infer the author's meaning. No matter how intelligent the reader, the text must be legible for it to be read. Analogously, for the participant in prelinguistic joint attention, the text read is not another's mind; the text read is bodily movement. Referential intent involves not mind reading but body reading, and that's why children don't learn the meaning of words when the speaker is bodily absent.

If a child does not become clued in to the way intentions become visible through the body, he or she can only learn the sounds of language but not its sense. The phenomenon of echolalia, which is especially common among autistic children, illustrates the problem. With echolalia, a child can repeat the sounds of words, sometimes entire movie scripts, but he or she does not understand the words uttered. Such children associate the sounds with various experiences and feelings but not the meanings of the words.[21] What ostension explains is the way objects become initially present to us intersubjectively; having learned the word, we can then talk about things in their absence. To make this point dramatically: a child whose sole exposure to language was the radio would have no way of learning words. The tone of voice would reveal the mood of the speaker, but the child would have no way to pair word-sounds and items in the world. Without ostension, we cannot explain how our intentions become mutually manifest prior to words.

One objection to the primacy of bodily movement would be the fact that blind children learn language quite well, and yet they cannot view the bodily movements of others.[22] Bodily movements, however, can also be perceived through touch. To take a famous example, Helen Keller learned the word "water" by means of her teacher making water present and naming it through tactile bodily movement.[23] Most blind children have the further benefit of hearing words, too. In this case, the child discerns the attentions of language speakers under the supposition that speakers are speaking about what the child is tactilely exploring. One study showed that parents of blind children took a more active role and entered into the child's frame of reference; they spoke more about the child than objects, and they "used their own speech to frame their babies' body actions and facial expressions."[24] Were adults to speak about only what was absent, the child could not learn any words. Blind children can be somewhat delayed in speech development, but they generally fall within the normal range of sighted children. Their situation is different, and bodily movement occurs within a narrower range, but it is still bodily movement that enables joint attention and word acquisition. A chief difference appears to be that whereas the sighted child can enter into the world of communication by reading bodily movement, the blind child relies more on her parents to read her bodily movements. Even here, however, the child must come to understand for herself what the parent is intending.

But is ostension always necessary? Consider the case of the rabbit bounding by that occasions a language speaker to say, "Look, a rabbit!" In this case, the speaker need not move at all, and yet the infant may still be able to discern the meaning, "rabbit." When confronted with the same scene, we generally attend to the moving item and not what remains the same. Even in such a situation, however, the body is still at work manifesting the intention. The child will attend to the posture and orientation of the speaker to make sure he is looking at the same moving thing. Were the speaker looking at his watch or the plane overhead, or were he facing the opposite direction, the child would not take the moving rabbit as the object of attention. Even when it is still, the body bears our intention, and it does so in contrast to other possible positions.[25]

2.3   The Ontogeny and Phylogeny of Joint Attention

Colwyn Trevarthen distinguishes two principal stages of intersubjective development, a schema that has been adopted and expanded by a number of other theorists.[26] The first stage of development is primary intersubjectivity, which involves the infant's understanding of others as "animate agents."[27] At this stage, animal action establishes an identity of agency across the difference of self and other, and the relations are dyadic. The newborn pays attention to human faces and interacts socially by imitating and turn-taking.[28] She understands others as fellow animate beings, and she soon can discern the meaning of more complex dyadic behavior. The infant interacts with another person or with something, or she sees another interacting with something. At this stage, the infant directly perceives the action of another as intentional. Meltzoff and Moore amass evidence that infants pay heed to purposive movement (what they call "human acts"), not physical motion per se. They conclude that "infants are not behaviourists."[29] The philosophers Gallagher and Zahavi remark: "Thus, before we are in a position to theorize, simulate, explain, or predict mental states in others, we are already in a position to interact with and to understand others in terms of their expressions, gestures, intentions, and emotions, and how they act toward ourselves and others."[30]

Developmentally, the second stage emerges around nine months of age with what Tomasello calls a "revolution." Infants begin to understand others as "intentional agents," a skill that differs markedly from that of other primates.[31] Such secondary intersubjectivity builds on the identity of primary subjectivity by introducing not only explicit difference but also the possibility of triadic relations.[32] The dyadic identification with an agent doing an action gives rises to a triadic differentiation of self-other-object. The infant comes to differentiate self and other in relation to some third thing, an item in the world. The infant's action is now not only purposive but also staged; the infant appears aware that multiple means can be employed to achieve the same goal.[33] The infant can complete an act that another fails to do, and she now enters into joint situations or contexts with others.[34]

The acquisition of language affords opportunity for further development. According to Bråten, language gives rise to first-order mental understanding of self and other and then to second-order understanding.[35] Tomasello says that at around four years children come to understand others as "mental agents," that is, no longer simply animate and intentional agents but specifically agents with beliefs that might not be manifest in their behavior.[36] At this point in development, children understand that people can have false beliefs. Gallagher and Zahavi sensibly maintain that narrative enriches the sense of intersubjectivity. The child develops the ability to situate an action within an overarching narrative.[37] The third and fourth stages are not relevant for ostension, though they are needed to round out the developmental account.

Ostension presupposes both primary and secondary intersubjectivity. Primary intersubjectivity makes us and our intentions immediately accessible to each other in our bodily movements. Early infant gestures, like those of chimpanzees, are dyadic and imperative.[38] Secondary intersubjectivity allows for joint attention, triangulation, and collective intentionality. With the development of secondary intersubjectivity, infants begin to make deliberate ostensive gestures such as pointing to some third thing just for the sake of joint attention.[39]

Gesture is thought to play an important role not only in how children acquire their first words but also in how our earliest human ancestors first instituted language. Such theorists as Armstrong, Wilcox, Stokoe, Corballis, and Tomasello valuably build phylogenic accounts around the role of gesture.[40] The appeal to embodied joint attention in this context raises important empirical and theoretical questions. For example, Tomasello criticizes Searle's "promiscuous attribution" of collective intentionality to all social animals, from ants to chimpanzees. A chimpanzee can follow gazes, and it makes sure that its gestures are in the line of sight of the trainer.[41] Nonetheless, chimpanzees appear unable to grasp we-intentionality as such—to understand that both animals are intentional agents who are mutually considering the same together.[42] "Rather, it seems that they do not understand the meaning of this cue—they do not understand either that the human is directing their attention in this direction intentionally or why she is doing so."[43] Chimpanzees can coordinate individual intentionality but not cooperate with joint intentionality. The latter more robust sense of collective intentionality is needed as a cognitive and social prerequisite for instituting and acquiring words. That is, a human child needs to be able to do more than follow gazes, postures, and gestures; she needs to recognize that these actions have reciprocal possibilities. Not only do others gesture to communicate, but the child can gesture too; not only do others speak, but the child can play the role of speaker as well. Intrinsic to collective intentionality, as Tomasello recognizes, is the mutuality of role-reversal imitation: "The child must not only substitute herself for the adult as actor (which occurs in all types of cultural learning) but also substitute the adult for herself as the target of the intentional act (i.e., she must substitute the adult's attentional state as goal for her own attentional state as goal."[44] As we will see, Augustine and Wittgenstein, along with Merleau-Ponty and Aristotle, work out a complex account for just how this reciprocity occurs through the interplay of bodily movement.

2.4   Mirror Neurons and Theory of Mind

Mirror neurons fire both when an act is seen performed by another and when the act is performed by oneself, and they fire only for goal-directed behavior. An object by itself does not arouse mirror neurons, nor does an action that does not appear purposive. Neuroscientists Rizzollati and Sinigaglia write that when a monkey "sees the experimenter shaping his hand into a precision grip and moving it toward the food, it immediately *perceives the meaning* of these 'motor events' and *interprets them* in terms of an *intentional act*."[45] Mirror neurons explain, on the neurophysiological level, the phenomenon of mirroring: "The mirror neuron mechanism captures the intentional dimension of actions, common to both the agent and the observer."[46] Rizzollati and Sinigaglia note that mirror neurons confirm

Merleau-Ponty's assertion that such an understanding happens without a "cognitive operation": "This understanding is completely devoid of any reflexive, conceptual, and/or linguistic mediation as it is based exclusively on the *vocabulary of acts* and the *motor knowledge* on which our capacity to act depends."[47] Accordingly, mirror neurons do not fire when humans see a dog bark, because barking is not part of the repertoire of human actions: "The activity of the mirror neurons is not linked to a specific sensory input; it is bound to the vocabulary of acts that regulates the organization and the execution of movements. Barking just does not belong to the human vocabulary of motor acts."[48] Rizzollati and Sinigaglia note two differences between human mirroring and nonhuman primate mirroring. First, human mirror neurons fire not only for transitive acts that engage an object but also for intransitive acts such as gestures that do not directly engage an object.[49] Second, human mirror neurons fire for the same amount of time as the perceived actor's.[50] In human beings, then, mirror neurons seem capable of supporting not just dyadic relations of actor and object but triadic ones of two humans gesturing. They accordingly speculate that mirror neurons, originally developed for coding transitive acts, might have been the "neural substrate" needed for intransitive and communicative acts.[51] In fact, Michael Arbib argues that mirror neurons enabled the development of the human "language-ready" brain.[52]

Alvin Goldman thinks the discovery supports his version of simulation theory, which is based on the premise that to understand another we have to adopt his or her point of view through a hypothetical mode of mimicry.[53] The neuroscientist Vittorio Gallese argues it supports a more direct yet reflexive view that he terms "embodied simulation."[54] By "embodied," he means that mirroring is a bodily and not a cognitive process. Moving farther in the same direction, Shaun Gallagher takes issue with the very term "simulation" and proposes the term "interaction" instead. On the interactive view, a primary intersubjectivity or what Merleau-Ponty calls "intercorporeality" plays across self and other, making reciprocal bodily manifestation possible. Secondary intersubjectivity, including such cognitive processes as inference and simulation, arises only later and constantly presupposes primary subjectivity:

This kind of perception-based understanding, therefore, is not a form of mindreading or mentalizing. In seeing the actions and expressive movements of the other person, one already sees their meaning in the context of the surrounding world; no inference to a hidden set of mental states (beliefs, desires, etc.) is necessary. At the phenomenological level, when I see the other's action or gesture, I see (I *immediately perceive*) the meaning in the action or gesture. I see the joy or I see the anger, or I see the intention in the face or in the posture or in the gesture or action of the other. I see it. No simulation of what is readily apparent is needed, and no simulation of something more than this is required in the majority of contexts.[55]

Gallagher accordingly regards mirror neurons as supporting primary, not secondary subjectivity. Gallese for his part accepts Gallagher's interpretation and agrees that the immediacy of mirroring rules out inference and hypothetical reasoning.[56] Mirror neurons, then, do not correlate with the two standard accounts of theory of mind: the theory-theory or the simulation model.[57] For higher-level phenomena, no doubt, some theory of mind is at work. In addition to seeing others as fellow animate agents engaging things in the world, we sometimes puzzle over certain behaviors and motives. We can do such complex reasoning, however, only because the other has already been made available to us by means of mirroring animate action. The discovery of mirror neurons confirms the work of the body in giving us immediate access to others through purposive bodily behavior or ostensive acts.

The presence of mirror neurons in other animals corresponds to the animate minds of primary intersubjectivity. At the same time, their difference in human beings enables a closer and more variegated identification with others, opening up the dimension of communicative gesturing and speech characteristic of secondary intersubjectivity. In the historical chapters, I will show that Wittgenstein, Merleau-Ponty, Augustine, and Aristotle understand the role of the animate mind in making joint attention possible. As Iacomboni comments, "Mirror neurons seem to explain why and how Wittgenstein and the existential phenomenologists were correct all along."[58] Rather than *explanation*, I would be more cautious and speak of a *correlation* between the phenomenon and the neurophysiological substrate.[59] In this way, the discovery of mirror neurons indicatively confirms the structure of the philosophical phenomenon. Specifically, the fact that they are keyed to purposive action and fire both for my action and for the action of another lends support to the manifestation account of ostension developed in the following chapters. Mirroring does not require mediation but instead involves a direct identity of self and other based on animate action. Simply by means of perceiving, each of us participates in the actions of others. In chapter 8, I will expound the philosophical approach to the mirroring of self and other necessary for ostension.

2.5   Pragmatics, Gesture, and Accidental Information Transmission

In philosophical circles, ostension names nonlinguistic means for learning words. In *Relevance: Communication and Cognition*, cognitive scientist

Dan Sperber and linguist Deirdre Wilson speak of "ostension" in a closely allied sense. To clarify my meaning, it will be helpful to discuss their use of the term. "We will call such behaviour—behaviour which makes manifest an intention to make something manifest—*ostensive* behaviour or simply *ostension*."[60] What I find valuable in this formulation is the language of manifestation. Despite this connection, my use of ostension differs in important respects. First, a communicative intention is not necessary for behavior to make our intentions manifest. Wilson and Sperber give an example of just such a disclosure, which they call an "accidental information transmission" to distinguish it from what they call ostension: "Mary speaks to Peter: something in her voice or manner makes him think that she is sad. ... This is not what Mary wanted: she was trying to hide her feelings from him."[61] As an example of ostension in their sense they give the following: "Peter asks Mary if she wants to go to the cinema. Mary half-closes her eyes and mimes a yawn. This is a piece of ostensive behavior. Peter recognizes it as such and infers, non-demonstratively, that Mary is tired, that she wants to rest, and that she therefore does not want to go to the cinema."[62] I think ostension in their sense logically presupposes what they call accidental information transmission. Here's what I mean. In the case of their "ostension," why does miming a yawn mean that she is tired? Because in general we yawn when we are tired. Deliberately yawning is revelatory of being tired only because in general nondeliberately yawning is revelatory of being tired. The communicative intention, in other words, does not grant the gesture additional powers of manifestation. (As I mentioned in the last chapter, deliberately communicative acts are generally exaggerated or caricatured versions of non-deliberate ones, and in that way they call attention to themselves as deliberate, but they are not thereby granted additional powers of manifestation. Whether she mimed a yawn or just happened to yawn at that moment, the revelation of tiredness would be the same.) On my view, ostensive behavior need not be intentionally communicative. Mary's tone is ostensive despite her intentions. This first difference is related to a second. Sperber and Wilson think that an ostensive act makes manifest an intention to communicate. When we take ostension more broadly as I do, what ostension manifests is not an intention per se but the target of an intention, namely, a publically available item in the world. Ostension, then, is behavior that makes manifest the target of our intentions, and it can occur either with or without an intention to communicate.

Gesturing has received considerable attention in connection with language. In some cultures, people point with their lips, whole hand, or variations of individual fingers.[63] A number of recent studies focus on the role of such gestures in communication.[64] In doing so, they take gesture in a restricted sense and work within the ambit of a communicative intention. For Susan Goldin-Meadow and David McNeill, gestures are hand movements that accompany deliberate speech acts. Adam Kendon's concept is somewhat broader and includes actions that appear to be done in order to be expressive. He excludes practical actions as well as involuntary ones, such as blushing. Such an understanding of gesture works for ostensive definition but not for ostension in which there is no deliberate intention to communicate. In what follows, accordingly, I will speak quite generally of bodily movement or behavior instead of gesture as that which is at work in ostensive learning.

Sperber and Wilson rightly point to the role of presumed relevance at work in following an ostensive cue. Since I have broadened ostension beyond deliberately communicative actions, I must broaden the assumption of relevance. I not only assume your ostensive gesture is relevant to me. I must assume that your behavior is relevant to you. "An act of ostension carries a guarantee of relevance, and ... this fact—which we will call the *principle of relevance*—makes manifest the intention behind the ostension."[65] They suggest a calculus according to which I think that you think the effort for me to understand will not outweigh the effect of that understanding.[66] Instead of such a calculus, I would put the matter more along the lines of Davidson's principle of charity.[67] In other words, I regard you as a fellow rational agent targeting a good, and therefore I am interested in your behavior as symptomatic of the good that you are pursuing and which I, too, might like to pursue. In chapter 9, I will flesh out this appeal to human nature, with its animal orientation to interaction, food, and play, and its rational orientation to the true and the good, because I think it is at work in helping to constrain the logical ambiguity of ostensive acts.

2.6   Why Ostension Is Necessary

Throughout this chapter and the last, I have examined claims by contemporary thinkers who regard triangulation or joint attention as necessary for first word learning. Some of these authors likewise emphasize ostensive acts as the prelinguistic means for triangulation or joint attention. Now, to conclude the discussion of contemporary resources, I would like to answer the following questions: Why is ostension necessary, and how necessary is it? Also, what is ostension, and how does it differ from ostensive definition?

When an accomplished language speaker happens upon an unknown word, she can turn to the sentential context as well as the broader context of the conversation to make sense of it; she can also ask for or look up a definition. But an infant cannot learn her first words this way, because definitions always presuppose an operative vocabulary. For example, an infant could not learn the word "dog" by being told "Dogs are four-legged mammals that bark." To understand such a definition, she would already have to know the other terms. Definitions work in terms of a network of language. They cannot explain the advent of the network. What can? Even before a child can speak, she interacts with others. This interaction occurs through regular patterns, reflects the natural desires of the participants, and admits turn-taking. Bodily action or ostension builds on this natural interaction and affords the possibility for first words to be learned. To see why, consider the following four scenarios.

First, consider a child who lives an otherwise normal life but never hears any words spoken in her presence. Naturally, such a child might improvise some vocabulary to use with her caregivers, but she would not learn the language of her caregivers (it turns out that they speak to one another, but bizarrely, they never do so in her presence). This scenario shows that simply being in the presence of other people's meaningful actions is not enough for learning their speech. Second, consider that child again. Now she receives a daily phone call from her grandmother, who speaks to her for hours and hours about everything under the sun. Will the child fare any better? She is exposed to speech-sounds, but they are not related to anything present. Even if the grandmother constantly spoke about what was around the child (let's say she's remotely watching on a surveillance camera) but the child could not see the grandma, she would have no reason to believe these sounds were relevant. She might learn word-sounds and parrot them or be moved by them, but they would be connected only with feeling, not with any other features of the world. Even if she did know they were relevant (an impossible supposition), she still would have no way to identify their meanings. Third, consider another scenario in which the child's caregivers are incessantly speaking but always about decidedly absent things: far-off places and events unconnected to the child's frame of reference. Here the child may as well be listening to a phone conversation or the radio. Patterns of sound might be gained, but nothing more. Finally, consider the real-life scenario: the child interacts with her caregivers while they incessantly speak, sometimes about absent things, but sometimes about present things. They are not necessarily trying to teach her any words. They are simply going through the day, occupied by cares and speaking to each other about things and practices that are sometimes relevant to the child. In this case, all the elements for word learning are available: not just speech about present items but also the bodily actions that show which items in the world are relevant to the one speaking. Ostension, we could say, is the Rosetta stone that grants the child entrance to language.

In highlighting the necessity of ostension, I am following mainstream Western philosophy and science, which denies that humans come normally equipped with telepathy or the power to read another's mind.[68] Telepathy is not logically impossible; one can imagine a kind of animal that evolved radio transmitters and receivers, for instance, or immaterial angels that could broadcast their thoughts. Telepathy's existence or nonexistence is a phenomenological and empirical question, and, for several reasons, I do not think human beings have such a power. First, whenever we think we know another's thoughts independent of his speaking, we can identify a *background awareness* of some gesture or expression or behavior that informs it. We generally have a background awareness of others in a room, just as a good driver has a background awareness of other cars nearby. If we hear someone behind us suddenly move or stop his movement, we might wonder what he is up to. The fact, then, that we might have a funny feeling that someone is staring at us need not be chalked up to telepathy; it can be handled by appealing to our perceptual awareness of others nearby and perhaps feelings of self-consciousness (that is, we are especially prone to such feelings if we are doing something unseemly that might motivate staring). In this way, there seems to be no awareness of what another is thinking independent of manifestation through speech or ostension. Second, in our daily interactions with people, we can tell how they are taking what we say *by means of looking at them.* Even something like a blank stare reveals a lot. In texting or emailing, by contrast, it is much more difficult to gauge another's understanding. That is why users inject "emoticons" and exclamation points. If we were telepathic, the bodily absence of the other would presumably make no difference for mutual understanding. To these empirical considerations, let me add two theoretical ones. Communication through speech, art, and ostension make evident use of our embodied sensory capabilities. We hear someone speak, we listen to music, or we see someone gesture. Mind reading independent of bodily sensory capacities would be an ability incongruent with typical human ways of communicating. Moreover, even if we were outfitted with a faculty of mind reading, it would be superfluous; ostension and speech enable our minds to meet without it. For these reasons, I do not think mind reading is part of the normal, everyday endowment of human beings. Because something like telepathy is out of the question, ostension comes to the fore as the means by which our minds can commune in a prelinguistic way so that our first words can be learned.

Ostension differs in important respects from ostensive definition. Some philosophers, such as Bertrand Russell, think language learning is a matter of providing ostensive definitions to initiates. On this view, ostensive definitions wed language to the world. I think this picture is mistaken for four reasons. First, ostensive definition presupposes an explicit learning situation consisting of teacher and student with a reciprocal purpose of teaching and learning words. However, such a situation need not obtain at all. Children can learn words even from language speakers with no intention of teaching, no intention of furnishing ostensive definitions. How can they be clued in? Patterns of action and expressive movements advertise meaning without any intention to teach. Ostension requires no explicit intention on the part of the language speaker, and it requires no explicit intention on the part of the language learner. Naturally and without deliberation, the child can follow the ostensive actions of the language speaker going about the world, and this furnishes the context for first words to be learned. Second, language does a lot more than represent the world; it includes such things as requests, apologies, expressions, and praise. To make sense of first word learning we need a richer panoply of actions than ostensive definition's pointing gesture. We need the full range of ostensive acts and behavior. Third, even when we are talking about the world, only certain sorts of things admit of ostensive definitions. One cannot ostensively define modalities such as hurrying, extremely large things such as the Earth, and extinct things such as the megalodon, but one can so define actions such as "whistling" and medium-sized objects such as "popcorn." Fourth, ostensive definition is ambiguous, because it is typically construed without reference to constraints and context. Ostension, by contrast, names the pattern of actions specified by human nature that sets the stage for words to be learned.

Ostensive definition   A deliberately communicative bodily movement, such as a gesture, that makes an item in the world jointly present and affords the opportunity for an interlocutor to identify a certain kind of item in the world and/or to learn the articulate sound used to present the identified item.

Such a definition can occur thanks to the initiative of the teacher or as a response to the inquiry of the learner. As with a linguistic definition, it presupposes a prior network of known words.

Ostension   An unintentionally communicative bodily movement, arising from a pattern of meaningful human action, that makes an item in the world jointly present and affords the opportunity for an eavesdropper to identify a certain kind of item in the world and/or to learn the articulate sound used to present the identified item.

Ostension does not wed language to the world. As we are already in a joint world of action and perception, ostension allows items in that world to be present to each of us together.

Granting that ostension is necessary in some cases to get speech going, how necessary is it for some other early words such as "uh oh" or "no"? Ostension is at work here as well. When a child hears an adult say "uh oh" while displaying frustration behavior or say "no" while taking something away, the child is positioned to understand the meaning of these terms. Of course, once an operative vocabulary has been acquired a child is also able to learn new words from sentential context and definitions. For example, one time my wife was telling our children about how skateboarding got started during a drought in California when all the swimming pools were drained. In the course of telling the story, she spoke of "the phenomenon of the drought," a phrase that prompted my six-year-old to ask, "What's a 'phenomenon'?" She replied, "It's something happening that's interesting." An abstract term such as "phenomenon" cannot be ostended; it can come to be understood only through sentential context or a definition, which might call upon other abstract terms such as "something," "happening," and perhaps "interesting." There is no way for children to learn highly abstract or recondite terms as their first words.

Ostension in first word learning cuts across the debate over reference. Whether one is a description theorist or a Kripke–Putnam causal theorist (or something in between), one has good reason to think that ostension plays a constitutive role in first word learning. On the one hand, description requires a stock of words to work. A child cannot describe Fido as "Jake's dog" unless she has words for "Jake" and "dog" and some sense of how they can fit together. The initial stock of words cannot be had by descriptions. They have to be learned by ostension. On the other hand, the ostensive definition of proper names and natural kinds tacitly takes advantage of already acquired language to handle the problem of disambiguation. To illustrate this, consider the difference in the following two scenarios. For a child's tenth birthday, her parents bring home a pet from the pound and proclaim, "This is Fido." The child should have no trouble identifying "Fido" as the proper name for her new dog, because among other things she already knows the relevant natural kind terms and the function of articles. Contrast this with another scenario. For a child's first birthday, her parents bring home a pet from the pound and proclaim, "This is Fido." Now, it just so happens that "Fido" would be the infant's first word. Will she think it means the particular dog Fido, a particular breed of dog (say, a Pekinese), any dog whatsoever, or even activities such as barking, jumping, and being loud? Considered in isolation, any act of ostensive definition is ambiguous. Causal theorists might not appeal to description to establish a reference, but the act of ostension at a naming baptism typically involves a network of operative language. Ostension in first word learning is a more radical problem than establishing reference, and it involves more acute troubles concerning disambiguation.

Now that the principal role of ostension is plain, new questions arise: What does ostension look like? What kind of bodily movement makes it possible? How is it disambiguated? What can be said of the movement that is at work in it? I take up these questions in chapters 7, 8, 9, and 10, respectively. But first, critical engagement with key examples from different philosophical traditions will make available to us a rich variety of resources (and some dead ends) for pursuing these systematic questions. The conversation about ostension has already spanned millennia. Before I make my own contribution, I want to appropriate the insights of some of the more significant contributions to that conversation.

II Historical Resources

3   Wittgenstein: Ostension Makes Language Public

One of the most dangerous of ideas for a philosopher is, oddly enough, that we think with our heads or in our heads.

—Ludwig Wittgenstein[1]

When G. E. Moore wished to refute skepticism about the existence of the external world, he proved the existence of two hands as follows: "By holding up my two hands, and saying, as I make a certain gesture with the right hand, 'Here is one hand', and adding, as I make a certain gesture with the left, 'and here is another.'"[2] Moore thought the proof worked because he knew that the premise was true. As readers of Wittgenstein's *On Certainty* are aware, Moore's use of the word "know" greatly troubles Wittgenstein. In thinking it through, Wittgenstein realizes that a skeptic simply has to take language for granted:

The fact that I use the word "hand" and all the other words in my sentence without a second thought, indeed that I should stand before the abyss if I wanted so much as to try doubting their meanings—shews that absence of doubt belongs to the essence of the language-game, that the question "How do I know ..." drags out the language-game, or else does away with it.[3]

While he takes issue with the proof itself, Wittgenstein comes more and more to appreciate the interweaving of words and gestures: "How curious: we should like to explain our understanding of a gesture by means of a translation into words, and the understanding of words by translating them into a gesture. (Thus we are tossed to and fro when we try to found out where understanding properly resides.)"[4] Wittgenstein shifts the philosophical conversation away from skeptical considerations, which dogged modern philosophy since its inception, toward ordinary language and the thicket of issues that surrounds it. In doing so, he retrieves the classical couplet of word and deed:[5]

The origin and the primitive form of the language game is a reaction; only from this can more complicated forms develop.

　　Language—I want to say—is a refinement, "in the beginning was the deed."[6]

Elsewhere, he puts it simply, "Words are deeds."[7] His celebrated notion of language games unites language and action, word and deed.[8]

Wittgenstein's recovery of the interplay of word and deed reveals the incoherence of any attempt to substitute a private language for one's ordinary language. There can be no private deeds and therefore no private words. He takes himself to be the defender of the ordinary language that each of us learned at our parents' knees:

Here we are in enormous danger of wanting to make fine distinctions. ... What we have rather to do is to *accept* the everyday language-game, and to note *false* accounts of the matter *as* false. The primitive language-game which children are taught needs no justification; attempts at justification need to be rejected.[9]

Although epistemological questions are out of place, other sorts of questions nonetheless arise. Every language "is founded on convention."[10] How can our first conventions be acquired? Wittgenstein identifies our language-acquiring abilities with natural abilities proper to our animal natures:

I want to regard man here as an animal; as a primitive being to which one grants instinct but not ratiocination. As a creature in a primitive state. Any logic good enough for a primitive means of communication needs no apology from us. Language did not emerge from some kind of ratiocination.[11]

Ordinary language originates from ordinary animal powers, and it bears the poverty of its origin. And yet: animals "do not use language—if we except the most primitive forms of language."[12] Language, a specifically human acquisition, emerges from primitive, animal forms of communication. With these questions of ontogeny and phylogeny, Wittgenstein insists he is not doing psychology. Rather, he is reflecting on the intrinsic intersubjectivity of meaning and its rootedness in our behavior and practices: "Am I doing child psychology?—I am making a connexion between the concept of teaching and the concept of meaning."[13] At the same time, his account has influenced child psychology. As I mentioned in the introduction, the psychologist Michael Tomasello agrees with Wittgenstein that word acquisition requires joint attention and intention reading within the context of everyday life and its routine social interactions.

　　In this chapter, I begin by examining Wittgenstein's rejection of private languages in view of ostension. I detail his adoption of Augustine's emphasis on ostension in first word acquisition. Then I exhibit his difference with

Augustine concerning the means for disambiguating ostensive gestures: Augustine's infant uses understanding and memory to disambiguate in a given context, and Wittgenstein's infant must simply be coached and corrected. To account for ostensive gestures, Wittgenstein does something novel and phenomenological: he reconfigures the inner and the outer, and denies inner evidence. The inner and the outer differ in their logic, not their evidence, and yet there remains an asymmetrical intersubjective hiddenness that behavior naturally reveals.

3.1 Background: Wittgenstein's Method and Context

My primary goal is not to open up new avenues in Wittgenstein scholarship. At the same time, I do think I am seizing upon a genuine possibility afforded by Wittgenstein himself, even if my aim does not correspond exactly with his own. My interpretation serves the function that someone like Aristotle presses his predecessors to play when, at the beginning of his treatises, he reviews what they have said, aware that he stands on their shoulders even if he claims to see something that they did not. For his part, Wittgenstein welcomes this kind of reading: "I should not like my writing to spare other people the trouble of thinking. But, if possible, to stimulate someone to thoughts of his own."[14]

Wittgenstein's thought can be divided into two periods: the early logical positivism of the *Tractatus Logico-Philosophicus* and the later ordinary language analysis of the *Philosophical Investigations*. It is the later Wittgenstein who makes significant contributions to the understanding of ostension. I will accordingly zero in on the later thinker and ignore all sorts of interesting questions beyond the scope of this book, such as the relation of the earlier to the later thinker and the shortcomings of the earlier analyses. For the same reason, I will have to pass over much that is interesting in the later Wittgenstein as well. In what follows, I will not examine his analyses of rule following or even much of what he has to say about the nature of meaning. Instead, I focus on ostension and how it works.

In the preface to the *Investigations*, Wittgenstein says that its reflections will be seen in the right light only if contrasted with his old way of thinking in the *Tractatus Logico-Philosophicus*. Wittgenstein likens language to a game in which the participants make up the rules as they go along.[15] Everyday language cannot be fixed to an established calculus as had been attempted in the *Tractatus*, not only because of its *ad hoc* and improvisational use of rules, but also because he who would ground language in something more fundamental must use language in the grounding: "When I talk about language (words, sentences, etc.) I must speak the language of every day. Is this language somehow too coarse and material for what we want to say? *Then how is another one to be constructed?*—And how strange that we should be able to do anything at all with the one we have!"[16] When we think we are reflecting *on* language, we are really reflecting *within* language. Reflections *on* language are something like the magician's sleight of hand: all our attention is focused in the wrong place—the real work is happening where he does not have us look. In this case, the philosopher looks at some word, sets it apart to make sense of its magical properties, while the whole time he is using language for analysis. But what if he were to reflect on his use of language while reflecting? Then he would need to reflect on this use, ad infinitum. Yet it seems we cannot be satisfied unless we fall into the absurdity of trying to ground the language we are using by using the language we are using: "Your very questions were framed in this language; they had to be expressed in this language, if there was anything to ask!"[17] When we set a proposition apart for examination, we have to ask how it is used in everyday language, for we "got it from there and nowhere else."[18] There is no getting behind the ordinary language of the everyday.[19] We must accept the ordinary as our particular *Lebensform*: "What has to be accepted, the given, is—so one could say—*forms of life*."[20] It cannot be rejected, because there is no alternative available. Our particular form of life, the language of everyday, is our ground. Wherever there is thinking, there is already language.

Wittgenstein believes philosophy arises when language stops working. Instead of language transparently presenting things, it can happen that the words themselves become reified. The philosophical pseudo-problem then arises: How can this word-sound be paired with something in the world? The philosopher invokes the indexical "this" to wed word and thing:

This is connected with the conception of naming as, so to speak, an occult process. Naming appears as a *queer* connexion of a word with an object.—And you really get such a queer connexion when the philosopher tries to bring out *the* relation between name and thing by staring at an object in front of him and repeating a name or even the word "this" innumerable times. For philosophical problems arise when language *goes on holiday*. And *here* we may indeed fancy naming to be some remarkable act of mind, as it were a baptism of an object. And we can also say the word "this" *to* the object, as it were *address* the object as "this"—a queer use of this word, which doubtless only occurs in doing philosophy.[21]

Wittgenstein thinks philosophers must renounce the task of legitimization and return to the standpoint of ordinary language. In the *Blue Book*, he cites an example of what this return might be like:

We seem to have made a discovery—which I could describe by saying that the ground on which we stood and which appeared to be firm and reliable was found to be boggy and unsafe.—That is, this happens when we philosophize; for as soon as we revert to the standpoint of common sense this *general* uncertainty disappears.[22]

Here Wittgenstein seems to equate philosophy with epistemology and epistemology with skepticism, and to assign himself the task of silencing philosophy before ordinary language. In this connection, Stanley Cavell writes that Wittgenstein was the first to recognize that the skeptical tendency of philosophy reveals the everyday, the ordinary, as that which it would deny.[23] Let me make a pointed criticism of Wittgenstein's project. I share his aversion to epistemology in its skeptical forms, but I think nonetheless there is more to philosophy (and epistemology) than he allows. Philosophy can do such things as contemplate the ordinary as ordinary, and it can give accounts of how we know things. It cannot replace the ordinary, but it can enlarge our understanding of it.

In the midst of this generally destructive program of criticizing his own earlier philosophy and seeking to extinguish the impulse to philosophize, a second Wittgenstein emerges, and it is this Wittgenstein that I find more interesting. Here and there throughout his later writings are hard-won insights produced from his own indefatigable efforts to wrestle with the phenomena in all their complexity. These various gems are something other than a mere return to the ordinary. They philosophically clarify the ordinary without attempting to substitute for it. In other words, I see Wittgenstein's philosophy contribute to a more ennobled understanding of philosophy than he himself articulates. It is not a matter of struggling philosophically against philosophy in order to return to the innocence of the ordinary. Nor is it a matter of rejecting the ordinary viewpoint as an outdated folk account lacking theoretical rigor. Rather, philosophy can rigorously examine the phenomena at work in ordinary experience and uncover its necessary structures. Philosophy is a way of showing the truth of the ordinary and correcting it when its self-understanding goes astray. Like others, I see Wittgenstein contributing toward this phenomenological project even though it goes beyond what he articulated as the task of philosophy.[24]

Wittgenstein's remarks about philosophical method as grammar hint at the more contemplative task I envision for philosophy. For him, philosophers exhibit everyday phenomena that are hidden in virtue of their everydayness. "Philosophy simply puts everything before us, and neither explains nor deduces anything.—Since everything lies open to view there is nothing to explain."[25] Putting things out before us constitutes the difficult task of philosophy, and the exhibition of the phenomenon is the only kind of justification available for such things.

We feel as if we had to *penetrate* [*durchschauen*] phenomena: our investigation, however, is directed not towards phenomena, but, as one might say, towards the *"possibilities"* of phenomena. We remind ourselves, that is to say, of the *kind of statement* that we make about phenomena. ... Our investigation is therefore a grammatical one.[26]

Philosophy not only seeks to silence itself; it seeks to silence itself before the integrity of the phenomena. I think philosophy can do more than analyze ordinary ways of speaking, but I also think ordinary ways of speaking often are more faithful to the phenomena than are theoretical reconstructions. I will say more about the phenomenological project and how it differs from a mere return to the ordinary in 7.5.

3.2   Ostension and the Unintelligibility of Private Languages

I read the private language argument as a refutation of the Cartesian egocentric paradigm. It thus motivates a return to the premodern emphasis on our social nature as linguistic animals. In this respect, I would likely fall into what Richard Eldridge calls the "neo-Aristotelian" school of Wittgenstein interpretation, comprising figures such as Anthony Kenny and Fergus Kerr.[27] When Aristotle confronts the denier of the principle of noncontradiction (PNC), he faces a hurdle. Because speech and argument presuppose the principle, he cannot offer the denier a proof. Yet he realizes that denying the principle is a grave sin against the truth, which effectively reduces the denier to a plantlike state, lacking not only linguistic distinctions but discriminatory perception and action as well. Animals do not regard other animals as both friends and foes at the same time and in the same respect, but the denier of the PNC is committed to denying even these differences. As I will show in chapter 6, Aristotle clears the hurdle by having the denier make the first move, which then provides the basis for arguing that his or her meaningful utterance involves discrimination and therefore implicitly acknowledges the authority of the PNC. Wittgenstein faces an analogous challenge when confronting the denial of the intrinsic publicness of language. He too recognizes it as a grave sin against the truth, which locks us into our heads and undermines the possibility of communication. Like Aristotle, he thinks behavior is a key ingredient in refuting the principle's denial. Wittgenstein rejects private language, because it is divorced from the manifestation of behavior, which he takes to be the origin of meaning. A private language would not be meaningful. Consequently, it would not be a language.

Wittgenstein targets the Cartesian egocentric predicament or the "brain-in-a-vat" scenario. On this view, each of us interprets the world on the basis of private sensations and "in a completely enclosed space."[28] By contrast, Wittgenstein places us out of our heads and in a public world of ostensive gestures. Normally and naturally, we unselfconsciously encounter items in a world that appears to each of us together.

Look at the blue of the sky and say to yourself "How blue the sky is!"—When you do it spontaneously—without philosophical intentions—the idea never crosses your mind that this impression of colour belongs only to *you*. And you have no hesitation in exclaiming that to someone else. And if you point at anything as you say the words you point at the sky. I am saying: you have not the feeling of pointing-into-yourself, which often accompanies "naming the sensation" when one is thinking about "private language." Nor do you think that really you ought not to point to the colour with your hand, but with your attention. (Consider what it means "to point to something with the attention.")[29]

In the place of the egocentric picture, he affirms the primacy of intersubjective experience. Two things follow from this. The private sensation is not the object of meaning, and language comes into being by means of our bodies. I will take each of these in turn.

Wittgenstein deploys a thought experiment to invite us to distinguish the public object of perception, jointly perceived, and the private dimension of perceiving. Suppose each of us had a box available only to our own introspection, and each of us called its content "beetle." We would have no way of knowing whether or not we were talking about the same thing. "Here it would be quite possible for everyone to have something different in his box. One might even imagine such a thing constantly changing. … [T]he thing in the box has no place in the language-game at all; not even as a *something*; for the box might even be empty."[30] The beetle in the box illustrates that the private dimension of sensation is "irrelevant" for meaning. The privatization of perception would undermine language, for we would have nothing in common to talk about.

Language, analogous to a game, functions in virtue of rules, which imply a context or system of signs. Just as a shrug of the shoulders may or may not signify something depending on the context, so words can have various functions in different games.[31] The use of the word, the way it works in a given game, is specified by the rule:

That means that language functions as language only by virtue of the rules we follow in using it. (Just as a game functions as a game only by virtue of its rules.)

And this holds, as a matter of fact, regardless of whether I talk to myself or to others. For neither do I communicate anything to myself if I just associate groups of sounds with random facts on an *ad hoc* basis.

I could also say that if the signs have been invented *ad hoc*, then a system, a rule, has to be invented.[32]

A one-time association of sound and fact would have no use; it would not be a move in a game. Instead of a shoulder shrug in response to a question, it would be like a shoulder shrug with no significance. Meaning requires connection to other moves, and this connection, formulated as a rule, has an identity and repeatability: "Every language-game is based on words 'and objects' being recognized again."[33] How are things recognized as the same?

Wittgenstein presents bodily movement as the natural vehicle for focusing interest. Words and deeds emerge from the public dimension of experience and bodily display, not from private processes. Our attentions are borne bodily toward things jointly perceived. Accordingly, there can be no ostensive definition of a word that is private in principle:

How do I recognize that this is red?—"I see that it is *this*; and then I know that that is what this is called." This?—What?! What kind of answer to this question makes sense?

(You keep on steering toward the idea of the private ostensive definition.)

I could not apply any rules to a *private* transition from what is seen to words. Here the rules really would hang in the air; for the institution of their use is lacking.[34]

Wittgenstein considers whether we could have a private language to name a recurring private sensation. Suppose we kept track of it in a diary with the sign "S." Now, no lexical definition of "S" is possible, but what about an ostensive definition? An inner ostensive gesture cannot yield the criterion of correctness that is necessary for meaning, because such an act lacks the normativity that comes from patterned bodily action.

A definition surely serves to establish the meaning of a sign.—Well, that is done precisely by the concentrating of my attention; for in this way I impress on myself the connexion between the sign and the sensation.—But "I impress in on myself" can only mean: this process brings it about that I remember the connexion *right* in the future. But in the present case I have no criterion of correctness. One would like to say: whatever is going to seem right to me is right. And that only means that here we can't talk about "right."[35]

The criteria for understanding reside in behavior.[36] I can tell someone understands a word by observing his use in the pattern of his behavior;

similarly, I can convey to another the meaning of a word through the pattern of my behavior; finally, I realize the meaning of a word through the pattern of my own behavior. Absent behavior, there is no pattern and therefore no meaning.

Wittgenstein considers the significance of behavior for word learning. Suppose, he says, humans lacked pain-behavior. Though we would still feel pain, we could not have a word for pain, since it could not be taught to others. A smart kid might make up a word for her own sensation, but it would have no use, and she could not explain its meaning to anyone. It would not have a place in the language game.[37] Without behavior, we could not institute and acquire words, because we could not institute or acquire the patterns for their identification. Lacking a method of identification, a private means of notation is not a language game. In rejecting the possibility of a private language, Wittgenstein expresses his fundamental belief concerning our natural starting point. What we can take for granted is the publicness of the world outside our heads, a world of joint perception, action, and meaning.

3.3   An Augustinian Emphasis on Ostension

If there is no private language, then the problem of the publicness of language comes to the fore: how can we come to share words when they exist by convention? Augustine provides the most influential account of word acquisition, and Wittgenstein, who had a great esteem for Augustine, engages the account repeatedly.[38] Wittgenstein makes three criticisms of Augustine's position. First, he regards it as a theory of meaning and argues that it applies only to naming but not to other kinds of meaning; as a result, the place of naming in language is misunderstood.[39] "When Augustine talks about learning language he talks exclusively about how we attach names to things, or understand the names of things. So naming here appears as the foundation, the be-all and end-all of language."[40] Naming, by contrast, is merely a preparation for use: "Naming is so far not a move in the language-game—any more than putting a piece in its place on the board is a move in chess."[41] Wittgenstein's target here is not so much Augustine as his own prior theory in the *Tractatus*.[42] Second, he regards it as a theory of word acquisition, and he argues that it involves ostensive *definition* and therefore the ability of the infant to ask a question in a mental language.[43] As I will argue in chapter 5, this is not an accurate interpretation of Augustine's account of word acquisition, which works by ostension, not ostensive definition; Augustine posits natural powers of understanding, willing, and remembering, but not a preexisting mental language. Third, Wittgenstein argues that ostensive gestures are impossibly ambiguous on their own.[44] Again, I will show in chapter 5 that Augustine was keenly aware of the ambiguity of gesturing.

Despite this pointed critique of Augustine's view of language, a critique that is in significant ways off the mark, Wittgenstein nonetheless largely adopts what he takes to be Augustine's account of first word acquisition. He rejects the associationist account of meaning, which relies on a mechanical process, because he regards intentional cues as necessary for guiding word learning.[45] Instead of *ostensive definition*, which he attributes to Augustine, Wittgenstein substitutes *ostensive training*. According to Wittgenstein, "ostensive definition" requires the ability to "*ask* what the name is,"[46] which in turn entails knowing "how to do something with it."[47] The infant, on Wittgenstein's view, lacks a prior language and such practical know-how. "Ostensive teaching of words," however, proves to be an indispensable part of training: "An important part of the training will consist in the teacher's *pointing to the objects, directing the child's attention to them, and at the same time uttering a word*; for instance, the word 'slab' as he points to that shape."[48] The ostensive gesture, though indispensable, is not sufficient, because the same gesture could mean any number of things depending on the training: "With different training the same ostensive teaching of these words would have effected a quite different understanding."[49] The training provides the disambiguating context for the gesture and specifies the use of the word. For Wittgenstein, Augustine's primitive form of language is part of the natural history of every language speaker: "A child uses such primitive forms of language when it learns to talk. Here the teaching of language is not explanation, but training."[50]

Wittgenstein introduces the notion of "language game" to correct the picture that words correspond to objects on a one-to-one basis. Instead, words function relative to each other and to a given pattern of behavior. In the same way that merely identifying the pieces of the game ("this is a pawn") is not yet a move in the game of chess, so ostensive training is not yet a move in a language game.[51] Merely establishing "This is a slab" does not specify how "Slab!" functions; the language speaker must still show what to do with the ostended item. In this case, when one says "Slab," someone brings one over.[52] How should we understand the relation between the ostension and the game? As I quoted above, Wittgenstein writes, "Every language-game is based on words 'and objects' being recognized again."[53] Ostension occasions an act of identification that allows the same word and object to function repeatedly across different performances of the same language game.

Wittgenstein thinks that we shouldn't misconstrue primitive linguistic expressions as shorthand for more complex ones as though the infant has a complex mental language lurking behind the simple utterances.[54] When a child says "Water!" and expects us to bring her some, we should not think to ourselves: "She says 'water,' but what she thinks is 'I am thirsty. Might I have some water to slake my thirst?'" After all, if an accomplished orator, wandering through a desert, collapses and is found by a caravan, all he or she might say and think is "Water!" Such an expression need not be used as a name; it can be used as a plaintive plea for drink. Only in contrast to subsequent grammar acquisition does the word's usage narrow down to a mere name; originally it is charged with verbal and affective meaning. In one sense, then, the difference between syntax and semantics breaks down for primitive language games; what appear to us as an object word may function as a complete sentence. In another, however, the distinction remains, insofar as subsequent learning will allow the child to take up the term into an unlimited variety of contexts and sentences. Let's suppose a child can't find her teddy bear, and she clues her mother into her sadness. The mother says, "Your bear's on the slab." If the child has participated in the slab game, she will potentially be able to know what in the world her mother is referring to, even though the mother in this case is not asking for the slab to be brought over. Later the child will be able to participate in more complex expressions: to understand and express not just protolanguage but language. The finite items and patterns of action to which she is exposed will come to afford her a palette of expression that is in principle unlimited.

How does ostensive training work? Wittgenstein employs a distinction between signs, which are voluntary, and symptoms, which are not. "In a conversation I can make a sad face as a *sign* of sadness, but it can also be just a symptom. Now in *this* case what does contorting one's face as a *sign* of sadness consist in? I would say: 'I did it on purpose and also ... to him.'"[55] Augustine's account in the *Confessions* has the infant discern the meaning of adults' signs and symptoms:

[1] When people named something and when, following the sound, they moved their body towards something, I would see and retain the fact that that thing received from them this sound which they pronounced when they intended to point it out. Moreover, [2] their intention was disclosed from the movement of their body, as it were, the natural words of all peoples, occurring in the [3] face and the [4] inclination of the eyes and the movements of other parts of the body, and by the [5] tone

of voice [6] which indicates whether the mind's affections are to seek and possess or to reject and avoid.[56]

Each of these Augustinian elements can be found in Wittgenstein. [1] First, he affirms that gestures enable infants to follow intentional cues and, when coupled with training, find their way into a language game. Ostensive gestures prove to be essential for the account: "It is only through explanations that a child *learns* one language by means of another. The language of words through the language of gesture."[57] Wittgenstein regards this necessity as a fact of human nature. Other sorts of beings (I suppose he has in mind angels or telepathic aliens) could handle the matter in a different way.[58]

Wittgenstein's gestural account of word learning raises the question of the learning of gestures. They are part of a system of signs that arise more or less naturally: "The language of gesture is a *language*, but we haven't learned it in the usual sense. That is: we weren't taught it deliberately.— And in any case not by having its signs explained."[59] How does the language of gestures come to be understood? [2] Human beings share a set of voluntary movements that reveal intentions: "There is a particular interplay of movements, words, expressions of face, as of manifestations of reluctance or readiness, which are characteristic of the voluntary movements of a normal human being."[60] The universality of such movements provides the reference point for acquiring language: "The common human way of acting [*Handlungsweise*] is the system of reference by means of which we interpret an unknown language."[61] For instance, he roots the ostensive gesture of pointing in human nature, regarding it as common as checkered board games and systems of writing: "It's in human nature to understand pointing a finger *in this way*. And thus the human language of gestures is in a psychological sense primary."[62] Like Augustine, Wittgenstein thinks we learn words through gestures, and he thinks gestures are rooted in human nature. He argues that gestures are not a kind of a priori language. First, they cannot be instantly understood but require immersion in a form of life. "We don't understand Chinese gestures any more than Chinese sentences."[63] Second, although the language of gestures enables word acquisition, it cannot substitute for them: "It sounds like a ridiculous truism if I say that anyone who believed that gestures are the primary signs that underlie all others would be incapable of replacing the most ordinary sentence with gestures."[64] At the same time, gestures have roots in the behavior of all animals. "What is the natural expression of an intention?—Look at a cat when it stalks a bird; or a beast when it wants to escape."[65]

The parallels to Augustine continue. [3] Wittgenstein regards the face as a gesture manifesting intention. We do not see one thing and make an inference to something else; rather, the play of expressions reveals the movement of another's consciousness:

Look into someone else's face, and see the consciousness in it, and a particular *shade* of consciousness. You see on it, in it, joy, indifference, interest, excitement, torpor and so on. The light in other people's faces.

Do you look into *yourself* in order to recognize the fury in *his* face? It is there as clearly as in your own breast.[66]

[4] Along with our facial expressions, the movements of our eyes betray our attentions to others:

We do not see the human eye as a receiver, it appears not to let anything in, but to send something out. The ear receives; the eye looks. (It casts glances, it flashes, radiates, gleams.) One can terrify with one's eyes, not with one's ear or nose. When you see the eye you see something going out from it. You see the look in the eye.[67]

Laying aside our prejudices and paying attention to the phenomenon, we can see the look of another. "If you only shake free from your physiological prejudices, you will find nothing queer about the fact that the glance of the eye can be seen too."[68] [5] He notes that the various modulations of the voice are ostensive: "There is a strongly musical element in verbal language. (A sigh, the intonation of voice in a question, in an announcement, in longing; all the innumerable *gestures* made with the voice.)"[69] The tone and tempo of speaking reveal the emotions: "A man talks angrily, timidly, sadly, joyfully etc., not lumbagoishly."[70]

Finally, [6] these various voluntary movements, facial expressions, eye movements, gestures, and tonal modulations serve to make manifest one's affections in the pursuit or avoidance of things: "One speaks of a feeling of conviction because there is a *tone* of conviction. For the characteristic mark of all 'feelings' is that there is expression of them, i.e. facial expression, gestures, of feeling."[71] How do these affections aid an infant in learning words? "One says to a child: 'Stop, no more sugar!,' and takes the sugar cube away from him. That's the way a child learns the meaning of the word 'no.'... In this way he has learned to use the word, but also to associate a particular feeling with it, to experience it in a particular way."[72] Gestures indicate the affective movement at work in words. They thereby enable the infant to undertake for himself the very same movement:

Isn't this the way we cause the child to attribute sense to words, without substituting another sign for them, and thus without expressing the sense in a different way?

Aren't we causing him, as it were, to do something for himself, which is given no outward expression, or for which the outward expression serves only as a suggestion?[73]

Wittgenstein remarks that when we cannot recall a word, we attempt to recall "characteristic accompaniments. Primarily: gestures, faces, tones of voice."[74] The child learns words by following the accompaniments of words and by undertaking, for himself, the requisite affective intentions. Such a comprehension is akin to listening to music; it requires a bodily involvement in the movement: "One says 'I understand this gesture' in the same way as 'I understand this theme; it speaks to me,' and here that means: I am involved with it, it engages me: I am involved in a particular way as I follow it."[75] The gesture belongs to a matrix of other gestures and cues:

What does *meaning* this movement as a shrugging of the shoulders consist in? Is what accompanies the movement, when we mean it this way, a certain feeling? Isn't it rather the entire *context* in which the movement is situated? What follows from it, so to speak—what I would say to explain it, or what I say or think to complement it? Would we talk about meaning, the intention of shrugging one's shoulders, for instance, if it occurred in isolation from all other modes of expression?[76]

3.4   An Alternative to Augustine: Disambiguating Ostension through Training

Wittgenstein adopts Augustine's view that ostension enables first word acquisition. The chief difference concerns the role of teaching in their accounts. For Augustine, the child teaches herself the meaning of words by following the intentions of language speakers at play in their gestures and behaviors. The intelligence of the child allows her to understand the gestures in the context of the everyday activities in which they occur. For Wittgenstein, the language speaker must teach the child by pointing things out and habituating her to certain activities. The teacher then looks for her reaction, her behavior and her use of the word, so that the ambiguity of the original ostension can be corrected and its use clarified: "I am using the word 'trained' in a way strictly analogous to that in which we talk of an animal being trained to do certain things. It is done by means of example, reward, punishment, and suchlike."[77] Wittgenstein's account only works for the modern Western model in which the language speaker must set out to teach the infant to speak; as I discussed in chapter 2, psychologists have shown this model to be mistaken. By contrast, Augustine's account of disambiguation explains the fact that children can teach themselves words by overhearing speech paired with ostensive cues.

Wittgenstein underscores the ambiguity of gestures: "Remember that by using the same ostensive gesture toward the same physical object the meaning of different kinds of words can be explained. For example: 'That means "wood,"' 'That means "brown,"' 'That means "penholder."'"[78] The ambiguity of gesturing leads to an unavoidable ambiguity in teaching words by means of gesturing. Wittgenstein thinks we sort out the ambiguity of ostensive definitions by means of a feedback loop. Subsequent use and reactions show whether or not the child made the right connection. In the case of ostensive training, the child must simply become habituated to a certain kind of behavior.

The child knows what something is called if he can reply correctly to the question "what is that called?"

Naturally, the child who is just learning to speak has not yet got the concept *is called* at all.

Can one say of someone who hasn't this concept that he *knows* what such-and-such is called?

The child, I should like to say, learns to react in such-and-such a way; and in so reacting it doesn't so far know anything. Knowing only begins at a later level.[79]

In this respect, Wittgenstein likens the first word acquisition of a human infant to the training of a dog, who learns to go to N when it hears "N." In this case, the dog doesn't "know" what N is called; rather, he has been trained to react in a particular way.[80] Language speakers train infants to speak through the triple of action, use, and reaction: "The children are brought up to perform *these* actions, to use *these* words as they do so, and to react in *this* way to the words of others."[81] Language games emerge from primitive reactions of glances, gestures, or other words.[82] The reaction of the student shows whether or not the teacher has been understood, and it leads to further teaching. Trainers habituate children to the use of words and simultaneously direct them to acquire the corresponding concepts.[83]

Once the infant acquires a primitive form of language, she can initiate the learning process herself and ask for ostensive definitions as well as verbal definitions. The teacher can determine whether the child has understood the ostension rightly by monitoring the subsequent use. Wittgenstein gives the example of teaching someone the meaning of the word "pain":

Perhaps by means of gestures, or by pricking him with a pin and saying: "See, that's what pain is!" This explanation, like any other, he might understand right, wrong, or not at all. And he will shew which he does by his use of the word, in this as in other cases.

If he now said, for example: "Oh, I know what 'pain' means; what I don't know is whether *this*, that I have now, is pain"—we should merely shake our heads and be forced to regard his words as a queer reaction which we have no idea what to do with.[84]

Gestures and actions establish the context in which the meaning can be explained, and the reaction of the learner tells the teacher whether or not the meaning has been understood. Understanding involves more than merely copying or imitating a gesture or sound; it involves grasping for oneself the meaning that is proposed, and this can be understood rightly, wrongly, or not at all. Wittgenstein generally regards the meaning of a word as specified by its use, but use does not exclude the importance of ostension.[85] Use and ostension are reciprocal signs of understanding, so if we explain something to someone by an ostensive definition, we can tell if he understood it by the use he made of it; similarly, if someone uses the word strangely, we can test his understanding by asking him for an ostensive definition.[86] Wittgenstein, then, complements ostensive training with the disambiguation of reaction and use.

One of Wittgenstein's criticisms of Augustine is that not all words are names. Many words behave in ways that do not lend themselves to ostensive gestures. How are these acquired? Wittgenstein recalls an example from his own childhood, filling in the details with speculation:

As a child I once asked about the meaning of the word "something" (or was it "perhaps"?). I was given the answer: "You don't understand that yet." But how should it have been explained! By a definition? Or should it be said that the word was indefinable? I don't know how I learned to understand it later; but probably I learned how to use phrases in which the word appeared. And this learning most closely resembled training [being trained].[87]

Training, then, habituates the child to the right use. But even here, one can wonder how he learned to use the word in different phrases. Certainly, he would have had to pay attention to the way others used it in the context of their interacting with the world, and such interactions would have afforded subtle ostensive cues indispensable to learning to use the word. Elsewhere Wittgenstein writes:

In which cases would you say that a word of a foreign language corresponded to our "perhaps"?—to our expressions of doubt, trust, certainty? You will find that the justification for calling something an expression of doubt, conviction, etc., largely, though of course not wholly, consists in descriptions of gestures, the play of facial expressions, and even the tone of voice.[88]

What affords the possibility of second language acquisition must be at work in first language acquisition. Without gestures, facial expressions, and the tone of voice, the young Wittgenstein could parrot the phrase, maybe even on the appropriate occasions, but he could not be said to understand it.

3.5   Ostension through Perception, Not Inference

How does ostension work? That is, what kind of theory of mind and view of the body make it possible? Wittgenstein articulates and criticizes the standard dualistic view according to which we see the actions of a body from the outside and infer that that body has inside it the evidence that can be known only from introspection:

The characteristic sign of the mental seems to be that one has to guess at it in someone else using external clues and is only *acquainted* with it from one's own case.

But when closer reflection causes this view to go up in smoke, then what turns out is not that the inner is something outer, but that "outer" and "inner" now no longer count as properties of evidence. "Inner evidence" means nothing, and therefore neither does "outer evidence."[89]

Why does the view go up in smoke? Our perception is not limited to the external. We say we perceive someone's doubts, but it doesn't make sense to say that the person perceives his own doubts.[90] "Indeed, often I can describe his inner, as I perceive it, but not his outer."[91] When it comes to emotion, too, he thinks he has good phenomenological evidence for rejecting the inferentialist account:

"We *see* emotion."—As opposed to what?—We do not see facial contortions and make inferences from them (like a doctor framing a diagnosis) to joy, grief, boredom. We describe a face immediately as sad, radiant, bored, even when we are unable to give any other description of the features.—Grief, one would like to say, is personified in the face.

This belongs to the concept of emotion.[92]

Our faces manifest our affects, and Wittgenstein says that we *see* the affective life of another: "In general I do not surmise fear in him—I see it. I do not feel that I am deducing the probable existence of something inside from something outside; rather it is as if the human face were in a way translucent and that I were seeing it not in reflected light but rather in its own."[93] Behavior puts our affective life on public display: "If I see someone writhing in pain with evident cause I do not think: all the same, his feelings are hidden from me."[94] Similarly, an avowal such as "I am in pain" is not the fruit of an introspective act that consults a private inner theater.[95] It is a learned extension of the natural expressiveness of pain-behavior: "You say you're in pain? I can tell."

Though Wittgenstein denies inner evidence, he does not reduce the inner to the outer, but rather regards them as distinct concepts: "What I want to say is surely that the inner differs from the outer in its *logic*. And that logic does indeed explain the expression 'the inner,' makes it understandable."[96] The writhing of a body in pain clearly involves not just the outward movement, "writhing," but also displays the inward experience, "pain." The two concepts belong together, so that without pain-behavior we are not moved to speak of pain experience. "'But doesn't what you say come to this: that there is no pain, for example, without *pain-behavior*?'—It comes to this: only of a living human being and what resembles (behaves like) a living human being can one say: it has sensations; it sees; is blind; hears; is deaf; is conscious or unconscious."[97] He wonders what we would have to do in order to deny inwardness to another body. He answers that we would have to see it acting purely mechanically:

How would a human body have to act so that one would not be inclined to speak of inner and outer states?

Again and again, I think: "like a machine."[98]

Normal human behavior, by contrast, naturally discloses inwardness, which Wittgenstein terms "soul." It leads us to adopt a particular attitude toward someone and to be quite certain about his inwardness: "My attitude towards him is an attitude towards a soul. I am not of the *opinion* that he has a soul."[99] In the midst of our everyday dealings with others behaving naturally, it is meaningless or strange to doubt their aliveness.[100] Why? Because movement manifests the life of the living thing:

Our attitude to what is alive and to what is dead, is not the same. All our reactions are different.—If anyone says: "that cannot simply come from the fact that a living thing moves about in such-and-such a way and a dead one not," then I want to intimate to him that this is a case of the transition "from quantity to quality."[101]

By means of movement that we may quantify, we come to perceive a qualitative difference in what we perceive. For example, human beings react in mostly unpredictable ways and the nuances of behavior are completely unpredictable: "*Important* fine shades of behavior are not predictable."[102] He counts words and ostensive cues among these unpredictable modes of behavior: "Perhaps language, along with tone of voice and the play of features, is the most subtly gradated behaviour of me."[103] Such movement clearly displays the life of a living being.

3.6 Comparison with Russell

Bertrand Russell keenly perceives the central role of ostensive definition for language learning, and he provides an extremely influential account of the problem of other minds that serves as a backdrop to ostensive definition. His account provides a good foil for bringing out just what Wittgenstein accomplishes. Russell points out that an infant's first words cannot be learned through other words, whether linguistic definition or verbal context. There must be an extralinguistic means for teaching words in order for word learning to be possible at all. He terms this extralinguistic means "ostensive definition" and defines it as "any process by which a person is taught to understand a word otherwise than by the use of other words."[104] He notes the ambiguity of ostensive definition; an infant, for instance, might reasonably confuse milk and bottle. He attributes an Augustinian motive to the infant: "Learning to utter words is a joy to the child, largely because it enables him to communicate his wishes more definitely than he had been able to do by crying and making gestures."[105] He also attributes Augustinian powers to the infant mind. He holds that an infant is intentional before it is a linguistic being.[106] He recognizes that acquiring a first language is an even greater cognitive challenge than acquiring a second language:

There are two stages in the acquisition of a foreign language, the first that in which you only understand by translating, the second that in which you can "think" in the foreign language. ... The infant, possessing as yet no language, has to begin with the second stage. His success does credit to the capacities of the infant mind.[107]

Wittgenstein, of course, criticizes Russell (and the early Wittgenstein) in the guise of Augustine. That is, the opening pages of the *Philosophical Investigations*, which scrutinize Augustine's account of word learning, are rightly taken to be a criticism of the kind of account that Russell offers. Wittgenstein points out that prelinguistic children are not capable of registering a definition at all, because definitions presuppose established linguistic competence; mature language speakers can make sense of an ostensive definition because they have a concept of "is called" and can know what to do with the word; prelinguistic infants, however, cannot break into speech through ostensive definitions, for definitions presuppose precisely what is to be explained: they presuppose established linguistic competence. Wittgenstein also finds a second problem with the appeal to ostensive definitions in general, whether for infants or mature linguistic speakers. The act of pointing at something is inherently ambiguous, so an ostensive definition just by itself cannot determine meaning.

This critique of Russell should not mask the substantial agreement between the two thinkers. First, Wittgenstein thinks that ostension, not ostensive definition, is at work in first word learning. The child cannot understand definitions, but nonlinguistic acts, such as pointing and everyday routines, are needed for first word learning. They are a necessary though not a sufficient condition. Second, Wittgenstein and Russell both think that infants must be taught language. They do not consider the Augustinian problematic of infants teaching themselves through overheard speech. Russell, like Wittgenstein, thinks the teacher disambiguates deliberate ostensive acts through correction.

Ostension serves to explain how we can understand the intentions of another person without language. To give an account of ostension entails giving an account of just how we can access another's intentions apart from language. Because Russell follows the mistaken modern Western model, he seems to think he need only account for the awareness that the linguistically competent teacher has of the infant's attention; he need not account for the infant's awareness of the language speaker's attention. Setting aside this defect for the moment, we can examine his account of how ostension occurs. He writes:

A spectator can see when a certain feature of the public environment is attracting a child's attention, and then mention the name of this feature. But how about private experiences, such as stomach-ache, pain, or memory? Certainly some words denoting private kinds of experience are learnt ostensively. This is because the child shows in behaviour what he is feeling; there is a correlation between e.g. pain and tears.[108]

In the last sentence, Russell speaks inexactly. His considered view is not that pain-behavior *shows* a feeling of pain. He thinks instead that pain-behavior occasions an inference to something that cannot be shown, namely, another's pain: "We cannot enter into the minds of others to observe the thoughts and emotions which we infer from their behaviour."[109] Such inference can occur in one of two ways. He thinks belief in another mind occurs in animals and nonphilosophizing humans through what he calls "animal inference," which spontaneously forms a belief on the basis of a sensation without any evident connection between the two.[110] In this case, the dog perceives petting behavior and automatically believes its owner to be positively disposed to him. Russell thinks the belief in other minds occurs in some philosophizing humans through what he calls "analogical inference," which is a scientific form of inference that establishes an evident connection between what is perceived and what is believed:

In animal inference, the percept A causes the idea of B, but there is no awareness of the connection; in scientific inference (whether valid or invalid) there is a belief involving both A and B, which I have expressed by "A is a sign of B." It is the occurrence of a single belief expressing a connection of A and B that distinguishes what is commonly called inference from what I call animal inference.[111]

In the case of other minds, the philosopher connects the visible behavior with an invisible other by means of establishing an analogy of mind and behavior. On the basis of inner evidence conjoined with the experience of moving my own body, I, the philosopher, view another body and infer that its movement correlates to hidden inner evidence from another person:

I now observe an act of the kind B in a body not my own, and I am having no thought or feeling of the kind A. But I still believe, on the basis of self-observation, that only A can cause B; I therefore infer that there was an A which caused B, though it was not an A that I could observe. On this ground I infer that other people's bodies are associated with minds, which resemble mine in proportion as their bodily behavior resembles my own.[112]

Let me connect Russell's account of other minds with his earlier account of ostension. On his view, the father might notice that his infant daughter ran into the table and is now crying and rubbing her head. Though he does not perceive her pain, he perceives her pain-behavior and spontaneously infers pain experience through an animal inference. If he is a philosopher, he can give some justification for this inference in terms of the similar behavior he displays when he experiences pain. He thereby infers that she is in pain and says something like the following: "Did the table give you a boo-boo?" He thereby tries to get her to learn the word "boo-boo" for pain, as well as comfort her in her experience of it.

Are there resources in Russell's account for assigning the infant a more active role in word learning? Might the infant clue in to the attentions of the adult? Clearly, analogical inference is out of the question, because the attempt to justify one's beliefs presupposes, among other things, linguistic competence. Moreover, Russell maintains that analogical inference of other minds presupposes animal inference of others:

The behaviour of other people's bodies—and especially their speech behaviour—is noticeably similar to our own, and our own is noticeably associated with "mental" phenomena. ... We therefore argue that other people's behaviour is also associated with "mental" phenomena. Or rather, we accept this at first as an animal inference, and invent the analogy argument afterwards to rationalize the already existing belief.[113]

He says that even young infants make such animal inferences, and he gives the example of an infant inferring the belief "Mother is angry" from the perception of a loud voice.[114] For Russell, infants could attend to adult intentions perfectly fine without recourse to epistemology and the argument from analogy. If we take this together with his earlier recognition that the cognitive skills necessary for acquiring a first language are more impressive than those necessary for acquiring a second language, we can see evident resources in Russell for having the infant teach herself language through eavesdropping.

Wittgenstein makes two trenchant criticisms of the kind of view espoused by Russell. First, the argument from analogy cannot get off the ground, because the mediating term is not the same. That is, the other's behavior and my own behavior are experienced in different ways and are not available, side by side as it were, to link together my experience of myself with the supposition that there is a hidden other behind the movements I see. Behavior cannot bridge the chasm from self to other. Second, even the appeal to animal inference problematically trades on the unfounded division between inner and outer evidence. Wittgenstein argues that we do not reason to another's inner states but perceive them as they are put on display through bodily behavior. The outer makes the inner perceptible. Wittgenstein does not occlude the difference of self and other. Rather, he realizes that the difference between self and other is not that one is given and the other is not. Both are experienced but in different ways.

3.7   Ostension Cancels an Intersubjective Hiddenness

If Russell is wrong that our minds are private, does it make sense to speak of hiddenness at all? Wittgenstein's analysis of the inner and the outer leads him to acknowledge hiddenness in terms of an "asymmetry of the game": "The inner is hidden from us means that it is hidden from us in a sense in which it is not hidden from *him*. And it is not hidden from the owner [*Besitzer*] in this sense: *he utters it* and we believe the utterance under certain conditions and there is no such thing as his making a mistake here."[115] Interlocutors perceive the same utterance, but one perceives it as his own and the other perceives it as belonging to his interlocutor. The speaker anticipates what he says and speaks to cancel a hiddenness. The auditor understands what he says as canceling the asymmetrical hiddenness intrinsic to intersubjectivity.

What holds for speech holds for other behaviors as well. Though others cannot predict my behaviors, "I foresee them in my intentions."[116] Behavior involves, then, a difference in perspective and a reciprocity of roles. For instance, I experience my own pain and that of others differently. Although both lead to my treating the pain, there are three differences. First, I cannot be in error about my own pain, and so I cannot be said to "know" my pain or thoughts: "I can know what someone else is thinking, not what I am thinking."[117] Wittgenstein does allow that I might be tempted to doubt my pain if I bracket "human behavior, which is the expression of sensation."[118] Without behavior, I would lack a criterion of identity and might be confused. Second, whereas others learn of my pain by means of my behavior, I do not learn of my pain at all: "Other people cannot be said to learn of my sensations *only* from my behaviour,—for *I* cannot be said to learn of them. I *have* them."[119] Third, I pay no attention to my own pain-behavior though I do attend quite interestedly to the pain-behavior of another in order to discern the site of the pain: "It is a help here to remember that it is a primitive reaction to tend, to treat, the part that hurts when someone else is in pain; and not merely when oneself is—and so to pay attention to other people's pain-behaviour, as one does *not* pay attention to one's own pain behaviour."[120] My pain is not hidden from me, because I feel it, and the pain of another, even though I do not feel it in the same way, is not hidden, because her pain-behavior reveals it. However, it is possible (though unusual) that I could not tell whether or not her behavior was in fact pain-behavior. In that case, her inner would be hidden from me. The reverse, though, is impossible, for I cannot be mistaken about my being in pain. So there is a kind of asymmetrical hiddenness: each of us cannot be mistaken about our own pain and normally we are not mistaken about the pain of others, but it is possible (though unusual) that the behavior of each of us might fail to make our pain manifest to others. What prompts the unusual case? Ambiguity.

In most cases, people's behavior effectively manifests their intentions, and then we are not aware of the hiddenness at all. Only when the gesture is ambiguous does the outer seem to hide an inner: "When mien, gesture and circumstances are unambiguous, then the inner seems to be the outer; it is only when we cannot read the outer that an inner seems to be hidden behind it."[121] Wittgenstein contrasts his complex view with the inferential view:

"In the inner there is either pain or pretence. On the outside there are signs (behavior), which don't mean either one with complete certainty."

But that's not the way it is. In an extremely complicated way the outer signs sometimes mean unambiguously, sometimes without certainty: pain, pretence and several other things.[122]

Wittgenstein regards such asymmetrical behavior as primitive or prelinguistic. "But what is the word 'primitive' meant to say here? Presumably that this sort of behaviour is *pre-linguistic*; that a language game is based *on it*, that it is the prototype of a way of thinking and not the result of thought."[123] The asymmetry of the game of behavior prefigures the game of language:

Being sure that someone is in pain, doubting whether he is, and so on, are so many natural, instinctive, kinds of behaviour towards other human beings, and our language is merely an auxiliary to, and further extension of, this relation. Our language-game is an extension of primitive behaviour. (For our *language-game* is behaviour.) (Instinct).[124]

The asymmetry of roles in language turns on the asymmetry of roles in behavior. Wittgenstein's picture now comes into focus. Children acquire language through habituation to ways of behaving. Teachers monitor behavioral reactions to discern whether children are making the right associations. Being human affords such prelinguistic opportunities for acquiring language. Our words take their bearings from deeds.

3.8 Conclusion

Wittgenstein tells us that he wants to conceive of the infant as an animal, rather than as a ratiocinating machine. At the same time, it seems like the animal he has in mind is more of a domesticated animal than one in the wild. What I mean is that his infant is passive in the process of training; through carrots and sticks, the animal is made subject to a way of life naturally foreign to it and for which it appears to have no natural inclination. By way of contrast, someone like Augustine envisions an infant ripe with desire to participate in the human conversation, an infant keenly interested in the world opened up in speech.

Despite the above criticism, I find it quite valuable that Wittgenstein recovers a sense of hiddenness that is not in principle private, a hiddenness capable of being canceled by a manifestation. He calls attention to behavior as the means of manifestation. Absent behavior, the hiddenness falls back into privacy. Instead of an opposition between public and private,

Wittgenstein recovers a sense of the interplay of hidden and unhidden. Against Russell, Wittgenstein argues that the human body and behavior do not occasion inferences but instead reveal the person and his or her affects. Interaction with other human beings affords the opportunity for us to come to understand each other and to share a language. The asymmetry of the interplay makes the game possible. Another twentieth-century thinker, Maurice Merleau-Ponty, likewise counters the privatization of the mind, but he does so with different philosophical resources. Instead of linguistic analysis, he brings to bear the phenomenological method. The results are complementary, as I will argue in the next chapter.

4 Merleau-Ponty: Gestural Meaning and the Living Body

For us the body is much more than an instrument or a means; it is our expression in the world, the visible form of our intentions.
—Maurice Merleau-Ponty[1]

Edmund Husserl, the founder of the phenomenological movement, focused his research primarily on the origin of mathematics, logic, and science. Yet the phenomenological method of investigation bore fruit in other areas as well. His *Ideas II*, which circulated in manuscript form to Heidegger and later to Merleau-Ponty, proved revolutionary for its inquiry into the living body and the surrounding world.[2] Heidegger finds attractive Husserl's new emphasis on the "experiential context as such."[3] Indeed, Merleau-Ponty avers that Heidegger's *Being and Time* "springs from an indication given by Husserl and amounts to no more than an explicit account of the 'natürlicher Weltbegriff' or the 'Lebenswelt' which Husserl, towards the end of his life, identified as the central theme of phenomenology."[4] I think this is somewhat of an exaggeration, but it shows the esteem Merleau-Ponty had for Husserl's later writings.[5] Merleau-Ponty found a different aspect of the manuscript fascinating. His interest was roused by Husserl's analysis of the animate body: its agency in perception, how it can only partially perceive itself, and the way it expresses our spiritual lives.[6] What Merleau-Ponty learned from Husserl proves to be directly relevant to the topic of first word learning.

Stimulated by Husserl's investigations and immersed in contemporary psychology, Merleau-Ponty develops a philosophical account of language acquisition. For him, word acquisition is not an isolated intellectual process of association. As in Wittgenstein and Augustine, it as an embodied, contextualized exercise that habituates the child to a form of life. His investigations focus on the ontology of first word acquisition. He wants to remedy the phenomenological failing that engenders both materialism and dualism, and he wants to identify the philosophy of mind that accounts for the display of intentions at work in ostension. To show the advantages of his analysis I briefly consider Heidegger's reflections on the same set of issues. Finally, I follow Merleau-Ponty into the phenomenology of inter-subjectivity and language. What he calls "flesh" includes others as well as myself and intertwines the visible body and the invisible intention. Flesh provides the basis for intentional display and the advent of speech. Children acquire language when flesh becomes word.

4.1   Background: Merleau-Ponty's Method and Context

Merleau-Ponty adopts Husserl's admonition to return to the things themselves and bring them into specific articulation: "True philosophy consists in relearning to look at the world."[7] He follows Husserl and thinks phenomenological method involves two elements. First, the phenomenologist enacts the *transcendental reduction*, which returns all things to their manner of givenness or how they are experienced. He thinks there is a need to recover the original innocence of the child who experiences the world without ideological blinders. According to Talia Welsh's suggestive formulation, the child is a "natural phenomenologist." As she puts it, "For the child, her experiences are not something she has 'about reality'; they *are* real."[8] Second, the phenomenologist does something the child does not: he or she employs the *eidetic reduction*, which seeks to conceptualize those manners of givenness. For example, the phenomenologist might attend to the difference in givenness between remembering and perceiving something and then seek to grasp the essential features of those two modes of presentation. Merleau-Ponty regards these essences in a realistic fashion: "The eidetic method is the method of a phenomenological positivism which bases the possible on the real."[9] His approach resembles Wittgenstein's respect for the primacy and integrity of ordinary life, but Merleau-Ponty goes further and maintains that philosophy can exhibit the necessary structures at work in the ordinary.[10] In doing so, phenomenology clarifies not only ordinary life but the activity of scientists as well.

Merleau-Ponty applies his phenomenological sensitivity to something our everyday awareness and scientific investigations take for granted: perception. "Perception is not a science of the world, it is not even an act, a deliberate taking up of a position; it is the background from which all acts stand out, and is presupposed by them."[11] In his view, only phenomenology is methodologically equipped to access this background as it is. In the phenomenological account, perception involves a triangle of self, other self, and thing. Each of us enjoys a vantage point on things, and things appear to each of us as simultaneously present to other vantage points. The animate body incarnates our vantage points and opens up the interpersonal world. On phenomenological grounds, then, he rejects the Cartesian restriction of self to consciousness. The animate body makes the triangular situation of perception possible:

For the "other" to be more than an empty word, it is necessary that my existence should never be reduced to my bare awareness of existing, but that it should take in also the awareness that *one* may have of it, and thus include my incarnation in some nature and the possibility, at least, of a historical situation.[12]

His critique is not limited to Cartesian dualism. He thinks one of phenomenology's great merits is to have navigated between the Scylla of idealism and the Charybdis of materialism. Before we ever philosophize, we enjoy the perceptual presence of a world imbued with meaning. Idealism misunderstands us as the originators of that meaning, but there can be no absolute Spirit, because our access to a joint world is always through our embodied natures. Conversely, materialism conceives of the world while neglecting the essential contribution of our joint perceptual presence. For Merleau-Ponty, phenomenology affords an alternative that affirms both the contribution of our points of view and the reality of meaning:

Probably the chief gain from phenomenology is to have united extreme subjectivism and extreme objectivism in its notion of the world or of rationality. Rationality is precisely proportioned to the experiences in which it is disclosed. To say that there exists rationality is to say that perspectives blend, perceptions confirm each other, a meaning emerges. But it should not be set in a realm apart, transposed into absolute Spirit, or into a world in the realist sense.[13]

Perception and the animate body it presupposes elude the traditional positions to be found in modern philosophy stemming from Descartes, whether dualism, idealism, or materialism. Merleau-Ponty therefore attempts a new beginning. In the next two chapters, I will show that this new beginning is in some sense a return to Augustinian and Aristotelian sensibilities, although he himself seemed unaware of the affinities.

Husserl carried out his mature phenomenological investigations with only passing remarks concerning the views of others. Heidegger remedies this neglect by scouring the history of philosophy for phenomenological predecessors, but he rarely engages his contemporaries. By contrast, Merleau-Ponty takes phenomenology into dialogue with contemporary psychologists. He employs psychological studies to get his bearings, deploys phenomenological accounts to complement the psychological investigations, and poses genetic questions that parallel the developmental questions pursued by psychologists. Merleau-Ponty models an interdisciplinary style of phenomenology that is quite attractive.[14]

4.2 Merleau-Ponty's Account of Word Acquisition

Word acquisition is puzzling, because language is a cultural and not a natural endowment.[15] In the lecture course "Consciousness and the Acquisition of Language," Merleau-Ponty discusses the transition from biology to culture in terms of the child's everyday context: "The child's relationship with his surroundings is what points him toward language. It is a development toward an end defined by the environment and not preestablished in the organism."[16] The environment in this case consists principally of other human beings with whom the child lives before the advent of speech. Language presupposes a context of communication established by our bodies. His account of word acquisition involves recovering the natural form of life inscribed in the natures of our bodies and expressed in such things as smiles and gestures.[17] In different ways, his position matches that of both Wittgenstein and Augustine.

With Wittgenstein, Merleau-Ponty rejects the "intellectualist" view of word acquisition in which the child suddenly grasps the relation of sign and signified. The child does not make rapid progress, she does not regard the word as a convention but as a property of the thing, and she lacks the ability to generalize in the same way as an adult.[18] Instead, Merleau-Ponty regards acquisition as a sort of habituation:

The employment of language ... does not appear to be founded on the exercise of pure intelligence but instead on a more obscure operation—namely, the child's assimilation of the linguistic system of his environment in a way that is comparable to the acquisition of any habit whatever: the learning of a structure of conduct.[19]

Habituation involves the child identifying herself with adults in her surroundings. Her experiences are theirs, and theirs are hers: "To learn to speak is to learn to play a series of *roles*, to assume a series of conducts or linguistic gestures."[20] By means of these roles, the child acquires the world: "At the same time that the child is assuming and forming his family relations, an entire form of thinking arises in him. It is a whole usage of language as well as a way of perceiving the world."[21] Children learn to speak by being habituated to the familial form of life.

Like Augustine and Wittgenstein, Merleau-Ponty calls expressive gestures "a first language," directly related to their context.[22] The gesture of another highlights an item from our surroundings and invites us to highlight the same item with our bodies:

The gesture which I witness outlines an intentional object. This object is genuinely present and fully comprehended when the powers of my body adjust themselves to it and overlap it. The gesture presents itself to me as a question, bringing certain perceptible points of the world to my notice, and inviting my concurrence in them. Communication is achieved when my conduct identifies this path with its own.[23]

Gestures are a peculiar way the body comes into play. They emerge from "the unco-ordinated movements of infancy."[24] Gestures indicate a third notion between motility and intelligence in which the body gains a "figurative significance."[25] The ability to gesture is an "open and indefinite power of giving significance—that is, both of apprehending and conveying a meaning."[26] Gestures, then, are essential to the form of life out of which we understand language. A gesture is intrinsically public, and it embodies an intention publically. Of course, gestures are ambiguous, but Merleau-Ponty rather matter-of-factly asserts that the human being is "a genius for ambiguity."[27] He says the ambiguity is manageable, because it is rooted in our shared bodily natures and joint activities. I think there is much more to be said on the problem than can be found in Merleau-Ponty, and I will give my own account of what makes it possible for us to be a "genius" at disambiguation in chapter 9.

4.3   The Elusive Nature of Gesturing

Word acquisition calls upon and transcends our natural powers, investing them with an instituted or cultural significance. Our bodies make possible ways of behaving, then gesturing, and finally speaking.

What then does language express, if it does not express thoughts? It presents or rather it *is* the subject's taking up of a position in the world of his meanings. The term "world" here is not a manner of speaking: it means that the "mental" or cultural life borrows its structures from natural life and that the thinking subject must have its basis in the subject incarnate.[28]

To account for speech, then, we need to understand how gesturing is possible. Merleau-Ponty underscores its reciprocity: "The communication or comprehension of gestures comes about through the reciprocity of my intentions and the gestures of others, of my gestures and intentions readable in the conduct of other people. It is as if the other person's intention inhabited my body and mine his."[29] Let's say I see you point to a seagull flying by. I will spontaneously consider the same seagull. Your embodied intention becomes my own. Our gesturing bodies mirror or echo each other. What theory of mind will account for this reciprocity and thus account for word acquisition?

Merleau-Ponty questions the adequacy of modern ontologies for making sense of gesturing. On his view, both materialism and dualism presuppose a separation of the inner and the outer. However, gestures cut across the inner–outer divide. He writes in his first major work, *The Structure of Behavior*:

From the moment behavior is considered "in its unity" and in its human meaning, one is no longer dealing with a material reality nor, moreover, with a mental reality, but with a significative whole or a structure which properly belongs neither to the external world nor to internal life.[30]

The structure of behavior calls upon an integral anthropology that distinguishes but does not separate soul and body. "In returning to this *structure* as the fundamental reality, we are rendering comprehensible both the distinction and the union of the soul and the body."[31] Causal relations among things cannot account for the revelation of meaning accomplished in the perception of behavior. Material forces are purely external; they cannot make intentions manifest. In the chapter "The Body as Expression, and Speech" in *Phenomenology of Perception*, Merleau-Ponty makes a bold proposal. For a gesture to work, the body must become the intention:

It has always been observed that speech or gesture transfigure the body, but no more was said on the subject than that they develop or disclose another power, that of thought or soul. The fact was overlooked that, in order to express it, *the body must in the last analysis become the thought or intention that it signifies for us*. It is the body which points out, and which speaks.[32]

The body does not represent or signify the intention as something external to itself. Rather, the body manifests our intentions; it is their visible form.[33] Word acquisition rests on a view of the body as essentially expressive.

Cartesian dualism, which splits mind and body, cannot account for gestures or word acquisition; the body does not display the mind. "The other is a for-itself that appears to me in things, through a body, hence in the in-itself. To conceive of this passage, one would have to elaborate a mixed notion, which would be unthinkable for Descartes."[34] According to Descartes, consciousness cannot be manifest in the body. The only motion the body can accomplish is physical force, not a motion that embodies the understanding. By contrast, Merleau-Ponty recovers a sense of animate movement: "Far from being a simple 'displacement,' movement is inscribed in the texture of the shapes or qualities and is, so to speak, the revelation of their being."[35] Ostension requires a philosophical anthropology outside of the opposition between physiological body and consciousness.[36]

Though he recognizes the limitations of Descartes, Merleau-Ponty does not return to pre-Cartesian philosophy of nature.[37] To account for the manifestation of our minds to others through our bodies, he makes a new beginning. He develops the interplay of within and without in terms of our belonging to a common world we each perceive together. He rethinks the body, no longer as a scientific object such as a "molecular edifice," but instead as the living body that we perceive; similarly he rethinks consciousness, no longer as a Cartesian "pure being-for-itself," but instead as an active, gesturing, perceiving being.[38] The resulting identity-within-a-difference is what he calls "flesh."

4.4   The Reciprocity of Gesturing and "Flesh"

Merleau-Ponty's thinking about reciprocity undergoes a development in the last decade of his life. At first, he approaches the phenomenon by appropriating the phenomenological investigations of Husserl and Max Scheler. Later, he seeks to identify the principle that makes the phenomenology possible. In "Consciousness and the Acquisition of Language," from the years 1949–1950, Merleau-Ponty discusses the reciprocity of gesturing in terms of imitation. He criticizes the intellectualist view for which imitation involves imitating the motor movement of others.[39] He follows the psychologist Paul Guillaume in thinking that the child desires the same end and so imitates the same action.[40] "To imitate is not to act like others, but to obtain the same result as others."[41] Merleau-Ponty accounts for this imitation in terms of a reciprocity of capability and action. The child finds in herself the capacity to do what she sees done: "Imitation presupposes the apprehension of a behavior in other people and, on the side of the self, a noncontemplative, but motor, subject, an 'I can' (Husserl)."[42] What allows us to identify the action of another with our own capability and vice versa is the corporeal schema or postural position: "The perception of *behavior* in other people and the perception of the body itself by a global *corporeal schema* are two aspects of a single organization that realizes the identification of the self with others."[43] The body of the other shows forth the same structure as my own and thus allows me to grasp the identity of an action as done by another and as done by me. Merleau-Ponty finds that Guillaume uses two notions that require philosophical clarification: the child's inchoate sense of self and her access to the other.[44] He turns to the phenomenological investigations of Scheler and Husserl to enrich the psychological perspectives of imitation and corporeal schema. Although Merleau-Ponty thinks both phenomenologists made essential contributions to intersubjectivity, he places them in opposition in order to set the stage for his own account.

Scheler revolutionized intersubjectivity by denying a privileged access to self and by affirming access to a common psychic stream. This allows a rehabilitation of expression as the very embodiment of consciousness: "Scheler's essential contribution is the notion of *expression*. There is no consciousness *behind* the manifestations. These manifestations are inherent in consciousness; they *are* consciousness."[45] Nonetheless, Scheler cannot account for individuation, which is Husserl's point of departure. Husserl presupposes a contrast between consciousness and intersubjectivity; he emphasizes that the other is given, albeit indirectly and problematically.[46] Merleau-Ponty sees Scheler and Husserl as two sides of the same dialectic between self and other. The dialectic destroys each term, undermining both self and other:

In minimizing consciousness of self, Scheler equally compromises consciousness of others. Husserl, on the contrary, wanting to retain the originality of the ego, cannot introduce other people except as destroyers of this ego. With Husserl, as with Scheler, the ego and other people are linked by the same dialectical relation.[47]

To avoid this tension, Merleau-Ponty underscores the importance of a shared situation as the basis for understanding both ourselves and each other.[48] In fact, he thinks this problematic from Scheler and Husserl thoroughly transforms our understanding of language acquisition by introducing the importance of context for understanding one another:

In the light of Husserl's and Scheler's conceptions, we no longer can consider language acquisition as the intellectual operation of reconstructing meaning. ... As a phenomenon of expression, language is constitutive of consciousness. From this perspective, to learn to speak is to coexist more and more with the environment. Living in this environment incites the child to recapture language and thought for his own means.[49]

Beyond the dialectic of self and other is a common context in which expressions embody our understanding. Imitation is possible, then, because of our belonging to a common world.

The next year, Merleau-Ponty returns to these themes in "The Child's Relation to Others."[50] He maintains that the basis of mind reading or joint attention is not association or analogy. He thinks these presuppose what they seek to explain: an access to the other as other. In addition, they invoke an inferential process too complex to be reasonably assumed in early infant development. Instead, shared attention occurs by means of conduct that is jointly understandable in terms of postural schema. The child identifies her bodily movement and the bodily movement of others. Merleau-Ponty now stylizes Scheler's and Husserl's views as two stages of psychogenesis, which correspond roughly to the distinction between primary and secondary intersubjectivity outlined in chapter 2.[51] There is first a "precommunication" stage in which there is an identification of self and other, which he finds in Scheler. For the child, "the other's intentions somehow play *across* my body while my intentions play across his."[52] Second is the Husserlian stage of pairing, which occurs when the child can achieve a perspective on her own body, especially in the mirror image, and when the child thereby recognizes the otherness of others.[53] For Merleau-Ponty, awareness of one's own body and awareness of the other emerge together: "The perception of one's own body creates an imbalance as it develops: through its echo in the image of the other, it awakens an appeal to the forthcoming development of the perception of others."[54] In this second phase, the child couples or pairs her body with others.

Reciprocally I know that the gestures I make myself can be the objects of another's intention. It is this transfer of my intentions to the other's body and of his intentions to my own, my alienation of the other and his alienation of me, that makes possible the perception of others.[55]

The second stage does not come to eclipse the first. Segregation is never total. Precommunication remains as the basis for reciprocal identification and communication.[56] The perception of self and of other imply each other and constitute a dynamic "form" (*Gestalt*), which "develops according to a law of *internal* equilibrium, as if by *auto-organization*."[57] Merleau-Ponty thinks this reciprocal, interpersonal movement is the basis for understanding.[58] In this writing, the other still retains something of the dialectical tension he saw earlier in Husserl and Scheler inasmuch as he sees alienation, aggression, and dominance as a natural result of pairing.[59]

A decade later in *The Visible and the Invisible*, Merleau-Ponty struggles to work out an ontology that supports the phenomenon of reciprocity. With his untimely death, the work remained unfinished and somewhat aporetic. Nonetheless, he outlines a clear development of this topic. He retains the notion of "corporeal schema," which he calls "the *hinge* of the for itself and for the other," but he transforms its terminology and deepens its analysis under the heading "flesh."[60] Breaking out of a dialectical tension of self and other, a tension he still sees in Husserl and Scheler, he finds in flesh a basic reversibility.[61] The other does not stand opposite my subjectivity.[62] Rather, each of us belongs to a common world in virtue of our living, perceiving bodies:[63]

There is here no problem of the *alter ego* because it is not *I* who sees, not *he* who sees, because an anonymous visibility inhabits both of us, a vision in general, in virtue of that primordial property that belongs to the flesh, being here and now, of radiating everywhere and forever, being an individual, of being also a dimension and a universal.[64]

The other provides needed perspective on my own bodily being. For example, my back can become visible for others although it will remain absent to me.[65] Flesh unites our living bodily being, which is structured posturally, and our perceiving, which is itself perceptible in our bodily bearing. By means of flesh, we are "two openings ... which both belong to the same world."[66] He thinks flesh dissolves the problem of intersubjectivity by uncovering our precommunicative basis. Flesh exposes us each to each other and establishes a reciprocity of intentionality.

What does Merleau-Ponty see in flesh? First, in perceiving the world, we perceive ourselves as embodied perceivers: "The flesh = this fact that my body is passive-active (visible-seeing), mass in itself *and* gesture—."[67] Flesh names the identity across difference of the body as *perceivable thing* and as *perceiver of things*: "Visible and mobile, my body is a thing among things; it is caught in the fabric of the world, and its cohesion is that of a thing. But because it moves itself and sees, it holds things in a circle around itself."[68] Second, flesh's identity across difference is itself something that comes to experience; it is not a rational construction: "The enigma is that my body simultaneously sees and is seen. That which looks at all things can also look at itself and recognize, in what it sees, the 'other side' of its power of looking. It sees itself seeing; it touches itself touching; it is visible and sensitive for itself."[69] Third, the fact that flesh is experienced means at the same time that the other person is genuinely experienced. Thanks to flesh, each of us appears as one to whom the world appears. Fourth, flesh acknowledges a difference in perspective without succumbing to a separation. The two dimensions of flesh are, "as the obverse and the reverse," two aspects of the same thing.[70] They are distinct but not separable, and they mingle without confusion. Fifth, flesh makes ostensive acts possible by enabling the body's "natural symbolism."[71] Flesh is not only a passive part of the world; it is also an active point of view on the world "capable of gestures, of expression, and finally of language, it turns back on the world to signify it."[72]

4.5   Comparison with Heidegger

The phenomenological movement offers other resources for puzzling out the reciprocity of interpersonal awareness necessary for word acquisition. Heidegger's 1929–30 lecture course, *The Fundamental Concepts of Metaphysics*, engages Aristotle and distinguishes the human and animal ways of being. Encountering the Aristotelian text *De interpretatione*, Heidegger provides his own account of word institution and acquisition: "Words emerge from that *essential agreement* of human beings with one another, in accordance with which they *are open in their being with one another for the beings around them*, which they can then individually agree about—and this also means fail to agree about."[73] Earlier, he had wrestled with the degree to which animal environments approximate the human world; in the context of that discussion, he rejected the Cartesian problematic for interpersonal relation. Human beings unproblematically dwell with others in a common world of things:

Indeed it appears much less questionable to us, indeed as not questionable at all, that in certain contexts and situations other human beings on average comport themselves to things exactly as we do ourselves; and furthermore, that a number of human beings not only have the same comportment toward the same things, but can also *share* one and the same comportment *with one another*, without this shared experience being fragmented in the process; it appears that it is possible, accordingly, to go along [*Mitgang*] with others in their access [*Zugang*] to things and in their dealings [*Umgang*] with those things. This is a *fundamental feature* of man's own immediate experience of existence.[74]

Given this state of affairs, how does one person relate to another? He suggests in passing that "the problem of the relationship of human being to human being does not concern a question of epistemology or the question of how one human being understands another. It concerns rather a problem of being itself, i.e., a problem of metaphysics."[75] To answer the question, Heidegger invokes his technical term, "Dasein," which combats the Cartesian picture of a self-enclosed consciousness. "Da-sein" literally means "being-here," and the "here" in this case is the shared world. Humans, as Dasein, dwell with other people among things in the world:

Insofar as human beings exist at all, they already find themselves transposed in their existence into other human beings, even if there are factically no other human beings in the vicinity. Consequently the Da-sein of man, the Da-sein in man means, not exclusively but amongst other things, being transposed into other human beings. The ability to transpose oneself into others and go along with them, with the

Dasein in them, always already happens on the basis of man's Dasein, and happens as Dasein.[76]

The question now becomes: How does transposition occur? Heidegger points to a particular kind of affectivity, which he terms attunement or fundamental moods. Such things as grief, good humor, angst, and joy are not things that happen "in" us. Rather, they affect the way the whole appears, and they are spontaneously shared. In *Being and Time*, he had credited Aristotle with treating moods as a feature of the way we share our lives together rather than as a psychological investigation into inner states. Aristotle's *Rhetoric*, he writes, is "the first systematic hermeneutic of the everydayness of Being with one another."[77] Now, two years later, he repeats the analysis: "Attunement is not some being that appears in the soul as an experience, but the way of our being there with one another."[78] Heidegger likens these moods to the weather, a comparison echoed by Gilbert Ryle.[79] Phenomenology gives us the courage to accept attunements just as they present themselves:

It seems as though an attunement is in each case already there, so to speak, like an atmosphere in which we first immerse ourselves in each case and which then attunes us through and through. It does not merely seem so, it is so; and, faced with this fact, we must dismiss the psychology of feelings, experiences, and consciousness. It is a matter of *seeing* and *saying* what is happening here.[80]

How does this "atmosphere" spread? He says simply that attunements are infectious like germs and catchy like tunes.

I see two fundamental shortcomings for Heidegger's account of the transposing and joint comportment necessary for word acquisition. First, he cannot say how attunement becomes co-attunement. He takes it to be a basic phenomenological fact that other people can depress or elevate our moods, but he seems to be wrong in accounting for how this occurs. "Attunements are *not side-effects*, but are something which in advance determine our being with one another."[81] How do attunements affect us in advance? Heidegger does not say, and his silence invites the belief that he really sees attunements hovering around the room. More careful phenomenological analysis, however, might have revealed that moods are borne by our bodily behavior and expression. Someone dampens our mood in virtue of his gait, the tempo of his speech, his fallen expression, his slightly retracted posture, the style of his gestures, what sorts of things he directs our attention to, and so on. What's more, when he shares his reasons for his mood, our own experience of the mood is quite often intensified. Heidegger's account of co-attunement is unsatisfactory. Second, even were we to grant its adequacy, co-attuning does not account for how a child comes to learn her first words. Why not? Because attunement is a global phenomenon, an atmosphere in which things appear. It constrains which things are relevant, but it still provides an extensive range of possible shared comportments. To account for first word acquisition, we have to say how the range becomes narrowed down to such things as balls and dogs. Heidegger's efforts are devoted to bringing the phenomenon of world to view, and attunement is necessary for this project. The question of first word acquisition concerns rather how particular things, actions, events, and the like come to be viewed, and attunements cannot explain this. At the risk of being distracting, I will put it this way: Heidegger cannot see the trees for the forest, but seeing the trees together is exactly what needs to be understood to account for triangulation and word acquisition. What more might Heidegger need? Because he neglects the body and bodily movement, he offers few resources for handling the question.[82] He asserts that we dwell with others among things, but he does not handle the specifics of shared comportment. Merleau-Ponty's identification of the living body as the hinge of the self and other affords the means to answer the question in a more adequate way.

4.6 Flesh and Words

With the terminology of flesh, what has Merleau-Ponty contributed beyond the psychology of corporeal schema? He maintains that the reciprocity he uncovers is not a truth of psychology but ontology.[83] It is not an empirical fact but part of the necessary logic of the manifestation of things. Our relation with others belongs to the very structure of experience: "For we must consider the relation with others *not only as one of the contents of our experience but as an actual structure in its own right.*"[84] To make this assertion, we need experience, but it is an insight that necessarily holds for all possible experience. It is a matter of ontology, not empirical science. Merleau-Ponty maintains that being necessarily involves structures of reciprocity. The reciprocity of flesh, which he terms "chiasm," shows that "every relation with being is *simultaneously* a taking and a being taken."[85] My body, bearing both a within and a without, corresponds to a twofold aspect of things. The reversibility of inside and outside accounts for the possibility of the visible revealing the invisible.[86] The subject of Merleau-Ponty's ontology is a vast and difficult topic, but for present purposes I need only show how it illumines the possibility of gesturing and word acquisition.[87]

An analogy of reversibility is at work in gesturing and in speaking. The interplay of gesturing prefigures speaking, and speaking recalls the interplay of gesturing:

In perceiving an organism which addresses its surroundings with gestures, I begin to perceive its perceiving because the internal organization of its gestures is the same as my own conduct and tells me of my own relation to the world—in the same way, when I speak to another person and listen to him, what I understand begins to insert itself in the intervals between my saying things, my speech is intersected laterally by the other's speech, and I hear myself in him, while he speaks in me.[88]

Speaking involves a basic reversibility of roles. To understand another I must understand his point of view for myself and in seeking to be understood I offer my point of view for another to consider. To learn to speak, then, is to grasp the reversibility of the roles of speaker and hearer.[89] Merleau-Ponty's chiasmic reversibility weaves together our points of view as part of the very logic of things. It establishes us in the world with others before the intelligibility of things. We are here, together, jointly speaking and understanding the manifestation of things, and this is thanks to the interplay of flesh. The identity in difference of flesh, which both perceives and is perceived, allows each of us to appreciate our perspective and the perspectives of others.

Plato's *Sophist* contains an insight for unpacking the ontological significance of flesh. Plato identifies the five great kinds that make intelligibility possible: sameness, difference, motion, rest, and being.[90] To be meaningful, a word must identify something determinate enough to exclude other meanings. For example, to be meaningful, "dog" must identify certain things in experience while necessarily excluding others, such as "cats," "bats," and "cars." Meaning requires sameness and difference, identity and contrast. Just as Plato discovered the play of identity and difference for meaning, so Merleau-Ponty discovered the play of identity-within-a-difference for the sharing of meaning. Specifically, our living bodies necessarily entail two different dimensions that come into play with each and every gesture. If I hold up my hands to stop you, you can understand this gesture as more than a physical movement of my limbs; it rather bears a meaning, an intention, which you can understand because my body has both an inward dimension of intention and an outward dimension of movement. The special insight of Merleau-Ponty is to have recognized that it is the body itself that unites these two dimensions and therefore makes possible the perception of these two dimensions in others. Gesturing, which involves the bodily manifestation of intention, is possible because flesh establishes the means of manifestation. Flesh answers the problem unanswerable within the confines of dualism and materialism. Access to the other occurs within a phenomenological transfiguration of the body: not as a brute physical thing that renders motion mute, but as flesh that allows movement to manifest intention. The fact that I not only appear but appear as one to whom the world appears allows another to appear as one to whom the world likewise appears. Our bodies are both part of the world and the null point of the world. The identity of the body, across these two dimensions, opens the possibility of multiple points of view, and it also establishes the possibility of gesturing. Within the reciprocity of points of view, bodily movement can outwardly bear inward intention.

In view of Merleau-Ponty's ontology and philosophical anthropology, how is word acquisition possible? The twofold or chiasm of flesh places each of us in a world together, enabling gesturing and joint attention. Flesh silently entwines the inward and the outward, allowing gestures to manifest intentions:

Speech does indeed have to enter the child as silence—... It is this fecund negative that is instituted by the flesh, by its dehiscence—the negative, nothingness, is the doubled-up, the two leaves of my body, the inside and the outside articulated over one another—Nothingness is rather the difference between the identicals—[91]

Flesh's identity in difference not only opens up different perspectives but provides the natural basis for word acquisition. Flesh and its chiasm open up a realm of joint action, joint attention, and joint speech. The reciprocity of action and capability displays in the figures of our bodies a natural meaningfulness, which enables an unlimited range of cultural forms of communication: "The body is the vehicle of an indefinite number of symbolic systems whose intrinsic development definitely surpasses the signification in 'natural' gestures, but would collapse if ever the body ceases to prompt their operation and install them in the world and our life."[92] A child learns words by means of flesh and the unlimited possibilities it affords us for cultural learning.

4.7 Conclusion

Merleau-Ponty works out his ontology and philosophical anthropology with word acquisition constantly in mind, and he was perhaps the only philosopher to have done so. His interest in the psychology of word acquisition occupied him in lecture courses and writings. His early work on behavior, which cut through the opposition of dualism and materialism, gave him the resources to account for the advent of speech. His engagement with psychology stimulated the manner and substance of his questioning. But it was his phenomenological expertise, especially in his ongoing dialogue with Scheler and Husserl, that elevated his concern from the merely empirical to the philosophical. He uncovered the dynamic by which word acquisition occurs by tracing the very possibility of communion to our joint bodily being.

In the previous chapter, I contrasted Wittgenstein's perceptual account of other minds with Russell's inferentialist account. According to Russell, other minds are hidden, but spontaneous animal inferences lead the infant and the average adult to certain beliefs about other minds—beliefs that they exist and beliefs about the kind of dispositions at work indicated by the specifics of their behavior. The philosopher can give some limited justification for this inference through analogy, which seeks to interpose one's own behavior and its causal antecedents as the linking term between the perceived behavior of the other and the inferred mind of the other. Wittgenstein found such justification to be unneeded. He pointed out that infants, children, and philosophers perceive other minds by means of behavior. The appeal to inference is mistaken and trades on the unfounded division between inner and outer evidence. The other is genuinely given, even though the self and other are given in different ways. In my view, Merleau-Ponty advances Wittgenstein's critique of inferentialism and the argument from analogy by clarifying the alternative: granting that self and other are given differently, how can they be given as interchangeable so that the interaction of play and conversation can take place? Merleau-Ponty turns to the animate body, which he terms flesh, as the middle term. Our bodies enable us both to have a world and to be had by others as one having a world. Russell wrongly conceived of behavior as something outer and experience as something inner. Merleau-Ponty recovers the richness of behavior: only by virtue of acting in the world do we have a world; in virtue of acting in the world we manifest to others our presence as ones to whom things are present. It is important to underscore this chief difference: Russell thinks behavior is of the same kind as anything else one meets with in the world of experience. Merleau-Ponty underscores that behavior is not itself a thing but the manifestation of another self to whom things are present. With Wittgenstein, he rejects inferentialism and its dualism of inner and outer evidence. Beyond Wittgenstein, he uncovers the interplay of self and other inscribed into the twofold character of the animate body.

Merleau-Ponty focuses his philosophical acumen on precisely that issue least developed in Wittgenstein, namely, how it is that the body is the best picture of the mind. He clearly sees the need to break from modern

Cartesian categories, and he begins the program of working out an alternative. At the same time, it is not clear that he was able to move "flesh" sufficiently beyond the metaphor stage of concept formation. He does not give a general account of just how the body can be twofold. I think the classical programs of Augustine and Aristotle, basically unknown to him, complement his anti-Cartesian sensibilities and give the resources to turn flesh into something more substantial. This is in keeping with the direction of Merleau-Ponty's own thoughts. In commenting on the later Husserl, he writes, "How to discover the emerging sense of philosophy? By expanding our thoughts, our lived philosophical situation, through those of the ancients, and those of the ancients by ours."[93] Merleau-Ponty seizes upon the animate body as the central means for sharing our lives together. In doing so, he complements Wittgenstein and hearkens back to perennial sources.

5   Augustine: Word Learning by Understanding the Movements of Life

What usefulness there is in that skill by which human society mutually communicates its thoughts, in order that the assemblies of men may not be worse for them than any solitude, if they cannot share their thoughts in conversation.

—Augustine[1]

Augustine is not only the first thinker to pose and answer the problem of first word acquisition; he is also the first to pose and answer the problem of other minds. Bodily movement, the movement native to living beings, establishes the natural prelinguistic context for us to share attention and thereby to share words. We acquire words by following the bodily movement of language speakers as they approach, point, and look toward what they are talking about. Wittgenstein famously criticized this account for several reasons. First, it applies only to certain kinds of words, not to all or even most of language. Second, it confuses initial language acquisition with the situation of an adult attempting to acquire a foreign language, but infants do not come equipped with "Mentalese." Third, ostensive acts are ambiguous on their own. Wittgenstein's own account of word acquisition emphasizes the role of context and habituation and recognizes the importance of "ostensive teaching" when coupled with training.[2]

It is commonplace to wonder whether Wittgenstein correctly interpreted Augustine's account of word acquisition, but I will do so on new grounds. Myles Burnyeat argues that Augustine's focus on bodily movement is epistemological; Augustine realizes the ambiguity involved in sorting out another's intentions, and he thinks no conventional agreement is possible apart from a divine guarantor.[3] Christopher Kirwan notes that Augustine displays full cognizance that language consists of more difficult items than names, and yet he thinks Augustine follows a simplistic model of thought-language isomorphism.[4] On my view, both Burnyeat and Kirwan miss the fact that Augustine is doing something novel in the *Confessions* account;

he is providing a *phenomenology* of word acquisition. His question is not epistemological and cognitive (whether and how knowledge occurs) but phenomenological and social (how shared understanding occurs). Augustine's illuminationist account of knowing does not exclude a phenomenological account of the sharing of conventions, which is, after all, a matter not of knowledge in the strict sense but of belief. That the word-sound "duo" should be what some people call *two* is not a necessary or eternal truth, but that "two plus two equals four" is. The latter requires divine illumination; the former does not. We do learn something from others, namely the conventions they use for the realities we see, and with these conventions we commune in a world jointly given via perception and understanding. As Saint Thomas Aquinas observed: "When Augustine proves that only God teaches, he does not intend to exclude man from teaching exteriorly, but intends to say that God alone teaches interiorly."[5]

Wittgenstein sought in Augustine "a particular picture of the essence of human language,"[6] but what Augustine offers instead is a theory of word acquisition. Recall from chapter 2 the two stages of first language acquisition: protolanguage (or words) and the acquisition of syntax. I think Augustine, in the *Confessions*, tackles only the first, not the second stage. Wittgenstein recognizes that Augustine's account applies to "a language more primitive than ours,"[7] and acknowledges that the account may be "one of those games by means of which children learn their native language."[8] In this sense, we can say that Wittgenstein's description applies to a more advanced stage of language acquisition.[9]

In the introduction and in chapter 2, I mentioned that the psychologist Paul Bloom thinks his account of word learning vindicates Augustine's. Children learn words by following the intentions of language speakers. Augustine goes further than Bloom by focusing on the way the animate body makes these intentions manifest in bodily movement. The infant comes to understand another's referential intent in his bodily movement when she discovers the power she has to display her intent through her own bodily movement. Bodily movement as manifestation of intention is the crucial understanding that enables word acquisition through shared attention. We acquire shared conventional terms on the basis of the natural manifestation of bodily movement.

In this chapter, I first situate Augustine's account within his larger philosophical project. Next, I sketch the problem of acquiring a conventional language as understood by Augustine and then present the role of bodily movement in establishing joint attention and enabling word acquisition. In the fourth section, I begin considering possible objections to his account.

I show that Augustine shares Wittgenstein's awareness of the ambiguity of ostension, and that he thinks it is controlled through memory and contextualized understanding. In the fifth section, I counter Wittgenstein's charge that Augustine's infant already has a mental language of his own that provides a crutch for conventional word acquisition. Finally, I argue that Augustine adopts an animate theory of mind that interprets bodily movement but does not need to handle false beliefs.

5.1 Background: Augustine's Method and Context

Augustine, a trained professor of rhetoric, became a Catholic philosopher in his thirty-third year and later a priest and bishop. His philosophical influence stems not only from the specifically philosophical dialogues he authored but also from his monumental theological works, *Confessions*, *On the Trinity*, and *The City of God*. Indeed, much of his original philosophical work can be found in these theological investigations. There are perhaps two extraphilosophical reasons for his being the first to pose the problem of word acquisition and other minds. First, he is one of the few philosophers with a professional training in the discipline of rhetoric. Among the factors classical rhetoric considered was the role of what we today call body language in public speaking. For example, the Roman rhetorician Quintilian, while reflecting on body language, had occasion to remark that gesturing is a universal means of communication: "In fact, though the peoples and nations of the earth speak a multitude of tongues, they share in common the universal language of the hands."[10] Second, Augustine the Christian philosopher came to Christianity through Saint Ambrose, who opened for Augustine a path to the hidden God. In "On the Duties of the Clergy," Ambrose calls bodily movement "a sort of voice of the soul," because it makes manifest "the hidden man of our heart (our inner self)."[11] Apparently, the central event of Christian faith, the becoming flesh of the eternal Word in order to make the hidden God manifest, serves to underscore the importance of our animate bodies for interpersonal communion.[12] Both rhetoric and Christianity are concerned with the role of the body in communication. Augustine appears to be the first to apply this theme to the philosophical topics of first word learning and the problem of other minds. I think Augustine's overcoming of skepticism provides a third, explicitly philosophical motive for thinking about these issues. In the *Confessions*, he reports that he abandoned skepticism when he realized that belief in the testimony of others is essential for human life: "Unless we believed what we were told, we would do nothing at all in this life."[13] Taking a page from

Cavell's reading of Wittgenstein, we can say that the failure of skepticism revealed to Augustine the interpersonal character of life.

To bring out the peculiar character of Augustine's philosophy, I would like to distinguish it from two philosophical approaches with which it is often associated: Plato's and Descartes's. The textbook claim that Augustine is a Platonist is correct but potentially misleading. Although Augustine embraced the metaphysical and epistemological hierarchical ascent of the Platonists, he did so in a decidedly Christian key by emphasizing that ascent can occur only through humility, divine self-emptying, and incarnation.[14] Since the time of Descartes, commentators have noted affinities between the two thinkers.[15] But I think the idea that Augustine was a Cartesian or Descartes an Augustinian is fundamentally mistaken. It is true that Augustine, like Descartes, employed the first-person point of view and refuted skepticism by appealing to the self-evidence of one's own existence. But it does not occur to Augustine to regard one's own existence solipsistically as a philosophical first principle. For Augustine, our existence is a bodily and perceptual one that presupposes a joint world of existence. Our inner world is not private but is constituted in dialogue with God, a dialogue we come to enjoy through the mediation of other people.[16] In this way, Augustine is not simply a Platonist and certainly not a Cartesian. He is a philosopher of the flesh, of the animate body in communion with others. In this way, Kerr's opposition of Wittgenstein and the supposedly Cartesian Augustine rests on a misunderstanding.[17] As I will show, Augustine is on the side of Wittgenstein.

How should we read him? Augustine pursues epistemological questions. He refutes skeptics, points to the inescapability of belief for everyday life, and appeals to divine illumination to guarantee eternal truths. He subscribes to the Platonic hierarchy of being and the classical doctrines of soul and animation. In the texts relevant for ostension and other minds, however, what particularly comes to the fore is not epistemology or metaphysics, although distinctions from these pursuits are at work (for instance, ostension and other minds are issues of belief, not eternal truths). What principally comes to the fore is a keen eye for just how the other's take on the world becomes available. That is, he exhibits a kind of phenomenological concern for questions of givenness.

Many of the most influential philosophers of the twentieth century had the highest regard for Augustine. Wittgenstein told Malcolm that he began the *Philosophical Investigations* in dialogue with Augustine, because any thought that was held by him must be worthy of serious engagement.[18] In fact, Malcolm averred that "the philosophical sections of St. Augustine's

Confessions show a striking resemblance to Wittgenstein's own way of doing philosophy."[19] Husserl began his phenomenology of time by recommending the reading of Augustine, a rare gesture for this philosopher of new beginnings.[20] Heidegger celebrated Augustine's analysis of care, a crucial ingredient in *Being and Time*.[21] Hannah Arendt wrote her dissertation on his concept of love, and Gadamer came upon the universality of hermeneutics by reading Augustine.[22] The fact that so many of these appreciators come from the phenomenological tradition testifies to the generally phenomenological character of his thinking. In this connection, Jean-Luc Marion rightly sees the *confessio* as a kind of transcendental reduction to givenness. In this case, the fundamental method of the *Confessions* is a question of the givenness of God to self and self to self through God to self.[23] For my purposes, I want to take this in a different direction from Marion and emphasize that the reduction to givenness also involves the horizontal dimension of human others. The question is not just the givenness of self through God but also the givenness of self through the human other that arises in experience. I think Augustine's phenomenological concern for givenness carries over to his other works as well.

Regarding his access to his own forgotten infancy, Augustine employs the natural ability "to understand oneself on analogy with others" (*ex aliis de se conicere*) and reflects on the lives of the infants he has observed.[24] "That this is the way of infants I have learnt from those I have been able to watch. That is what I was like myself, and they, not knowing, have taught me more than my knowing nurses."[25] The counterintuitive thought that teaching can be unintentional lies at the heart of Augustine's account of ostension. He learns from infants with no intention to teach him that they learn language from language speakers with no intention to teach them. In both cases, such unintentional teaching occurs by means of heeding the meaning of bodily movements, which are intrinsically ostensive.

5.2 The Problem of Conversation by Convention

In the *Confessions* (397–399), several paragraphs before the passage famously quoted by Wittgenstein, Augustine sketches the basic problem of human conversation. We are born without language. An infant instinctually cries to manifest the presence of an unfulfilled desire, but further specification requires something more than instinct. Augustine says that the dawning of awareness involves desires and the desire to express them to others: "Little by little I began to be aware where I was and wanted to manifest [*ostendere*] my wishes to those who could fulfil them."[26] His desire, however, met with frustration, because others could not perceive his inwardly felt wishes: "And I could not, for my desires were inside me; other people were outside and had no means of entering into my soul."[27] The infant Augustine, like any infant, naturally attempted to manifest his desires by bodily movement and sounds. This, too, met with failure, because there was no natural correspondence or similarity between the movements and the things he desired: "So I threw my limbs about and uttered sounds, signs resembling my wishes, the small number of signs of which I was capable but such signs as lay in my power to use: for there was no real resemblance." The attempted "signs" did not resemble his desires, and so they failed to manifest his desires to others. Augustine develops his theory of first word acquisition to account for the problem of the outward manifestation of the inward dimension of meaning.

A sign, Augustine writes in *De doctrina Christiana* (396), a book roughly contemporary with the *Confessions*, is a presence that directs our attention toward something: it is "a thing which of itself makes some other thing come to mind, besides the appearance [*speciem*] that it presents to the senses."[28] We can employ signs to reveal our affections: "Given signs are those which living things give to each other, in order to show, to the best of their ability, the movements of their mind, or anything that they have sensed or understood."[29] Shared consideration involves outwardly manifesting our inward attention so that another may inwardly attend to the same thing: "There is no reason for us to signify something (that is, to give a sign) except to express and transmit to another's mind what is in the mind of the person who gives the sign."[30] Augustine envisions this not as the movement of a concept from one person to the other but instead as the achievement of a shared apprehension of reality. In *The Free Choice of the Will* (395), he says that what we sense and understand is public. It is common to all who sense and understand it, but the powers to sense and understand belong uniquely to each one of us: "Yet each one sees it with his own mind, not with mine or yours, or with anyone else's mind, since what is seen is present to all alike who behold it."[31] Words, then, allow us to commune in a shared reality that is jointly though individually given via perception and understanding.

In *De doctrina Christiana*, Augustine makes two sets of distinctions directly relevant for posing and answering the problem of first word acquisition. First, he distinguishes two ways signs occur: *given* signs are employed deliberately in order to show affections, whereas *natural* signs automatically betray them. Second, he distinguishes two origins of signs: by *nature* or by *agreement*.[32] The distinction between deliberate and nondeliberate signs calls for elaboration. As a natural sign, smoke automatically reveals fire: "It does not signify fire because it wishes to do so; but because of our observation and attention to things that we have experienced it is realized that there is fire beneath it, even if nothing but smoke appears."[33] Similarly, our faces outwardly bear the inward dimension of our experiences whether we would like them to or not: "The expression of an angry or sad person signifies the affection of his soul even if there is no such wish on the part of the person who is angry or sad, and likewise any other movement of the soul is revealed by the evidence of the face even if we are not seeking to reveal it."[34] Natural signs allow us to learn something about something or someone independent of their intentions. By contrast, given signs, such as gestures, pantomimes, flags, tunes, and words, are subject to the intentions of those who employ them.[35] Although bodily movement can betray affections, it can also be used deliberately to reveal affections: "When we nod, we give a sign just to the eyes of the person whom we want, by means of that sign, to make aware of our wishes. Certain movements of the hands signify a great deal."[36] The most important given signs are words, because they are the principal means for human communication. They are also practically infinite and recursive: "I have been able to express in words all the various kinds of sign that I have briefly mentioned, but in no way could I have expressed all my words in terms of signs."[37] Speech allows us to theorize in ways that tunes, flags, and natural gestures do not. Again, Augustine also distinguishes signs that arise by nature and those that arise by convention. A word, for instance, signifies what it does "not by nature but by agreement and convention."[38] He notes that the same phoneme can mean two entirely different things for different language groups:

All these meanings, then, move the soul according to the agreement of each with a particular social group. As this agreement varies, so does their movement. People did not agree to them because they were already meaningful; rather they became meaningful because people agreed to them.[39]

Augustine, then, makes two sets of distinctions. First he distinguishes deliberate (given) from nondeliberate (natural$_1$) signs. Then he distinguishes instituted (conventional) from noninstituted (natural$_2$) signs.

Augustine's discussion of signs in *De doctrina Christiana* allows us to formulate the problem of word acquisition. If given words, as conventional signs, are arbitrary, how can they be instituted and acquired so that conversation can occur? Augustine looks for the answer not in the signs themselves but in the reality they signify. We must first jointly attend to the thing signified, and then we can learn the meaning of the word, that is, the connection between the sound and the reality the speaker signifies. In *De magistro* or *The Teacher* (389–390), he writes, "As I have stated, we learn the meaning of a word—that is, the signification hidden in the sound— once the thing signified is itself known, rather than our perceiving it by means of such signification."[40] The poverty of a conventional sign is that it cannot give experience of a thing. Rather, it manifests something only by singling it out from the field of present or past experience. Absent shared consideration in establishing conventions, we may agree about reality but appear to disagree because our words single out different objects.[41] Dis-agreement, after all, presupposes some agreement without which "we can't carry on a conversation at all."[42] Shared consideration of things enables the institution or acquisition of conventional signs. The problem of first word acquisition, then, is the problem of shared attention. But without language, how can we share attention? To share attention and thus learn her first conventions, an infant follows the natural meaning of deliberate and nondeliberate bodily signs.

5.3 Bodily Movement, Manifestation, and Word Acquisition

In the *Confessions*, Augustine develops a theory of first word acquisition that solves the problem of shared attention. Motivated by the desire to express himself, the infant Augustine sought to acquire the conventions of others:

Yet I was no longer a baby incapable of speech but already a boy with power to talk. This I remember. But how I learnt to talk I discovered only later. It was not that grown-up people instructed me by presenting me with words in a certain order by formal teaching, as later I was to learn the letters of the alphabet. *I myself acquired this power of speech with the intelligence which you gave me, my God.* By groans and various sounds and various movements of parts of my body I would endeavour to express the intentions of my heart to persuade people to bow to my will. But I had not the power to express all that I wanted nor could I make my wishes understood by everybody.[43]

It is important to stave off a misunderstanding that thrusts itself upon us as modern Westerners. Just because Augustine's caregivers did not try to teach him language does not mean they were indifferent to his well-being and development as Mulhall suggests: "It is as if the child acquires language despite the indifference of his elders, as if he is forced to pick it up by stealth—to steal it rather than being gifted with it, inheriting it."[44] On the contrary, Augustine makes it clear that these elders opened up the possibility of his learning by means of their playing games with him. The context is one of love expressed through joyful activities, "from my nurses caressing me, from people laughing over jokes, and from those who played games and were enjoying them."[45] In fact, Augustine expands this list of activities later in the *Confessions* when he discusses friendship, suggesting that the infant acquires speech through intimate exposure to others, the very basis of friendship:

There were other things which occupied my mind in the company of my friends: to make conversation, to share a joke, to perform mutual acts of kindness, to read together well-written books, to share in trifling and in serious matters, to disagree though without animosity—just as a person debates with himself—and in the very rarity of disagreement to find the salt of normal harmony, to teach each other something or to learn from one another, to long with impatience for those absent, to welcome them with gladness on their arrival. *These and other signs come from the heart of those who love and are loved and are expressed through the mouth, through the tongue, through the eyes, and a thousand movements of delight, acting as fuel to set our minds on fire and out of many to forge unity.*[46]

The context in which Augustine teaches himself language is a context of interpersonal affection nourished by expressive bodily movements. Why, then, do not Augustine's elders try to teach him? They and the adult Augustine do not think that first words can be taught, but that does not imply that the child steals the words. Language is an inheritance of our joint human nature, which allows the child to participate in life's activities with those who love him and affords opportunities for the child to teach himself the conventions others use for the things around them.

Augustine says his elders revealed their affections through a full range of directed bodily movement. He has in mind much more than just pointing. In the terms of *De doctrina Christiana*, the child is discerning the natural meaning of bodily movement whether deliberately or naturally disclosed. By discerning the meaning of such movement, Augustine can teach himself the meaning of words that others use. First, the intentions of language speakers were manifest through the natural meaning of deliberate or *intentionally communicative* bodily movement:

My grasp made use of memory: when people named something and when, following the sound, they moved their body towards something, I would see and retain the fact that that thing received from them this sound which they pronounced when they intended to point it out [*ostendere*].[47]

Second, their intentions were manifest through the unconventional meaning of natural or *unintentionally communicative* movement:

Moreover, their intention was disclosed from the movement of their body, as it were, the natural words of all peoples, occurring in the face and the inclination of the eyes and the movements of other parts of the body, and by the tone of voice which indicates whether the mind's affections are to seek and possess or to reject and avoid.[48]

When we read this passage against the backdrop of the earlier statement of the problem, we see that Augustine is contrasting two movements: his own inadequate ones that failed to disclose his affections and those of his elders who successfully disclose theirs. The infant's chaotic movements are unlike the inward movements of attention; the elders' directed movements disclose the movements of attention. Augustine unravels the puzzle of acquiring unknown conventional meanings by highlighting the mediation of natural, bodily display. Bodily movement, whether intentionally communicative or not, provides a vehicle of manifesting the thing intended and thereby furnishes the possibility of sharing conventional terms. What preexists the conventions is a desire that seeks articulation and discovers the ability to do so by understanding the bodily movement of language speakers as they go about life, pursuing, possessing, rejecting, or shunning things. The natural vocabulary of all people is the display of determinate bodily movement.

The earlier text, *The Teacher*, highlights the peculiar role of bodily movement in word acquisition. In contrast to explaining one sign by another, bodily movement furnishes the opportunity to understand the sign in terms of some present, visible thing: "Aiming a finger is certainly not the wall. Instead, through aiming a finger a sign is given by means of which the wall may be seen."[49] Of course, the wall was visible beforehand, but the same wall is now seen in a new light: *as intended by another*. The bodily movement is "a sign of the pointing-out itself rather than of any things that are pointed out. It's like the exclamation 'look!' [*ecce*]."[50] Bodily movement, then, does not directly grant knowledge to the child. It does not explain the spoken sign or afford an ostensive definition. Instead, it is an ostensive act that advertises the language speaker's intention. It provides the opportunity for the child to turn to the matter spoken of by another and to understand it for himself.

For Augustine, the natural language of the body, realized in different contexts, enables word acquisition. He concludes the *Confessions* account as follows:

Accordingly, I gradually gathered the meaning of words, occurring in their places in different sentences and frequently heard; and already I learnt to articulate my wishes by training my mouth to use these signs. In this way I communicated the signs of my wishes to those around me, and entered more deeply into the stormy society of human life.[51]

Augustine's infant desires to be a part of the intercourse of human life and therefore actively discerns the conventional meanings of words across sentences as they are spoken in the course of life. Augustine underscores that the child is hearing ordinary language, formed into ordinary sentences, accompanied by ordinary gestures, and spoken by adults with no intention of teaching. The child wants to be part of the language game, and he becomes part of it by watching how it is ordinarily played. To do so, he invokes no extraordinary powers, just insight into bodily movement as manifestation of intention.

5.4 The Ambiguity of Ostension

Readers of Wittgenstein may be surprised to learn that, as Burnyeat and Kirwan have already noted, Augustine is keenly aware of the ambiguity of ostension. In *The Teacher*, in fact, he clearly affirms the ambiguity of ostensive definitions. Suppose we are asked about an action we are now performing and try to ostend it by altering it in some way. Let's say I'm walking while you happen to ask me what "walking" is. If I hurry up in order to ostend "walking," you might easily believe that "walking" means hurrying. Augustine writes, "Don't you know that *walking* is one thing and *hurrying* another? A person who is walking doesn't necessarily hurry, and a person who is hurrying doesn't necessarily walk. We speak of 'hurrying' in writing and in reading and in countless other matters."[52] Later, he acknowledges even more difficulty:

How shall I guard against his thinking that it's just the amount of walking I have done? He'll be mistaken if he thinks this. He'll think that anyone who walks farther than I have, or not as far, hasn't walked at all. Yet what I have said about this one word ["walking"] applies to all the things I had agreed can be exhibited without a sign.[53]

In *The Teacher*, Augustine handles this ambiguity by appealing to intelligence and its ability to grasp what is essential in a given situation.[54]

Now, if Augustine is so keenly aware of the ambiguity of ostensive acts, why is there no mention of it in the *Confessions* in which ostension comes to the fore as the natural language of all peoples? Burnyeat has said it is "inconceivable" that Augustine would have ignored or forgotten his earlier magisterial treatment of these issues in *The Teacher*.[55] Why, then, does the ambiguity of ostension merit no mention?

Perhaps the answer—and I should underscore that this is highly speculative on my part—comes from the difference between situations envi-
sioned in the two works. *The Teacher* highlights the ambiguity of gesturing
for ostensive definitions, but it does so in the context of two adult philosophical interlocutors discussing epistemology (Augustine is speaking to
his adolescent son, Adeodatus). As Wittgenstein notes, such discussions
are prone to mischief: "I am sitting with a philosopher in the garden; he
says again and again 'I know that that's a tree,' pointing to a tree that
is near us. Someone else arrives and hears this, and I tell him: 'This fellow isn't insane. We are only doing philosophy.'"[56] The ambiguity of gesturing would normally be controlled by context, but instead Augustine
emphasizes the practically unlimited logical possibilities of a given gesture.
Augustine appeals to intelligence to disambiguate, but he does not say just
how this might occur.

Ten year later, the account of the *Confessions* is quite different. Rather
than the artificiality of a philosophical conversation, abstracted from
desires and everyday concerns, Augustine envisions infants bereft of a
native language seeking to acquire one, and all they have to go on, besides
their ability to understand, are the gestures and expressions of adult speakers as they go about life. The adults are not trying to teach the infants
through ostensive definitions. Rather, the infants discern the adult's meaning by observing their bodily movements in the context of life. As I mentioned above, Augustine has in mind such pedestrian situations as the
following: "my nurses caressing me, ... people laughing over jokes, and
... those who played games and were enjoying them."[57] The infant is an
affective being, who experiences disappointment, jealousy, and desire. And
affectivity involves a cognitive dimension; the infant wants certain items
(warmth, food, etc.) brought close and certain other items (coldness, hunger, etc.) removed. The child recognizes that there is a pattern of human
life going around him that consists of regular actions and sounds that make
differences in what is brought close and what is removed. The child wants
to participate further in this pattern of action. Perhaps in the *Confessions*
Augustine does not highlight the ambiguity of gesturing, because the gesturing occurs within the disambiguating context of everyday affective life
and not the artificiality of a philosophical conversation. He does indeed
learn from others the conventions they use, not by having them teach him,
but by overhearing their conversation in the context of everyday routines.

But can this be the answer? Can the radical ambiguity of ostensive acts,
flagged by *The Teacher*, be handled by understanding everyday contexts,
routines, and desires? Burnyeat and Matthews don't think so. They maintain

that the Augustinian infant teaches himself language through divine illumination.[58] For justification, they point away from the *Confessions* to *The
Teacher*. Are ostensive gestures disambiguated through divine illumination
or through an affective understanding of context? Four considerations support the latter position. First, in the *Confessions'* account of word learning, Augustine appeals not to divine illumination but to expressive bodily
movement as the language of all peoples. Certainly, divine illumination
is equally available to all peoples, yet Augustine does not invoke it in this
context, although he does frequently throughout the *Confessions*. Instead
he focuses all attention on bodily movement, an extremely puzzling move
for a Platonic philosopher. Since the body is involved, Augustine must not
be asking an epistemological kind of question, but something else instead
(what I am calling "phenomenological"). Second, in the *Confessions*, Augustine deploys his account of bodily movement manifesting affectivity, developed in *De doctrina Christiana*, in which he clearly maintains that some acts
transparently display mental states even in the absence of a communicative intention. To harmonize these texts, we can simply say that expressive
bodily movements are generally unambiguous; ambiguity enters in not so
much in the bodily movement as in the correlation of the term of movement and a given word-sound, and Augustine thinks it is everyday contexts
and games that control ambiguity. Third, in *The Teacher*, Augustine appeals
to intelligence to disambiguate ostensive definitions without specifying
how intelligence can accomplish this feat. In a minor work, *The Divination
of Demons*, Augustine makes some relevant remarks in the context of wondering how demons or fallen angels can know our thoughts. Such beings
exceed human intelligence, and Augustine accordingly speculates that they
are able to know our thoughts because their increased intelligence *makes
them more able to perceive the way our bodily movements betray our thoughts*.[59]
He later retracts the claim about demons, but the passage does illumine
why he thinks intelligence can disambiguate ostensive acts: he regards
intelligence as a kind of perception or receptivity to what is given rather
than a means for forming hypotheses. Fourth, a major theme from *The
Teacher* is the fact that to learn a word, as a mere conventional sound, is
not to learn something about the world. A word comes as an invitation to
look and learn (and thereby be illuminated by God), but another's word does
not convey knowledge. The implication is clear: the meanings of words fall
outside the subject of knowledge. They are an issue of belief, and belief for
Augustine is what makes possible our shared lives together (as I noted in
6.1, this insight comes to him in overcoming skepticism). And therefore
it does not make sense to invoke the divine guarantee of illumination to

undergird a mere belief. It is, in fact, no wonder that Augustine does not do so in his account of first word learning.

Augustine does well to emphasize that our bodily desires and everyday contexts provide the horizon for disambiguating ostension, but he does not give a complete account of what psychologists of word acquisition call the "object bias," that children naturally tend to take adults as talking about a whole, for example, "rabbit," and not incidental features, such as "furry," "white," and so on.[60] To puzzle this out would require an account of the nature of perception and the kinds of features it naturally profiles. At the same time, Augustine specifically envisions children learning words by hearing sentences, suggesting he is aware that syntactical cues play a role in disambiguation.[61] In chapter 9, I will draw from Augustine and Aristotle to give my own account of disambiguation.

5.5 Mental Language and Word Acquisition

Throughout this chapter, I have emphasized that Augustine appeals to joint reality, revealed by directed bodily movement, in order to account for word acquisition; a mental language does not enter into his account. This interpretation contrasts strongly with Wittgenstein's charge: "Augustine describes the learning of human language ... as if the child could already *think*, only not yet speak. And 'think' would here mean something like 'talk to itself.'"[62] Wittgenstein takes Augustine's account of word acquisition to involve not just ostensive training (as in Wittgenstein's own) but ostensive *definitions*, which imply the ability to "*ask* what the name is" and to know "how to do something with it."[63] If children learn their native tongue from ostensive definitions, they must have an inborn mental language. Now, some of Augustine's texts in fact exhibit a decided tendency toward mental language or Mentalese. For example, Augustine writes in *The Trinity*, "For the thought formed from that thing which we know is the word which we speak in our heart, and it is neither Greek, nor Latin, nor of any other language, but when we have to bring it to the knowledge of those to whom we are speaking, then some sign is assumed by which it may be made known."[64] I think we should read such passages with two considerations in mind. First, he talks about the experience of thought preceding speaking only when discussing the identity of the eternal Word before and after the Incarnation. The search for a human analogue for this theological mystery colors the analysis. Second, Augustine's discussion of the inner word is charged with affectivity. We always have more we want to say, and that is what drives us to speak endlessly to others. Gadamer puts the thought this way: "One cannot express everything that one has in mind. ... That is something I learned from Augustine's *De trinitate*."[65] What is the role of the inner word in his account of first word learning? Matthews, for one, concludes that Augustine was under the assumption that he "had a quite fully developed capacity to think and reason long before he had acquired a public language in which to express his thoughts and desires."[66] Is Wittgenstein right that Augustine's infant learns a native tongue by a process of translation?

In the *Confessions*, Augustine underscores that his "thoughts" or "concepts" are affective. While the child is born in ignorance knowing little more than how to suck,[67] he or she gradually grows in knowledge, and knowledge of a thing is a prerequisite for learning the meaning of a word. "My own heart constrained me to bring its concepts to birth, which I could not have done unless I had learnt some words, not from formal teaching but by listening to people talking; and they in turn were the audience for my thoughts."[68] As we have seen, however, these "thoughts" are wants, not theoretical propositions. Indeed, he first learns the words he does by understanding adult gestures as revealing their affections in the pursuit, possession, rejection, or avoidance of things. Mentalese has no natural connection with bodily movement, but desire does. In this way, I think that desire and bodily behavior provide the horizon for understanding what Augustine means by thoughts and concepts in his account. To learn language, infants need certain cognitive abilities, and they need to be able to understand the suggestive expressiveness of bodily movement; but they do not need to talk to themselves in a private language. Language emerges from desire and bodily manifestation, not ratiocination.

In *The Teacher*, Augustine points out that language can guide thought. Knowledge is a prerequisite for learning the meaning of a word, but a word which signifies something we do not know invites us to look and see what we might discover for ourselves. The unknown word comes "in order that I might direct my attention, that is, in order that I might look for what I should see."[69] Similarly, in *The Trinity*, he says the unknown word inflames us "with the desire of knowing the thing of which it is the sign."[70] Surely the infant is mostly in just such a situation, invited to make distinctions that he or she has not yet explicitly made. Augustine does not say as much in the *Confessions*, perhaps because he envisions the child as principally attentive to known items relevant to the child's desires, such as food and comfort. But he is well aware that the advance of knowledge and the advance of speech occur in tandem. In *On Merit and the Forgiveness of Sins, and the Baptism of Infants* (411–412), for example, he observes that parents find the speech of infants amusing even though they would not find the same speech amusing in a grown child: "But such things can only belong to such young children as are just stammering to lisp out words, and whose minds are just able to give some sort of motion to their tongue. Let us, however, consider the depth of the ignorance rather of the new-born babes, out of which, as they advance in age, they come to this merely temporary stammering folly—on their road, as it were, to knowledge and speech."[71] The infant acquires words as it acquires knowledge on a slow and arduous path toward enlightenment. The infant, then, does not learn words by translating a ready mental language into a conventional one.

We might suppose that Mentalese could help with the problem of disambiguation by equipping the infant with theoretical powers of hypothesis and inference, but I think Mentalese exacerbates the problem of disambiguation. As an Augustinian example of everyday context, consider the game "Head, shoulders, knees, and toes," in which the parent taps each part of the infant's body as he sings the song. Here the infant learns a whole pattern of activity and speech in which certain parts of her are correlated with certain word-sounds. If the infant were a philosopher (or just running full-blown Mentalese), she'd have to ask herself in her private mental language, "Is the word-sound 'head' meaningful or is it just a sound like 'fa-la-la'? If it is meaningful, does it refer to what I call 'the top of my body,' 'the part opposite my foot,' 'my hair,' 'a tapping gesture done to my head,' 'head,' or something else entirely?" But as we have seen, Augustine does not think the infant is a philosopher; in this primitive language game the infant is invited to section off her body into regions, which we have no reason to believe she has already accomplished privately in a more sophisticated manner.

5.6   An Animate Theory of Mind

Whereas I have defended Augustine by arguing that Wittgenstein misunderstood him, Jerry Fodor defends him by arguing that mental language is absolutely necessary to explain word acquisition.[72] If I am right that Mentalese does not figure into Augustine's account of word acquisition, then what theory of mind is required? With Fodor, Augustine recognizes a prior ability required for discerning the attentions of language speakers, but he does not think such an ability is principally mental, since what needs to be explained is the extramental disclosure of attention. The prelinguistic "language" of disclosure is bodily movement as manifestation of intention.

What is involved in the child's perception of adult intention through bodily movement? As Matthews has observed, Augustine seems to be the very first thinker to have posed and answered what today we call the problem of other minds.[73] In my view, it is no accident that the first thinker to pose the problem of word acquisition would be the first to pose the problem of other minds, because they emerge from the same problematic. For Augustine, as I have said at the outset, this problematic is not epistemological: just as conventional terms are a matter not of knowledge but of belief, so perception of others is a matter of belief, not of knowledge. That is, his question is not whether I can be certain that there are other minds, but how other minds can be given through experience, when sensation, strictly considered, gives bodily, not mental, being.[74] The answer to his phenomenological question of other minds is the same as the answer to his phenomenological question of word acquisition: bodily movement manifests the minds and intentions of others. For him, access to other minds is a fact of ordinary experience that evokes wonder and elicits philosophical contemplation. He does not subscribe to the Cartesian program that aims to replace the legitimacy of everyday experience with some kind of technique.[75]

In *The Trinity*, Augustine insists that we do in fact perceive other minds, not through our eyes, but through bodily movement:

For we recognize the movements of bodies also from their resemblance to ourselves, and from this fact we *perceive* that others live besides ourselves, since we also move our body in living, as we notice these bodies to be moved. For even when a living body is moved, there is no way opened for our eyes to see the soul [*animus*], a thing which cannot be seen with the eyes; but we perceive that something is present within that bulk, such as is present in us, so that we are able to move our bulk in a similar way, and this is the life and the soul [*anima*].[76]

We might be tempted to think that Augustine, like Russell, believes we must *infer* that the sensed body before us is populated with a mind. Indeed, in *The Trinity*, he suggests that we conjecture another on the basis of our own, a conjecturing that nonetheless brings about a givenness to thinking: "[A] living man whose soul indeed we do not see but *conjecture* [*conicimus*] from our own, and from the corporeal motions *gaze also in thought* upon the living man, as we have acquired knowledge of him by sight."[77] In an early work, he uses this verb, *conjecture*, in a semiotic sense to mean becoming aware of something on the basis of something else. Smoke signifies fire; accordingly, smoke, seen, makes us conjecture or become aware of fire, unseen.[78] Analogously, we can say that bodily movement signifies soul; accordingly, bodily movement, seen, makes us aware of soul, unseen. In *The City of God*, he is even clearer that this semiotic conjecturing leads to a perceptual givenness of the signified. Against the Platonic separation of sense and intellect, Augustine forcefully states:

Now in this present life we live among fellow-beings who are alive and display the movements of life; and as soon as we look at [aspicimus] them we do not *believe* them to be alive, but we *see* [uidemus] them to be alive. We could not see their life without bodies; but we observe [conspicimus] it in them, without any ambiguity [remota omni ambiguitate], through bodies.[79]

Bodily movement does not occasion an act of reasoning or a principle of association; rather, such movement presents us with another living being. Augustine makes the noninferential character of this perception of others even clearer by identifying it with an ability enjoyed by nonrational animals. To return to the passage from *The Trinity*:

Nor is this [perception of others] the property, so to speak, of human prudence and reason. For even beasts perceive the fact that not only do they themselves live, but also that they live with others like them and the one with the other, and that we ourselves do so. Nor do they see our souls [animas] except through the movements of our bodies, and that at once and very easily by a sort of natural concord.[80]

Interanimal awareness is rooted in what he calls "inner sense," which is a power common to humans and other animals.[81] Augustine does not say that humans or philosophers know about others through reasoning and animals know about others in an analogous way; rather, he says that human beings are aware of other living beings in the same way that other living beings are, namely, by inner sense.[82] According to the theory of inner sense, such awareness accounts for animals' purposive movement: "For if the beast were not aware of its act of perception, it could not otherwise direct its movements toward something, or away from it. This awareness is not ordered towards knowledge, which is the function of reason, but towards movement."[83] Animal movement reveals the animal's inward awareness of its perceptual field. "The inner sense enables the animal to seek and acquire things that delight and to repel and avoid things that are obnoxious, not only those that are perceived by sight and hearing, but all those which are grasped by the other bodily senses."[84] Movements, then, disclose these inward affects. On his view, bodily movement does not occasion a rational *inference* about the presence of life; rather, such movement *reveals* life and its peculiar affections. Augustine's infant perceives inner sense at work in the bodily movements of others.

What is necessary for understanding bodily movement as disclosive of intention? At first, Augustine's infant lacks motor control, and he simply flails his limbs.[85] As time progresses, however, the infant grows in control and comes to understand what is at stake in purposive bodily movement, namely, the manifestation of willed intentions: "The soul in wonderful ways is mixed with the body, to vivify it, by the same incorporeal volitional power with which it also gives commands to the body by a certain intention, not by physical force."[86] In this way, Augustine seems to have in mind something like the Aristotelian understanding of directed movement, which reveals the inwardness of desire and perceptual discrimination. In developing motor control, infants develop an understanding of the natural language of the animate body.[87]

Augustine's account of word acquisition calls upon the developed ability of inward awareness to make the movements of life reciprocally manifest. However, he also invokes the properly human triple of understanding, memory, and will. It is not enough merely to be aware of movement; the child must also understand its intended object and remember the instituted conjunction of sound and sense. Only then can the child communicate his will. Now, understanding and will are likely more familiar as distinctively human attributes, but Augustine's inclusion of memory might seem strange. In fact, Augustine distinguishes between two grades of memory, one proper to other animals, and one proper to humans. Specifically human memory is "not of things that have become habituated by repeated acts, but of the countless things that have been attained and retained by observation and illustration," including "the invention of so many symbols in letters, in words, in gesture ... the languages of so many people, their many institutions."[88] The contrast, then, is between a memory of mechanical habituation, proper to other animals, and a memory of insight into institutional reality, proper to humans.

Understanding allows the child to grasp the intention borne by the gesture and achieve insight into institutional reality. Without such understanding, a gesture would simply be puzzling; its movement would likely attract attention but only with the result of mystification.[89] Burnyeat puts this problem as follows: "No-one can achieve my understanding for me, not for the trivial reason that it is mine, but because to internalize the requisite connections is to go beyond what is presented on any occasion of so-called teaching."[90] Understanding allows us to see a bodily movement as an act of intentional communication and not just as an attention-getter. Finally, the will is a necessary ingredient for word acquisition. In *De doctrina Christiana*, Augustine distinguishes natural signs such as smoke signaling fire from given signs employed deliberately to manifest intentions. The child's own will and desires allow him or her to discern the communicative will of others, not just their unintended indications. The will directs our attention from this object to that object, and it directs our actions.[91] More-over, the will provides the essential motivation for the child to discover the meaning of words. In the *Confessions*, Augustine strongly contrasts the acquisition of his first language, learned willfully, and his second language, learned through drilling and punishing: "This experience sufficiently illu-minates the truth that free curiosity has greater power to stimulate learning than rigorous coercion."[92] To learn his first language, the child sought to enter into a world of speech about things, and he did so by unearthing the significance of animate movement.

Augustine does not invoke inferential powers to account for prelinguis-tic shared intentionality. All that is needed is the understanding of bodily movement as it is lived by us and displayed by others. The movements of life include willed movements, and they naturally display intentions. The child, with her understanding, discovers that will is at work and made man-ifest in bodily movement. Such a discovery comes by virtue of being alive and directing movement and recognizing that the directed movements of other living beings reveal intentions. In this way, we could say that in Augustine's view the infant is not an alien detective observing and infer-ring; rather, she is a perceptive witness, who discovers speech by having discovered the disclosive power of bodily movement. Augustine's theory of mind is founded upon the discernment of bodily movement. Without it, we could not commune at all: "It is utterly impossible for us either to perceive or to understand his will unless he makes it known by some corpo-real signs, and even then we believe rather than understand."[93] Augustine's account of word acquisition requires not only understanding, memory, and will but these three in the domain opened up by inner sense and the corporeal signs its movement makes possible. Understanding, memory, and will allow the child to recognize, retain, and employ the intentions manifest in bodily movement.

5.7   Conclusion

Wittgenstein presents language acquisition as inauguration into a habitu-ated way of acting. He writes that human beings "agree in the *language* they use. That is not agreement in opinions but in form of life."[94] Augus-tine sensibly maintains that the form of the body, outwardly manifesting inward affections, enables inauguration into the stormy intercourse that is our form of life. His robust sense of nature allows him to accord the infant a more active role in learning than does Wittgenstein. The infant is not habituated to an alien form of life through punishments and rewards;

the infant desires to participate more fully in a particular version of the human form of life, and she can do so by understanding the natural patterned actions unfolding all around her. Initiated bodily movement brings particular affects to the fore and allows them to be specified by conventional terms. Though life appears without ambiguity, context is important for disambiguating revealed intentional movements. Word acquisition involves three things: (1) affectivity, (2) purposive bodily movement, and (3) the contextual interpretation of movement via desire, understanding, and memory. Our bodies give us an ambiguous, suggestive expressiveness, a learned but natural way of acquiring words.

Despite the optimism that words can be learned and that language speakers share a world in speech, Augustine is deeply realistic about the prospect of mutual understanding achieved by means of our shared meanings. That is, he holds both to the communal character of words and to the great difficulty in understanding another human being. In fact, for Augustine there is even a great difficulty in understanding ourselves. The human being is "a vast deep," and "it is easier to count his hairs than the affects and movements of his heart."[95] Even with the purest of motives, mutual understanding is beset with difficulties.[96] "Men may speak, may be seen by the operations of their members, may be heard speaking; but whose thought is penetrated, whose heart is seen into? ... Do not you believe that there is in man a deep so profound as to be hidden even to him in whom it is?"[97] For Augustine, despite our common language, understanding others or even ourselves is no easy task.

6 Aristotle: Natural Movement and the Problem of Shared Understanding

He who thus considers things in their first growth and origin, whether a state or anything else, will obtain the clearest view of them.

—Aristotle[1]

Augustine provides a compelling account of word learning through ostension, complete with descriptions of animate intersubjectivity and rigorous awareness of the problem of disambiguation. Animate movement advertises affects to other animate minds in the context of sharing a life together. In developing this account, Augustine makes liberal use of "life," "nature," and "animate movement," but he does not unpack these concepts. It is here that Aristotle's expertise recommends itself. My consideration of Aristotle is not intended to be of merely historical interest. As I detailed in the first chapter, I join a variety of thinkers, both analytic and continental, in finding Aristotelian principles relevant in the contemporary context.

Aristotle differs from Wittgenstein, Merleau-Ponty, and Augustine in that he offers no explicit account of word learning and our awareness of other minds. However, he was the first person in the history of philosophy who had the conceptual resources for doing so. The pre-Socratic philosopher Cratylus still advocated the primitive idea that words are natural copies of things. Against this view, Plato was the first to underscore the conventional character of words. According to Aristotle, Cratylus also faithfully maintained the doctrine of universal flux, and he therefore denied the principle of noncontradiction (PNC). The denier is unable to speak meaningfully or even point; consequently, Cratylus just waved his finger about like a plant blown in the wind. Though Cratylus was an extreme figure, he was influential, and Aristotle tells us that even Plato was a lifelong believer in Cratylus's doctrine of universal flux.[2] Plato accordingly advocated looking beyond the conventions of words and the flux of the visible to grasp the unchanging, self-identical forms. In this way, he affirmed both the flux of the visible and the identity of meaning required by the PNC. Aristotle agrees with Plato that language is conventional and that the PNC cannot meaningfully be denied, but he disagrees that the realm of nature is one of universal flux. He develops a strategy for finding intelligibility in change and movement.

In this chapter, I would like to return to the critique of Cratylus. Specifically, I would like to propose a problem that arises in Plato's rejection of Cratylus's primitive idea of words as natural copies, and which Aristotle's rehabilitation of natural movement is the key to solving. If words are conventional, how can they first be instituted or acquired? New words can be acquired on the basis of previous conventions, but how can the first conventions come about? In order to acquire the first conventions, we must have a natural way of sharing attention. Despite Plato's forceful rejection of natural meaning, his interest remains in the cognitive achievement of grasping the forms.[3] In the *Cratylus*, Plato limits the body's revelatory character to artificial movements: "The only way to express anything by means of our body is to have our body imitate whatever we want to express."[4] He has us gallop to represent a horse or raise our hands heavenward for celestial phenomena, but such pantomimes do not explain how first words are ordinarily learned. In Aristotle's discussion of Cratylus, reduced to silence and purposeless movement, we find the key to sharing attention and acquiring conventions. Bodily movement naturally manifests our intentions, which is why Cratylus, doggedly refusing to grant the PNC, must deliberately wave his finger about. Were he to rest his finger he would be pointing, a movement that naturally displays intention. In short, first word acquisition is possible because of natural movement, which displays our attentions and thereby allows the coordination of attention required for word acquisition.

Animate movement, appropriated by human understanding and freedom, is the central insight in Aristotle's account of how intentions appear in experience. A living being, displaying the movements of life, also displays its intentions. Such movement reveals both a power to move and perceptual discrimination. Although such movement is ambiguous, it is complemented by Aristotle's account of the structure of perceptual experience, which prioritizes universals and substances over particulars and accidents. Aristotle's understanding of animate movement and perception provides a robust account of word acquisition. Searle, for his part, believes that thinkers from Aristotle onward "take language for granted" in their discussion of institutions.[5] To show that this is not the case, I will gather together an Aristotelian account of the first acquisition of language and the prelinguistic collective intentionality it requires. This chapter exploits Aristotle's resources for handling a problem he did not quite broach, although he could have. Because of its speculative nature, the project appears to be without precedent in the secondary literature.[6]

I begin by reviewing Aristotle's defense of the PNC, the supreme principle of intelligibility. To refute its deniers, Aristotle invites them to say something both for themselves *and others*. The negative proof of the PNC, then, involves not just intelligibility but shared intelligibility. Next, I consider the problem of shared intelligibility in the context of Aristotle's account of the conventional character of language. Then, I show that Aristotle's understanding of movement provides resources for understanding how intentions can be borne and shared. To bring out the value of Aristotle, I compare his view with Descartes's restriction of motion to mechanical principles that offer no resources for prelinguistic joint attention. Returning to Aristotle, I examine the difference between animal coordination of attention and human collective intentionality. Finally, I argue that Aristotle's understanding of the logic of perception controls some of the ambiguity of ostension famously highlighted by Wittgenstein and Quine.

6.1 Background: Aristotle's Method and Context

Aristotle's father was a physician, and his teacher, Plato, a metaphysician. Aristotle saw himself as the heir to two traditions: the pre-Socratic inquiry into the principles of nature and the Socratic–Platonic inquiry into definitions, ethics, and metaphysics. He accordingly sought to return to the investigation of nature and marry the pre-Socratic material cause to the Platonic formal cause in order to give a causal explanation of the patterns exhibited by natural phenomena.[7] He was a polymath, who did dissections, formalized logic, and discovered the reality of sensible things.[8] In logical works, he prioritized demonstration as the proper method of science. Aristotle thinks we can be said to know something only when we not only understand *that* it is the case but can additionally specify the causal reason *why* it is the case.[9] He points out that the ultimate starting points of demonstrations cannot themselves be demonstrated. Instead, first principles must be known through experience.[10] The most important philosophical inquiry concerns these principles. In his investigations on nature, soul, and being, we accordingly find few demonstrations. Instead, he employs historical reviews to motivate his own causal analyses, critical distinctions, analogies, and analyses of examples.

At the dawn of modernity, thinkers such as Bacon, Galileo, and Descartes sought to overthrow the dominant Aristotelian inquiry into nature. In the main they were right in the judgment that contemporary Aristotelians, in their efforts to master Aristotle's texts, often failed to look up from the page and consult the book of nature.[11] But Galileo at least thought his opponent was not so much Aristotle as his degenerate followers. For example, he wrote that Aristotle's mistake about celestial phenomena followed not from some limitation of his method but simply from his lack of a telescope.[12] I agree with Galileo that Aristotle's limitations came not from his principles but from his instruments. Because Aristotle was limited to the naked eye, much of what he said is now obsolete. But when it comes to the topic of the everyday manifestation of life through action, our instruments are no more sophisticated than they were in his day nor, in principle, than they can ever be. It is not a matter of trying to see the microscopic or the telescopic, but of seeing those phenomena that Wittgenstein and Merleau-Ponty say are right there before our very noses: the basic ways of everyday manifestation. In this regard, Michael Thompson makes a remark concerning the contemporary relevance of Aristotle with which I heartily agree:

Nature in general, we may say, he approaches with the categories derived from the representation of life and action. This is very bad news if you are envisaging, say, a mathematical physics. But if your topic is precisely life and action, and these as objects of philosophy, then things are evidently otherwise. It is in the sphere of action and life that we find legitimate place for the forms of philosophical reflection that led Aristotle to introduce his peculiar concepts of *substance, capacity, activity, form, matter, unity, process, final cause,* and so forth—even if these particular concepts are not just exactly the ones we ourselves need.[13]

Ostension concerns the philosophical question of how a particular kind of action, intending, can be shared with other living beings. Therefore, Aristotle is directly relevant.

Aristotle regards action as a crucial constraint on the kind of ideas we might entertain about philosophy's starting point. The more exotic claims of sophists and skeptics do not square with the natural actions of an intelligent, animate being:

But such inquiries are like puzzling over the question whether we are now asleep or awake. And all such questions have the same meaning. These people demand that a reason shall be given for everything; for they seek a starting-point, and they wish to get this by demonstration, while *it is obvious from their actions that they have no conviction.* But their mistake is what we have stated it to be; they seek a reason for that which no reason can be given; for the starting-point of demonstration is not a demonstration.[14]

Aristotle thinks our starting point must be what is most manifest to us, the world of natural movement, although such a beginning will lead us to ultimate causes that are not immediately evident: "So we must follow this method and advance from what is more obscure by nature, but clearer to us, towards what is more clear and more knowable by nature."[15] That is, we must begin with sensible experience of moving things and then proceed to their causes. At the same time, the advance in understanding does not consist in denying the reality of the beginning; Aristotle sensibly holds that experience and reason must cohere, and his philosophy consists in bringing out the at times hidden harmony. For example, Parmenides held to the principle "Nothing can come from nothing" and argued against the reality of change. Aristotle agrees with the principle, but he denies that it should lead us to reject our manifest experience. Parmenides's error came from inexperience: "The first of those who studied philosophy were misled in their search for truth and the nature of things by their inexperience, which as it were thrust them into another path."[16] Change is a real feature of our experience, and Aristotle saves its reality by introducing further principles to make sense of it. Capacity and activity are correlative principles that make change possible; something comes to be from a prior potentiality, not from absolutely nothing. Aristotle's principles and his fidelity to experience furnish rich resources for understanding the manifestation accomplished by natural movement.

6.2   Sharing Intelligibility

Aristotle accounts for intelligibility in a twofold manner. First, he handles the cognitive dimension in terms of the actualization of the potentiality to understand, which occurs at the summit of *epagōgē*: perception compounds into memory, memory compounds into experience, and experience yields to the act of understanding.[17] Though Themistius, a fourth century commentator, uses the example of acquiring language in commenting on this process, Aristotle himself sticks closely to cognitive rather than linguistic achievement.[18] Second, Aristotle treats the metaphysical dimension in terms of the actuality of form realized in the potentiality of matter. The PNC is the supreme principle of intelligibility, which clarifies the formal identity through difference required for signification. The PNC holds that it is impossible that something be and not be in the same respect and at the same time. Revisiting Aristotle's account of intelligibility, especially as it concerns this supreme principle, will allow the problem of shared intelligibility to come to the fore.

Now, the full content of the PNC becomes manifest in the difficulties encountered by anyone who attempts to deny it. Although Aristotle maintains that we cannot prove any first principle, we can nevertheless refute the PNC's denier by showing how he must presuppose the principle in order to engage in any meaningful activity.[19] The heart of the refutation is contained in the following text, which I will quote in full before discussing in detail:

[1] The starting-point for all such arguments is not the demand that our opponent shall say that something either is or is not (for this one might perhaps take to be assuming what is at issue), but that he shall *signify something both for himself and for another*; for this is necessary, if he really is to say anything. For, if not, such a man will not be capable of speech [*logos*], either with himself or with another. [2] But if any one grants this, demonstration will be possible; for we shall already have *something definite*. [3] The person responsible for the proof, however, is not he who demonstrates but he who listens; for *while disowning reason [logos] he listens to reason [logos]*.[20]

The first matter for our purposes is the request that the opponent "signify something both for himself and for another." The opponent need not assert which of two contradictory properties inheres in a subject; he need only signify something. This might seem a peculiar request unless we consider a passage from *De interpretatione*:

When uttered just by itself a verb is a name and signifies something—the speaker arrests his thought and the hearer pauses—but it does not yet signify whether it is or not.[21]

Speaking is a movement that effects rest.[22] Aristotle bids his interlocutor to signify not only for himself but for another, because he wants to bring about a public display of this movement-effecting-rest, and because joint signification establishes a sameness between us.[23] When someone says something, we attend to what she says. Our own train of thought pauses, and we think about the same. Ignorance of the meaning is the only thing that would keep us from acquiescing.

The second important point is that the act of joint signification necessarily introduces "something definite." To signify is to identify one thing in contrast to others.

For not to have one meaning is to have no meaning, and *if words have no meaning discourse with other people, and indeed with oneself has been annihilated*; for it is impossible to think of anything if we do not think of one thing; but if this *is* possible, one name might be set [*tithēmi*] to this thing [*pragma*].[24]

In this way, there is a kind of syntax built into a single signification: "The formula [*logos*], of which the word is a sign, becomes its definition [*horismos*]."[25] The word means *either* something *or* another, and this distinction can be formulated in a definition.[26] Naming follows upon the initial act of distinguishing one thing from another. If we fail this initial act, we cannot converse with ourselves or others.

The third feature worth pursuing is the claim that the cause of the proof is the listening. We can take this in two ways. It could be that the denier is refuted through hearing his own word and thereby arresting his thought on a single meaning. We both speak and hear ourselves speaking; as Plato observed, thinking is dialogical.[27] It could also be that the PNC's denier has simply heard our request to signify and in doing so arrests his thought on a single meaning with us. Either way, the denier is refuted, because he has, for a moment, stopped with some one meaning that is necessarily not some other meaning.

Three interplays come to light in refuting the denier of the PNC: [1] movement and rest, [2] sameness and difference, and [3] speaking and listening. To signify is to make *a movement which effects rest* by *distinguishing one thing from others*, and this rest is *achieved for the speaker and the hearer together*. The PNC governs our conversations by making intelligibility possible. However, it fully accounts not for the possibility of *shared* intelligibility, but only for intelligibility *simpliciter*:

> And it will not be possible for the same thing to be and not to be, except in virtue of an equivocation, just as one whom we call "man," others might call "not-man"; but the point in question is not this, whether the same thing can at the same time be and not be a man in name, but whether it can in the thing [*pragma*].[28]

In the refutation, Aristotle insists on the importance of shared intelligibility, but the PNC itself only accounts for intelligibility, not shared intelligibility. What ensures shared intelligibility? What is the principle of "nonequivocation"? How can we acquire a convention so that we might mean something both for ourselves and for another?

6.3 The Problem of Shared Intelligibility

Aristotle thinks that animals communicate with one another according to natural significations. In the imagination, a movement initiated by perception issues in a natural signification: a wolf inspires fear, and warning calls sound among the sheep of the flock.[29] For humans, a newborn's cry functions similarly. It naturally belongs to animals to be able to communicate according to these signs. Humans also possess a higher possibility of communication that allows them to share insights into far more than what is currently pleasurable or painful. Specifically human life unfolds from the unique possibilities of communion afforded by the power of speech:

Nature, as we often say, makes nothing in vain, and man is the only animal who has the gift of speech. And whereas mere voice is but an indication of pleasure or pain, and is therefore found in other animals (for their nature attains to the perception of pleasure and pain and the intimation of them to one another, and no further), the power of speech is intended to set forth the expedient and the inexpedient, and therefore likewise the just and the unjust. And it is a characteristic of man that he alone has any sense of good and evil, of just and unjust, and the like, and the association of living beings who have this sense makes a family and a state.[30]

The natural openness of human speech involves more than nature alone provides. For our communication is not a natural process like metabolism.[31] Rather, it occurs by convention, when a sound becomes a symbol. "No name is a name naturally but only when it has become a symbol. Even inarticulate [*agrammatoi*] noises (of beasts, for instance) do indeed reveal something, yet none of them is a name."[32] Human speech, then, surpasses the communication of pain and pleasure, and it does so by expanding beyond the template of possibilities specified by animal needs. Central to this transcendence is the institution of conventional terms. Now, what is problematic about shared conventions?

The problem can best be formulated on the basis of Aristotle's famous though difficult discussion of convention at the beginning of *De interpretatione*. He identifies the place of conventional terms within the structure of experience. He calls perceiving and understanding "affections," and he says they target things we deal with in the world:

Now spoken sounds are symbols of affections in the soul, and written marks symbols of spoken sounds. And just as written marks are not the same for all men, neither are spoken sounds. But what these are in the first place signs of—affections of the soul—are the same for all; and what these affections are likenesses of—actual things—are also the same.[33]

We share an intelligible world with others via our own individual "affections" (*pathēmata*). To each of us the world appears, and to each of us it matters. Aristotle says the affections are the same for all, but they nevertheless must occur for each of us individually. Indeed, this text illumines why Aristotle invites the PNC's denier to signify something both for himself and for another, namely, because the identity of meaning acknowledges the sameness of affection and thing. If we understand "cat" together, we are both targeting the same perceived and understood thing; our affections are identical and so is the thing. The affections are the way each of us receives the public world; they put us with others out among things. It is through our own affections that we have a shared world.

When it comes to joint intelligibility, two kinds of ignorance must be surmounted. First, each person needs to know the thing, and second, each needs to know which of the many known things the word designates.[34] Aristotle handles the first with affections and the second with signification. Acquaintance with the thing is a necessary but not sufficient condition for understanding the word. For that, we must coordinate our attentions, coordinate our experiences, so that at the sound of the word we consider the same experienced thing. As a minimal account of the problem of word acquisition, then, we need a thing, the experience of it, and its signification. The thing can be both experienced and signified; to be signified, experience must be coordinated, so that the same thing appears to each of us together. What is the difficulty of this coordination? Although affections are not somehow "inside" us, they do involve an ineluctably "inward" dimension, which is closed to others, although it can be made manifest.[35] That is, the affections are hidden, because they occur for each of us individually.[36] Such hiddenness is the reason we need language and do not automatically or telepathically share each other's thoughts. The reality of hiddenness invites reflection on just how affections can become manifest and shared.

When we turn to the world that appears to each of us together, we find that our senses, especially vision, "bring to light many differences in things."[37] Animals have smelling, hearing, and seeing for self-preservation: "But in animals which have also intelligence they serve for the attainment of a higher perfection. They bring in tidings of many distinctive qualities of things, from which knowledge of things both speculative and practical is generated in the soul."[38] Human perception affords us a world ripe with intelligibility. We share a perception not just of shape and color, but of the nature or intelligibility of a thing, and words come into play precisely here with the issue of intelligibility. Human perception exceeds our animal needs and opens up a limitless horizon of meaning. Confronting so many and varied sensible and intelligible things, how can we consider the same thing and thereby achieve a shared symbol? Our experiences reveal the same basic structures of things, but each of our symbols must target only one experienced item from the vast field of shared experience. Open to the same world, how can we target the same *pragma* via our own affections so that my "man" is not your "not-man"? There must be some nonconventional or natural way that our affections can be mutually manifest.

6.4   Sharing Attention through Bodily Movement

Aristotle's discussion of the PNC again provides direction. In order to be a consistent denier of the PNC and affirmer of universal flux, Cratylus refuses to signify something for himself and another and instead resolves to do nothing more than move his finger. In doing so, he shows the way to sharing intelligibility through bodily movement. Cratylus, Aristotle reports, "finally did not think it right to say anything but only moved his finger, and criticized Heraclitus for saying that it is impossible to step twice into the same river; for *he* thought one could not do it even once."[39] Were Cratylus to stop moving his finger, he would be pointing, and pointing is an intentional movement that advertises the focus of one's attention. It is analogous to the act of signifying that brings about a shared consideration, a peculiar kind of rest. Aristotle likens Cratylus's existence to a plant, because animals, no less than rational animals, evidently discriminate.[40] The squirrel moves toward the acorn and away from the cat, distinguishing what appears good from what appears bad. We do not perceive the squirrel's perceptual affections, but its purposive actions reveal them. "In this way living creatures are impelled to move and to act, and desire is the last cause of movement, and desire arises through perception or through imagination and thought."[41] Determinate movement, which targets a good or avoids a bad, reveals a power to initiate this movement, a power not only to effect movement but to discriminate between alternatives: "For all living things both move and are moved for the sake of something, so that this is the limit of all their movement—that for the sake of which."[42] Aristotle viewed such natural movement as most manifest in experience: movement reveals the power to move.[43] Nature is the inward principle of movement and rest that belongs to the thing in virtue of its whole.[44] We see the squirrel seeking to rest in a good and initiating movement for this end, and we understand that the squirrel has the power to do what we see it doing. Cratylus, then, denies not only his intellective soul but also his sensitive soul power. Unlike the squirrel, he cannot distinguish friend from foe.

According to Aristotle, animals display discriminatory behavior. What more is required for the coordination of attention necessary for human word acquisition? Suppose that instead of waving, Cratylus pointed. What would his pointing achieve? The act of pointing, like the action of the squirrel getting an acorn, is a determinate movement. It is a movement effecting rest. The arm moves outward in relation to the body, and the index finger moves outward in relation to the hand. The gesture is announced by the movement and achieved in the rest of an extended arm and hand.[45] The movement displays a power to move, and the rest a power to discriminate. However, unlike the action of the squirrel resting with an acorn, the act of pointing achieves no immediate good. Rather, it establishes a line of sight. It reveals an intention that extends beyond the gesture to something in the world. Its meaning, as Wittgenstein and Augustine emphasize, depends on context, but the gesture nonetheless excludes much more than it includes. When other people gesture, we naturally follow their movement beyond its rest to the item targeted by their affections. Their organic body, organized into a front and back owing principally to the place of sight and the natural orientation of the bodily plan toward forward movement, situates their attention within the perceptual environment.[46] Their gaze is directional and indicated by their posture and eye movement. A specific gesture emerges from this already determinate bearing upon the world and further restricts the possible items of attention. Their contemplative action of gesturing has us turn with them toward the highlighted item in our surroundings.

Movement that effects rest, that is, movement that brings about the good of shared intelligibility, is made possible at first by the organized plan of our bodies and the revelatory character of posture and gesture. Our natural bodies, then, are important conditions for our sharing the world in speech, because they manifest our inward affections. The specific character of natural movement, in contrast to the modern physics of movement, is that it reveals a power to move. In the case of animal movement, which targets a good and avoids a bad, the power is clearly discriminating. In the case of deliberate human gestures, movement invites us to look beyond the movement and its rest in order to rest in another's attention. The animal ability to discriminate is presupposed and elevated to serve a contemplative stance of considering something with another.

In section 1.5, I introduced Gadamer's phenomenological reading of Aristotelian nature as self-expression through play. That reading is rooted not only in natural movement but in first philosophy as well. At the heart of Aristotle's metaphysics is a distinction between *kinēsis* and *energeia*, between movement and activity.[47] Both movement and activity have a fundamental phenomenological property of manifesting a *dunamis*, or ability, but activity is even more robustly expressive. It reveals not only abilities to discriminate and move; it reveals the substantial being of a living thing. Two studies of Aristotle bring this to light. In *Activity of Being: An Essay on Aristotle's Ontology*, Aryeh Kosman underscores the expressive quality of activity:

Since an ability and its exercise are the same being, its exercise indeed constituting an ability's manifest presence and preservation, the relationship between *dunamis* and *energeia* thus understood is maintained even in the fullest moment of realization. ... A person whose eyes are open still has the ability to see, and a person who is actively engaged in speaking French is still able to speak French. At the moment of exercise, abilities of this sort are indeed most fully realized, called forth into the fullest and most active form of their being. Here realization does not replace ability. It manifests ability and expresses it, and it is, in contrast to the unstable and other-directed expression of ability that defines motion, the occasion for the fullest and most active self-expression of the ability that it is.[48]

Movement expresses self relative to another; activity expresses self from itself.[49] In *Doing and Being*, Jonathan Beere begins with an epigraph from Gerard Manley Hopkins that identifies doing and being: "Each mortal thing does one thing and the same: / Deals out that being indoors each one dwells."[50] His study points to a fruitful tension at the heart of Aristotelian *energeia*: "For this way of being is supposed, on the one hand, to be a way of *being*, but it is also supposed to encompass doing and changing."[51] Aristotle's *energeia* expresses the fact that the actions and activities of an animate being reveal its dynamic powers of being.

6.5 Comparison with Descartes

"I hope that readers will gradually get used to my principles, and recognize their truth, before they notice that they destroy the principles of Aristotle."[52] For Aristotle, movement encompasses growth, alteration, and change of place, but Descartes restricts motion to change of position: "By 'motion,' I mean local motion; for my thought encompasses no other kind, and hence I do not think that any other kind should be imagined to exist in nature."[53] He thinks the Aristotelian definition of motion is rife with obscurity, and he proposes his own definition as follows: "*Motion is the transfer of one piece of matter, or one body, from the vicinity of the other bodies which are in immediate contact with it, and which are regarded as being at rest, to the vicinity of other bodies.*"[54] By substituting mechanical motion for animal movement, Descartes represents a sharp contrast to Aristotle.

In part 1 of the *Principles of Philosophy*, Descartes says that conventional words can obscure the natures of things: "The thoughts of almost all people are more concerned with words than with things; and as a result people very often give their assent to words they do not understand, thinking they once understood them, or that they got them from others who did understand them correctly."[55] He then observes that the issue of conventional meaning cannot yet be handled since the body has not been discussed: "This is not the place to give a precise account of all these matters, since the nature of the human body has not yet been dealt with—indeed the existence of any body has not yet been proved."[56] He recognizes that the body is the means for words to be acquired. What does he make of it?

Descartes thinks that even living bodies are essentially automatons or machines. Just as there is no affectivity—no appetite or awareness—at work in a machine, so there is no affectivity at work in animals. For example, clocks just are, and they move in terms of the mechanical forces of their parts; no awareness of time need be posited to account for the fact that they mark its passage.[57] By the same token, the cat chasing a squirrel is not experiencing and desiring it; rather, a complex chain of mechanical causality, of inputs processed into outputs, is at work in explaining the motion of the cat. Descartes arrives at this parsimonious view by applying his new understanding of motion to perception. He paradoxically likens sight to the cane of a blind man, which conveys to its speaker awareness of the extension of things and their position but does not convey sensible qualities that inhere in things: "In just the same way, when a blind man feels bodies, nothing has to issue from the bodies and pass along his stick to his hand; and the resistance or movement of the bodies, which is the sole cause of the sensations he has of them, is nothing like the ideas he forms of them."[58] Descartes collapses sight into touch, and he reduces touch itself to mere mechanical impact.[59] The mechanism of light and the mechanism of the nervous system convey brute motion, not sensible qualities.[60] Perception, then, no longer entails sensory awareness. For Aristotle, a sheep seeking grass and avoiding a wolf discloses an inner power of discrimination, and hence of sensory awareness and appetite. For Descartes, the very same behavior can be explicated without recourse to felt awareness and appetite—simply in terms of the interaction of purely mechanical parts.[61] Certain impacts on its nervous system trigger pursuit mechanisms and certain impacts trigger flight mechanisms. Bodily movement no longer discloses an inner principle of movement and affectivity.

At first blush, it might seem that Descartes is denying something to animals that he affirms of humans, but that is only partially true. There is no sensory awareness built into the human machine. In fact, he justifies the claim about animals in terms of our experience of automatic motion and reflexes, which he reasons are due to the mechanisms of our bodies and not our thinking:

Now a very large number of the motions occurring inside us do not depend in any way on the mind. These include heartbeat, digestion, nutrition, respiration when we are asleep, and also waking actions as walking, singing and the like, when these occur without the mind attending to them. When people take a fall, and stick out their hands so as to protect their head, it is not reason that instructs them to do this; it is simply that the sight of the impending fall reaches the brain and sends the animal spirits into the nerves in the manner necessary to produce this movement even without any mental volition, just as it would be produced in a machine.[62]

Alongside these mechanical powers, which humans share with animals, humans also have mind, which is a uniquely human attribute:

Since we believe that there is a single principle within us which causes these movements—namely the soul, which both moves the body and thinks—we do not doubt that some such soul is to be found in animals also. I came to realize, however, that there are two different principles causing our movements. The first is purely mechanical and corporeal, and depends solely on the force of the spirits and the structure of our organs, and can be called the corporeal soul. The other, an incorporeal principle, is the mind or that soul which I have defined as a thinking substance. Thereupon I investigated very carefully whether the movements of animals originated from both these principles or from one only. I soon perceived clearly that they could all originate from the corporeal and mechanical principle, and I regarded it as certain and demonstrated that we cannot at all place the presence of a thinking soul in animals.[63]

Animals, lacking mind, have all the mechanisms of perception and movement but no felt awareness.

Why does Descartes overlook the obvious affinity of humans and other animals? Descartes does consider an argument based on the morphological similarity of the human and animal machine: "I see no argument for animals having thoughts except this one: since they have eyes, ears, tongues and other sense-organs like ours, it seems likely that they have sensation like us; and since thought is included in our mode of sensation, similar thought seems to be attributable to them."[64] He rejects this reasoning, because animals communicate only passions, never thoughts, about things:

Within a single species some of them are more perfect than others, as humans are too. This can be seen in horses and dogs, some of which learn what they are taught much better than others; and all animals easily communicate to us, by voice or bodily movement, their natural impulses of anger, fear, hunger, and so on. *Yet in spite of all these facts, it has never been observed that any brute animal has attained the perfection of using real speech, that is to say, of indicating by word or sign something relating to thought alone and not to natural impulse. Such speech is the only certain sign of thought hidden in a body.* All human beings use it, however stupid and insane they may be, even though they may have no tongue and organs of voice; but no animals do. Consequently this can be taken as a real specific difference between humans and animals.[65]

If speech alone reveals the "thought hidden in a body," what does he make of the prelinguistic infant? Is she, like the animal, simply a mindless machine? Descartes responds in the negative by appealing to the common nature of infants and adults: "Infants are in a different case from animals: I should not judge that infants were endowed with minds *unless I saw that they were of the same nature* as adults; but animals never develop to a point where any certain sign of thought can be detected in them."[66] Because thinking is the essential attribute of human beings, and even the youngest child is a human being, the youngest child is thinking. Descartes's appeal to human nature is puzzling for two reasons. First, he identifies his own nature with consciousness that is only available to introspection and not to observation, but here he says that he is able to *see* that another has the same nature he enjoys.[67] Second, his understanding of the natural world specifically excludes natures or the formal differences among things; such differences, on his account, are superficial, but here he inconsistently appeals to them in a substantive manner.[68] Mention of human nature appears to be an ad hoc move inconsistent with his broader philosophical program. It is more Aristotelian than Cartesian.

Descartes has little to say about the advent of speech, but he insists that even "the stupidest child" can speak better than the brightest monkey.[69] He sketches two stages of childhood development relevant for first word learning. The first stage involves a kind of sensory overload in which the infant mind has no opportunity for referring or word learning, because he or she is totally consumed by experiencing sensations: "In our early childhood the mind was so closely tied to the body that it had no leisure for any thoughts except those by means of which it had sensory awareness of what was happening to the body. It did not refer these thoughts to anything outside itself."[70] Rather, it merely felt pain and pleasure and had sensations of qualities and shapes. This stage did not yet distinguish things from their appearances. The second stage enables word learning, because it involves the differentiation of the mind from the world and appearances from things, a differentiation occasioned by discovering movement and the satisfaction or frustration of desire: "The next stage arose when the mechanism of the body, which is so constructed by nature that it has the ability to move in various ways by its own power, twisted around aimlessly in all directions in its random attempts to pursue the beneficial and avoid the harmful; at this point the mind that was attached to the body began to notice that the objects of this pursuit or avoidance had an existence outside itself."[71] The undifferentiated realm of sensing is now differentiated into sensing and sensed. Descartes sees our philosophical problems begin at this point, because the child naively attributes its rich variety of sense experience to the independently existing things, an attribution that grows habitual in time and becomes a deeply engrained prejudice in the adult. The child takes the star to be no bigger than a candle and thinks the Earth is flat and motionless. In differentiating herself from her surroundings, the child discovers a world she erroneously believes is ripe with sensible qualities, and she encounters other human-looking beings presumably manifesting that intelligibility in speech. For Descartes, the world of speech is illusory, because it is grounded in the private sensations that each projects upon a mechanical world altogether devoid of sensible qualities.

On the Cartesian view, living beings are nothing but extremely complex machines or robots, exhaustively explained in terms of the single concept of mechanical motion. Can the input–output, stimulus–response of machines afford entrance to shared meaning? For Descartes, the infant must project her subjective experience onto things and into people. She cannot discover meaning in every animate movement she sees. She also has to use a concept of human nature to identify conspecifics, but such a concept is simply without foundation in Descartes's philosophy of nature. Aristotle, by contrast, thinks of the child as a human animal. The infant finds herself in a world of fellow animate beings whose actions reveal their affective engagement with things. Although Aristotle does recognize the Cartesian analogy of animal and machine, he underscores a central difference. Unlike machines, all animals undergo bodily changes that reveal affectivity: "However, in the puppets and the toy wagon there is no change of quality. ... This change of quality is caused by imaginations and sensations and by ideas."[72] Joint attention involves the manifestation accomplished by changes in qualities. It is not reason alone that provides inwardness; reason develops within a prior animal awareness. Few today would accept Descartes's denial of animal affectivity, but it follows directly from his consistent restriction of movement to mechanical motion. He is no doubt correct that semantics and experience are not possible for a machine, but I think he is mistaken to think of an animal only in terms of mechanical motion. Acquiring semantics seems to call for something more than brute motion; it seems to call for the aboutness of animate movement and perception. In chapter 7, I will argue that the Cartesian conception of other minds and the inference it recommends is mistaken about the phenomenological facts. In chapter 8, I will advocate a view of mind that breaks free of the dialectic of inside and outside occasioned by Descartes's mechanical reduction of movement. In chapter 9, I will advance the view that an understanding of human nature is tacitly involved in making sense of others. In chapter 10, I will argue that it is necessary to distinguish mechanical motion from phenomenological movement, something Aristotle did not have occasion to do. In that chapter, I will also suggest a way to think of light, the brain, and the nervous system that does not foreclose the possibility of interpersonal manifestation. There is much to celebrate in the Cartesian philosophy of nature, but it is suited to the realm of planets and projectiles, not animate nature.

6.6   From Revelatory Movement to Collective Intentionality

What more needs to be added to animate movement in order to arrive at collective intentionality proper? Aristotle identifies certain cognitive powers and motivations specific to humans that appropriate movement as a means of sharing a world, the prerequisite for the advent of speech. For present purposes, it is imitation that is central, for he says it is what enables children to learn: "Imitation is natural to man from childhood, one of his advantages over the lower animals being this, that he is the most imitative creature in the world, and learns at first by imitation. And it is also natural for all to delight in works of imitation."[73] The role reversal intrinsic to imitation requires a ground in the very structure of experience, and this is where a creative retrieval of Aristotle can help. Again, Aristotle has the denier of the PNC signify something both for himself and for another, and in speaking he hears himself. Similarly, not only can we see someone point, we can understand the gesture as it were from the inside, knowing that we too can gesture with the same result. The reversibility of *movement to mover* and *mover to movement*, of activity to capacity and back again, is rooted in the nature of living form, which outwardly exercises inward powers, and inwardly experiences outward movement.[74] In Aristotelian terms, it is the understanding of organic form, with its levels of life and characteristic actions, that make shared intelligibility and imitation possible.

The difference between perception and intellection proves relevant in this context. Intellection grasps what it is to be a thing in its universality, but perception is geared toward a particular sensible good or bad.[75] Great apes can be trained to gesture, which involves taking the natural revelation of movement and deploying it to reveal one's attention. Their gestures, however, remain within the horizon of the particular sensible good or bad, and they freely gesture in order to indicate what they would like to enjoy.[76] Human infants, by contrast, not only gesture toward what they would like to eat; they gesture in order to share the intelligible world.[77] That is, gestures are not restricted to requesting, but also include deictic gestures, which share attention, and iconic gestures, which pantomime an action. The target of attention for humans, a precursor to speech, is the very intelligibility of things in the context of sharing a life together. The difference, as Aristotle underscores, is that the human being is not just a social but a political animal, and the political animal does not just live with others, but shares beliefs about what makes for a good life with them. Sharing beliefs requires language, which, in turn, requires the recognition that others, like oneself, can share understanding.

In the corpus of Aristotle, mutual sharing of understanding seems clearest in the celebrated discussion of friendship in the *Nicomachean Ethics*. The discussion culminates in an account of the goodness of good friends. Does a virtuous person, by definition self-sufficient, need to have friends? Naturally, Aristotle reasons that he does. His most profound argument, rooted in "the nature of things," trades on a basic reciprocity of understanding between friends. He spells this out in steps. To perceive involves perceiving one's self in the act of perceiving another; similarly, to understand involves understanding oneself in the act of understanding another: "If we perceive, we perceive that we perceive, and if we think, that we think."[78] This self-awareness, in turn, involves awareness of one's life or existence, which is good and pleasant in the case of virtuous people. Good friends multiply and amplify the perceived goodness of life: "He needs, therefore, to be conscious of the existence of his friend as well, and this will be realized in their living together and sharing in discussion and thought; for this is what living together would seem to mean in the case of man, and not, as in the case of cattle, feeding in the same place."[79] Aristotle's discussion of the goodness of good friends presupposes the cooperative character of human existence. The peculiarity of human living together comes to the fore, and the account of reciprocal awareness applies to every human encounter. In perceiving and understanding, humans have self-awareness, and in perceiving and understanding each other, there is mutual awareness. If, as Aristotle says in *On the Soul*, understanding is the "place of the forms," then mutual awareness involves the reciprocal recognition of each as affording a place for the intelligibility of things.[80] Since humans share discussion and thought not principally about each other but about a shared world, they understand each other in the very act of understanding a shared world. In the case of friends, this reciprocal understanding is enjoyable; in the case of others, it may be pleasant or painful, and it can be because, as human, it is first cooperative or reciprocal.

Allow me to expand on these Aristotelian themes. Living with others outwardly displays through bodily bearing and dealings our own inward experience of the world and the things within it. To *be alive* is to have an organized body; to *perceive* is to have that organized body open upon its surroundings; to *understand* is to be able to articulate the world that appears to the organic body through perception.[81] Understanding cannot be conceived in isolation from these other natural dimensions of life without imperiling joint intelligibility; it is only on the basis of our bodily bearing within the world that our inward affections are outwardly borne. The bodily interplay of perceiving and being perceived, of perceiving nature and being natural, affords the context for our understanding to be understood. Soul or animate form, inwardly experienced in perception and understanding, outwardly experienced in shape and movement, is the interface between the two poles of experience, inward and outward, and it makes the soul's thing-directed affections available to others for joint meaning. Understanding, in turn, is the crucial ingredient for elevating coordinated animal behavior into cooperative human action.

How can a symbol first be acquired? Gesturing and speaking are meaningful movements directed to the rest of considering the indexed and signified thing. Thanks to our bodies, this movement-coming-to-a-rest does not occur simply in our thoughts. Rather, our bodily movements put our affections on display by putting them into play within the world. A conventional word effects rest by recalling the natural movement effecting rest that occurred at its institution. That is, we can share a common semantic field by means of the fact that our natures are on display and that our movements reveal not only the power to move, but the power to discriminate, both in perception and in intellection. Accordingly, we not only coordinate our attentions but cooperate, recognizing the reciprocity of perspectives afforded by our organic bodies.

6.7   The Ambiguity of Ostension and the Logic of Perception

One problem with the Aristotelian account is the ambiguity of ostension, an ambiguity made famous by Wittgenstein and Quine. I can find in Aristotle several factors scattered throughout his works that constrain some of the unlimited ambiguity they envision. These constraints naturally profile certain features of the world. Let me gather them together here and mention them in cursory fashion. Then, when I return to this topic in chapter 9, I will give a systematic exposition that appropriates some of these Aristotelian insights. The first constraint I find in Aristotle is the context of a shared way of life. As we have seen, animate movement discloses to other animate beings a mover, desire, and affections. Human life in particular is a shared life, constituted by shared actions and eventually shared speech and beliefs about the world. Second, Aristotle says that natural movement is most manifest in experience. The rabbit hopping by naturally calls attention to itself simply because it is moving. Similarly, someone could silently make a gesture toward a motionless rabbit and thereby draw our attention to it. Either way, movement is conspicuous. Third, Aristotle says that the universal is more manifest in perception than the particular: "Though one perceives the particular, perception is of the universal—e.g. of man but not of Callias the man."[82] The child who learns a symbol accordingly joins it first to the universal before the particular:

It is a whole that is more knowable to sense-perception, and a universal is a kind of whole, comprehending many things within it, like parts. Much the same thing happens in the relation of the name to the formula. A name, e.g., "circle," means vaguely a sort of whole: its definition analyses this into particulars. Similarly a child begins by calling all men father, and all women mother, but later on distinguishes each of them.[83]

Fourth, Aristotle remarks that the denier of the PNC reduces all substances to accidents with the resulting absurdity of a predication of one accident to another that would proceed to infinity.[84] For example, one and the same plant can be green or brown, robust or withered, wet or dry, small or large, warm or cold, among many other accidents. We can achieve an alignment of our attention by means of pointing out substances principally, for these are finite whereas accidents are infinite. In the *Categories*, he thinks pointing or the demonstrative applies most properly to the composite or primary substance: "As regards the primary substances, it is indisputably true that each of them signifies 'this something'; for the thing revealed is individual and numerically one."[85] Secondary substance, the universals, can seem to be "this something," but since they are not numerically one, but apply to many, it is not accurate to designate them in this way. The child, then, enters into shared intelligibility by means of the primacy of universals in experience, which are pointed out and given a conventional name. Only later can the child grasp the composite and the primary significance of "this something." Fifth, Aristotle does not, like the modern empiricist, restrict perception to the atomic moment. Rather, he sees it compound into memory and experience, a movement that progressively diminishes ambiguity. Aristotle, then, reduces the ambiguity of gesturing by means of living together, the natural manifestation of movement, the priority of universals, the priority and finitude of substance, and the density of experience. Psychologists call these cues for interpreting intentions "lexical constraints."[86] The advantage of Aristotle's approach is that these constraints are rooted in the nature of perception and reality, not in a priori or innate conceptuality. Although he does not provide a complete theory of lexical constraints, he does indicate a strategy that locates them in the dynamics of perceptual experience.

6.8 Conclusion

In Aristotle's refutation of the PNC's denier, three interplays come to the fore: movement and rest, sameness and difference, and speaking and listening. These interplays prove to be essential to an Aristotelian account of collective intentionality and word acquisition. Movement reveals a power to move, and rest reveals a discrimination or highlighted difference. Principally, these are universals following the logic of perception. The movement is understood when it is grasped as something reversible or interchangeable: the child understands pointing as a power the child too can employ to effect rest and highlight a difference in things for another. Similarly, the child acquires speech when she understands it as a possibility for sharing the world together.

Aristotle helps to clarify what Searle calls the "biologically primitive sense of the other person as a candidate for shared intentionality."[87] He does so by rehabilitating natural movement after Cratylus's critique. Living organisms outwardly bear their inward affections through their natural movement. Such awareness of others is not a supposition of the background but a primitive fact of our experience in which movement discloses movers and gestures disclose intentions. The institution of the symbol requires more than imagination and perception; it requires the ability to identify the natures of things. Though such words originate by institution and not by nature, once instituted they have an identity and power of their own; they reveal the things they name, rather than merely stand for the things in question. This revelation recalls the gestural movement that first disclosed affections.

Aristotle's efforts to refute the PNC's denier give us grist to formulate a companion principle, the principle of shared intelligibility. To signify is to make a movement that effects rest by distinguishing one thing from other things, and this rest is achieved for the speaker and the hearer together. We can share intelligibility thanks to the disclosive power of natural movement, which outwardly bears our inward affections. The togetherness of speaker and hearer has roots in the togetherness of natural, organic form, which weaves together inward and outward, two dimensions of the same organism. Aristotle might not have worked out an account of word acquisition, but he does provide the resources, corroborated recently in many details by empirical science, to sketch the animal and human capabilities that enable joint understanding.

III Philosophical Investigations

7 Phenomenology: Discovering Ostension

More is involved in being, for example, angry than simply showing the symptoms and feeling the feeling. For there is also the display or manifestation.

—J. L. Austin[1]

In the American elementary school activity called show-and-tell, children bring something interesting from home to show to their classmates. Attention focuses on the item shown, and the presence of the item serves as the point of departure for the child to speak about it. "This is Santa on a surfboard. It's something my mom bought in Hawaii when she was a girl. Every Christmas, I get to hang it on our Christmas tree." Telling can speak about many absent things, but it begins with something present: the shown thing. The interplay of showing and speech in this game recalls the interplay at work when children learn to speak. Ostension is a kind of showing that sets up the possibility of speech.

The Aristotelian themes from the previous chapter go a long way toward completing Augustine's account of ostension through manifestation and disambiguation through context by specifying the way mind is manifest in bodily movement and by suggesting at least certain constraints built into perception. In the chapters that follow, I will make the above heritage my own by appropriating, defending, and amplifying the insights of Wittgenstein, Merleau-Ponty, Augustine, and Aristotle. These are representatives of what Sellars calls "perennial philosophy," those who articulate and safeguard what he terms the "manifest image."[2] In my project of taking over their insights, I am at the same time articulating and safeguarding the so-called manifest image. In this chapter, I examine the disputed question concerning whether or not ostensive acts are directly perceived, and I argue that they are. Ostension works because bodily movement makes intentions perceptible—there is no need to infer the presence of invisible intentions. In chapter 8, I turn to the animate philosophy of mind that makes direct perception possible. The interplay of animate self and other makes intentions mutually available in our animate bodies. In chapter 9, I argue for the superiority of a joint Augustinian–Aristotelian account of disambiguation over Wittgenstein's reliance on training and correction. Human nature comes with certain inclinations that make ambiguity naturally manageable. In the final chapter, I relate direct perception or manifestation to the nature of language and to the nature of the scientific enterprise, and I argue for the integrity of the manifest image.

While reviewing the opinions of others, I found two accounts of ostension: the manifest and the latent. On the manifestation account, the child sees another animate self engaging items in the world. The other is genuinely given in his bodily movement. The latent view, on the other hand, gives more muscle to the mind, having it guess about the unseen on the basis of the seen. Davidson has the child react to the world, see another body reacting, and then invoke analogy to posit another self that moves the other body. Russell has the child spontaneously infer the invisible other on the basis of perceived behavior. In both cases, the other self is latent and so must be inferred from what is in fact given. For convenience, I call the view that ostension makes another mind manifest "OM," and the view that ostension prompts an inference to a hidden other mind "OI."

Both OM and OI agree to the analogy thesis: we understand bodily movement as intentional in relation ourselves. They agree that the child understands herself and the sway she has over her own bodily movement. But they differ on the evidence available for the other. OM thinks more is given. In perceiving bodily movement, the child perceives the other mind and the intention at work. OI holds that all that is given is the other body. The other mind and the intention at work must be inferred via analogy, because the other is not perceived. The difference between the two can be clearly stated in terms of the following propositions:

1. The intention of the other is made present in bodily movement.

2. The intention of the other is inferred on the basis of bodily movement.

OM thinks (1) is true and so does not need (2). OI thinks (1) is false and therefore posits (2) to fill in the gap. For OM, both self and other are given, but in different ways; for OI, analogy warrants the cognitive move from a self that is given to another that is not given.

Augustine, as we know from chapter 5, is a good example of OM. Let me repeat a characteristic passage here:

Now in this present life we are in contact with fellow-beings who are alive and display the movements of life; and as soon as we look at them we do not *believe* them to be alive, but we *see* them to be alive. We could not see their life without bodies; but we observe it in them, without any ambiguity, through bodies.[3]

Russell provides a classic expression of OI:

We cannot enter into the minds of others to observe the thoughts and emotions which we infer from their behaviour.[4]

Both agree that mind reading or telepathy is out of the question. Bodily behavior is what we have to go on. But does the behavior allow us to observe or just infer the thoughts and feelings of the other?

In this chapter, I defend OM, which is the view I found at work in the historical studies of Wittgenstein, Merleau-Ponty, Augustine, and Aristotle. To do so, I will call upon the resources uniquely afforded by phenomenology. The divide between inner and outer evidence is an unfortunate residue of Cartesian method that still infects our contemporary mindset. To this end, I propose we modify the expression "joint attention," which suggests the alignment of two inner things. Instead, I favor "joint presence," which suggests a public world jointly given to each. I conclude the chapter by discussing the method appropriate for understanding the truth of appearances, because a general suspicion of appearances erodes confidence in OM. The phenomenological finding of this chapter invites further exploration in the next. If, as I argue, the intentions of the other are in fact made manifest in bodily movement, the question becomes how it is that bodily movement can accomplish this feat. In the next chapter, I unpack the logical structure of ostension and the philosophy of mind it presupposes.

7.1 Manifestation

OM problematizes the divide between inner and outer evidence by observing that the inner of another is very often made manifest in outer appearance. Outward movement reveals inward experience. A number of philosophers have recognized this quite clearly in the case of emotions. Wittgenstein observes, "If I see someone writhing in pain with evident cause I do not think: all the same, his feelings are hidden from me."[5] To see such behavior is to perceive that someone is experiencing pain. To see it just as an action that is extrinsically connected to pain requires a specific act of theoretical abstraction. When we look upon a living body engaging the world we do not see a machine and infer an inward life. The inward life is on display in the way the animal engages and is engaged by things in its surroundings.

Table 7.1
Chapter 7: The phenomenological problem.

T2.1	Manifestation, not inference, accounts for ostension.
T2.2	"Joint presence" names what ostension achieves more aptly than "triangulation," "collective intentionality," or "joint attention," which suggest a purely mental alignment.

In the perception of emotion, J. L. Austin valuably distinguishes the symptoms of an emotion from the display of it. He rightly points out that *symptoms* of an emotion such as anger occur only when an emotion is rising or suppressed: "Once the man has exploded, we talk of something different—of an *expression* or *manifestation* or *display* of anger, of an *exhibition* of temper, and so forth."[6] The italicized terms are phenomenological terms. In an actual display of anger, we do not have symptoms on the basis of which we infer hidden emotions. Rather, the feeling of the emotion is manifest. Austin regards the manifestation as belonging to a whole *pattern* of events entailed by an emotion, including symptoms, occasion, and feeling.[7]

Emotion, as its etymology implies, involves being moved out of oneself. As Austin realizes, one's body advertises the movement of emotions to all those who have eyes to see. What holds true of emotion holds true for other potentially ostensive acts. To perceive something, I have to do something. I have to turn toward it, approach it, draw it near, and get an angle on it. But all these activities, undertaken by the perceiver in perceiving, are on display to other perceivers. That is, when Ava sees James turn, walk, and pick up a novel object, turning it over in his hands, she sees him engaging that item. Finally, action or play involves means and ends. To see someone pick up a bucket, walk into the water, scoop up water and return, carrying the bucket of water, is to see that someone is fetching water, although why she is doing so (to build a sandcastle, to surprise her spouse, etc.) might not be immediately clear.

One motive for denying OM is the fact that bodily movement appears to be radically dissimilar to felt experience. The outer and inner seem to belong to separate domains. How can something make manifest something so different? We are moved to say, then, that it occasions an inference to the dissimilar thing. Descartes, for instance, noted that just as a conventional word bears no resemblance to the thing it signifies and just as the physics of light bears no resemblance to its perception, so bodily expressions bear no resemblance to their felt experience.[8] The red face is nothing like embarrassment, but nature has established a kind of "convention" according to which reddening signifies embarrassment, tears sadness, and laughter joy. In this respect, there is no difference between conventional words and natural bodily expressions. Both are *radically* unlike what they signify.

Two considerations defuse this motive. First, the movement of music is radically unlike the movement of felt experience, and yet the movement of the former reflects and affects the movement of the latter. Music can elevate or dampen our mood. Music, felt deeply, spontaneously overflows into dance. Although there is no discernible similarity between movements of music and movements of minds, there is clearly no inference from music to affect (what would the evidential basis of the inference be? There is no supposed analogy as in the case of intersubjectivity and the sway over one's own limbs). Rather, as T. S. Eliot phrases it, "You are the music / While the music lasts."[9] Music carries its own movement; it embodies its own motivation. To hear it is to participate in its movement, to be affected by it. Similarly, ostensive acts carry their own movement and embody their own motivations. To recognize one is to participate in its movement. Second, I think the dissimilarity of bodily movement and felt experience is exaggerated. Our bodily movements go toward and away from things, and much of our felt experience concerns feelings of interest or aversion. Wittgenstein thinks children learn the meaning of "no" by means of removing something from their presence: "One says to a child: 'Stop, no more sugar!,' and takes the sugar cube away from him. That's the way a child learns the meaning of the word 'no.'"[10] The movement of a gesture can embody the negative movement of the mind. The same can be said for perceiving something. If we think about what it should look like to see someone else seeing something from a different angle from ourselves, we will realize that it should look just like it does. There is no sense in saying that the other's posture, gaze, and movement are dissimilar to the act of perceiving. They are necessary and natural accompaniments of it. They belong to the pattern of events characteristic of perceiving something. Emotion involves some arbitrary properties, such as blushing or being pale. But in general, the tenseness or ease, the lashing out or the quiet repose, are like the feeling, which makes sense, since the movement is part of the feeling.

Whether it be emotion, perceptions, or actions, our intentions are made manifest through our bodily movements.

7.2 Inference Lacks the Appropriate Evidence

Inference is a cognitive operation that moves from something given to something not given, from something present to something absent, from something manifest to something hidden. OI presupposes a divide between inner and outer evidence. A given outer movement occasions an inference to a hidden inner state. Though the other inner is ineluctably hidden behind the outer, each of us experiences our inner from within. We use inference to yoke together the present outer and the absent inner on analogy with our own inner experience and outer behavior.

Before I explain why inference is unable to bridge the gap created by the denial of manifestation, I first want to identify the Cartesian character of OI.[11] A phenomenological chasm exists at the heart of Descartes's philosophy between an object, which is manifest to many, and a subject, which is ineluctably hidden to others but most manifest to itself. As he writes in the *Second Meditation*, "I can achieve an easier and more evident perception of my own mind than of anything else."[12] While illustrating the contribution of understanding to perception, Descartes claims that, strictly speaking, other people are not experienced by us. Instead, a certain shape and kind of motion occasions a judgment on our part that attributes thought to others:

But then if I look out of the window and see men crossing the square, as I just happen to have done, I normally say that I see the men themselves, just as I say that I see the wax. Yet do I see any more than hats and coats which could conceal automatons? I *judge* that they are men. And so something which I thought I was seeing with my eyes is in fact grasped solely by the faculty of judgment which is in my mind.[13]

The object of perception in this case is a self-moving machine, or, in contemporary language, a robot. What motivates our judgment that these robots are human, that is, populated by minds? I am a privately manifest mind tethered to a publically manifest body, and another person is a publically manifest body tethered to an ineluctably absent mind. To solve the problem, Descartes proposes a simple test: "Speech ... alone shows the thought hidden in the body."[14]

OI accepts the Cartesian bifurcation of internal and external evidence, but it looks to inference instead of the language test in order to close the gap between someone's outside and his hidden inside. (Descartes himself found the appeal to analogical inference unpersuasive.)[15] For OI, an infant attending to an adult sees behavior, but the behavior does not disclose perception and desire; strictly speaking, it only displays something purely outward. How can the infant learn the meaning of words in this view? Let us grant her full-blown Cartesian intelligence and assume that she has an innate idea of conventional language. Peering out at the world, she encounters a babbling machine and decides to attempt to decode its speech. What does she have to go on? Can inference do the job?

Normally, inference requires some kind of experience as its basis. If I see smoke and infer fire, it is because I have experience that confirms that smoke comes with the presence of fire. If I had no experience of fire, however, I would have no reason to infer fire in the presence of smoke, unless perhaps someone who had experience of fire causing smoke told me. If I see presents under the tree, I can only infer that Santa left them, because someone told me that a fellow named Santa would leave presents. Had I no such information, the presents would not lead me to infer the existence of Santa Claus. A child without language cannot be told that understanding accompanies bodily action. What is the basis, then, for her supposed inference from overt behavior to covert intention? In effect, OI expects the infant to infer fire from smoke, having never experienced fire before.

Let me make the same point by using Wittgenstein's beetle example in a somewhat different sense: Suppose everyone I know has a box, but I only know what is inside my box. Shall I infer that what is in my box can be found in all the other boxes as well? But the situation is in fact even trickier. How is it that I take these other boxes as boxes at all? That is, how is it given that these sensed items have a hidden "inside"? The infant finds herself unproblematically inhabiting a world. How does it occur to her that there is more than the perceptual environment, that there is something hidden in those sounds she hears? Is it because there is something in the sounds she utters? Is it because she feels pain and hears herself crying that a bridge is made between the inside and outside of the box? But here she would only have the association of *her* inside and the outside. What would prompt the reversal of perspective whereby the outside can occasion an inference to *another inside*? *Her* inside she directly and unproblematically experiences, but *another* inside is not experienced at all. Moreover, why should she regard *her* inside as an "inside" unless she experiences other "insides"? Where can she get the idea of an inside in general to serve as the vehicle for the inference?

In his critique of Descartes, Gilbert Ryle provides some of the best statements of the insoluble character of this predicament. As is well known, he decries "the Ghost in the Machine" picture of Cartesian dualism and rightly argues that, absent some sixth sense, it affords no way for minds to commune: "But mental happenings occur in insulated fields, known as 'minds,' and there is, apart maybe from telepathy, no direct causal connection between what happens in one mind and what happens in another. Only through the medium of the public physical world can the mind of one person make a difference to the mind of another."[16] The public and private domains cannot be correlated because no possible experience could unite them: "Direct access to the working of a mind is the privilege of that mind itself; in default of such privileged access, the workings of one mind are inevitably occult to everyone else. For the supposed arguments from bodily movements similar to their own to mental workings similar to their own would lack any possibility of observational corroboration."[17] He argues that Cartesian dualism leads naturally to solipsism. Ryle rightly rejects Descartes's Myth, but merely rejecting the Myth does not yet show how others are given to us.

Alasdair MacIntyre makes a parallel observation in a somewhat different context: "Descartes's misunderstandings were as much about humans as about nonhuman animals. What misled Descartes was his view that our beliefs about the thoughts, feelings and decisions of others are wholly founded on inferences from their overt behavior and utterances."[18] Rather than inference, MacIntyre advocates a kind of interpretive knowledge based on involvement. I think MacIntyre is right about the limits of inference, but he does not develop the disclosive character of movement as the proper antidote to Cartesianism. As we saw with Aristotle and Augustine, interpretive knowledge requires animate movement at work in our limbs.

OI assumes a flawed framework in which the terms *inside* and *outside*, *private* and *public*, *self* and *other*, are mutually exclusive. The chasm separating these two domains cannot be bridged by endowing the infant with mind-boggling powers of inference; it can be bridged only by uncovering the perception of animate movement. On this view, the infant appears more naturally as an understanding animal, not an inferring scientist.

Inference does play a role in understanding the intentions of others. The question is where the line between inference and perception really lies. I suggest it lies here: Ordinarily, we perceive others engaged with items in the world and their affections are thereby made palpable. Occasionally, this engagement is clearly perceived but the item engaged and/or how it is engaged is not. I see you looking intently skyward, and, without looking up myself, I infer that you see a bird because I don't hear a helicopter or plane flying overhead. Or, as we speak about a pleasant topic, I see you grimace. I perceive that you are affected by something unpleasant, and I infer that you are thinking about something other than the topic of our conversation. Or, I catch you making a strange Mona Lisa smile and I simply don't have any idea what to make of it, and I guess at various explanations and interpretations. These examples hardly exhaust the possibilities; inference and guesswork happen frequently, but they are based on the perception and palpability of the affections in the first place.

7.3   Answering Objections to the Manifestation Account

First Objection: Since no prelinguistic infant can do phenomenology, we cannot know what it is like for them to follow the intentions of others. In this case, phenomenology is impossible.

Reply: Phenomenology is not ineluctably tied to one's own first-person point of view. It asks not how something appears to oneself, but how something appears to anybody. Therefore, we do not have to get into the mind of the infant; we need only turn to the phenomenon that that mind accesses, namely, the appearance of another's intention. This phenomenon is not different for us simply because we are outfitted with language. Language enables us to articulate the phenomenon, but it does not affect the way the phenomenon is given.

Second Objection: The availability of intentions is a subpersonal or nonconscious process and is not available for phenomenological investigation.

Reply: I grant that most of the time we do not pay explicit attention to the play of intentions in bodily behavior, but that doesn't mean it is not phenomenologically available. Consider driving a car: the skills employed react to the things in the background of one's attention, although they can easily be foregrounded and done not just intentionally but also attentively. If something unusual occurs within our field of perception while driving, we clue in and pay attention. When a car suddenly pulls out, a deer runs across the street, or a car in front of us oddly slows to a stop without using a turn signal, we tune in. The automatic background handling of the problem becomes referred to explicit attention (or at least it should, if we are going to be good defensive drivers). Philosophically, we can make use of this modulation between background and foreground to train attention on the very way in which intentions are available in behavior. We usually perceive other's expressive behavior in the background and attend instead to what those expressions reveal, but this priority can be deliberately reversed. There is a phenomenology of driving, and there is a phenomenology of ostension.

Third Objection: Perception itself is an inferential process, so it does not make sense to say that the intention is perceived rather than inferred.

Reply: Perception is routinely taken to be a basically inferential process of modeling whereby consciousness works up sensory input into a representation of the world.[19] The reason this is taken to be necessary is the poverty of sensory stimuli, which includes blind spots and only a small range of detail in the visual field, when compared to the richness of experience. To this, I would make two remarks. First, those who employ an inferential account of perception would not, I take it, wish to deny the difference between perception and inference. On their view, perception is an inference from stimuli to world, whereas inference is an inference from stimuli to world *to something else*. In other words, an inferentialist about perception can still agree that there is a difference between perception and inference. Second, I think the inferentialist account of perception cannot be right, for reasons well adduced by advocates of the enactive theory of perception and the phenomenology of perception. I agree with Noë: "We don't conjecture or infer how things are from how they look. In actively encountering the way in which how things look varies with movement, we *directly* encounter how things are."[20] Perception is not something that happens inside us; perception is something we accomplish in the world. It affords the public presence upon which inference can begin. I'll have occasion to say more about perception in 7.5 and 10.2.

Fourth Objection: A habituated inference is phenomenologically identical to a perception. Therefore, the phenomenological account cannot decide between them.

Reply: The objector is right that habituation affects the phenomenology of an experience. For example, there is an obvious difference between seeing Fido chew the pillow to pieces and inferring, on the sole perception of a damaged pillow, that Fido chewed the pillow. If the experience is unusual or hasn't happened before, it might take a moment for us to infer the right cause for the given effect. But if this is a regular practice, we will move quite automatically, without effort, from perception of the damaged pillow to realization of the absent cause, Fido. The lack of deliberation would make it seem like no inference was taking place. In the case of ostension, am I confusing a habituated inference from bodily movement to mind with a perception of mind in bodily movement?

I think not, for two reasons. First, perception is prior to inference. Let's suppose that we never saw Fido chew on a pillow. We would still infer that it was Fido if there were no other likely candidates (no other animals in the house and no open window to let another in). But suppose Fido never chewed anything at all. We would still think he was the culprit, but it would be puzzling. Now suppose we never saw Fido at all (he was a stray dog that snuck in through the window and was now gone). Would we have any reason to think it was Fido? Obviously not, but we might infer that it was an animal of some kind and quite possibly that it was a dog. But suppose we had no reason to believe that chewing behavior belonged generally to dogs or other animals. In that case, we would not know what to make of the chewed pillow. An inference to an unperceived cause, on the basis of something perceived, is nourished by past experience; without such experience, it cannot make any headway. Applied to the present case, we can say: we must have some experience of the intentions of others in order for us to be able to make inferences about them. If that is so, there is no reason to deny OM. Put differently, OI presupposes the experiential access that OM claims.

Second, there is still a phenomenological difference between an experience in which we *see* Fido chewing the pillow and a habituated inference in which we see only the chewed pillow and automatically *infer* the cause. They are in fact distinguishable. One involves the perceptual presence of the cause and the other involves something present that enables us to reason to the absent cause. We say, "I *saw* Fido chew the pillow" and not "I *know* Fido chewed the pillow." By the same token, it is open to phenomenological investigation whether the intentions of the other are present in their active engagement in the world or whether some kind of absence is involved.

Fifth Objection: Perception reports sensible qualities, and the intention of another is not a sensible quality. Therefore, the intention of another cannot be perceived.

Reply: In humans, perception occurs together with the understanding. To see something and to see it as something belong to the same act.[21] Consider what occurs when someone comes into a new room and looks around. He or she cannot see sensible qualities except by seeing them as qualities *of things*. There are not color impressions and noises swirling about chaotically, but a richly textured world of people, animals, and things in play. Wittgenstein's duck–rabbit example illustrates the same point more simply. We can see it either as a duck or as a rabbit but not as neither one nor the other. We have to reason to the bare figure, and even then we will see it as a particular shape and not as mere blotches of black pigment. The act of perception-understanding differs from inference. We don't see the sensible qualities of a duck and then infer that it is a duck. If it walks like a duck and quacks like a duck, we understand it to be a duck. Inference comes in only when the perception is evidently ambiguous. Perception has a horizon of anticipation and a horizon of retention. It takes place against the backdrop of one's past experiences. When we perceive someone's intentions, we do not do so by scrutinizing a frozen image, like a picture, but by seeing the person engaging items in the world. Such an engagement is dynamic and often quite complex. Only in the moving image is the intention perceived.

Sixth Objection: What about social robots? Humans spontaneously ascribe feelings and intelligence to things based on very little: a gaze, a gesture, an expression. Doesn't this fact show that humans make inferences on the basis of signs rather than perceive intentions at play in bodily movement?

Reply: We need to distinguish the phenomenological question, concerning how ostensive acts are given, from the epistemological question, concerning our reasons for confidence in that manifestation, and the ontological question, concerning the status of the agent we perceive. Here we will address only the phenomenological question by agreeing with Austin: "For why on earth should it *not* be the case that, in some few instances, perceiving one sort of thing is exactly like perceiving another?"[22] For example, from afar, a mound of salt might look like a pile of snow, and therefore they can be mistaken for each other depending on the context. Let's say I am walking across campus in late winter and remark, "Look, I can't believe the snow hasn't completely melted yet." My colleague corrects me, "That is not snow; that's salt." Though I misunderstood what I perceived, I didn't infer that it was snow. I really did perceive the pile of white crystals; I simply misunderstood what it was.[23] Similarly, robots and actors can give an appearance of feeling without the corresponding feeling.[24] We are not wrong to think that they appear to have the feeling. There may be no way, intrinsic to an experience of real feeling and feigned feeling, to distinguish them. To account for this lack of distinguishability, however, it is not necessary to invoke inference for the same reason that inference is not necessary for mistaking ice and snow. Rather, I misunderstood what I perceived; I misconstrued an appearance.

In this connection, Gadamer rightly distinguishes between two kinds of mere appearance: the imitation of an actor and the feigning of emotions in a social situation. Acting involves a wish not to deceive but to be understood as an imitation; feigning involves a wish to deceive. About artistic imitation, he writes, "Such imitation is not feigned, is not false show, but on the contrary is clearly a 'true' showing, 'true' as a show. It is perceived just as it is intended, namely *as show, as appearance*."[25] Actors and social robots present a true appearance. It is worth noting that someone can give the false appearance of sympathy or affection only because sympathy and affection truly appear. Rather than undermine appearance, such behavior presupposes it. In a related way, Searle points out that a radio appears to be intelligent insofar as intelligible speech regularly issues from it; however, we do not attribute intelligence to it because we have a basic idea of how it works.[26] We shouldn't allow the mere appearance of intelligence in such things as radios and social robots to undermine our confidence in the appearance of intelligence in such things as fellow human beings. We also shouldn't think that the sounds coming out of radios do not appear intelligent.

7.4   Replacing Inner and Outer with Joint Presence

If OM is right, as I argue, then we have reason to review and revise some central terms. Ostension is not a matter of coordinating the mental lives of different people by means of physical behavior; it is rather a matter of perceiving other people perceiving the world. To do justice to this phenomenon, I would like to adopt a term from Aristotle. In the *Eudemian Ethics*, he discusses the need for friends to live together in order to facilitate the sharing of a world that is necessary for friendship. In doing so he employs a felicitous expression, "the activity of joint perception." He writes:

As to our seeking and praying for many friends, while we say that the man who has many friends has no friend, both are correct. For if it is possible to live with and share the perceptions of many at the same time, it is most desirable that these should be as numerous as possible; but since this is most difficult, the activity of joint perception must exist among fewer.[27]

In this expression, Aristotle uses "perception" broadly to indicate that the same item is present to each. For example, friends discussing the ideal city are achieving joint perception even though no such city is there to be bodily perceived. I would like to broaden this activity of joint perception or presence beyond Aristotle's view of friendship to include any situation in which two people consider an item in the world together.

Joint presence says that the same item (thing, aspect, event, etc.) is present to both of us together. "Joint" suggests the reversibility of our bodily schema as well as the role of movement. "Presence" suggests the manifestation of an item as a result of movement. The target of joint presence is an item in the public world. Let me disentangle the senses of presence involved in the term. The present item can be spatially or temporally absent to one or another or both of us while yet being present in awareness to each of us. Suppose you and I recall the lecture we just attended. Although the lecture is temporally absent it is present in awareness to each of us together. On the phone, I describe a meal I am making; that meal is jointly present even though it is spatially absent to you. Such joint presence also involves mutual awareness, the presence of each of us together. You and I might be spatially present yet seeing or thinking about something else, in which case joint presence would not take place. You are admiring the frame and I the painting; you are on the phone and I am checking my watch. You and I can be temporally absent to one another yet think about the same thing. I come home and read the note my wife wrote earlier about dinner; though absent temporally, we achieve joint presence about the dinner. You and I can be spatially, temporally, or attentionally absent or present to one another and to things. Even if we find ourselves in spatial or temporal proximity, our awareness might be mutually absent to each other (we might be regarding the same item in the world but be oblivious to that fact, and that would not qualify for joint presence). Whereas joint presence tolerates a lot of absence, it requires a minimum of presence (the same item must be present in awareness to each of us, and this mutuality must present itself to at least one of us).

As I discussed in the opening chapters, a child must tune in to the embodied intentions of language speakers in order to learn the meaning of her first words. The terminology of joint presence allows us to state this condition with phenomenological precision. The same item must be present in awareness to both her and the language speaker, and at least she must be aware of this. Speech, once acquired, allows joint presence across spatial and temporal absence, but without speech, joint presence requires spatial and temporal proximity. A prelinguistic infant cannot achieve joint presence with someone on the telephone, nor can she achieve joint presence with a recorded speaker. Even if a remote voice tries to achieve joint presence with a child, the child will not figure it out; researchers put children in a room with a new object while a voice from the other room identified that object as a *modi*, yet children did not make the inference that the voice was relevant to the item they were viewing. Prelinguistic joint presence, essential for first word acquisition, requires that the language speaker be spatially and temporally present; but there is more. Suppose a child got exposed to a lot of speaking adults, but the speaking adults always talked about things that were absent and never when they were present. The child could never learn any first words. Once a network of words are acquired, she can ask questions: what is a president, what is an election, what is the United States of America, and so on, but until then talk of absent things will not bring about joint presence with the child. To learn her first words, then, the infant needs language speakers to be spatially and temporally present, talking about spatially and temporally present things, or talking about things that will become spatially and temporally present and giving signs of recognition when they are made present. The child, too, needs to be aware of the fact that the same item is present to each. As Davidson observes,

Language fills in and enriches the base of the triangle, and of course language soon reaches far beyond what can be immediately and jointly experienced. But the ability to talk and think about what is too small or distant or abstract to be seen or touched rests on what we have been able to share directly, for the experiences we register as communal tie our words and thoughts to the world.[28]

Without language, joint presence does not tolerate much absence; with language, joint presence reaches out into the vast regions of absence.

In my view, the term "joint attention" is too mental, and it suggests the coordination of two private things. For example, the psychologist Eve Clark says that first word learning requires not just joint attention but also "physical co-presence, the actual presence of the object or event at the locus of attention."[29] But this suggests that attention and physical presence are externally related. In fact, there is no prelinguistic locus of joint attention without something being physically present. Attention and presence belong together originally. In this way, I like the way Davidson describes triangulation: "It is only *in the presence of shared objects* that understanding can come about. Coming to an agreement about an object and coming to understand each other's speech are not independent moments but part of the same interpersonal process of triangulating the world."[30] Joint presence, like triangulation, focuses on the presence of shared objects, but it does so by emphasizing the phenomenological (rather than cognitive) process that makes this possible.

It may shed further light on the matter to distinguish prelinguistic joint presence from co-occurrence. Terrence Deacon, for instance, employs the term "co-occurrence" to name Hume's second rule of association: contiguity of time or place.[31] Thinking of the Lincoln Memorial might lead us to think of Martin Luther King, Jr., because his historic "I Have a Dream" speech took place on its steps. What I mean by joint presence, however, is irreducible to co-occurrence. First, it is not only closeness in space and time that brings about presence let alone joint presence. The item must also be of concern to someone at a given moment. Consider a couple sitting on a rock overlooking the Grand Canyon. The closest things to them at that moment, physically speaking, are the clothes on their backs and the rock under them, but quite probably neither is present to them at the moment. What is present instead is the canyon, stretching over a mile down and eighteen miles across.[32] Second, the nearby item of concern must be actually available to be present. I might be looking for something that is in my pocket, but unless I notice it, it is not present to me; even if I am looking for it, it is absent though it might be pressed up against me. The presence of joint presence involves an item that is engaging and available to someone at a given moment. Thus, presence has perspective built into it; it is not just the juxtaposition of two things. By spatial presence and absence, then, I mean presence and absence relative to the personal activity of exploring. By temporal presence and absence, I mean presence and absence relative to the personal activity of experiencing.

Ostension achieves prelinguistic joint presence. The infant and the language speaker are spatially and temporally present, and the language speaker talks about something spatially and temporally present (or presentable and soon-to-be-presented). Even if the adult does not intend to teach, his movements betray his attention. Ostensive cues open up prelinguistic joint presence and make it possible for infants to learn their first words. Ostension works because we are not only datives of manifestation but agents of manifestation. Our actions advertise to others our take on the world. By "agent of manifestation," I mean that each of us appears within the world, and we do so in a dynamic manner. That is, we are not merely an object in the world over against subjects; rather, we actively manifest ourselves as subjects by means of our actions, whether vital or deliberate. The closest thing my body can come to being a pure object in the modern sense is when it is no longer alive and when it appears as a cadaver; but even this is only an approximation, because it remains a vestige of the human form, the residue of my agency in the world. Descartes wonders whether his neighbor is not a machine bereft of consciousness. However, if we renounce the chasm between inner and outer and recollect the Aristotelian and Augustinian understanding, we will see that the neighbor is alive and actively manifesting herself.

7.5 How to Handle Appearances

If the phenomenon of manifestation is so obvious, why do many philosophers deny it? They do so, I submit, because they do not handle appearances in the right way. In our ordinary experience, we focus on things and only episodically on appearances. Consequently, when many philosophers think about appearances, they mistakenly treat them in an ordinary way as another class of things. Taking appearances as things has a disastrous consequence. The appearance-things cannot be "out there" among real things like dogs, cats, and sticks of butter, so they migrate indoors. They become things that take place in the private confines of our heads. In the end, they stand between us and the public world, and inference is invoked to bridge one mind or brain and another. I would like to suggest a different way to handle appearances that does not "short-circuit" perception but allows it to do what it naturally does: present the public world to each of us together.

In our everyday dealings and thoughts about our dealings, we occasionally pay attention to how these things appear. For example, we sometimes take note and say to someone, "You *look* tired," "annoyed," or "pleased," and we might say, "The car *looks* a little beat up." But to focus explicitly on the topic of appearance requires a unique habit of mind. Marketers, artists, politicians, magicians, actors, and philosophers are among the curious bunch that pays attention to it. Most of these think little about how things appear in general; they concentrate on manipulating appearances for their own special purposes. Such manipulation does not escape the distinctions of ordinary language use. When someone makes mere appearance his theme, we call him "showy," "ostentatious," "superficial," or a "spin doctor," depending on the context. But appearance need not be *mere* appearance. Artists and some philosophers are uniquely concerned with contemplating in a more or less systematic way how things appear in their truth.[33] Art does so by imitating, philosophy by conceptualizing, how things appear. Art is self-consciously concerned with the truth of appearance as such. A play, for instance, is truthful as a play or show, even though the actors and actresses must suppress their real identities in order to appear as the characters they depict. To watch the display is to delight in it as a display; it is not to be deceived. Philosophy, especially in its phenomenological form, pays explicit attention to how things appear in the ordinary course of experience. It seeks to identify and conceptualize the various ways things are and can be given to us.

Wittgenstein and ordinary language philosophers are right to see a genuine access to truth occurring in our everyday experience. However, what they do not realize is that philosophy can do more than guard the integrity of ordinary experience and language. Philosophy can pay attention to dimensions of experience we ordinarily pass over and do not conceptualize, and philosophy can clarify nuances in experience that escape everyday speaking. In this way, the task of philosophy does not consist in going away and letting the ordinary be; the task of philosophy consists rather in raising the truth of the ordinary into explicit elucidation. Philosophy, as I take it, amplifies and magnifies the theme of appearance.

At the same time, Wittgenstein and ordinary language philosophers are right to recoil before the way philosophers typically present appearances. If we try to handle appearance according to our natural perspective, we are prone to make the appearance itself into a thing; we are prone to reify the appearance into a representation or mental entity. Indeed, philosophers as diverse as Descartes and Hume take appearances to be representatives. Hume thinks all philosophers must accept that the appearances of things are mental entities existing within the private sphere of our consciousness, and we have no way to tell how these private entities hook up with or relate to the objects with which we deal in our everyday activities: "The mind has never anything present to it but the perceptions, and cannot possibly reach any experience of their connexion with objects."[34] Phenomenologists, by contrast, tend to be suspicious of conjuring up mental entities; instead they suggest that appearances, rather than being something merely mental, rightly belong to the object that appears. For them, Descartes and Hume didn't handle appearances from the right philosophical perspective.

Phenomenology, as its name implies, seeks to bring phenomena into explicit articulation. It focuses its analytic attention on how something is given, on how it appears. Phenomenologists insightfully distinguish profiles, aspects, and sides in the way things are perceived.[35] Consider a circular painting that each of us is viewing (to make it more colorful, imagine that we are in Florence at the Uffizi viewing Michelangelo's bold painting of the Holy Family). From your position, the circular side facing us appears under an ovalish aspect; from my own position, the side appears under a different ovalish aspect. Of course, we can also take turns standing directly in front of the painting. Then the same circular side we saw before under an ovalish aspect now appears under a circular aspect. The aspect is a public dimension of things. The same side can be viewed under the same aspect by each of us, but of course not at the same time. How can we account for the difference at work in the perception when each of us takes a turn viewing the same side from the same aspect? Phenomenologists talk about the difference in terms of profiles. As I continue to experience something, I take in various profiles of the aspect and sides of a thing. These profiles are temporally individuated such that, even though I can see the same side and aspect again and again, each time I take in a new profile. So when we take turns standing in front of Michelangelo's *Holy Family*, we take in the same side from the same aspect or perspective, but we do so under different profiles.

On the topic of perception, let me make one further clarification. As Noë points out, we should not think that when we are off center and the circle appears ovalish that this is an illusion, deception, or mere appearance. On the contrary, this is precisely how a circle appears and should appear when viewed from an angle; having ovalish aspects belongs precisely to the being of a circular side.[36] This is a crucial point in the history of epistemology.

The empiricists did not make the right distinctions when they handled perception and so felt compelled to say that the input is stimuli and that the mind (or brain) must construct the apparent world on that basis. Hume, for instance, rightly observes, "The table, which we see, seems to diminish, as we remove farther from it: but the real table, which exists independent of us, suffers no alteration."[37] But he wrongly concludes that considering this fact should undermine the following belief, which he thinks is inscribed in human nature: "This very table, which we see white, and which we feel hard, is believed to exist, independent of our perception, and to be something external to our mind, which perceives it. Our presence bestows not being on it: our absence does not annihilate it."[38] For Hume, appearance happens in our individual minds. Phenomenology and the enactive theory of perception instead invite us to regard perceptual appearance as a public dimension of things. The table and its sides are publically available by means of the aspects through which the sides are given. Our presence does not bestow being on it, but our presence does allow us to come to know it.

Phenomenology works out the logic of the interplay of presence and absence that is constitutive of experience. Such things as perception, memory, and anticipation involve different blends of presence and absence, and they interact with things such as imagination and expression in interesting ways. I perceive a tree being chopped down across the street. Later, I recall the event, considering the same tree, which is now absent; I reanimate the earlier perceptual experience but in a different register, as past. Now I narrate the event for people who didn't see it. They are led to think about the same absent tree; if my description were particularly vivid, they might imagine the contractor sawing its trunk, in which case there would be a grade of presence, a grade still less than their having seen it in the flesh. If I were talented enough, I might draw a picture or perhaps just show a photograph that I took; in that case, there would be a genuine presentation of the tree's demise, but again, such a presentation falls short of full presence. If the tree were particularly meaningful to me, I might hold onto a bit of bark as a memento; seeing it would remind me of the tree and its felling, but it would do so as an indication, not as a presentation. In all these cases—perceiving, remembering, narrating, picturing, and so on—the same single item is intended. All these appearances belong to the event narrated. When I tell you about the event that you did not witness, you think about the same tree even without seeing it; and, what's more, if both of us saw the tree and now, in its absence, talk about it, we are not relating to private mental entities inside each of our heads, for then we wouldn't be talking about the same tree. Rather, our intentions target a public item: the tree being cut to pieces. The language of presence and absence is indispensable to phenomenological investigation, and it has the advantage of recovering the publicness of what we intend. We intend public things, not mental entities.

The present question is the phenomenology of ostension. What is the peculiar interplay of presence and absence that is characteristic of this phenomenon? Bodily movement makes our intentions present. Such movement is not an indication or symptom, which points to something ineluctably absent; it is not a symbol or memento that represents the absent thing; it is not a picture of the intention that gives something less than bodily presence. The presence accomplished by the movement cancels the hiddenness or the absence just before the movement. Consider the following scenario: I tell you that I don't have the paper due today. As you hear my words, the warmth in your face fades and a stern expression comes over it. This movement makes your affectivity present. Had you remained the same, a different modality of affectivity would likewise have been made manifest. Our bodily being continually makes present our affective lives and our engagement with things.

My approach to phenomenology differs in important ways from the Husserlian tradition. First, I think something like natural philosophy is possible and necessary. Phenomenologists tend to think that they can talk about the body only as it is experienced from the first-person perspective. I think there is phenomenological substance to an Aristotelian approach that characterizes how nature is made manifest. In this respect, a phenomenological account of how something appears is, to my mind, complemented by a more causal account of how mind is in fact made manifest through bodily movement. In the next chapter, I will make good on this claim by sketching such an account and by speaking of the sense of nature at work in it. Second, my principal concern is not how something appears to me (the problem of intentionality) or even how a perceived body can appear as a fellow person (the problem of intersubjectivity), but how the world about us appears not just for me or for you but for both of us together. I am working within an exclusively public register, so even terms such as intentionality are potentially misleading. Better, I think, to speak of items in the world being jointly present in a prelinguistic way.

8   Mind: The Logic of Ostension

Our proper expression belongs to a sphere different from that of the animals: it is a "controlled" expression, which is superimposed on the relics of a system of spontaneous manifestation.

—Adolf Portmann[1]

In *Charlie and the Chocolate Factory*, chocolatier Willy Wonka lets his guests peer into a room full of a most curious treat: "There you are! Square candies that look round!"[2] The children protest that the candies look square, not round, but thereupon Wonka flings open the glass doors and all the candies look round to see who has entered the room. (The little sugar cubes have tiny pink faces painted on them.) The word "look" involves a kind of mirroring. It can mean the act of turning to see what's there, or it can mean what appears there to be seen. We say we go and "take a look." When we do so, we might compliment someone on his "new look" or caringly inform him that that he "looks tired." The word "face" has a similarly dual perspective. We face the world with our faces and find there others facing the world with theirs.[3] I can turn to face you; when I do, my face meets yours, face to face. The semantic range of such words as "look" and "face" invites us to consider the phenomenon they highlight, namely the reciprocal interplay of manifestation.

In *Other Minds*, Anita Avramides reviews the history of the problem of other minds from an analytic point of view. She distinguishes the epistemological problem of other minds from the conceptual problem and argues for the priority of the latter. Before each of us can ask what kind of justification we might give for believing that a given body is populated by another mind, we must have available to us a concept of mind in general that could be ascribed to another. However, if all we have is our own case, how can we have a concept of mind applicable to another? I would like to distinguish a third philosophical problem beyond the epistemological and conceptual problem. It is the genetic question of access: how are minds given to us? This is the most fundamental question, presupposed by both the conceptual and the epistemological analyses, and it is the question that occupies phenomenological approaches to the topic.[4] Avramides thinks that the conceptual problem stems from the incommensurability of the first-person and third-person points of view. She recommends avoiding this problem by beginning with a concept not rooted in a point of view, a concept of mind so general that it can be applied regardless of the perspective. She is right that the Cartesian or solipsistic starting point is a dead end, not only for the epistemological but also for the conceptual problem. But she is wrong to think that the solution to the incommensurability problem is to begin with a sufficiently general concept of mind that ignores points of view: "The lived position just is a position in which our concept is general and where we understand this generality by appeal to our actions and our common human natures."[5] In fact, the lived position is otherwise: action and life intrinsically involve points of view. This does not entail solipsism. The first-person perspective is not given via introspection but is, like the second-person perspective, embodied. What gives rise to the incommensurability problem is not the inclusion of a point of view; it is the exclusion of the other's point of view in the initial sketching of the problem.

Wrong question: How can *I* move from a visible *it* to some invisible other *I*?

So conceived, the problem of other minds admits of no solution; a point of view cannot be wrested from no point of view. The solvable question of other minds involves rather the *second-person* perspective: the mirroring of the first-person perspective that occurs in every face-to-face encounter or joint presence. We cannot conceive of ourselves as being entirely alone.

Right question: In what way do *you* encounter *me* and *I* encounter *you*?

The other person I encounter appears to me and I to her *from embodied points of view that mirror each other*. With this question, Augustine's classical appeal to the animate mind joins with Merleau-Ponty's concept of flesh to complement Wittgenstein's understanding of self and other. Animate, embodied actions advertise one's mind to other animate, embodied actors. Ostension requires that minds be available to others in a prelinguistic way. In this chapter, I sketch the view of minds that makes this availability intelligible.

Table 8.1
Chapter 8: The intersubjective problem.

T3.1	Prelinguistic joint presence happens thanks to the mirroring of bodily movement or animation.
T3.2	Bodily movement, whether deliberate or not, makes manifest our affective engagement with things.
T3.3	Such manifestation occurs against the background of the reciprocal mirroring of animate self and animate other.

8.1 A Different Kind of Analogy

In this section, I pose two questions before specifying a unique role for analogy in supporting the perception of other minds. First, how is it possible to deny OM, the view that ostension makes other minds manifest? That is, what is the experiential basis for thinking that inference is necessary for understanding ostensive acts? Second, what motivates this experiential basis?

In answering the first question, let me make my own a comment of Wittgenstein:

How would a human body have to act so that one would not be inclined to speak of inner and outer states?

Again and again, I think: "like a machine."[6]

Wittgenstein is right that the machine ontology is the alternative to OM. I think such a view need not be a response to the artificiality of someone's behavior; it can also arise from theoretical considerations, as I have experienced firsthand. Once I was drawn into a conversation with two bioethicists on aggressive organ transplants. One of them recounted the claim of a doctor who maintained he could indefinitely prolong the life of a body or a head even though they were not attached to one another. As the bioethicist expounded on this possibility, I could not help but vaguely imagine it as a possibility for the human now before me, and I noticed that he seemed to do the same. At least it appeared to me that he now viewed me differently, and I know I viewed him in a different register. As I grappled with the suggestion that his head could be severed from his body without any difference, he appeared bizarrely puppetlike instead of a fellow agent. It was an uncanny experience. Strangely, we can shift from perceiving someone as an animate mind to perceiving him as a machine.

What are we to make of this shift? It is tempting to say that the perception is the same in both cases; the difference comes merely from how we understand the perception. But that's not right. I do not perceive the same thing in both cases. When viewing my neighbor as a machine, his eye looks glassy and opaque. I notice accidental features like the sagging skin of his throat. When viewing him as an animate mind, I see life and feeling in his eyes. I gauge his interest in what I say by his look and bearing. I attend to what he says. How we understand something frames the perception and allows something different to be given. Yes, the same one embodied person is there before me, but how I perceive him, that is, what I attend to and notice and what significance that has, differs quite dramatically.

I think OI—the view that ostension prompts an inference to a hidden other mind—and its epistemological appeal to analogy originates in this reduction of the other to a machine. We cannot simultaneously view the actions of others as expressive and as mechanical. To view others as machines is to view them as devoid of evident interior life. Once we make such a move, it then becomes necessary to bring them back to a simulacrum of life through some kind of artifice. Think of the way a ventriloquist makes his dummy speak, and recognize the parallel with OI: inferential analogy makes brute motions meaningful by projecting hidden experience into them. Inference becomes necessary only when the natural expressiveness of bodily movement has been first put out of play through mechanical modeling.

Now, we come to the second question: what motivates this shift from perception of another animate being to perception of a machine possibly inhabited by consciousness? Several recent phenomenologically minded philosophers, such as Edith Stein, Hans Jonas, and Evan Thompson, have defended the view that life can be perceived only by life.[7] I can perceive animate action because I have desires that can be fulfilled and frustrated. Without experiencing such desires, I could not make sense of the actions of others. Perhaps I could narrate the actions in terms of a series of linked mechanical motions, but the inward dimension of meaning-fulfillment that the actions reveal could not be comprehended. If we ignore our own bodily aliveness, we will not be able to perceive life in others. We will instead face a world populated exclusively by machines. For example, Descartes overlooks life in his characterization of the *cogito*: "But what then am I? A thing that thinks. What is that? A thing that doubts, understands, affirms, denies, is willing, is unwilling, and also imagines and has sensory perceptions."[8] In fact, he expressly excludes animation from its nature: "But what of the attributes assigned to the soul? Nutrition or movement? Since now I do not have a body, these are mere fabrications."[9] It comes as no surprise, then, that he denies life and animate movement to others; they appear to him as machines, although speech reveals that some machines are populated with minds. Denying one's own life renders one incapable of perceiving the life and animate movement of another. If my point of view is not intrinsically embodied, then no one else's body will be able to manifest the point of view of another person.

I would like to underscore the artificiality of this denial of animate movement. The natural perspective is to perceive fellow animate minds at work. Let me review some developmental psychology that supports this claim. Children can be quite generous in their attribution of action intentions. One-year-olds will even follow the "gaze" of a faceless robot if it seems to act purposively, but they will ignore it if it does not.[10] They will not imitate the motion of a machine doing an action, even though they will imitate an adult performing the same action.[11] In other words, infants discriminate between a mere motion and a purposive movement, and the criterion for discrimination is not its physical property. Infants are just as adept at achieving the goal of an action when an adult fails to achieve the goal; infants, that is, imitate purposive action, not a particular motion. Meltzoff and Moore accordingly distinguish between a psychological description of behavior and a physical description, calling the former "human acts" and the latter "motion." The distinction is crucial, but I think the term "human" is misleading in this context. The infant follows animate acts, that is, acts done to obtain a desired goal. There is nothing specifically human about this, for purposive action is proper to all animals. Infants live in the milieu of animate acts, not brute physical motion.[12] They regard others as animate agents, not machines. It takes a great deal of theoretical coaxing to apply the understanding of mechanical things to perceived people. Imaginative scenarios must be sketched or biological facts marshaled. Normally and naturally, animate movement puts us into spontaneous communion with one another. The machine view is neither natural nor primary.

I come now to the central contention of this section. I agree with the above phenomenologists that to perceive life in another requires awareness of life in oneself, but I also think the converse is true: to be aware of life in oneself requires us to perceive its display in others. The manifestation of life is intrinsically reversible from the first-person perspective to the second-person perspective. Our point of departure is not the self, then the other; indeed, the perception of life in another is even more manifest in our experience than the tacit awareness of our own lives. An analogy, mirroring, or interplay of self and other is at work. This analogy is ontological, not epistemological. It enables perception; it does not support theoretical positing. In chapters 4 and 5, I showed that Merleau-Ponty and Augustine subscribe both to the phenomenological claim that the intentions of the other are perceived in bodily movement and to the claim that such perception is supported by an analogy of animate self and animate other. Their invocation of analogy functions differently from Russell's or Descartes's: it does not make up for what is absent in the perception. Rather, it enables the perceiver to perceive what is there to be perceived.

Analogical perception (ontological): Someone is seen as another living being. *Analogical inference* (epistemological): Something seen is taken to be an unseen someone on analogy with myself.

In the remainder of the chapter, I want to show how analogical perception works.

8.2   Manifestation I: Animate Action Discloses Affects

"Manifest" comes from the Latin *manifestus*, which means "caught in the act" and includes reference to the *manus* or hand.[13] Being "caught in the act" differs from being literally "caught red-handed." The former entails the direct perception of a crime's performance; the latter involves an inference from some present perception (say, a bloodied hand) to an unperceived criminal act (say, a murder). For example, Augustine's friend, Alypius, was caught red-handed for a crime he didn't commit; he heard a window breaking, went to the scene (the real robber had already fled), absent-mindedly picked up an axe he found there, and was taken to be a criminal by the mob of people that arrived. Augustine tells us that "they gloried in having caught him in the act [*manifestum*]," but as a matter of fact they had only caught him red-handed.[14] They perceived correctly that he held the weapon, but they wrongly inferred that he had done the deed. To be caught in the act involves a direct exhibition of the action.

Manifestation is the direct perception of another's affective life, and it occurs through action broadly construed. How does it work? First, we have to see movement to perceive intentions. That doesn't mean that sitting still isn't expressive. It just means that even sitting still is what it is in contrast to other possible behaviors. If one always sat still like a statue, one's behavior would cease to be expressive—cease, in fact, to be behavior. Wittgenstein observed, "Expression could be said to exist only in the play of the features."[15] So a certain kind of movement or play is necessary to make intentions perceptible. This is a case of aspect perception: we see someone's evident feelings by means of his or her bodily expression. We could not see them without the movement, but through the movement we perceive the feeling.[16]

What kind of bodily movement is necessary for ostension? Automatic bodily movements, such as metabolism and cell division, are unrelated to intention and therefore do not make any intentions perceptible. Routine bodily movements, such as regular breathing, do not disclose intentions or affections. Occasional movements, however, respond to and engage items in the world and thereby make intentions manifest. Quick breathing, for example, typically accompanies fright and excitement. Other such movements include the glance of the eye, turning toward or away from someone or something, and turning something over in one's hands. "Occasional" denotes not the frequency of the movements but the fact that they vary in engaging items in the world. To be alive is to be continuously making occasional movements. I will call these occasional movements "animate movements," and distinguish them from automatic animate processes, such as digestion. What makes one's intention perceptible in these animate movements?

As I argued in the two chapters concerning contemporary resources, no communicative intention is necessary to make one's intention perceptible. In fact, animate movements need not be deliberate at all. For instance, the person who stubs her toe and hops around on one foot muttering under her breath is not trying to make her felt pain manifest and would rather not be exhibiting such behavior. The person who turns bright red with embarrassment is not intending to make his feeling palpable. His bodily movement reveals his affections independent of his intentions. The biologist Adolf Portmann sees such "spontaneous manifestations" as characteristic of the higher animals.[17] These manifestations form the basis of the rich repertoire of gestures involved in animal life:

The whole posture of the animal nearly always expresses the mood of the moment as well. Rest, tension or fear; threat, or readiness to attack; and many other inner conditions manifest themselves in typical external changes. True gestures are produced by a raising or lowering of the head, or by movements of the tail.[18]

I think what holds for emotions also holds for perceptual items of interest. If we see someone in an art gallery walk up to a painting and look intently at it, we can tell what is occupying her interest. She does not engage in such behavior in order to show others which painting she's looking at; she simply is trying to get the best view of the painting. A less constrained example: an infant sees her father go to the refrigerator and remove a bottle of milk.

She can see that the milk, rather than the ceiling fan or the mayonnaise, is engaging his interest.

In what follows, I distinguish three interrelated types of animate movement: (a) actions in general, (b) actions involved in perception, and (c) emotions. By these movements, our affective engagement with items in the public world is made manifest to others. By "affective," I recall Augustine's *affectiones* and Aristotle's *pathēmata*. For both of these thinkers, "affection" names the soul's undergoing or suffering experience. It includes whatever has been sensed, understood, and felt. Michel Henry regards such affectivity as the essence of life, and he thinks affection always involves manifestation of life to itself.[19] In doing so, this phenomenologist recovers a classical insight: to experience something is at the same time to experience oneself as the one who undergoes the experience. He points out that such an experience undermines a Kantian or early Heideggerian conception of self-positing. The self is radically passive in the experience. Despite these insights, Henry sees only one side of the phenomenon. Limiting perception to objectivity, he remains within the Cartesian framework and thinks the manifestation of life occurs only to each for himself and never to another. By contrast, I think the full significance of affectivity emerges by attending to animate movement: not only is affectivity a revelation of life to oneself, but it is a revelation of life to all others who have eyes to see, ears to hear, or hands to touch. To be an animate being means to have certain desires, inclinations, and propensities to respond to the items in the world in a certain way. A given natural movement intrinsically includes the manifestation of a corresponding inward affect that targets an item in the world. One naturally imagines anger together with anger behavior, perceiving together with perceiving behavior, and action together with action behavior, although one can certainly distinguish them in thought. Animate action naturally reveals our affective engagement with items in the public world.

(a) *Action in general.* Action makes sense in terms of desire and awareness. I take action in the broadest sense to include the activity of animate agents, whether they be lions, tigers, or humans. I am setting aside specifically human actions that presuppose linguistic competence. In animate agency, the agent wants something that it sees is available by means of a certain activity. The giraffe moves toward a tree, because it desires the food it perceives there. In the infant world, actions include desiring the presence of a parent and crying to bring it about or perceiving the parent get the bottle to feed the child. To perceive an action as an action is to see it as the expression of affectivity and agency. Desire functions negatively as well. The giraffe perceives the lion and runs away because it fears harm. The infant hears a loud noise and cries out, because the noise instills fear. Animate beings desire for good things to be near and for bad things to be far away, and they act accordingly.

(b) *Actions involved in perception.* For several reasons, I think it is valuable in this context to regard perception as a kind of action. First, all action requires perception. An agent acts by navigating through her surroundings: she walks across the room, picks an item up, swings a bat to hit a ball, and the like. Perceptual engagement is a necessary feature of all action in such a way that it is hard to say where the action leaves off and the "mere" perception begins. Second, perceiving involves the logic of action. If people are looking at something, it is because they desire to look at it, and their looking is the means to fulfill that end. (Of course, they could just have a blank stare as they imagine something; the point is that all "live" looking is a kind of action that betrays desire.) Third, perceiving involves the same kind of means-end logic employed in all action. If I want to perceive a given thing, I have to find the best vantage point. For example, we say we want to "see" a novel object, meaning we want to turn it over in our hands and examine it closely. The enactive account of perception rightly underscores that perception is not a passive reception of the world, but a kind of deed; animals have to do something, engage the world, in order for it to appear to them. As Noë puts it, "Perceiving how things are is a mode of exploring how things appear. How they appear is, however, an aspect of how they are. To explore appearance is thus to explore the environment, the world."[20] On the enactive view, the entire person is the agent of perception: "It is not the brain, it is the animal (or person), who sees. It's the person, not the brain, that has semantic powers."[21] I would like to make explicit something that is implicit in the enactive account. Because perception requires a kind of activity involving moving about, getting the right angle, and so on, and these movements are perceptible from different points of view, perception makes our engagement with things manifest to others. Perception, as a kind of action, shows up in the world.

(c) *Emotions.* Feeling or desire is a modality of action. First, our rich affective life is a response to items in the world. Our feelings are either the result of an action or the beginning of one. Romeo and Juliet meet, fall in love, and marry. They sorrow at the perceived death of the other, and are moved to take their own lives. Emotions are interwoven with action and therefore can be the object of dramatic representation. Second, emotions are tied to certain bodily expressions. Austin makes the point in an admirably clear manner:

And it is to be noted that the feeling is related in a unique sort of way to the display. When we are angry, we have an impulse, felt and/or acted on, to do actions of particular kinds, and, unless we suppress the anger, we do actually proceed to do them. There is a peculiar and intimate relationship between the emotion and the natural manner of venting it, with which, having been angry ourselves, we are acquainted. The ways in which anger is normally manifested are natural to anger just as there are tones naturally expressive of various emotions (indignation, &c.). There is not normally taken to be such a thing as "being angry" apart from any impulse, however vague, to vent the anger in the natural way.[22]

Nor is there a "being afraid" or "being in love" without an impulse to vent the emotion in a natural way. Wittgenstein, too, as I mentioned in 3.7, thinks avowals concerning one's own emotions are rooted in a natural expressiveness that already makes one's emotions manifest to others. To say "I am angry" is not to issue a report about an inner Cartesian theater of consciousness; it is to express verbally what is already explicit in one's behavior. There is a third way that emotion is at work in our actions. How an action is performed expresses its felt emotion. Even the icily cool countenance I maintain as I respond to your jibe betrays something of the suppressed anger I feel. When I feel jubilation or joy, the tempo of my voice escalates, there is a bounce in my step, and so on. Fourth, action requires feeling. If I do something, it must be because I desire it, and when I complete an action I show signs of satisfaction. Without feeling, I would do nothing; if I do something, affectivity must be present.

To bring out the special dynamic of animate movement, let me contrast it with a kind of movement that does not disclose affects. Consider an outdoor flag that is mostly hidden unless the wind is blowing. As Francis Scott Key wrote in the *Star-Spangled Banner*: "What is that which the breeze, o'er the towering steep, / As it fitfully blows, half conceals, half discloses?" Here the movement originates from outside of the flag, making more of the flag visible. In the case of animate movements, both stillness and movement, originating from within, disclose not just more of the body but the person's affective engagement with items in the public world. Animate movement is self-movement that makes plain an affective self. Disclosed is a new dimension, which is somewhat akin to the moment of seeing the unfurled colored cloth as a symbol of America. The meaningfulness of the flag is not a physical feature of the flag, but it is not inferred from the flag. Rather, when it is seen, it is seen as the symbol in a case of aspect perception. Similarly, bodily movement is seen as manifesting animate affectivity. A notebook entry from Nietzsche captures this insight: "Movement is symbolism for the eye; it indicates that something has been felt, willed, thought."[23]

8.3   Manifestation II: Mirroring Disclosure

In chapter 2 on promising research in science, I detailed the discovery of mirror neurons, a neural correlate for action identification and comprehension. Animals that see others act have activated, at a lesser intensity, the same neurons that fire when they perform the action themselves, and they do so only for actions that are taken to be purposive. This suggests an immediate action identification that is specifically goal-directed. The way another engages something is a possibility I might engage in for myself. The mirroring of action is something the philosophers in our historical studies likewise examine, although from a philosophical perspective. Wittgenstein, for example, underscores the asymmetrical character of interpersonal manifestation: I attend to your pain behavior, not my own. Merleau-Ponty points to the chiasm or reversibility of bodily being, bearing within itself two dimensions of inner and outer; such intertwining establishes the reciprocity of self and other that makes gestures understandable. Augustine's infant discovers the ability to move purposively in his own members and thereby comes to discern the ability to move purposively in the members of others; thereafter another's movements put another's affections on display. For Aristotle, human beings can build upon the natural propensities of their shared human form to share a life, and imitation is a chief instrument of this shared life.

Ostension requires not only animate movement, but also the mirroring of such movement. Let me say something as to why "mirroring" recommends itself as the right term in this context. When I look into a mirror, I see myself from the outside, as it were. My normal perspective is inverted, and I see myself as another sees me. One of the things that makes me think the image is my own is that the movement of the mirror image corresponds with my own felt movement; I feel myself smiling and see a smile. When someone tries to "mirror" us by exactly reproducing our actions back to us, we get an uncanny feeling that we're somehow seeing a mirror image of ourselves. The movement of the other in the mirror plays toward us movement that we are playing out from ourselves. When we think about a mirror, we think of it as a means for seeing ourselves. But more precisely, it is a way for us to see ourselves as if we were another.

When I first conceived of this book, I thought to follow Heidegger and call this central phenomenon "self-transposition."[24] As I read others and thought about it, I realized that this term, contrary to Heidegger's intention, was still bound to the individual subject as its point of departure and suggested that it took a specific cognitive action to place ourselves, as it were, in another's point of view. "Mirroring" has the advantage of suggesting a process entirely spontaneous and yet open to experience. It also underscores that the individual subject is not the point of departure, for it leaves dynamically open which is the image and which the original. In this vein, Wittgenstein observes, "Think, too, how one can imitate a man's face without seeing one's own in a mirror."[25] What is mirrored in this context is of course not the particular looks of someone but instead possibilities of animate movement and expression. Mirroring underscores that our animate lives are on display for each other in a dynamic interplay.

The mirroring of disclosure happens by means of an identification and difference. The same pattern of manifesting action—originating from another, targeting one or more items in the world, and terminating with another—is understood as being the same across a difference in perspective. That is, I could originate the manifesting action, involving the same one or more items in the world, so that it terminates with me. The child sees her father look at her with wide eyes and a smile and then pick up a ball and throw it to her; she picks it up and throws it back with a look of engagement and delight. They are undertaking not only a reversal of action, but a reversal of interpersonal manifestation, reciprocally advertising their reciprocal take on things.

Our animate bodies can provide the vehicle for intersubjective disclosure, because they localize us and specify an orientation in the world. We could not be agents of manifestation without visible or tangible bodies. Moreover, our visible or tangible bodies do more than localize; they also display directionality, which is important for perception and action. Our front is what it is because with it we face the world and because it is the direction in which we principally can and do move. If we were perfectly spherical, we would have no such orientation; were Wonka's candies without faces, no one could tell they were turning to look around. The fact that our bodies are not partless wholes but articulated wholes gives us purchase on the world from a particular point of view. Such a perspective is crucial for making sense of ostensive acts. We not only understand the target of the other's action, we understand it as mirrored into our field of action. We mirror the act that occurs in another's field into an act that can occur in our own. We do so because our bodily orientation, facing another, mirrors another, facing us. Without the directional character of our lived bodies, we would not be able to experience or enact movement, foreclosing the possibility of shared understanding.

Nietzsche saw the role of mirroring in word learning. In *Human, All Too Human*, he writes:

Imitation of gesture is older than language, and goes on involuntarily even now, when the language of gesture is universally suppressed, and the educated are taught to control their muscles. The imitation of gesture is so strong that we cannot watch a face in movement without the innervations of our own face (one can observe that feigned yawning will evoke natural yawning in the man who observes it). The imitated gesture led the imitator back to the sensation expressed by the gesture in the body or face of the one being imitated. This is how we learned to understand one another; this is how the child still learns to understand its mother.[26]

He is right that the basic mirroring of bodily self and bodily other and the advertisement of affectivity it presupposes cannot be taught, because it appears to be the original means of communication and thus teaching. Moreover, empirical investigation shows that newborns can imitate expressions even though they have never seen themselves in a mirror or seen expressions before. They cannot be inferring from their own behavior to the other's behavior and affections, nor could they have learned of the expressions through experience.[27] We might learn some of the fine points of expression through experience, but the fact of expression and its basic vocabulary must be inscribed into our bodily way of being.

8.4 Manifestation III: Reciprocal Roles of Disclosure

With the last two sections, I have discussed how each of us engages the world in such a way that our engagement is potentially available to others.

Mirrored Action: As your animate action engages x, so may x be engaged by my animate action.

I would like to formulate the move from this mirroring of action to prelinguistic joint presence in the following way:

Joint Presence: Either my animate action engages x, and, understanding this, you engage x via your animate action, or your animate action engages x, and, understanding this, I engage x via my animate action. x is thereby animately engaged by each of us together.

Through mirrored action, we can jointly engage items in the world. (1) If you lift a glass of water to your lips, I see that you are thirsty and drinking water. (2) I see your act of drinking water as something I could do to quench my own thirst. (3) I can follow your drinking or you mine, or one of us can point out a glass of water. By mirroring disclosure we recognize the *same* item as jointly present. I can then register candidates in your word-sounds for "water," "thirst," and "glass," if, that is, you happen to be talking about what you're doing. In what follows, I would like to bring out various aspects of joint presence.

(a) *Presence is potentially joint presence.* "Presence" is a relative term in that it logically entails someone for whom it happens. There is no presence without presence *to* someone. Let us consider what makes it possible for presence to occur. First, someone must do something for presence to occur, whether that is see, hear, touch, and so on; presence is an achievement. Second, this exploring of the world necessarily unfolds from an embodied vantage point: to smell this rose, that is, to have it present, requires that flowers in other gardens, other lands, or other possible universes are not present. Things are present not just to someone but to some *body* in a particular time and place. Exploring involves a first-person point of view on the world, but this point of view is rooted in a bodily engagement that advertises the first-person point of view at work to others present. As an achievement of the animate body, presence is potential joint presence.

Can there be presence without embodied animate action? Consider the case of a movie camera. While it is filming, the characters pay no attention to the camera; it unobtrusively observes a scene. The moviegoer, in turn, can see the scene, but she is not part of the scene because she enjoys the vantage point of the camera. In Cartesian fashion, cannot each of us be like the movie camera, unobtrusively allowing the world to be manifest, without ourselves being manifest to others? I think this is impossible for several reasons. First, each camera enjoys one and only one vantage point, and it enjoys that vantage point because it is itself a part of the world. Second, those in the scene could see the camera, even though they act as if they cannot. Third, it is not the camera that sees but first the director, then the cameraman, and then the moviegoer, and each of them sees by means of animate engagement. The world not only appears to me but I appear within it, and it can appear to me only because I appear within it. The unique character of our animate bodies establishes the possibility of joining presence.

(b) *Joint presence involves turn-taking.* In conversation, we can either listen to another or speak but cannot do both at the same time (though we do hear ourselves speaking in such a way that we can detect mistakes in what we say, we cannot hear another while we speak, nor can we hear more than one person at a time). Even in a group of people, conversation is dialogical. In action, of course, we not only can act or watch someone acting; we can undertake joint action in which we do the same action at the same time. There is nonetheless a turn-taking here, for I can alternatively be the initiator of disclosive action or the one who follows another's initiation; it is not possible to initiate and follow at one and the same time. Turn-taking is part of finitude, the fact that the presence in which we live and move and have our being is limited.

(c) *Joint presence is regularized*. Animate action reciprocally discloses our affective engagement with items in the world. Acts do not just episodically establish joint presence. Rather, only because the world is always already available for each of us together such that our animate bodies continually advertise our engagement to others is it possible for a particular item to engage both of us together in a way that is manifest to one or both of us. In other words, particular ostensive acts are what they are only in virtue of a background of habitual experience. What Sellars said about the social dimension of cognition can analogously be said of ostension: there is no ostension apart from a common pattern of action, which relates what I would do in a given context to what anyone else would do in a given context (and vice versa).[28] In a related way, Meredith Williams argues that the flexible yet normative character of human action-patterns exceeds biological teleology to prefigure the normative character of human speaking.[29]

(d) *Joint presence needs understanding and freedom*. With Augustine and Aristotle, I would like to say something of the cognitive skills requisite for meeting the social and normative situation of joint presence. In addition to the animate powers of perception, desire, and awareness, specifically human powers are needed for handling manifestation. Understanding allows us to perceive the animate actions of others not just as actions but also as manifestations of affectivity. It equips us to make sense of others and thereby enables us to join another's presence whether or not that person is explicitly inviting us to do so. The will allows us to explicitly invite another to join in our presence and allows us to decide to join in another's presence.

(e) *Friendship motivates joint presence*. To raise mirrored action to joint presence requires a unique suite of motives—practical, social, and contemplative. We need help to satisfy our needs, we want to share our lives with others, and we want to share an understanding of the world with others. Augustine and Aristotle give us a way to grasp the unity of these motives in one word: friendship. Augustine thinks friendly encounters afford the opportunity for the child to acquire speech; Aristotle speaks of friendship broadly to include anyone who shares a life together, whether family members, unrelated individuals, or fellow citizens. Friendship, broadly construed to include these various situations of shared living, names the natural, human motive for participating in joint presence. The natural teleology of human life, we could say, is friendship.

A memorable passage from the *Confessions* illustrates these themes. Augustine tells us of an episode involving his best friend Alypius, who was forced by his friends to attend gladiatorial shows. Alypius foolishly tells them: "If you drag my body to that place and sit me down there, do not imagine you can turn my mind and my eyes to those spectacles. I shall be there as though absent, and so I shall overcome both you and the games."[30] Here, Alypius distinguishes joint presence from physical and temporal proximity. As readers of the *Confessions* know, Alypius's resolve failed when the crowd roared. Overcome by curiosity, he opened his eyes to see what others saw, and he drank in the carnage. We need not see Alypius's failure as the mark of some deep sinful tendency; he simply failed to consider the pull of animate action. The interest of others on display in their bodily movements naturally attracts our own attention. An inclination to joint presence is inscribed into our animate natures.

(f) *Joint presence builds on animate action.* In the scientific resources, I discussed two stages of intersubjective development, and in the historical resources, I detailed the developmental speculations of the philosophers in question. Augustine, for example, contrasts his first erratic movements that were ultimately uncommunicative with his subsequent ability to follow the animate movements of others, and Merleau-Ponty stylizes Scheler and Husserl as two stages of psychogenesis: identification and pairing. Now I would like to relate the developmental account with the analysis of this chapter. The first stage, primary intersubjectivity, corresponds to the first two aspects I identified, disclosure and mirroring. The second stage, secondary intersubjectivity, corresponds with the advent of my third aspect, reciprocal roles for establishing joint presence. Philosophers such as Quine and Davidson who recognize the centrality of ostension are nevertheless prone to ignore the roots of secondary intersubjectivity in primary intersubjectivity. In doing so, they assign to purely cognitive processes such as "triangulating" what belongs originally to the animate dimension of mirroring disclosure. By contrast, I want to say: we humans can acquire speech and accomplish our tremendous feats of intersubjective rationality because we are in the first place animate beings who share the world of mirrored disclosure in virtue of that fact.

8.5   Other Animate Minds

Throughout this chapter, I have made the case that ostension works thanks to animate action, which makes our affectivity manifest to each other. I argued above that OI presupposes the reduction of others to something like a machine, and the problem with such a position is that it attempts to square a circle: to wrest a point of view from none at all. What does OM presuppose? I think it presupposes the natural perspective: the other is *another animate being* whose activity manifests his or her affectivity. Points of view, my own included, are essentially embodied, and we know of this in the first place through the mirroring of self and other that occurs in experience; it is not something arrived at first through reflection. How does the mirroring of animate being fare in traditional accounts of mind?

In chapter 6, I detailed Aristotle's analysis of natural movement in terms of activities manifesting capacities, a position commonly referred to as *hylomorphism*.[31] A distinctive feature of his approach is that the causal principle, form, has fundamental phenomenological properties that are discernible both inwardly and outwardly. There is a distinction but no separation between the two. As I detailed in sections 6.5 and 7.2, Descartes replaces these categories of animate nature and movement with a fundamental ontological and phenomenological *dualism* of the inner and outer worlds. On the one hand, there is mind, which is immaterial, free, self-conscious, and manifest only to itself. On the other, there is matter, which mindlessly obeys mechanical force laws in a way that is publically available. Animals, constructed solely from mechanistic matter, are essentially mindless machines. Descartes makes an important exception for the human being, which has, alongside its mindless robotic body, an immaterial mind available to introspection. Philosophers who subscribe to such dualism call upon inference to yoke together self and other. As I discussed in chapter 7, the Cartesian picture cannot be right; dualism does not support the embodied viewpoint necessary for joint presence. Does materialism fare better than dualism in supporting joint presence? Nietzsche, an avowed materialist, uncharacteristically praises Descartes:

As regards the animals, Descartes was the first to have dared, with admirable boldness, to understand the animal as *machine*: the whole of our physiology endeavors to prove this claim. And we are consistent enough not to except man, as Descartes still did: our knowledge of man today goes just as far as we understand him mechanistically.[32]

Nietzsche's *materialism* still accepts the Cartesian dualism of inner and outer evidence. It replaces the ontological dualism of mind and machine with the research program of mechanistic monism. We investigate the parts of the body on the supposition that mind is reducible to matter. Despite his fine comments on gestures that I quoted in this chapter, Nietzsche's mechanistic monism leads him to lose confidence in the reality of manifestation:

In an animated conversation I often see the face of the person with whom I am talking so clearly and so subtly determined in accordance with the thought he expresses, or that I believe has been produced in him, that this degree of clarity far surpasses my powers of vision: so the subtle shades of the play of the muscles and the expression of the eyes *must* have been made up by me.[33]

Joint presence through the manifestation of animate movement appears illusory, because the mechanical movements of the body are too complex to be perceived. On the question of manifestation, then, such materialism fares no better than dualism. Is there an alternative that is more hospitable to the phenomenon? Concerning joint presence and embodied points of view, I do not find mitigated forms of dualism and materialism to be better positioned.

Property dualism exploits the Cartesian separation of inner and outer evidence to its own advantage: minds are available only to introspection, which is a necessarily private act. Points of view are essentially disembodied. Consider one of its principal arguments, the logical possibility of zombies. As David Chalmers describes it: "A zombie is just something physically identical to me, but which has no conscious experience—all is dark inside."[34] Of course, zombies are logically possible only in the case of other beings; we know from the inside that our light is on. Chalmers therefore asks, "How do we know that others are not mindless zombies?"[35] He thinks Russell's inferential analogy is the best means available for answering the question, and he thinks it is obvious that zombies are logically possible. My own view is that the specter of the zombie is neither natural nor intuitive. Rather, it trades on the theoretically motivated mechanical conception of bodies to which a mind may or may not be clandestinely present. Zombies will appear as an *obvious* possibility if and only if you have already accepted the Cartesian separation of the inner and outer. Now, I do think the phenomenological claim that movement naturally makes affectivity manifest is compatible with the metaphysical claim that, despite the appearance, it is logically possible that in a given case the manifestation is an illusion; in reality nothing is there to be made manifest. As I pointed out in section 7.3, this is the case with social robots and, in a different way, with actors. My point, following Evan Thompson, is just that what makes zombies an obvious possibility is the Cartesian denial of animate movement.[36]

Nonreductive physicalism, as articulated by John Searle, suffers similar defects. I focus on Searle because I agree with much of what he says. As I mentioned in section 1.3, he does not think that we infer that people or animals are conscious; he thinks we just respond to them as conscious beings. Searle formulates his account of collective intentionality according to the dictates of methodological solipsism. An intentional act is directed toward the world even if it happens in a disembodied brain artificially stimulated by scientists: "But I could have all the intentionality I do have even if I am radically mistaken, even if the apparent presence and cooperation of other people is an illusion, even if I am suffering a total hallucination, even if I am a brain in a vat."[37] I do not find it problematic that Searle entertains the logical possibility of such a scenario. I find it problematic that his materialism leads him to think it is—in some sense—true:

My basic assumption is simply this: ... The brain is all we have for the purpose of representing the world to ourselves and everything we can use must be inside the brain. Each of our beliefs must be possible for a being who is a brain in a vat because each of us is precisely a brain in a vat; the vat is a skull and the "messages" coming in are coming in by way of impacts on the nervous system.[38]

Naturally, I do not doubt the scientific facts and the causality of the brain in cognition. I just wonder about its relevance when discussing meaning and the way it is socially acquired through joint presence. Searle rightly thinks that our points of view are embodied, but he wrongly buries the point of view under our skin. If each of us is in some sense a brain encased in a vat, what becomes of the presence and cooperation of other encased brains? How can we coordinate the stimuli in two people's brains when we have so little to go on? As Davidson argues in his critique of Quine, proximal stimuli cannot support joint presence and word learning: "Proximal theories, no matter how decked out, are Cartesian in spirit and consequence."[39] Biological facts *seem* to put us "inside" our heads. Word learning, however, requires us to be outside our skin with others, among things. As we have seen, this happens thanks to animate movement. Searle is not wrong to talk about brains; he just does so prematurely, before finishing up the requisite phenomenological and logical analyses of how we are available to each other. In section 10.2, I will suggest a strategy for understanding the biological and philosophical facts in a complementary way.

Informing the basic assumption of both property dualism and nonreductive physicalism is a Cartesian blindness to interpersonal manifestation and joint presence. To make sense of our sharing the world, I advocate scuttling the Cartesian framework.[40] To do so, I suggest adopting a principle articulated in different contexts by Sokolowski and Noë, respectively:

The way things appear is part of the being of things; things appear as they are, and they are as they appear.[41]

How things look ... is precisely a feature of the way things are.[42]

Appearances are not necessarily private; they can belong to the public natures of things. I would like to apply this approach to appearance in the present case. For the perception of other minds, we need something more than brains, consciousness, and mechanical motion. We need the appearances at play in facial expressions, gestures, and purposive movements. Points of view are essentially embodied. I think that hylomorphism, enriched by phenomenology, uniquely supports interpersonal appearance. Because "phenomenologically enriched hylomorphism" is unwieldy, I propose the shorter term "animate mind." According to the animate mind, the appearance of mind in animate movement is simply an aspect of what mind is. With phenomenology, the animate mind would reconnect the inward and the outward and reclaim the genuine perception of other animate minds. With the perennial tradition, it would articulate a unity across two dimensions: inward experience and outward manifestation. Activities and movements reveal capacities to discriminate, desire, and act. The mind is not incidentally attached to a body; the mind is essentially embodied and on display in animate action. This sort of account affords resources for joint action, joint perception, and joint contemplation. At the same time, the manifestation of mind remains unthematized in traditional hylomorphism. Its proponents, following Aristotle, are typically concerned with giving a causal account of the substantial unity of an organism rather than developing its intersubjective potential.[43] In this connection, Augustine and Merleau-Ponty provide a needed phenomenological development of hylomorphism. The enrichment is reciprocal, for despite their fruitful phenomenological investigations, neither gives an adequate account of the nature of the animate mind. For example, more explanation is needed concerning how the phenomenological properties of mind relate to the underlying material substrate that science can investigate.[44] I also think hylomorphism gives us the ability to accept Wittgenstein's sensitivity to manifestation while avoiding his behavioristic leanings. In section 10.3, I will say more about the concept of animation operative in this account of mind and why I don't think it can be straightaway identified with the subject matter of biology.

9 Epistemology: Disambiguating Ostension

I cannot open the eyes of my readers or force them to attend to the things which must be examined to ensure a clear knowledge of the truth; all I can do is, as it were, to point my finger and show where the truth lies.

—René Descartes[1]

Many years ago during a visit to the beach, my grandfather picked up a broken conch shell. He called his grandchildren around him and solemnly declared, "This is a *Pingus pangus pongerongus*." Now that he has passed away, there is a heated disagreement among us: is a *Pingus pangus pongerongus* any broken shell, or does it have to be a broken conch shell of the same shape and size? His humorous ostensive definition was ambiguous, and what's true of *Pingus pangus pongerongus* is true of all ostensive definitions, as Quine, Wittgenstein, and Augustine argue. One and the same gesture might point to a piece of paper, its whiteness, or its surface. One and the same gesture might point to a rabbit, its fur, or its undetached rabbit parts. A major question of ostensive definition is epistemological: how can it be disambiguated? What's true of ostensive definitions appears to be true of ostension more generally. Gestures, gazes, and actions admit of a plurality of interpretations; their targets can be parsed in more than one way. Not only is the target of the action potentially ambiguous (is the adult filling up the bottle or just emptying out the milk jug?), but the language spoken while performing these actions might have no bearing on the actions themselves (perhaps it's just talk about this year's prospects for the Cleveland Indians). At least with an ostensive definition, the definer is trying to control the ambiguity through context, cues, and by proper set up. How can ostensive acts be useful for prelinguistic infants when they are infected with such ambiguity?

The astonishing fact is that children are pretty good at disambiguation. They figure out ostension and learn words. The question is, philosophically speaking, what must be at work in their expertise? As I pointed out above, the disambiguation of ostensive definition is much simpler than the disambiguation of ostension more generally. For this reason, I begin this chapter by examining the problem of ostensive definition. My remarks in this section could also be taken to solve what Michael Devitt and Kim Sterelny call the "*qua*-problem" in Kripke, which is a localized version of the problem of disambiguation. An act of ostension cannot establish a rigid designator absent some constraints that specify just what is being identified: the dog *qua* dog, the dog *qua* cocker spaniel, the dog *qua* Fido, and so on.[2] Although the item of ostension need not be subsumed under a rule or description, it does need to be disambiguated along the lines I suggest. After I discuss the problem of ostensive definitions, I take up the problem of ostension. Context, repetition, and the logic of perception provide the right kinds of lexical constraints or biases that make disambiguating ostension possible. My contribution in this chapter stems from the phenomenology of joint presence and the mirroring of action disclosure. Experimental psychology can contribute much to the particulars of the question; here I want to identify the broad logical and phenomenological contours of the process. What background biases and abilities put the relevant items in the foreground, thereby establishing prelinguistic joint presence?

9.1 Disambiguating Ostensive Definitions

An ostensive definition occurs in a conversational context. It involves a communicative intention and some means for establishing prelinguistic joint presence. Most characteristically, it involves a gesture, such as picking up a novel object and bringing it to view, or pointing or nodding in the direction of the item; but such gestures are not necessary. An ostensive

Table 9.1

Chapter 9: The epistemological problem.

T4.1	Ostension is considerably more ambiguous than ostensive definition, because the learner must identify ostensive acts on her own and disambiguate them for herself.
T4.2	Understanding everyday contexts and routines helps us disambiguate ostensive acts.
T4.3	The inclinations of our joint human natures constrain our desires and highlight certain features of the world over others.
T4.4	Ostension affords the learner the opportunity to identify a thing, and this identification is organically related to further growth in understanding the thing in question.

definition can occur in response to an inquiry, when someone else asks, "What is that?" And the other person need not even formulate a question. We might just see her staring at something with a quizzical look. For example, to illustrate for my students the difference between animal perception and human perception, which is accompanied by understanding, I bring into class a heavy, nonrepresentational sculpture my sister made out of clay. As soon as I bring it into the classroom, they stare. Some ask, "What is it?" but everyone looks puzzled. In response to their query, whether verbalized or not, I can tell them what it is. What allows for this prelinguistic joint presence?

(a) *Movement is an attention getter*. Either the definer or the questioner can use movement to make an item present: here is an item. But neither need do anything. The item itself, by virtue of its own movement, might elicit our attention. The airplane flying overhead or the bunny bounding by gets our notice. There is no logical necessity to this. It is perfectly conceivable that an inhabitant from Alpha Centauri might be found who would do the reverse: ignore movement and pay attention to what was still. Of course, this would be a very inefficient way of achieving joint presence, because generally speaking most of the things in our surroundings are still, while fewer are on the move. One of the things that enable the disambiguation of ostensive definition is simply the fact that movement and things that move in a manifest way are, generally speaking, interesting.

(b) *Difference is an attention getter*. Imagine being at the beach with wave after wave crashing, or sitting at a bus stop on a busy street while car after car zips by. We will not have any motivation for thinking that our companion is thinking about this particular wave or that particular car, since the movement is routine or patterned and is in that respect not a movement. Now, imagine that a huge wave came crashing in, one much bigger than the rest, or imagine that an antique car with giant rocket fins drove by. These things are different and novel, and so are attention getters. It is not movement itself but the difference of something moving that makes it jointly present. If I constantly made a pointing gesture, you would rightly cease to pay my pointing any mind. The new and the different are prominent in our experience.

In the next chapter, I will say more about how movement and difference help make the same item jointly present. Now I will pursue a slightly different question: how can we further tell just what it is about the item present that is relevant? That is, when we are presented with the same rabbit, what about it—the fur, the rabbitness, the composition of parts, and so on—is being defined? Ostensive definition, it seems to me, is helped by several constraints on the target of joint presence.

(a) *Bias toward the novel.* Let's suppose that two friends are on a walk through the woods. A snake slithers by and one reports that it is an "elephant trunk." Since the other sees that it is a snake and thinks the companion is a meaningful fellow, he will likely take the ostensive definition as introducing him to one of the 3,000 species of snake he has never heard of before. (Of course, the companion might just mean that it looks like an elephant trunk, so he'd have to ask to be sure or just look to see whether the fellow looked like he had delivered an amusing comment or an informative one.) Absent indicators to the contrary, we naturally attend to what is novel in the experience. This tendency is helped when we are in the company of someone who knows quite a bit about what we know and don't know, but it still works for someone we've just met who can rely on general patterns of what is usual and unusual for human beings.

(b) *Perspectival bias toward an object of a certain size in the perceptual field.* We carve up the perceived world into wholes and are prone to regard ostensive cues as targeting entire objects, rather than their parts. We generally say, "There's an airplane," not "There's a wing." In our perceptual field, the number of wholes is much more manageable than the number of parts. If we see something from far away, we are likely to refer to it as a whole. Say we're at the zoo looking for the animal in the exhibit: "There's the bear." The child can follow the adult's gaze and spot the creature poking out from behind the crop of rocks. The child does well to think the parent is talking about the bear and not any bear parts. But suppose we were at the nature center looking at the stuffed bear looming large right in front of us. Now, we might talk about some part of the bear: "Look at those massive teeth and those fearsome claws." Similarly, if we are standing on the runway during an airshow right next to the plane, we would more likely talk about the wing or the landing gear because they are larger portions of the visual field. There is a flexible perspectival bias toward a certain range of sizes. Let's suppose that we have some novel object before us, for example, a broken shell, and we point to its missing piece. A secondary pointing for something already present focuses attention to its part.

(c) *Bias toward a certain kind of thing.* Ostensive definitions work best for basic actions and present things. You can give an ostensive definition of some simple act, such as gulping, drinking, or jumping jacks, but it is well-nigh impossible to ostend modalities of action. For instance, if you wanted to define, "sallying," you would do well to give a verbal definition. *Merriam-Webster* defines it as "a venture or excursion usually off the beaten track."

You obviously cannot ostend something that is absent, so most things we talk about don't admit of ostensive definitions. My point is that if I know you are trying to give an ostensive definition, I'll look for basic actions or present things that can be easily defined in that way.

(d) *Bias toward essential properties.* My grandfather was joking when he defined the *Pingus pangus pongerongus* as a broken conch shell. What made it funny was the fact that we define things in terms of their essential properties, not their accidental ones. There is no word for "broken shell," because we name things for what they are, not what incidentally happened to them. If we named things in terms of their accidental properties, ostensive definition would be radically ambiguous: is this just a shell picked up on this day and hour, is it something with a streak of brown, a chip, or that is hard to the touch? Further, is it something that fits in your hand, weighs a certain amount, or looks a little like a rhinoceros? I am just scratching the surface, of course, regarding the infinite number of accidental properties potentially indicated by a single ostensive gesture. But, as Aristotle rightly points out, essential properties are not so numerous. Absent indicators to the contrary, we will naturally look for essential properties.

(e) *Bias toward a certain level of generalization.* Does the ostension intend this singular shell, this particular kind of shell, an example of shellness, an example of something found on the beach, or an example of a physical object? Absent other specifying information, we tend to take an ostensive definition as specifying low levels of generalization: this particular kind of shell or shell in general. We don't define particulars, and we do not define abstract terms such as "something found on the beach." Absent indicators to the contrary, we'll naturally look toward a certain level of generalization.

(f) *Conversational context.* Suppose you wanted to define a term that required resisting one or more of the above biases. For example, how could you ostensively define an accidental property? Unlike ostension in first word learning, ostensive definitions occur amid speech. They normally happen in a conversation or in reference to a previous conversation. "Do you remember when we were talking about raccoons? Well there's one now." The conversational context could specify that what was being defined was not a thing but an accidental property of things: "Here's something that is broken." Moreover, linguistic markers such as articles indicate whether the word should be taken as an abstract term or a particular. Without conversational context, the biases toward novelty, essential properties, or low levels of generalizations are generally in play. With conversational context, these biases can be reversed or further specified.

9.2   Disambiguating Ostension

In ostensive definition, the ostender takes strides to ensure that the ostendee follows the ostensive act. As such, the ostender looks to see whether or not the ostendee rightly comprehends the ostended item. This can be done visually: does the ostendee look in the right direction, is he puzzled, or does he display a look of recognition? It can also be done verbally: the ostender listens to the ostendee speaking and corrects his or her word use, if necessary. Correction constitutes an additional support for ostensive definition, a support lacking ostension. Let me give an example. With the fall time change, my children were awake after the sun set for the first time in many months. Looking out the window, I pointed to the dark sky and told my children, "Look at the moon." I noticed that my eighteen-month-old was looking into the foreground at the dark mess of trees and whatnot with a puzzled look, so I pointed again, this time exaggerating the upward movement, and said, "*Moooooooon.*" When he looked upward toward the luminous moon, a look of recognition came across his face and he smiled to see something new.

Wittgenstein thought that correction was the principal means of disambiguating ostension, but this cannot be. First, because he presupposes that children must be taught their first words, but in fact they can learn them through eavesdropping. There must be a way to disambiguate ostensive cues besides correction, because correction presupposes training but language learning does not. Second, correction is rarely needed. Children generally do not make mistakes when making sense of what is being ostended. The most common error is error in extension, but in such a case the right item is understood but under the wrong level of generalization. For instance, at first my son called all liquids, whether milk, water, or urine, by the same name, "milk." He was right that we were speaking about a liquid when we used the term "milk," and not a host of other things, such as the cup, the activity of drinking, the Cheerios, and so on. For him, the word "milk" meant what we call "liquid." Milk is only milk in contrast to terms for different kinds of liquid. Absent these other terms, he rightly "overextended" milk. But such overextensions are rare. Where correction is needed is in fine points of grammar, such as word order and pronoun usage. In learning first words, the child seems quite capable of disambiguating without correction from an instructor.

It is not just the lack of correction that makes ostension more difficult to disambiguate than ostensive definition. With ostension, the infant has no linguistic context for help; she cannot ask for an ostensive definition, and she would not know what to do with an ostensive definition. Ostensive definitions target a particular class of things that lend themselves to being pointed out and thereby taught; the teacher is trying to teach and tries to teach only those things that are teachable. With ostension, however, the language speaker is not trying to teach, not trying to disambiguate his ostensive cues. The infant, then, is in an extremely ambiguous situation: eavesdropping on speech accompanied by occasional ostensive acts not necessarily intended to be ostensive. Unlike a traveler to a foreign land, the infant does not have a reference language with which to attempt to translate the strange new language. She does not already know how language might carve up the world. The infant just has these strange sounds to parse and pair with occasional and ambiguous ostensive cues. How can this overwhelming ambiguity be managed? Children do learn words even in situations when they are not being deliberately taught. So, we know the challenge is surmountable. Logically speaking, what is there to go on?

On a plane ride, I was given a taste for the infant's situation by watching television programming without earphones. Of course, the camera showed you where to look to follow the action, and the action is exaggerated and stereotypical; infants naturally do not have the benefit of either camera angle or genre understanding. Still, the expressions of emotion and the people's reactions to various situations were quite palpable. With the audio on, I would naturally have attended to the speech and only secondarily and in the background to the action; with the audio off, the action and gestures came to the fore. The child finds herself within a perceptually given field of experience. Within the field, various items of possible interest are available. Take the typical living room for an infant in the West. There's something big to climb and sit on, something small to hold with buttons to press, something to push and roll around, bounce, or toss, something to stack; there are also a host of other things whose function is less clear: the novel texture of the something below, the shapes up above and all around, the green something she is always prevented from touching; most interesting of all is the parent or sibling who is engaging these things and making sounds while doing so. Now the child can operate in two modes: as a dyadic engager of things or as a triadic observer of others engaging things. By manipulating things, she gets a sense for them: how they feel, smell, look, taste, how they react to different motions, what you can do with them. By watching others, she gets a sense not only for what can be done with these things but for what words clothe them. When in observer mode, how might an infant tell which item from the field of experience is relevant to the words she hears? Ostensive cues are crucial, but how can she make sense of them to tell which of the many items and aspects of items are relevant?

The infant who follows ostension has a number of things likewise available to the adult who disambiguates ostensive definitions. Movement and novelty tend to be conspicuous. The child, moreover, will naturally seek to pair novel words with novel items, to attend mainly to wholes over parts, to look for particular kinds of objects, to look for essential features, and to look for items on a middle level of generality. Infants must make sense of ostensive cues in terms of their own active engagement with the world. They will make distinctions between things based on manifest sensible qualities, whether tactile or visual. They will distinguish bears from airplanes based on the difference in shapes and sounds and visual behaviors characteristic of each. They will not regard "bear" as referring to "something crouching behind a rock" or "something that makes me scared" but instead to "something of a particular shape that is brown and furry and growls." They will not regard OJ as "something bought at the store," "something orange in color," "something stored in the refrigerator," "something cold," and so on, but as "some sweet orange drink." Moreover, the child is inclined to take words to name natural kinds, not particulars. For example, for a while my son called all dogs "Tia," the name of his grandparents' dog. The child understands that "tickling" means tickling anyone, not just the child. Beyond these similarities to ostensive definition, ostension requires some unique disambiguating clues. All three of the following constraints are in Augustine.

(a) *Natural wants.* Children are not machines but animals, who experience a range of desires that specify practices. For example, the child gets hungry, and she is fed. When she feels hunger, her attention narrows to this felt need. When the caregiver hears the cry of the infant, her felt need becomes present to him, and they achieve joint presence. Desires, signaled by cries and other prelinguistic cues, establish joint presence. Perhaps Wittgenstein had something like this in mind with his cryptic remark: "If lions could talk, we wouldn't understand them."[3] If some creature with a radically different set of desires had a language, we would have less to go on in making sense of their practices and thereby their words (indeed, if it were radically different, the creature could lack the human desire to understand and communicate; it would therefore lack language).

(b) *The context of everyday routines and games.* Children disambiguate ostensive cues in reference to established everyday routines and games. The child learns the word for mother and father in terms of the care they give. Words for food and drink are established through routine care giving.

Words for ball and swing, brother and sister, come about in the context of regular play. Play and action specify certain items as ends and others as means, which makes them available for ostension. For example, the child might overhear the following in the course of routine caregiving: "Can you please get me a diaper?"

(c) *Repetition across various contexts.* Children can learn words on a single occasion, but most of their first words will be heard on multiple occasions and in different contexts. The play of identity and difference will then help disambiguate ostensive cues. Children can pair the novel object or action with the novel word. Repetition, of course, is itself puzzling. Different contexts progressively narrow down the range of meaning. How should we construe this? Perhaps, we think that either something is clear, or that it is hopelessly ambiguous. A clear ostensive cue could be understood at one go, but what good would repetition do for hopeless ambiguity? Repetition would simply yield more ambiguity. Another way to construe this is to think that we form a mental range of possibilities that subsequent experiences systematically narrow until the ostensive meaning is clear: it is either $a, b, c, d, \ldots,$ or z, but now it must not be z, so it is either $a, b, c, d, \ldots,$ or y. I think the phenomenon of vagueness, however, allows us to see the elimination of ambiguity in a more natural and less theoretical way.[4] Experience has a cumulative effect. At first things might be vague, but subsequent experience brings greater clarity. It is the force of experience itself and not an act of reasoning that eventually brings to the fore the relevant target of an ostensive cue repeated in various contexts.

What do the above biases add up to? Children are animals with desires that wed them to the world and profile certain features related to those wants. Contexts and routines bring to the fore some items and activities, letting others recede into the background. Perceptual experience naturally focuses on wholes (or parts of a certain size in the visual field), and it tends toward a smaller number of essential properties rather than the infinite number of inessential properties of things. Finally, on the cognitive level a child begins geared toward a certain level of generalization. When the child overhears speech about the world, and this speech is accompanied by ostensive cues, she is able to disambiguate them through desire, context, and biases native to perception and cognition.

9.3   The Nature of the Conversational Animal

In the preceding sections, I have made much of biases. I owe the reader an explanation of them. Are they a priori constraints? If not, how do they arise? I think the Aristotelian concept of nature can be helpful here. I have in mind the following. To be human is to have a human nature. Now, nature for Aristotle is not something static but is instead a dynamic propensity for development. To be an oak tree is to have a determinate vector of growth that nonetheless gives much leeway for individual variation (for example, all oak trees have acorns and the same pattern of leaves, but their sizes and shapes vary, as do the arrangement of their branches). In human beings, nature is even more dynamic, and Aristotle distinguishes between first and second nature. First nature gives us the capacity to develop certain abilities, and second nature designates those abilities once acquired.[5] In English we say that our habits become "second nature," by which we mean something quite Aristotelian: piano practice gives us the propensity to play the piano, batting practice gives us the propensity to hit the ball, smoking gives us the propensity to smoke, and doing good deeds gives us a propensity to do further good actions. Virtue ethicists make much of second nature in the practical realm, but second nature is not limited to habits of action. As McDowell has recently emphasized, second nature has a specifically cognitive dimension as well.[6] Our understanding of things is not something given; it is something that must be developed. Second nature is what it is thanks to the free development of first nature, and I think first nature can help us make sense of the biases I have identified.

For Aristotle, first nature comes with certain capacities to develop habits, and these capacities constitute a kind of *inclination* toward the development of these habits. In a similar way, John Stuart Mill speaks of a natural tendency to maturation: "Human nature is not a machine to be built after a model, and set to do exactly the work prescribed for it, but a tree, which requires to grow and develop itself on all sides, according to the tendency of the inward forces which make it a living thing."[7] Thomas Aquinas broadens inclinations in a way I find suggestive. He thinks human nature specifies a range of inclinations. Like any substance, we humans desire self-preservation. As with other animals, we humans desire to eat and reproduce. The presence of rationality also introduces into the human animal inclinations toward community, truth, and God.[8] My purposes are different from Aquinas's insofar as I am not in this context interested in the origin of morality but in the possibility of human communication. I think Aquinas's intuition, here, is quite helpful for my present concern, for the inclinations of human nature specify a range of human interest.

Above, I argued that disambiguating ostensive definitions is helped by several factors. First, movement and difference are naturally conspicuous.

Second, perceptual experience naturally profiles items that are novel, a certain size of the visual field, and at a particular level of generalization. Third, the context of the conversation, whether linguistic, perceptual, or behavioral, provides clues to understanding. Additionally, I argued that ostension is helped by natural wants, everyday routines, and differential repetition. Now I would like to argue that these biases and contexts are inscribed in human nature as inclinations. We learn of these inclinations by having them, not by attending to a network of a priori concepts. We need never pay any attention to them. Human nature, experienced from within by means of having certain desires and engaging the world in a certain way, guides the infant in making sense of others. Such guidance does not, I think, entail specific beliefs: to be human means to desire *x* or to do *y* by means of *z*. Rather, the guidance belongs to infant's background understanding. As she progresses in engaging the world, she mirrors others and progresses in understanding the way other animate beings engage items in the world. It takes quite a bit of experience to restrain the universal projection of a human way of being on anything that moves meaningfully, such as other animals and robots.

When I make these claims about natural human inclinations, I have in mind the concept of "life-form" recently expounded by Michael Thompson. He thinks the life-form is described through a natural-historical judgment, which is logically distinct from other kinds of judgment. To say, for instance, "Dogs have four legs," is different from saying, "Most dogs have four legs" or "Dogs should have four legs."[9] The judgment is not about Fido, Zeus, or Mopsey, any of which, after all, might be dogs with just three legs. The judgment rather describes the life-form of the species. There is a philosophical approach to human nature as a natural kind. In the present case, I think it is necessary to say: the human life-form has certain inclinations that aid disambiguation. It is not that most humans have these inclinations or that they should if they do not. Rather, the human life-form is something we necessarily use to make sense of each other. To see why this must be the case, consider an insight from Anscombe on the possibility of communication. She writes:

I am sitting in a chair writing, and anyone grown to the age of reason in the same world would know this as soon as he saw me, and in general it would be his first account of what I was doing; if this were something he arrived at with difficulty, and what he knew straight off were precisely how I was affecting the acoustic properties of the room (to me a very recondite piece of information), then communication between us would be rather severely impaired.[10]

Let's say an alien scientist arrived whose foreground was the acoustic properties of the room, something that naturally belongs to our human background. We could never communicate without some common fore-grounding inclination such as an inclination to understand action in terms of intentions rather than physical effects. I would turn to the rabbit hopping by, and the alien would be paying my ostension as much mind as my metabolism. As the ancient saying goes, he would be absent while present. Ralph Waldo Emerson rightly said, "In all conversation between two persons tacit reference is made, as to a third party, to a common nature."[11] The common nature functions by naturally profiling certain features of the world and thereby inclining us to joint presence.

9.4   Indeterminacy and the Publicness of Perception

The merits of my appeal to nature can be clearly seen by contrasting it with Quine's approach to inclinations. He acknowledges that some kind of bias is at work in the famous case of the linguist disambiguating "gavagai." He suggests that a sensible linguist would take the native's expression as referring to the rabbit owing to an implicit maxim of the priority of moving bodies for attention. "The implicit maxim guiding his choice of 'rabbit,' and similar choices for other native words, is that an enduring and relatively homogeneous object, moving as a whole against a contrasting background, is a likely reference for a short expression."[12] Quine thinks that the linguist should follow such maxims but that he would be wrong to think the maxim expresses anything universal: "The maxim is his own imposition, toward settling what is objectively indeterminate."[13] As a rationalist, Quine seems to fall prey to the following confusion. Because he recognizes that there could be an exception to the maxim, he denies that it has universality. But if the maxim is understood as an inclination rather than a universal proposition, it can admit of contrary cases. The everyday saying, "The exception proves the rule," similarly holds that rules and maxims can admit of exceptions and still be rules and maxims. Quine's suggestion that exceptions undermine the objectivity of the maxim expresses a failure to recognize the kind of maxim or rule at work here. It is not the universality of a physical law, which admits of no exception, but the formulation of a natural inclination, which holds, as Aristotle observed, either always or maybe just most of the time.[14] Because he has this confusion, Quine shifts the maxim from nature to subjective imposition, but this generates the following puzzle: how can a subjective imposition be useful in understanding another human being's expression?

Only, it seems, if the subjective imposition corresponds to something common in the other subject.

Quine thinks the ambiguity of ostension is radical. It is not just the ambiguity of a gesture, which he thinks can be controlled through repetition in various contexts. For instance, whether someone was pointing to paper rather than whiteness could easily be decided by his or her pointing to one more object that was white but not paper or that was paper but not white. The ostendee could then tell what the ostender was ostending. But Quine thinks he is raising a more radical problem of disambiguation, beyond that of Wittgenstein (or Augustine, for that matter). The problem is ontological relativism. We cannot understand the native's "gavagai" as "rabbit" unless we have come to know the rabbit as a unit, and ostension cannot teach that to us.[15] How can we know that anyone else individuates the world in the same way we do? Quine thinks we can imagine some word that would systematically be used differently by two people, but no ostensive cues would ever show it. Someone could go through life using "rabbit" to mean what another calls "undetached rabbit parts," and neither would ever know it. What should we make of his suggestion? Well, as Augustine emphasized, ostension does not grant knowledge; it merely directs us toward things we know or might learn about while giving us a means for having that known thing be jointly present in its absence. To share the world through ostension, each of us must rouse our own resources to learn about the items to be found in it. Now, Quine asks, how can we know how others know the world? Here again a substantive commitment to human nature can help. Human nature affords certain ways of generalizing and profiling. It is our common nature that specifies a human style of individuating things. This claim, of course, raises a further question. How do we know what is to be found in human nature?

The biggest obstacle Quine faces in his attempt to mesh words with understanding is his continual interpretation of perception in terms of stimuli. Things impinge upon our sensory awareness, and sensory stimuli are radically particular. I think the project of marrying words and understanding is helped along by the richer, nonreductive account of perception I sketched in 7.5. Here let me underscore two salient points. First, the concept of stimulus is ambiguous, as Davidson observes; it can mean something like private evidence or something publically available in the world. What is relevant for joint understanding is the publically available item in the world; we can profitably drop mention of "stimulus" in the context of speaking about perception in service of speech. Second, what are publically available to serve as the backdrop for speech are not flashes of color and impacts on our sensory receptors. What are available are complex states of affairs: articulated wholes doing things in relation to other things. We really do perceive the cat being on the mat. Aristotle saw part of this; for him, perception puts us into contact with wholes: things having a particular shape, characteristic movement, and so on. Phenomenologists have developed this analysis of perception further by broadening perception over the categorial sphere.[16] I don't experience sensory impacts that I model into a cat and a mat and then a cat being on the mat. I experience the cat, the mat, and the cat being on the mat. All this can be given to each of us together. If I am trapped in my skull interpreting sensory impacts, then of course I have no idea of a common human nature. But if we perceptively dwell within a richly articulated interpersonal realm, the idea of a common human nature is much more compelling.

How does a common way of perceiving connect with the question of individuation? A common manner of perceiving suggests a common manner of conceiving what is perceived. If we perceive wholes together and perception is the basis for understanding, then it is natural to think that we individuate the world in the same way. But have I dodged the thrust of Quine's question? Granted that not all of our words suffer from indeterminacy, could it be that one word does? Yes, but I would make this qualification: I cannot imagine a given indeterminacy that is not in principle open to being exposed through the right kind of experience or conversation. Since humans perceive and think along the same lines, prioritizing perceptual wholes to parts, it is strange to think someone would have a word for undetached rabbit parts without having a word for rabbit. Moreover, conversation about something such as how to trap and skin a rabbit might expose the indeterminacy.

It is noteworthy that Quine wanted to attend to the possibility that cultures might carve up the world in different ways. I would put the thought in this way. The natural inclinations are tendencies that constrain ostension, but these inclinations themselves are affected by the language acquired. Language can develop a kind of second nature for these inclinations. For example, suppose a non-Western culture was more relational in its generalization. The bias toward a certain level of generalization would be channeled in a non-Western way. The inclinations might be flexible, and a given language could exercise a backward control. But such relativity takes place only against the backdrop of a common nature. Children take parents to be talking about things present, although just what it means to be a thing is a matter of some cultural elasticity. The child comes to conceptualize the world in a culturally specific way only through the advent of a lot of speech.

9.5   Words, Identification, and Understanding

Augustine sensibly maintained that we cannot learn the meaning of a word without knowing something about the item meant, and yet an unknown word can prompt us to inquire into its meaning and perhaps make a new discovery about the world. Certain differences among things, no doubt, would get the attention of children who were not exposed to language that registered those distinctions. If there were a language without a word for "ball" spoken among a people who played with them, even a child would likely note its identity without linguistic prompting. Such is the case with things like mamma, dada, milk, dog, truck, and other manifest features of the child's world. But other items show up as such only thanks to language. For example, the chances that someone would have had occasion to explicitly grasp the item identified by the word "magenta" without being invited to do so by another are, I think, extremely low. Yes, there was a person who first coined it, so it is not impossible. But I think most people wouldn't identify magenta as such unless invited to do so by hearing the word spoken by others. Here I agree with Nietzsche: "What is originality? *To see* something that has no name as yet and hence cannot be mentioned although it stares us all in the face. The way men usually are, it takes a name to make something visible for them.—Those with originality have for the most part also assigned names."[17] In this way, I do not think Wittgenstein is entirely correct when he maintains that an ostensive definition does not say anything "*about* the object to which it directs our attention."[18] What, on my view, are we saying about the ostended magenta? That it is a unique and interesting shade of color, one that is worth the effort of identifying. Ostension does not specify an essential property, but it does necessitate an act of identification. The one who follows the ostensive action must risk an act of identification: to look and see what is being sampled by discerning the identifying marks of the ostended item. We do not care much about the convention itself but the distinction the convention invites us to recognize. Consider a child learning the word "poodle." We shouldn't think the child follows the pointing finger and says to herself, "Oh, so that's what people mean when they say 'poodle.'" Rather she is charged with the wonder of new discovery: "Wow, a poodle." The recognition is focused on the presented item in the perceptually available world in its manifest uniqueness;

it is not focused on the word-sound that can later be used to present the item in its absence. Language and meaning is self-effacing. It transparently presents the world to understanding while not calling attention to itself.

Kuhn speaks about the relation of thought and language in a manner I find quite natural. He describes the way a father might invite his son to divide up his understanding of birds into more precise groups, consisting of swans and geese, among others. He says this can happen during an afternoon walk that is peppered with ostensive definitions and corrections:

When he began his walk, the neural program highlighted the differences between individual swans as much as those between swans and geese. By the end of the walk, features like the length and curvature of the swan's neck have been highlighted and others have been suppressed so that swan data match each other and differ from goose and duck data as they had not before. Birds that had previously all looked alike (and also different) are now grouped in discrete clusters in perceptual space.[19]

Language learning fuels the learning of natural kinds. It's not that the child already has concepts for geese and swans and then learns the conventions; rather, the conventions direct him to look and discover what there is in nature to be understood. So, it's not that the child just learns the conventions of a particular people; in general, those conventions illumine reality, although which parts are registered might reflect the idiosyncratic interests of a people. Despite this agreement, let me note some displeasure with the way Kuhn expresses himself in the above passage. Kuhn should not say that these identifications happen on the level of a neural program, which wrongly suggests that the child was passive in the process; the ostensions and corrections rather prompt him to make a new distinction for himself. He is invited to carve up the natural world in a more precise way, but he alone can figure out the distinction for himself. Commenting on Augustine, Burnyeat phrased this well: "No-one can achieve my understanding for me, not for the trivial reason that it is mine, but because to internalize the requisite connections is to go beyond what is presented on any occasion of so-called teaching."[20] It is the child's act of identification that rewrites the neural program.

Just what is necessary for identification? Ostensive acts make our intentions apparent; and, in doing so, they make present to each of us the appearances of things. Wittgenstein writes that shape is important for understanding the target of an ostensive act: "An important part of the training will consist in the teacher's pointing to the objects, directing the child's attention to them, and at the same time uttering a word; for instance, the word 'slab' as he points to that shape."[21] In ruling out the possibility of a private language, Wittgenstein also stresses the importance of the "shape" or pattern of bodily behavior at work in the ostension. Without such a pattern, a word lacks the requisite criterion for its identification. By calling attention to shape, Wittgenstein recovers a theme from the perennial philosophical tradition. For Aristotle, *morphē* is critical for understanding a thing; the shape is the outward display of a thing's nature or intelligibility.[22] In taking over this theme from Wittgenstein and Aristotle, I am construing shape quite broadly. For example, the shape of an animal includes not only its appearance at rest but also its characteristic movements. The shape of a squirrel, for example, is made especially manifest not by our staring at a dead specimen but instead by our viewing a live one going about the world actively engaging things: climbing trees, searching for acorns, and playing with other squirrels. Actions, too, have a characteristic shape or contour; we identify the difference between crawling and walking or walking and running by the differences in the way they appear. Now, shape is a property of a thing, although it is not its essence.[23] By means of its shape, we can identify something and set the stage for understanding what it is. Color is part of identification, no doubt, but it is not as important as shape. We might think of swans as white, but if we see a bird of the same shape that is black, we will be inclined to regard it as a black swan. By contrast, were we to see a white bird of a different shape, we will give it a different name. The act of identification that learning a name involves especially latches on to the shape of a thing. When we learn a name, we gain the ability to foreground something for ourselves and another. Identification, then, is not just an issue of knowing; with language, it becomes an issue of making something present for recognition.

The primacy of shape can be highlighted by examining Descartes's confused efforts to marginalize it. In the *Second Meditation*, he deploys an ostensive act: "Let us take, for example, this piece of wax."[24] He observes that exposing the piece to fire changes its shape, color, and fragrance. Despite this radical difference in appearance, our act of understanding easily allows us to identify it as the same bit of wax. He wants us to do what he did: "distinguish the wax from its outward forms—take the clothes off, as it were, and consider it naked."[25] To my mind, Descartes is right to emphasize the role of understanding in the act of identification, but he is wrong to suggest that shape is as dispensable as clothing. In the "Fifth Set of Objections," Pierre Gassendi insightfully calls attention to the fact that such a position allows for neither presence nor joint presence: "The alleged naked, or rather hidden, substance is something that we can neither ourselves conceive nor explain to others."[26] In reply, Descartes claims he was misunderstood: "I did not abstract the concept of the wax from the concept of its accidents. Rather, I wanted to show how the substance of the wax is revealed by means of its accidents, and how a reflective and distinct perception of it (the sort of perception which you, O Flesh, seem never to have had) differs from the ordinary confused perception."[27] Descartes's considered position is that such things as shape *reveal* the nature of a thing. He can ostend wax for us precisely because such things as shape serve as the means for identification.

The importance of shape raises the issue of stability. If Cratylus's doctrine of universal flux were right, we could not achieve prelinguistic joint presence. There would be nothing to identify and recognize in the chaos. Presence and joint presence require the interweaving of change and rest. A rabbit hops by us; even in its movement, it remains the same rabbit with the same dynamic shape and parts, and it shows up against the backdrop that remains the same. In the *Physics*, Aristotle works out the dialectic of stability and change that makes possible the intelligibility we experience in the world. Identification requires some continuity. For example, my wife and I were watching a television show detailing the conquests of Cortez. The host walked the bustling streets of Mexico City and said things like, "Here is where Cortez met Montezuma." The streets looked like the streets of any other contemporary city. There were no Aztec ruins to serve as reference points, and there was no historical plaque or other marker. The identification, then, became a bit attenuated. It was not entirely undermined, however, because the host mentioned that the contemporary streets follow the routes of the ancient city. The city has the same plan or shape. Had the entire city been razed and replaced with a nature preserve, the identification would have been still more tenuous: "There in the middle of the thick grove of pine trees is where Cortez met Montezuma." Identification requires some continuity to stick.

The ostensive act affords the interlocutor or eavesdropper the opportunity to achieve something like a *nominal definition*, that is, an understanding that allows him or her to identify the spoken item and distinguish it from other sorts of similar things. It does not provide a *real definition*, that is, an understanding that allows him or her to know what is essential to the spoken thing. For example, the published sketches of a naturalist who discovers a new species effectively furnish others with the sample necessary for ostending the species. To progress beyond the initial act of identification, naturalists would need to observe the new species' behavior, diet, internal organization, and so on.

What is the relation between this initial identification and the subsequent knowledge of essence? I think Kripke is right that there is an organic relationship between the initial identification and the subsequent understanding; our identification of something by distinguishing it from others admits of intensification through understanding what is essential to it. Let's say you ostend x to me, and I understand the ostension by seeing how I think it differs from y and z. Later, you start to tell me much more about x: not just how it differs from y and z for the purpose of identification, but in terms of its behavior and constitution. One day my six-year-old saw me cleaning out the lint collector on the dryer. He said, "You're cleaning the dust out of there?" I said, "This is not dust but lint." As a result of an explicit ostensive definition or correction, he can figure out for himself the difference between lint and dust. I can't say what distinction he made: perhaps it is that lint is the fluffy stuff in the dryer, and dust is the fluffy stuff under couches. Later, no doubt, he'll learn more about their differences: lint is made up of particles of clothing, whereas dust is mostly dead skin cells, and that sort of thing. Such an understanding will be a continuation of and intensification of the initial understanding he has of dust and lint. Kripke uses a different example. Initially, the interlocutor or eavesdropper is given the window to see that this is gold, differing in its manifest properties from things like silver and bronze. But these manifest properties are of course not enough to distinguish gold from iron pyrite or fool's gold. When we further specify the properties that distinguish true gold from its mere appearance, we have not redefined gold; rather, we have come to a greater understanding of the same item originally ostended to us.[28] Kripke's point is that an ostensive act does not yield certain knowledge concerning the properties of a thing but establishes a rigid reference to someone, something, or some kind of thing.

Young children can solicit an ostensive act of naming. The human child naturally thinks words clothe the item in question, and she wants to know how to speak of something she finds interesting. Wittgenstein denied ostensive powers to the infant, because he thought such powers presupposed a preexisting mental language. But in fact the infant need not think to herself something like "I wonder what people call that?" Instead, she need only experience wonder in the presence of something. Perhaps she spies something hop around on the sidewalk and then fly away. In wonder, the child points and makes a sound of urgent interest. The parent says, "That's a *bird*," and the child might repeat, "bird." The child already finds items in the world interesting and wants to find out what they are. How should we make sense of this? I think cognition and language are not independent of each other, because understanding is naturally a social activity. My infant son, for example, does not tire of announcing, with unmitigated enthusiasm, the presence of every airplane that flies overhead or every lawnmower he can hear. He found airplanes and lawnmowers interesting even apart from having words to speak about them, but having words to speak of them fulfills the inner trajectory of his interest, for he does not find them interesting just for himself but interesting per se, and so he naturally wants to share the interest with all those around them. Words give him that power. Words, in this perspective, emerge from the same wonder at the world that prompts knowledge, a wonder that is communal. Think, for example, about how it is impossible for young children to keep a secret—say, information about a Father's Day present—because their natural inclination is to share what they find interesting about the world.

It is philosophically tempting to think our epistemological apparatus runs independently of language. In this way, we envision the child interacting with items in the world in a dyadic way. On this view, language and social awareness comes to serve a merely utilitarian function of allowing us to transfer to others the ideas we arrived at in this independent fashion. However, I urge a dramatically different picture, in which the epistemological apparatus and the sociality of language are interwoven. The child finds herself in a world saturated with distinctions a comparatively few of which the child naturally thinks relevant enough to monitor. But the speech of others excites her to look and register distinctions she would not otherwise have made, and, moreover, words give a way for those distinctions to be registered and remembered with ease. The fact that each of us has operative vocabularies in the tens of thousands, registering all sorts of distinctions among items in the world, happens thanks to the sociality of language. By ourselves, attending to our immediate environs, we would not understand nearly as much. Considerably more effort is involved in making a distinction for the first time than in adopting a distinction first made by another. Of course, Plato was right to point out that language is liable to mislead as well as to lead; the problem is that the coiners of words were not always insightful.[29] So language is not a storehouse of knowledge. It is rather a storehouse of invitations for each of us to turn and see for ourselves whether the distinctions it makes in fact obtain. We learn our first words by operating on the natural assumption that the distinctions are illuminating.

Some philosophers do attend to the social dimension of cognition. Putnam, for example, speaks of a "division of linguistic labor" in which lay people defer to experts to ostend, say, the difference between gold and

fool's gold or, more interestingly, all the abstruse objects of scientific investigation.[30] When I say "H$_2$O," I mean what a scientist can identify as the
molecular properties of water. The lay person here need not have the ability
to analyze water for himself and need not have a mastery of the periodic
table of elements. But he can say "H$_2$O" meaningfully by deferring to the
ostension of the appropriate scientist. Just as we can refer to Julius Caesar
by participating in a causal chain founded on an original ostension of Caesar (we can't ostend him ourselves, since he's absent from us), so we can
refer to water as "H$_2$O" by participating in a causal chain founded on an
original ostension of H$_2$O. I take a somewhat more generous approach to
the division of labor by recognizing that a wide variety of experts—and not
just scientists—identify things for us. Many of our words are learned and
used in this way (not our first words, which require joint presence, but the
sorts of words we learn through sentential context, definition, and reports).
Historical figures, differences between natural kinds beyond ones close
to us, abstract terms such as *justice* or *love*, terms from our economic and
political systems, and so on, enable us to participate vaguely in a conversation regarding terms many of which we have not personally understood
deeply. The communion of minds, nourished by original ostensive acts,
affords the opportunity to refer to experts or witnesses who were present
to things that we ourselves could not be or as a matter of fact are not. Plato
distinguishes two classes of words: "When someone utters the word 'iron'
or 'silver,' don't we all think of the same thing? ... But what happens when
we say 'just' or 'good'? Doesn't each of us go in a different direction? Don't
we differ with one another and even with ourselves?"[31] Plato thought this
second class gives rise on the one hand to the power of rhetoric to sway
public opinion and on the other to the need for philosophy to clarify terms.
When it comes to a topic such as justice, we can defer to the amateurish
identifications of a rhetorician or the expert identifications of an accomplished philosopher. Of course, if we happen to be a philosophical expert,
we may be in a position to follow an ostension and achieve joint presence
on a given topic, but we will still have to defer to the expertise of others to
identify other abstruse matters.

Infants disambiguate ostensive cues and spontaneously achieve joint
presence. Like other parents, I have observed that children, surrounded by
a room of toys, will stand still until one makes a move and chooses a toy
of interest. The other child will then suddenly develop an overwhelming
desire for the same object, even though it is only one item of interest in a
room full of fascinating toys. The second child, following the movement of
the first, spontaneously experiences the perceived interest of the first child

overflowing into her own. Language speakers going about the world make available to the infant the language they speak. In doing so, they reveal to infants just what is fascinating about the world. Even though it is our common nature that affords us a common linguistic world, the language so afforded presents us with a world much broader and richer than the confines of our own human nature. It gives us a world charged with intelligibility and wonder.

10 Metaphysics: Movement, Manifestation, and Language

Could he, whose rules the rapid Comet bind, / Describe or fix one movement of his Mind?

—Alexander Pope[1]

Woody Allen joked that he was expelled from college because he cheated on a metaphysics exam: "I looked into the soul of the boy sitting next to me."[2] In this book, I have followed the mainstream position of Western philosophy and science that literal mind reading or a "sixth sense" is not a natural human endowment. Instead, animate movement effectively enables our minds to commune so that we can subsequently share the world in speech. In this chapter on metaphysics, I wish to clarify conceptually the resources involved in sharing the world.

In the phenomenological account of chapter 7, I argued that ostension works by manifestation rather than inference. It makes items in the world jointly present rather than occasioning conjectures about unavailable mental states. In the analysis of chapter 8, I maintained that manifestation trades on the reciprocal roles established by mirroring disclosive animate movement. Such movement affords joint presence. In the epistemological reflections of the previous chapter, I considered the difficulty of identifying the target of ostensive acts. I pointed to inclinations, rooted in human nature, that limit the ambiguity inherent in our animate movement. In this final, more speculative chapter, I wish to focus on a fundamental concept operative in the foregoing analyses, and I wish to connect this concept to some larger themes in philosophy. To this end, the chapter first addresses the term *animate movement,* by relating it to the history of philosophy and by distinguishing it from the kind of movement represented by modern physics. Then, I examine the implications of manifestation for our understanding of human nature and of language in general. I conclude by applying insights about ostension to the perennial question concerning philosophy's starting point. Philosophy is, among other things, a conversation that takes as its necessary point of departure everyday speech acquired by ordinary means. The logic of ostension, I argue, is not a ladder that can be kicked away once we've climbed up it; the logic of ostension is more like our own two legs, because it is intrinsic to what we are as embodied or animate minds. It should for this reason inform our most abstruse conversation about the ultimate natures of things.

A note on method: by "metaphysics," I designate the inquiry into first principles and causes that Aristotle called "first philosophy." Drawing on classical metaphysics, I offer a phenomenologically enriched presentation of the principle of manifestation. In light of this principle, I examine topics in language, mind, and ontology. I will touch on themes in contemporary philosophy, but I am not situating this discourse relative to trends in analytic metaphysics or in the continental overcoming of metaphysics. The topic of ostension constrains my choice of metaphysical themes as well as my vocabulary and approach; it is what makes this chapter peculiar and unusual, qualities that are, thankfully, potentially virtuous in philosophy, if not in social circles.

10.1   Animate Movement and Joint Presence

I would like to begin this chapter with a basic question: "How is manifestation logically possible?" That is, what are the essential ingredients necessary for it to be what it is? To answer the question concerning the logical possibility of manifestation, we'll have to turn our attention away from what is made manifest and focus on manifestation itself. On this most difficult topic, I think a creative appropriation of classical philosophy is helpful. As I recounted in chapter 6, Aristotle's refutation of the denier of the principle

Table 10.1
Chapter 10: The metaphysical problem.

T5.1	Ostension as manifestation is a philosophical kind of movement irreducible to the mechanical movement of physics and physiology.
T5.2	Language continues to move in the dimension of joint presence first opened up by ostension.
T5.3	Being human involves appropriating the animal power of manifestation for the sake of making a world jointly present.
T5.4	The publicness of language, rooted in our joint animate natures, cannot meaningfully be denied.
T5.5	Manifestation and joint presence have a substantive and not merely methodological priority.

of noncontradiction (PNC) involves a kind of dialogue. Aristotle invites the denier to say or do something meaningful both for himself and for another, and if he does so, he acknowledges the sovereign character of the PNC. Why? To be meaningful, he must say or do some one thing that is different from others. In doing so, he achieves a kind of rest for himself and his auditor together. They achieve joint presence. There are three couplets in play: (1) *sameness–difference*, (2) *movement–rest*, and (3) *speaking–listening*. The first two couplets recall Plato's discussion in the *Sophist*, in which he articulates the five great kinds that underlie all intelligibility: *sameness* and *difference*, *movement* and *rest*, and *being*.[3] Plato says that were it not for these couplets nothing could be understood. For example, if apples were not the same as other apples, and were apples not different from oranges and all other kinds of things, they could not be understood as apples; sameness and difference underlie the intelligibility of all things. I would like to expound this Platonic theme in an Aristotelian manner, by underscoring that Aristotle's third couplet, *speaking–listening*, is made possible by means of the other two couplets, *sameness–difference* and *movement–rest*. Plato's great kinds not only provide the ultimate principles of intelligibility; they also make possible joint intelligibility or joint presence.

Joint presence or the correlation of speaking and listening is itself a kind of *moving rest*. It is achieved by effecting a change in presence by means of movement, and it leads to a new presence as its terminus. Let's say that you had been thinking about the weather or the chances of the Cavaliers winning tonight or how to discipline your child, but then, when I introduced a *movement* by speaking, lo, there we are together out in the shared world thinking about the same thing; we, as it were, *rest* in that shared item as long as we think about it and not something else. Joint presence also works with the interplay of *sameness* and *difference*. My speech and my gestures invite you to consider with me the *same* greenness of the pasture and the tree or the *different* flavor of chocolate and butterscotch chips; my movement invites you to move and rest jointly in an intelligibility constituted by sameness and difference.

Manifestation is logically possible because we naturally attend to perceived movement and difference rather than what is at rest or the same. If I say, "What was that?" you will ignore a thousand things perceptually around you and naturally think I am talking about what just hit the window. Ostensive acts are ostensive because of this phenomenological priority of movement and difference. We not only passively attend to something moving or different; we can introduce a movement to make present a sameness or difference. With the aid of speech we can attend to the same thing even while absent. Because of the phenomenological priority of movement and difference, the Platonic matrix of intelligibility is also a matrix of manifestation, making it possible for us to share a world in speech. Without this matrix, we would point and no one would pay it any mind. With the matrix, we can turn and speak and these actions come to the foreground because they occur against the backdrop of rest and silence. Quine recognizes in passing the role of movement and difference in making ostension possible: "Pointing ... contributes by heightening the salience of a portion of the visual field. Primitively this salience is conferred on the pointing finger and its immediate background and neighborhood indiscriminately, through the familiar agency of movement and contrast."[4]

How can movement and contrast make things manifest? Difference and movement can be significant, because there is more sameness and rest in our experience than difference and movement. We are geared to the new because the old is relatively more predominant.[5] If we were confronted with an almost universal flux, we'd likely attend to what wasn't in flux. As it is, the world of experience is one of relative stability punctuated by occasional localized movements. It is one of relatively familiar kinds of things peppered with some different or novel items.

Hume's three principles of association—resemblance, contiguity in time or place, and cause or effect—cannot be the last word.[6] Imagine a student daydreaming about his spring break plans while in philosophy class. He thinks about the warm weather, then what clothes he should pack, then the fact he needs to do laundry, then about the girl he met last time he did laundry, and then how she reminded him of a girl from home. This train of thought would have continued, freely following associative principles except for one thing. A voice from elsewhere has arisen. Looking about him he feels all eyes on him and he feels flush with embarrassment. Deliberately he calls to mind what he had just heard without attention: "What about you? Would you have sentenced Socrates to death?" What interrupted the zigzag flow of associative thinking was the introduction of a new presence through movement. We naturally attend to movement; if we did not, we could not communicate. The teacher would talk, and no one would listen. The car might pull in front of us, but we would pay it no mind. The parent would engage the world, and the infant would learn nothing. However, the ostensive movements of others do elicit our attention. The priority of movement over rest and difference over sameness are deep phenomenological constraints rooted in the structure of experience.

Plato argues that both movement and rest are necessary for understanding. Movement names the activity of the soul coming to understand, and rest names the necessary attribute of what is understood. He regards movement and understanding as proper to life. Hence, he thinks the denial of living movement renders understanding impossible. Absent such movement, "nothing anywhere possesses any intelligence about anything."[7] Plato accordingly raises the alarm to rouse would-be philosophers to the task of defending manifestation and thus the possibility of understanding. "And we need to use every argument we can to fight against anyone who does away with knowledge, understanding, and intelligence but at the same time asserts anything at all about anything."[8] He rightly regards as absurd the view that intelligibility is not intrinsically related to movement, understanding, and life.[9] To Plato's discussion of the five great kinds we must add—with Aristotle, Augustine, Merleau-Ponty, and Wittgenstein—the *animate body*. Capable of fulfilling its desires by means of its articulated structure, it enables ostension, the manifestation of our presence to others. Things are intelligible for each of us together because of our joint bodily and animal being, which situates us in a world and makes our intentions available to others in a prelinguistic way.

10.2 Relating Mechanical and Phenomenological Movement

In the *Monadology*, Leibniz rightly argues that the machinery of perception cannot account for the phenomenology of perception. To make his case, he envisions taking any machine reputed to have perceptions and making a scale copy of the machine as big as a mill so that we could walk into it and look around: "Assuming that, when inspecting its interior, we will only find parts that push one another, and we will never find anything to explain a perception."[10] The push and pull of forces differs in kind from the manifestation of things that is perception. Leibniz accordingly inserts an immaterial consciousness or monad at the terminus of the machinery to explain perception. This might explain the fact that there is something it is like to undergo experiences, but it does not account for the availability of minds one to another: "The monads have no windows through which something can enter or leave."[11] As readers of Leibniz know, he "solves" this problem by invoking an elaborate prearranged harmony of one windowless mind to another in which interactions play out within each of us. My proposal, by contrast, is to open up some windows. I have done so by arguing that mechanism is not the only kind of movement.

We cannot simply restate the classical doctrine of the animate mind, because modern science has given us so much information concerning the physiology at work in living beings. How can the classical emphasis on animation be updated in light of what we now know to be the causal processes involved in perception? I think we need to make a distinction unknown to the classical mind between *phenomenological movement* and *physical motion*. For communication and intelligibility, the kind of requisite movement is animate movement or the kind of movement that is phenomenologically discernible. Here movement is disclosure, the canceling of a hiddenness. The second kind of movement is that which physics can model and predict. In this case, movement is the physical transfer of matter and energy within space and time. The two belong to different dimensions of experience. Let us say that I have just told you a bit of good news. You light up. Your response manifests your affectivity, canceling its hiddenness. Now such a disclosure obviously involves quite a bit of neurology and physiology. You could not have followed my meaning if you lacked a central nervous system that duly conveyed stimuli to the brain or if the terminus of the nerves was not a brain but, as Wittgenstein once fancifully imagined, a pile of sawdust. The interpersonal interaction requires a long chain of mechanical motion to take place, which we could describe crudely as follows: I utter acoustic blasts, the sound waves of which impact your sensory receptors, which translate them into nerve stimuli, which travel to the brain, where they are processed by neurons, thereby leading to the stimulation of facial nerves that lift your eye brows and curl your lips upward; thereafter, light rays reflect off your face and enter my eye, impacting my rods and cones, and so on. The physical path of motion does not enter into the dimension of disclosure. It rather moves in time through spatial positions. This is what Wittgenstein calls "the transition 'from quantity to quality.'"[12] Phenomenological movement needs all this physics to happen, but it is something other than the physical happening. By the same token, all this physical happening needs the phenomenological movement in order to be understood as anything.

Someone like Nietzsche saw both the importance of appearance and the conflict between it and mechanical motion. However, he came too soon and could not avail himself of the phenomenological method to sort it out. In the preface to the second edition of *The Gay Science* (1886), he wrote the following paragraph. Its significance can be gleaned from the fact that two years later he would include it as the final passage in *Nietzsche Contra Wagner*, the last book he ever wrote:

Oh, those Greeks! They knew how to live. What is required for that is to stop courageously at the surface, the fold, the skin, to adore appearance, to believe in forms, tones, words, in the whole Olympus of appearance. Those Greeks were superficial— *out of profundity*. And is not this precisely what we are again coming back to, we daredevils of the spirit who have climbed the highest and most dangerous peak of present thought and looked around from up there—we who have looked *down* from there? Are we not, precisely in this respect, Greeks? Adorers of forms, of tones, of words? And therefore—*artists*?[13]

Nietzsche rightly understood the importance of appearance, but he wrongly understood appearance to be mere appearance. Recovering the Aristotelian sense of nature and employing the phenomenological method enable us to do something Nietzsche could not: regard ourselves as receptive to the manifestation of things.

Phenomenology began with Husserl's two volumes of *Logical Investigations* in 1900 and 1901. In the work, he does two important things. First, he argues that psychologism, which takes truth to be a physical process, undermines the validity of truth and amounts to a self-defeating relativism.[14] Second, he analyzes the interplay of language and experience and finds that truth does involve a kind of movement, the fulfilling intuition of something that was emptily intended.[15] Truth is irreducible to psychology and physics but yet belongs to experience. Heidegger's distinction between the ontic and the ontological names the difference between these two irreducible senses of movement. Heidegger glosses Plato's inclusion of movement in the five great kinds as follows. Movement is necessary for there to be understanding, namely, "a living disclosure, the carrying out of the uncovering of beings themselves."[16] The difficulty of these phenomenological writers stems not only from the German penchant for obscurity but also from the challenge of thinking the difference between these two kinds of movement. For example, Heidegger's technical term for being human, *Dasein*, means "to be the agent and dative of such movement" or, in Greek, *kinēsis*: "Thus if *kinēsis* is the theme of the dialectical consideration, that means the theme is nothing else than human Dasein, life itself, insofar as it expresses itself and addresses the world in which it is."[17] Manifestation involves a dimension other than the play of physical forces.

Making the distinction between physical motion and phenomenological movement invites the speculative question concerning the relation of the distinguished terms. Phenomenologists have made various proposals. Heidegger, in his dialogue with psychologists, says that physiological motion is a *necessary* but not *sufficient condition* for our encountering other people.[18] Paul Ricoeur, in his dialogue with the neuroscientist Jean-Pierre Changeux, likewise maintains that the mechanical causality of the brain and central nervous system constitute the condition for the causality of thought or manifestation.[19] Beyond Heidegger, Ricoeur emphasizes a correlation between physiology and manifestation. He suggests we regard the brain as the substrate for thinking; all our thoughts then indicate a neuronal structure.[20] In dialogue with contemporary analytic authors, Noë sounds a note of caution regarding such a suggestion. He argues, with Searle, that the program of finding neural correlates of consciousness rests on a confusion. So far, researchers have located correlates for particular conscious acts, say the perception of a physical object, but they overlook the fact that consciousness was already in play beforehand. What is identified, then, is not a neural correlate for consciousness in general but only a neural correlate for a particular act. He points out that correlation without further specifying the causal connection does not warrant our terming the neural activity a substrate or necessary condition. Noë instead argues that we should conceive of the brain and central nervous system in light of our dynamic interaction with items in the world: "Consciousness is a phenomenon that occurs only against the background of the active life of the animal. There is no good reason for assuming that the only relevant background is the activity of the brain."[21] We should understand the role of the brain in light of our openness to perceived items in the world and not vice versa. How might we conceive of this relation?

Sokolowski proposes a simple but powerful way to do so. He suggests that we think of the relation of physiology and perception by means of the concept of "lensing."[22] He invites us to consider an ordinary glass lens such as you might find in a pair of glasses. You can either look through the lens at something or look at the lens itself. He recommends we regard the brain, nervous system, and senses as a lens. In our ordinary experience, it serves as a transparent medium through which we access things, but it is also possible, thanks to modern science, to make the lens into an object of investigation in its own right. The fact that we take the brain, nervous system, and senses as an object does not mean that it cannot make the world genuinely available to us. What the senses receive and convey to the brain are not mere mechanical impacts from the surrounding world. The energy involved in all the senses is a kind of ambient energy, energy that is configured by the items in the environment. As configured or patterned, the energy bears the appearance of the things it encounters.[23] For example, the light that hits the rods and cones on the back wall of the eye is organized by the visual objects in the perceptual field. Horses and parakeets look different because the light, as configured, conveys a different appearance to us. There is more to sensation than physical force, and therefore we have good reason to think that the lens of our senses, central nervous system, and brain allows us to access public items in the world.

Stephen Hawking and Leonard Mlodinow also describe the brain as a kind of lens, and it is helpful to contrast their view with Sokolowski's. They write: "Our perception—and hence the observations upon which our theories are based—is not direct, but rather is shaped by a kind of lens, the interpretive structure of our human brains."[24] Sokolowski regards the lens as supporting the directness of perception, and hence it is worth examining their justification for regarding perception as indirect. They give two reasons:

There is a blind spot where the optic nerve attaches to the retina, and the only part of your field of vision with good resolution is a narrow area of about 1 degree of visual angle around the retina's center, an area the width of your thumb when held at arm's length. And so the raw data sent to the brain are like a badly pixilated picture with a hole in it. Fortunately, the human brain processes that data, combining the input from both eyes, filling in gaps on the assumption that the visual properties of neighboring locations are similar and interpolating.[25]

I do not think these two reasons, the hole and the pixilation, warrant viewing perception as indirect. What about the 1 degree of rich detail in the middle of the visual field not interrupted by a blind spot? Is that, too, indirect? No argument has been adduced for its being so. Perception is not principally a global apprehension of everything in one's surroundings all at once. That occurs in the background, and detail is hardly important. Principally, perception is engagement with something in the foreground. Our interest does not concern the trees in the background or the whole pond, but now just the couple of waterfowl diving for food over yonder. And when we apprehend those ducks, we don't just stare; rather, the saccadic movement of our eyes ranges over them, providing rich detail regarding their activities. The detail of the middle of the field unobstructed by a blind spot is where the principal work of perception takes place, and that is direct. We can therefore say with Sokolowski that the lens comprising the senses, nervous system, and brain transparently makes the world available to us. (One further objection: what about the rest of the visual field besides the rich center? Is that indirect and modeled? Let's say I take a photograph of the tree in my front yard and upload it to Photoshop on my computer. There's a black mark obscuring the image from a piece of dust on the lens; no problem, I'll just use the stamp tool to borrow a visual pattern from nearby and fill it in. The picture is just a little out of focus, so I apply a filter to sharpen it up. With the stamp and the filter, I've corrected mechanical distortions to make it a more faithful presentation of the original. The result is not an *artistic illustration* of the tree, i.e., an indirect model, but a *photograph* of it, i.e., a direct presentation. What holds for the photograph holds true for the lens's enhancement of the visual field that is at work in perception.)

I would like to connect lensing with Davidson's rejection of proximal evidence in word learning. The brain, nervous system, and senses can function transparently to present things to us, or, in a change of perspective, can be regarded as objects in their own right. Of course, when we take them in this way, they no longer are self-effacing; they no longer serve to make public items in the world available. Now, so-called proximal evidence is the result of taking the lens as an object. We think of the brain as a thing in a vat or skull that is interpreting mechanical impacts on its sensory receptors. The input is then something private, and it is all we have to go on. By contrast, when we take the brain, central nervous system, and senses as a diaphanous medium, our focus turns to "distal" evidence, namely the publically perceived objects themselves. The object is there as an object manifesting itself to both of us together. The concept of lensing allows us to see that two points of view are at work, the mechanical and the phenomenological. It is the phenomenological perspective that yields public evidence and therefore the possibility of speech and scientific investigation. The metaphor of lensing allows us to reconcile the personal and impersonal points of view, what grammarians call the first and third persons. I think lensing can be expanded in its application to accommodate the interpersonal or second-person perspective. That is, I can view another's movement as diaphanous, transparently revealing his affective engagement with things, or opaque, in which the movement becomes the object in its own right. The first corresponds to phenomenological or animate movement, the second to physical motion.

10.3   The Ostensive Animal

At the end of *Action in Perception*, Noë looks to biology and the theory of evolution to solve the problem of how unconscious states give rise to conscious ones.[26] I think this is a mistake, because consciousness is irrelevant to the biological investigation of nature. Methodologically speaking, biology is equipped to examine the mechanics of life but not its phenomenology. This division of labor need not be controversial. In dialogue with the analytic tradition, Michael Thompson defends the legitimacy of a philosophical approach to life. Concepts requisite for understanding life and action admit of only philosophical, not biological explanation.[27] In a similar vein, we can say that a philosopher, as philosopher, is not equipped to uncover the mechanics of life; a biologist, as biologist, is not equipped to uncover the manifestation of life. One might develop a kind of phenomenology of evolution and life, as does Evan Thompson, but such a venture, although informed by life sciences, is not itself a contribution to those sciences. By the same token, one might develop a biological account of the remarkable "aboutness" characteristic of complex unicellular eukaryotic cells, as does W. Tecumseh Fitch, but such an account requires a philosophical analysis to be understood as a precursor of manifestation.[28] In this section, I would like to follow both Thompsons in making a nonbiological contribution to our understanding of living beings such as ourselves. My point of departure will be Merleau-Ponty's concept of "flesh," which weaves together the inward and the outward. I don't think he worked out the concept; as it is, it remains on the level of a metaphor, but it serves to connect phenomenological concerns, physiological findings, and classical sensibilities. Ostension is possible only for an animate or enfleshed being.

All living things are agents of manifestation and, insofar as they have awareness, are likewise datives of manifestation. They make themselves manifest to others and others are manifest to them. According to the classical view, language and rationality afford humans a higher mode of animal life. Speaking and thinking are not something layered on top of animal life but a higher way of being an animal.[29] Augustine, for instance, writes that by valuing human rationality "you have not preferred anything else to life, but have placed the better life above just any form of life at all."[30] That human life belongs to life in general is, of course, a decidedly non-Cartesian notion, but it is one that evolutionary theory recommends. In the first chapter, I noted that a number of recent philosophers emphasize, with Aristotle and Augustine, the continuity of life without undermining the uniqueness of speech and reason. Among these I mentioned Evan Thompson, Maxine Sheets-Johnstone, and Shaun Gallagher. The phenomenological angle of these thinkers makes them attentive to manifestation, inwardness, and the experience of life as well as the new dimension opened up with reason.

Ostension is a uniquely human power that nonetheless draws upon abilities shared widely with other animals and indeed all living beings. Every level of life affords resources. On the cellular level, the plasma membrane establishes a fundamental demarcation between self and other, within and without. The distinction is not simply spatial, for what is inside *belongs* to the cell in a way that what is outside does not. What is inside contributes to the identity and subsistence of the organism. To maintain itself, the organism must continually take in and synthesize new matter.[31] The physicist Erwin Schrödinger describes the process this way: "Thus the device by which an organism maintains itself stationary at a fairly high level of orderliness (= fairly low level of entropy) really consists in continually sucking orderliness from its environment."[32] The self subsists by means of a dynamic interchange with what it is not; for a single-celled organism, it is the plasma membrane that demarcates self and other. To the degree to which the organism perceives, a further differentiation occurs. In perception, the organism achieves a surrounding world of nearness and farness, a domain of potential actions. Its need to metabolize drives it outward. The organism perceives a relevant item at a distance, and, desiring it, acts to bridge that distance and satisfy the desire. The giraffe sees the leafy food and moves to eat it. The organism dwells in the interplay of perceptually given distance and nearness achieved through action.[33] The organism moves in the dynamic of frustrated or satisfied desires. Here again the perceptual domain is not simply spatial, because the perceptual environment belongs to the perceiving organism. Owing to its vantage point and the particularity of its biological apparatuses for perception, any given organism has access to only a small slice of the world of existing things. Perceptual experience occurs for each organism individually, even though organisms relate to a publically available world by means of perception. Metabolism and the difference between inside and outside put the organism into the world; perception opens that organism to a world of distant but desired items able to be obtained by action. A grade of manifestation and communication opens up with action. The biologist Adolf Portmann, for instance, distinguishes simple isolated marine animals, such as sea anemones and tube-worms, from the higher animals that share their inner lives through "spontaneous manifestation."[34]

For human understanding, the basic distinction between within and without and the higher distinction between something distant that is desired and something near that is enjoyed becomes translated into presence and absence.[35] Humans are organisms with a within and a without; they are animals, having perspectival surroundings and an appetite for acting; they are also specifically human, having presence and absence together with others. Our basically animal bodies, hungry for nourishment, longing for touch and engagement, open up a world of action capable of being jointly understood. This, in turn, provides the context for gesturing, speaking, and being understood. To be human, then, is to be the animal that shows and is shown a world of intelligibility—the one who, through gestures and words, makes items of the world manifest, thereby enacting an

Table 10.2
The scale of intersubjectivity.

Level of Life	Interplay	Intersubjective Possibility
1. Metabolism	Inner—Outer	Joint Ecosystem
2. Perception, Desire, and Action	Desire—Satisfaction	Joint Action
3. Understanding and Speaking	Presence—Absence	Joint Presence

absence-canceling presence. To be human is a new way of being an animate being.

10.4 Words Are Ostensive

The disclosive power of ostension reverberates in words. Bodily movement shows us things, thereby allowing words to be learned. Once learned, words harbor the same power of showing, with this difference: they show irrespective of the bodily presence or absence of the thing in question. Davidson appropriately calls language "a mode of perception,"[36] and Heidegger calls speaking a mutual showing: "To speak *to* one another means: to say something, show something to one another, and to entrust one another mutually to what is shown."[37] I would like to clarify the sense in which speech is a kind of showing by answering a charge made by the sophist Gorgias against the very possibility of speech.

Gorgias famously argues the following: Nothing exists; even if it did exist, it couldn't be known; even if it could be known, it could not be communicated. For our purposes, the third claim is the most interesting: even if we could know the world, speech would not enable our knowing minds to commune. He reasons as follows. We communicate by way of speech, but speech cannot generate an experience of the item spoken about:

When, therefore, one has not a thing in the mind, how will he get it there from another person by word or any other token of the thing except by seeing it, if it is a colour, or hearing it, if it is a noise? For he who speaks does not speak a noise at all, or a colour, but a word; and so it is not possible to think a colour, but only to see it, nor a noise, but only to hear it.[38]

If I talk about the Amazon milk frog, *Trachycephalus resinifictrix*, which I saw at an exhibit over the weekend, you do not thereby see its brown and white coloring or hear its distinctive croak. You can gain an understanding of it, but not an experience of it.

Gorgias is right that speech does not give an experience of a thing. What he misses is that speech shows something in the modality of experiential absence, and it does so precisely in such a way that it can enter into its presence. Let's say I vividly describe the experience of attending a Mississippi State home football game. I do not thereby give an experience of it; you do not see the massive crowds or hear the deafening roar. Yet it is genuinely presented to you. After describing it, we go to Starkville and attend the game. You then experience firsthand the thunder of thousands of cowbells clanging. You understand it to be the same experience I spoke about before in its absence. Now, over the noise, we talk about the game and thereby show something to each other that is experientially present. Later, enjoying a slice of pecan pie at a restaurant, we can recall this or that feature of the game, and we can talk about it with our waitress, who wasn't there. Speech is a form of showing that achieves joint presence even regarding experientially absent things.

In one of Charlotte Brontë's novels, a character mentions the disclosive power of speech: "It was his nature to be communicative; he liked to open to a mind unacquainted with the world glimpses of its scenes and ways ...; and I had a keen delight in receiving the new ideas he offered, in imagining the new pictures he portrayed, and following him in thought through the new regions he disclosed."[39] Our ability to follow a novel is an example of just such a power to show that is characteristic of all speech.

Although speech cannot give an experience, it can give knowledge. Before GPS devices, if you were lost you might ask for directions. The person giving the directions would use words that were familiar enough, but they were describing something you might never have seen before. You might try to visualize what they were describing to help yourself remember it: Take a sharp right at the third stoplight after the fire station. As you drive, you realize that the fire station is not as you pictured it and the sharp right is trickier than you imagined, but none of that matters. By means of speech, the person conveyed knowledge of how to go where you needed to go. Words, acquired at least in part through joint experience, allow us to show each other things that may or may not be jointly experienced.

Speech also gives us knowledge that in some instances could not be acquired in any other way. I see you looking off into space, your thoughts occupied. There is nothing around us that is obviously puzzling. I have no way to know what you are thinking about unless you tell me. Even if we are confronting the same scene, I don't necessarily know what about it you are considering from moment to moment. I can make some educated guesses, but when you start talking, you let me know just what it is you are thinking about. Speech, then, cannot give experience, but it can give knowledge about things and about what we are thinking about. It can show things absent to our experience, and therein resides its great power.

In a second line of attack against the possibility of communication, Gorgias wields sameness and difference to argue for the incoherence of joint presence. If our perspectives are different, what we perceive must not be the same:

For the same thing cannot be present simultaneously in several separate people; for in that case the one would be two. But if ... the same thing *could* be present in several persons, there is no reason why it should not appear dissimilar to them, if they are not themselves entirely similar and are not in the same place; for if they were in the same place they would be one and not two.[40]

Gorgias's objection dissolves when we realize that there is an identity given through a manifold and that our positions are given as interchangeable. We can see the same touchdown pass even if from different angles. As I pointed out in section 7.3, perceptual objects are just the sort of things that admit of multiple angles. Moreover, when we see something from one perspective, we simultaneously perceive that there is more to be seen about the thing than we presently perceive from our perspective, and we understand that we could see it from other perspectives. Against Gorgias, I maintain that speech shows things without thereby giving them to experience and that joint presence is possible.

Ostension is the prelinguistic means for establishing joint presence. Does that make it the primary language? Merleau-Ponty regards gestures as constituting the vocabulary of a primary language, which we then translate into the conventional terms of our native tongue. Wittgenstein rightly observes regarding this position: "It sounds like a ridiculous truism if I say that anyone who believed that gestures are the primary signs that underlie all others would be incapable of replacing the most ordinary sentence with gestures."[41] For a variety of reasons, gestures cannot be words. Words are highly specific, show absent and not just present things, and enter into semantic and syntactical relations. Gestures do not do these things, except when formalized into a conventional language of their own (such as American Sign Language). Emma Borg writes of the difference between ostension and speech as follows: "The meaning of a non-linguistic ostensive act seems ineliminably tied to its context in a way that the meaning of a linguistic act is not."[42] However, there is yet another way for gestures to be primary signs—not as a more fundamental language but as the original form of the disclosive power proper to speech. Wittgenstein seems to make just such a connection: "It isn't the colour red that takes the place of the word 'red,' but the gesture that points to a red object or to a red colour chip."[43] The showing of gestures grants entrance to the showing of speech, which extends showing into absence and specifies what is shown. Ostension prefigures speech only insofar as ostension shows, and showing is the essence of language.

Speaking harbors within it the force of its original ostensive institution. To speak of dachshunds, for example, is not simply to select one class of things from among others. It is also to present that class as an item of interest for yourself and your interlocutor. To say "dachshunds" in this way bears an ostensive significance that we could formulate as follows: "Behold a dachshund" or, in their absence, "Remember beholding a dachshund," "well, they have long bodies and short legs like all other hounds." Of course, you may never have seen one, in which case I will be reanimating the joint presence of hounds or dogs in order to give you the appropriate definition of dachshund. That is, I will begin with what you have seen, before making the appropriate modifications to introduce the new species. Perhaps you are from a remote island and have never seen a dog. If I did not have a picture to show you, I would have to begin with your experience of animals before making the right adjustments (walks on four legs, wags its tail, fetches, and so on). All language acquisition builds on the words first learned through ostension.

Everyday speech bears the power to show, because our bodies naturally advertise what is present to us. In chapter 8, I discussed the mirroring disclosure and reciprocal roles of agency at work in the perception of ostension. The same logic plays out with the nature of language as well. That you speak while I listen, and you listen while I speak, hearkens back to the reciprocal interaction characteristic of prelinguistic infants. The turn-taking of speaking continues the mirroring of action disclosure. Action sets up ostension, which sets up conversation.

10.5   Manifestation Makes Language Public

I have argued that ostension is necessary for first word learning on the supposition that language is something essentially public. Because language is shared but acquired, there must be a prelinguistic way for us to share the world in an articulated manner. Ostension, or the reciprocal disclosure of animate activity, makes this possible. Now, I would like to turn to the publicness of language. Can I give it any justification?

I think the publicness of speech is a properly basic principle presupposed by all verbal communication. Like the principle of noncontradiction, it does not admit of a standard proof, because any proof would have to make use of it. But that doesn't mean it is merely a belief on par with other beliefs that don't admit of proof (I cannot, for example, prove to you that I am not overly fond of American cheese; you'll have to take my word for it). We can take a page from Aristotle's defense of the PNC and offer some support for the publicness of language by showing the impossibility of meaningfully denying it. The belief, "Language is not public," cannot be communicated, for communicating the belief to another person would presuppose the publicness of language. Were someone to believe in the privacy of language, that belief would have to remain in the privacy of his understanding (even if the belief were universal, no one could know that it was universal since it could not be communicated). Nietzsche, a latter-day disciple of Gorgias, can serve as our Cratylus in this respect. In an early notebook, he experimented with the thought that "language is a lie,"[44] and he argues that this follows directly from mechanistic physiology, since it leads to a proximal view of evidence. For him, what we know are concepts generated from images, which are generated from private nerve stimuli. How our private concepts relate to public things is simply unavailable. Language presupposes a joint world, but there is no joint world. Therefore, language has no truth-value. Nietzsche represents a possible intellectual position sincerely held on the basis of informed scientific evidence, but he cannot possibly be right.

What is presupposed by speaking? When we speak, we presuppose that our words are actually *or potentially* meaningful to our hearer(s). The act of speaking involves a tacit sense for the presence of others who understand not just the world but also the words with which we present the world to each other. To speak is to presuppose the public character of language. (Note: this need not entail the belief that the listener has the exact same vocabulary; just that any meaning can potentially be shared.) If an interlocutor understands the claim "language is a lie," or "language is not public," the claim must be false. That is, if the proposition is meaningful to anyone else, language must be shared and so must be public.

Can we give further support for the publicness of language besides the impossibility of communicating that claim?

There's no difference in meaning between merely thinking "language is not public" and saying "language is not public." The same words are used in both cases; the only difference is that one is voiced and the other is not.

But surely the person who maintains that language is not public does not mean to say that it may or may not be voiced. He rather wants to say that words mean what they do relative to each one of us. So, invite the person who would maintain the privacy of speech to voice his thoughts. If he is right that speech is private, then merely voicing his thoughts should make no difference. Now the person is not intending to communicate, and so is not engaged in a performative contradiction (denying the possibility of communication while communicating). But we do at least have the claim available for analysis. Now that it has been aired, the question becomes whether we can agree or disagree with the claim. If we can, that means the claim is meaningful to each of us together. We are not contemplating an abstract painting, each of us finding it meaningful in our own way. It is something that each of us can agree or disagree about. But if there is agreement or disagreement (it does not matter which), then the claim that language does not exist for both of us together is manifestly false. Of course, the denier of the publicness of language will have to deny that we can agree or disagree with him. He'll have to say something like, "Because language is private, you don't know what I mean when I say, 'Language is private.'" But here we have him: his disagreement with us presupposes the agreement of meaning accomplished by speech. If we are aware of a disagreement, we must be aware of a common meaning.

Now, someone might wish to distinguish the claim "No language is public," refuted above, from the claim "A private language is possible." Let's take a look at the second. As is well known, Wittgenstein argued for the publicness of language by denying the possibility of a private language (or private word), and he did so by calling attention to the constitutive role played by ostension in the institution of a word. I would now like to show the impossibility of a private language (or private word) in my own way. Every meaning is at least *potentially* public even if it is not actually so. Here's why.

Suppose I am alone in a cabin in the woods. I decide to invent a new, private language (Privatese) to replace the English of my youth. How might I proceed? I could institute words through English equivalents. "X" could be Privatese for "dog," for instance. But a private language would have to be one that is not in principle translatable, so I cannot create it by means of translation. Alternatively, I could institute words for things specifically absent in English. "X" could mean "something tight-fitting," for instance.[45] But in this case, the meaning would be determined by English and would be easily defined in English; in effect, it would be a new English word. To really start *de novo*, I would have to set English aside. Without English or some other existing language, there's nothing to keep track of the movements of consciousness and its flow of presentations, so I wouldn't be able to start institutions there. Instead, I'd have to begin in the perceptual world about me. Where should I begin? I'd want to talk about things I noticed: the warmth of the fire, the fact that it needs another log, the coldness outside, the hunger I felt, the food I needed, the tranquility of the scene, and so on. Privatese would be instituted in terms of a basically human form of life that would be publically discernible. I could deliberately deny the relevance of my human concerns and formulate Privatese to speak about abstract and irrelevant things, say, the acoustic properties of objects, but I could hardly dwell there; I'd need a host of other words about more tangible things to manage my human affairs and keep my human interest, and these abstruse terms would be woven together with these public concerns and actions. To institute a truly private language as the medium for one's thoughts would be to institute a nonhuman form of life or, in fact, to renounce the relevance of life altogether. Privatese might be possible for a Cartesian consciousness, but such a thing does not in fact exist; it is not possible for the animal that is a human being.

10.6   Philosophy's Manifest Starting Point

A perennial question for philosophy concerns the basis for philosophical inquiry. Aristotle, for instance, replied to naysayers about the existence of nature by maintaining that nature, as an inner principle of movement, is the most manifest feature of the world and as such cannot be proven on the basis of any more manifest principle. The world in which we take part is a world of natural change. He thinks it is theoretically possible to deny nature just as it is theoretically possible to talk about color if you were born blind and lacked all color experience. The denier of nature simply lacks experience about which sorts of things need to be proven.[46] In modern philosophy, the question of beginning becomes a source of great perplexity. Descartes engineers a change from the manifestation of nature to consciousness alone in a mechanical world. Subsequent philosophers begin inside the head and seek justification for moving to a world outside. Hegel, wrestling with the same problematic, titles a chapter of his *Science of Logic* "With What Must the Science Begin?" Though he rejects the artificiality of the Cartesian starting point, he retains the primacy of thought.[47]

One challenge to the manifestation of nature comes from the modern version of consciousness, which seeks to motivate belief in the primacy of inner evidence. I agree with Norris Clarke that the "we are" of dialogue is a more fruitful starting point for philosophy than is the Cartesian *cogito ergo sum*.[48] We can share the world in speech because we first share the world through animate movement. A second challenge to the manifestation of nature comes from a certain way of construing the findings of modern science. In Cartesian fashion, it reduces everything other than consciousness to mechanical motion. The neuroscientist Antonio Damasio complains that Descartes "persuaded biologists to adopt, to this day, clockwork mechanics as a model for life processes."[49] The geneticist Richard Lewontin goes even further and says that Descartes's machine metaphor supports "the entire body of modern science."[50] The Cartesian denial of animate movement can seem to support the idea that knowers act independently of each other, but this is an illusion. As a matter of fact, science is a collaborative effort rooted in interpersonal dialogue and prelinguistic bodily presence. Were scientists to adjust some of their conceptual language, the apparent opposition between science and the manifestation of nature would vanish.

In the last century, Sellars distinguished between the "manifest image" and the "scientific image." The manifest image is the apparent world of persons and things, the world studied by the perennial or Aristotelian philosophy as well as by phenomenology and ordinary language philosophers.[51] He rightly points out that the manifest image is scientific in its own sense; the only thing it does not avail itself of is the "postulation of imperceptible entities, and principles pertaining to them, to explain the behavior of perceptible things."[52] The scientific image, by contrast, is a total understanding of the world, gradually certified by the march of investigations and rife with appeals to imperceptible causes known by indirect means. Sellars, like many analytic philosophers (Quine and Searle are two other prominent examples of those whose ideas inform the present book; Michael Thompson would be an important exception), argues for the substantive primacy of the scientific image. At the same time, Sellars, like Quine, acknowledges the methodological priority of the manifest account; science and philosophy presuppose the manifest view just to get off the ground. However, Sellars cautions that we should not construe this methodological priority as justification for a substantive priority:

The fact that each theoretical image is a construction on a foundation provided by the manifest image, and *in this methodological sense* pre-supposes the manifest image, makes it tempting to suppose that the manifest image is prior in a *substantive* sense; that the categories of a theoretical science are logically dependent on categories pertaining to its methodological foundation in the manifest world of sophisticated common sense in such a way that there would be an absurdity in the notion of a world which illustrated its theoretical principles *without also illustrating the categories and principles of the manifest world.*[53]

Sellars grants the methodological priority of the manifest image but rejects the substantive priority, because he thinks the scientific image is a complete view that is therefore in conflict with the manifest account: "Thus although methodologically a development *within* the manifest image, the scientific image presents itself as a *rival* image."[54] He accordingly recommends replacing the manifest image with the scientific one. But his opposition of the two strikes me as just plain mistaken. Among other things, science cannot in principle replace the manifest image, because it cannot help itself to the concepts requisite for its understanding.

To reconcile the two images, we might want to say that science describes the objective world and phenomenology the subjective experience of the world. Science describes what is the case, and phenomenology appends experience to it. But when we focus on ostension and manifestation, phenomenology no longer appears as incidental to the work of understanding the world. The first scientist, Thales, investigated things and found moisture in them. He published his theory, "All is water." Immediately, other scientists disagreed. Empedocles said there were four elements: water, fire, air, and earth. In the 2,500 years since, scientists have made a great deal of progress on the basic constitution of the material world. They have done so in part by publishing their findings, learning from each other, and correcting each other. We stand on the shoulders of giants, from Thales through Dmitri Mendeleev, owing to our ability to communicate with one another using conventional words aligned by prelinguistic joint presence established through ostensive acts and our animate bodies. Were it not for joint presence, each us would be limited to Thales's first groping investigations of nature. (Even this is not quite right, for Thales could make the first start in theoretical understanding only by means of repurposing the words for "water," "all," and "is," which he learned from other animate minds.)

Ostension may not be just a remote presupposition for science in affording a joint language; it may be an immediate presupposition for its method. Kuhn, for one, thinks it is the ostension of examples that plays the constitutive role in establishing a scientific paradigm or disciplinary matrix. Again, he illustrates the way ostension works here by considering how a young child might learn to identify geese and swans. On a walk, the father ostends a swan. The child later wrongly calls a goose a "swan" and is corrected. After several such trials, the child is just as capable of distinguishing geese from swans as his father. The point is that rules, criteria of identity, or definitions, such as "swans are white" need not be at work; the ostended sample embodies the reference point, and new samples are understood by similarity. In an analogous way, Kuhn thinks that working through ostended examples such as the inclined plane and the conical pendulum is precisely how one becomes introduced to Newtonian physics.[55]

Joint presence is a condition for the possibility of scientific discourse. There can be no scientific account of joint presence, because in the canons of scientific causality there is no such thing as presence and jointness. *Presence* requires first-person experience, and *jointness* requires second-person experience. Their interplay requires something other than physiology; it requires the manifestation of the animate body. I do not regard this as a shortcoming of science, any more than it is a shortcoming of mathematics that it doesn't account for the principle of noncontradiction, even though it employs it throughout. Manifestation gives us items in the world to be explained; science goes a long way toward explaining those items, but it does not go so far as to explain how manifestation gives us the items in the world. I therefore think that the priority of the manifest image is not only methodological but substantial. It gives us the primary (and not merely preliminary) understanding of what the human being in the world really is.[56] In making the world jointly present, manifestation exercises a genuine causality that cannot be derived from the push and pull of physical forces. The scientific image cannot rival manifestation precisely because it must constantly make use of it while not being able to make sense of it. However high scientists might climb, they do so on the two feet afforded by manifestation.

Given the substantial priority of the manifest image, philosophers have no reason to adopt the scientific image as either their point of departure or their point of return. In the linguistic division of labor, it falls to philosophers to ostend dimensions of experience such as joint presence and animate movement. Everyone lives in these dimensions, but only the philosopher wonders and thinks about something so pedestrian that it is at work in all of our activities in an inconspicuous way. By being faithful to this topic, philosophers can make a genuine contribution to the task of understanding the world, a task that includes understanding the place of joint understanding in it.

11 Conclusion: The Origin of the Human Conversation

Once the new way of thinking has been established, the old problems vanish; indeed they become hard to recapture. For they go with our way of expressing ourselves and, if we clothe ourselves in a new form of expression, the old problems are discarded along with the old garment.

—Ludwig Wittgenstein[1]

"Has philosophy lost contact with people?" wondered Quine in a 1979 *Newsday* column. He was responding to Mortimer Adler, an Aristotelian and Great Books enthusiast, who maintained that professional philosophy no longer appealed to the general literate public. Quine acknowledges that the menu of philosophy has become exotic, and only connoisseurs will appreciate its offerings today. But Quine takes umbrage at the suggestion that this specialization should be taken as a shortcoming. It rather constitutes philosophy's maturation into a scientific discipline. The linguistic turn had the great merit of undermining modern introspective notions, which proved inadequate for accounting for our understanding of the world: "Control is gained by focusing on words, on how they are learned and used, and how they are related to things."[2] I would like to respond to Adler's charge in a somewhat different manner. Quine is right that the linguistic turn marks a great advance over the framework of modern epistemology, but I think a narrow approach to language is problematic.

At the start of this book, I recalled the return to dialogue as the proper starting point for philosophy. Davidson and Gadamer take philosophy to be speaking to others about things. Insofar as the linguistic turn is at the same time a dialogical turn, it is not quite as recondite as Quine would suggest. Rather, it is in some sense ordinary and pedestrian. It includes reference to the basic experience of conversing with people, and what drives conversation is a quest for mutual understanding of the truth. "To converse" originally meant to share a life. It derives from the Latin verb, *conversari*, which means "to turn oneself about, to move to and fro, pass one's life, dwell, abide, live somewhere, keep company with."[3] The restlessness of conversation, its incessant movement back and forth, is rooted in the natural aims of human life. To reflect on language in terms of conversation is to reflect on those who desire to converse with one another, with those who desire to share a life with one another. The turn to conversation necessarily involves the question concerning human nature. Plato asks, "What is the human being? What actions and passions properly belong to human nature and distinguish it from all other beings?"[4] I ask the question about human nature in terms of language learning and conversation: "What is the human being? What actions and passions enable human beings to show each other things and thereby share the world in speech?" In turning to language and conversation, philosophy has lost contact with the practical concerns of people, but it has not lost contact with people or their desires. In a purely theoretical or contemplative key, it does something analogous to what Aristotle did in the *Metaphysics*: it asks about the condition for the possibility of dialogue about things. It does so out of wonder and not out of any need or advantage.

Children learn language principally by eavesdropping or overhearing the conversation of their parents and caregivers as those parents and caregivers go about their everyday routines. The actions of the speakers *show* children what the parents and caregivers have in mind, and often they will be speaking about the items made manifest by their actions. The human way of life, specified by the dynamic inclinations of our nature, constrain the natural ambiguity of such showing. Showing itself is a kind of animate movement different from such things as planetary movement and physiological processes. Phenomenology provides the means for its analysis.

11.1   Behold the Animate Mind

When I try to explain this book to those outside of philosophy and psychology, its topic appears trivial at first. "How do children learn the meaning of their first words? Children learn words by reading body language." My interlocutors look at me with an expression that says, "Of course they do," and I have to explain to them why the topic is worth pondering. In the first place, philosophers, like anyone else, are prone to misconstrue the phenomenon. Locke treats first language acquisition as merely an associative process, leaving out the crucial question of what guides the association. Wittgenstein uncritically adopts the modern Western model and thinks parents have to teach children the meaning of their first words. He seems to have confused the experience of teaching mathematics and spelling, which does involve training, with the learning of first words, which happens naturally without any coaching being necessary. But it is not to correct the suppositions of philosophers that this book takes as its aim. It is above all to accomplish the following: to begin to rethink philosophy and human nature in light of ostension.

Few among us are sympathetic to Descartes's system. But despite our intentions, we have failed to climb out of the basically Cartesian categories of thought that have led us to misunderstand what we in fact experience. In truth, when we see another, we are not inferring another subject on the basis of the perception of a basically mechanical body. Rather, animate movement makes animate minds mutually manifest. The child is not a scientist forming hypotheses about some foreign species. Nor is language a gift from caregivers to the child. The child is the human version of an animate being, attuned to the world by means of her desires, and clued in to her parents and caregivers by means of the actions that embody desires. Language is an inheritance of our joint human nature. Ostension is a showing that requires us to adopt a phenomenological vocabulary of manifestation and the interplay of presence and absence. The language the child acquires is not a code for translating something that happens in one person's skull to what happens in another person's skull. Language, born by ostension, continues to move in the dimension of manifestation: language achieves joint presence even regarding absent things. Our bodies are not outside us. Our language is not extrinsic to us. We humans are the ostensive animal.

Ostension is puzzling even apart from the troubling Cartesian legacy. Augustine finds it provocative within the compass of classical concepts of nature. Here the question is not insoluble, not a matter of squaring the circle in some attempt to wrest publicness from private sensations. Nor is it a matter of conjuring into existence some kind of faculty or module to explain the inexplicable (such as "telepathy" or Russell's "inference instinct"). Rather, the question is phenomenological and logical. What is body language? How are intentions bodily borne? For there is a genuine difference between your experiencing something and my experiencing something. Experience is not private and yet it is owned by each one of us. How can you experience my experiencing something? My experience is not given to you as it is given to me, but it is, for all that, still genuinely given to you that it is given to me. Augustine happens upon the social character of human experience as a complement to the overarching epistemological and metaphysical concerns of the philosophical tradition.

11.2   New Wine in New Skins

Let me review some of the novel moves I make. To account for first word learning, I shift focus from ostensive definition, presupposing as it does a broad linguistic competence, to ostension, and I defined *ostension* as any expressive bodily movement regardless of whether or not a communicative intention is employed. This shift aims to overturn the paradigm that has so captivated modern philosophers up to the present. As a matter of fact, infants do not need to be taught language, a point Augustine keenly observed. Infants can understand the meaning of bodily movement even when language speakers do not assume the role of teacher. How? Our animate bodies achieve a communion on the basis of which conventional language can be learned. To combat the picture of hermetically sealed minds or brains trying to coordinate mental ideas or synaptic events (and associated ideas of "mind reading," "joint attention," or "inference instinct"), I urge a phenomenological and public vocabulary of *joint presence*. In this phenomenon, the same public item is present to each of us, and at least one of us but not necessarily both of us is aware of that fact. Typically, one of us has taken the lead and the other has clued in, but it can also happen that some feature of our environment (a barking dog, for instance) leads us to be jointly present without one of us having taken the lead. The turn-taking of joint presence expresses a *mirroring* of animate action at work in our animate natures. By means of prelinguistic joint presence, we can learn speech that allows us to achieve joint presence even regarding absent things (we can, for instance, talk about the salt content of the Dead Sea). Discussions of ostensive definition typically focus on the radical ambiguity of any gesture, and I argue that ostension is even more ambiguous, because it is undertaken without any attempt to teach or correct. I propose that some *inclinations* proper to human nature help constrain the ambiguity, so that disambiguation happens thanks to a human form of life that expresses or realizes these various human inclinations. The term "inclination" recommends itself because of its dynamic flexibility, which allows exceptions; it also fits in with the overall emphasis on affectivity. Infants are in the first place animate beings with desires; they are not, so to speak, computing devices. Infants will not puzzle about abstruse items in the environment, such as might be on the radar screen of an alien scientist, and they will not miss out on anything, because the human speakers around them are going to be talking for the most part about things interesting to the lives of human beings. I take seriously the fact that ostension is a kind of showing or manifestation based on bodily movement that carries over into the words that are learned. I reflect on the status of this *animate movement* by contrasting it with the sort of motion that can be explained through concepts available to the physicist or biologist. Philosophy, I argue, has a unique role to play in giving an account of this domain of manifestation and language.

11.3   A Glance Back

The first two chapters sought to show what is valuable and yet questionable in contemporary philosophy and science concerning ostension. In doing so, I answered the first philosophical problem of word acquisition (P1), namely, what is the principal prelinguistic means by which infants learn the meaning of words. Ostension, understood broadly to include expressive action undertaken without a communicative intention, enables first word acquisition, and a phenomenology of action equips us to explore just how this occurs. In the historical resources, I explored how four prominent philosophers from diverse traditions who point to ostension as the answer to P1 handle four other philosophical problems of first word acquisition: P2 on its phenomenology, P3 on its philosophy of mind and intersubjectivity, P4 on disambiguation, and P5 on its metaphysics. On my interpretation, all four thinkers agree in the answer to P2: ostensive actions allow us to be acquainted noninferentially with the mental states of others. They offer complementary accounts of the philosophy of mind at work, each filling in needed gaps. They provide contrasting and generally inadequate accounts of disambiguation. Finally, they raise questions about the nature of movement and language. The contemporary and historical resources motivate the questions of ostension and afford various strategies for answering those questions.

In the final four chapters, I developed and defended answers to the philosophical questions that arise with ostension. In chapter 7, I focused on the phenomenological question (P2), and I argued that ostension involves the perceptive understanding of another's intentions on display in his or her bodily movement; no inference from something present to something absent is at work. In chapter 8, I asked what kind of theory of mind is at work in making our intentions available to others in a noninferential way (P3). Ostension logically entails reciprocal roles established by the mirroring of purposive movement. In chapter 9, I addressed the problem of epistemology (P4). Disambiguation occurs via an infant's understanding of contextual relevance aided by an experience of being human; correction is not central to the infant's learning process. In chapter 10, I approached the metaphysics of ostension (P5). Animate movement enables ostension, that is, prelinguistic joint presence, and thereby first word acquisition and language more generally. Ostension requires the interweaving of inner and outer; every kind of mechanistic divide between inner and outer undermines ostension and therefore the publicness of language.

11.4   The Conversation about Conversation

One of Descartes's most famous critics, Thomas Hobbes, wondered about his claim that the nature of a thing is revealed by the mind alone. Doesn't this suggest that we can know only our conventions for things, not the things themselves? Descartes agrees with Hobbes that if our insight is confined to the conventional meaning of words, reasoning about things will be impossible. While he thus recognizes the force of the objection, he thinks it can be avoided simply by asserting that conventional terms do target the same thing:

Who doubts that a Frenchman and a German can reason about the same things, despite the fact that the words that they think of are completely different? And surely the philosopher refutes his own position when he talks of the arbitrary conventions that we have laid down concerning the meaning of words. For if he admits that the words signify something, why will he not allow that our reasoning deals with this something which is signified, rather than merely with the words?[5]

Hobbes asks a good question about how our minds access things when our senses no longer contribute to understanding, and Descartes renders this unproblematic by insisting that ideas are innate. But there is a related problem that cannot be avoided through epistemological conjuring: how can our words, meaning what they do through convention, come to be acquired in the first place? A philosopher who cannot account for word acquisition surely refutes his own position.

Philosophy is, among other things, a conversation, and, as a conversation, it takes its place among other human conversations.[6] What provides entrance to conversation is a common symbolic language, and such an entrance occurs in part thanks to ostension. The phenomenological or manifest account of ostension, couched in terms of the classical philosophical tradition, suggests that the manifest image provides the framework in which we can converse with one another. Because we can converse, we can enter into specialized conversations with specific methodologies; that is, we can do things like science and philosophy. As Wittgenstein puts it, "The picture we have of the language of the grown-up is that of a nebulous mass of language, his mother tongue, surrounded by discrete and more or less clear-cut language games, the technical languages."[7] Part of the work of philosophy must consist in giving an account of what philosophy presupposes: the entrance into a joint language in which specialized conversations can commence. I argue that such an account includes a phenomenology of ostension and certain categories of natural philosophy. The prelinguistic perception of intentions trades on understanding natural movement as purposive. Historically speaking, it is necessary to join Merleau-Ponty and Augustine to Aristotle. That is the only way to do what Wittgenstein grasped as our imperative: to keep language what it is, that is, public. Against Cartesianism and a certain way of construing the scientific data, we must maintain that animate movement makes affectivity manifest. There is a kind of movement that physics cannot know but which phenomenology can: animate movement, and it is the way we share our lives together.

This book draws from different traditions and disciplines to carry out a philosophical analysis of ostension in all its implications. Because there are so many tributaries, there is something for readers of all theoretical persuasions and intellectual traditions to enjoy. By the same token, I am keenly aware that so many tributaries likewise offer much for readers to find irksome. Those operating in the Anglo-American tradition might puzzle at the reach of my claims in the last chapters. Poststructuralist readers might well wonder why I put such confidence in concepts such as presence. Historically minded readers might very well find objectionable my habit of seeing phenomenology at work in thinkers outside the phenomenological school of philosophy. Phenomenologically minded readers will likely be bothered by my avoidance of the method's technical vocabulary. Empirically minded readers might wonder at the novel conceptuality I employ, and theoretically minded ones might be bothered by all the empirical engagement.

Ostension is a phenomenon that calls for this diversified approach despite the inherent risks of such an undertaking. The various traditions each make an essential contribution to its understanding. I have sought to be faithful to its richness as far as my necessarily limited powers and background allow. Thinking seriously about ostension leads us to abandon the Cartesian picture in which language is taken for granted. Such a picture is an illusion of perspective, akin to thinking that the Sun moves about the Earth just because we don't appear to be moving ourselves. Though our own linguistic origins are shrouded in the mystery of forgetfulness, we can consider those of children. When we do so, we can undertake a kind of Copernican revolution in human nature. We do not originate language; we are its inheritors. We come to understand the world and ourselves thanks to those who have gone before us and opened up so many possibilities for understanding. At the same time, we can come to understand others only thanks to animate movement and the inclinations at work in our joint human natures. Contemplating the child in this way can be the starting point for a richer sort of philosophy, one that is more mindful of what it is to be human.

Notes

Introduction

1. Nietzsche, *Thus Spoke Zarathustra: A Book for All and None*, ed. Adrian del Caro and Robert B. Pippin, trans. Adrian del Caro (Cambridge: Cambridge University Press, 2006), 22.

2. Plato, *Seventh Letter*, trans. Glenn R. Morrow, in *Complete Works*, ed. John Cooper (Indianapolis, IN: Hackett, 1997), 341c. Plato also writes: "Only when all of these things—names, definitions, and visual and other perceptions—have been rubbed against one another and tested, pupil and teacher asking and answering questions in good will and without envy—only then, when reason and knowledge are at the very extremity of human effort, can they illuminate the nature of any object." Ibid., 344b.

3. Descartes, *Discourse on Method*, in *The Philosophical Writings of Descartes*, vol. 1, trans. John Cottingham, Robert Stoothoff, and Dugald Murdoch (Cambridge: Cambridge University Press, 1984), hereafter CSM I, 116.

4. Both wrote dissertations on Plato's *Philebus*. See Gadamer, *Plato's Dialectical Ethics: Phenomenological Interpretations Relating to the* Philebus, trans. Robert M. Wallace (New Haven, CT: Yale University Press, 1991), and Davidson, *Plato's* Philebus (New York: Garland, 1990). Davidson calls attention to the relation in "Dialectic and Dialogue," in *Truth, Language, and History* (Oxford: Clarendon Press, 2005), 251–260, and "Gadamer and Plato's *Philebus*," in *The Philosophy of Hans-Georg Gadamer*, ed. Lewis Edwin Hahn (Chicago: Open Court, 1997), 421–432. In Gadamer's response to Davidson, he cites the above passage from the *Seventh Letter* as illustrating the priority of conversation for communicating. "Reply to Donald Davidson," in *The Philosophy of Hans-Georg Gadamer*, 434–435. On the relation of the two thinkers, see John McDowell, "Gadamer and Davidson on Understanding and Relativism," in *Gadamer's Century: Essays in Honor of Hans-Georg Gadamer*, ed. Jeff Malpas, Ulrich Arnswald, and Jens Kertscher (Cambridge, MA: MIT Press, 2002), 173–193, and Jeff Malpas, "Gadamer, Davidson, and the Ground of Understanding," in *Gadamer's Century*, 195–215.

5. Wittgenstein, *Philosophical Investigations*, 2nd ed., trans. G. E. M. Anscombe (Oxford: Blackwell, 1958), §1; Quine, *Ontological Relativity and Other Essays* (New York: Columbia University Press, 1969); Sellars, "Language as Thought and as Communication" and "Some Reflections on Language Games," in *In the Space of Reasons: Selected Essays of Wilfrid Sellars* (Cambridge, MA: Harvard University Press, 2007); and Cavell, *The Claim of Reason: Wittgenstein, Skepticism, Morality, and Tragedy* (New York: Oxford University Press, 1979), 168–190.

6. Heidegger, *The Fundamental Concepts of Metaphysics*, trans. William McNeill and Nicholas Walker (Bloomington: Indiana University Press), 309; Merleau-Ponty, *Consciousness and the Acquisition of Language*, trans. Hugh J. Silverman (Evanston, IL: Northwestern University Press, 1973); Habermas, *The Theory of Communicative Action*, vol. 2: *Lifeworld and System: A Critique of Functionalist Reason*, trans. Thomas McCarthy (Boston: Beacon Press, 1987), 1–46; and Sokolowski, *Phenomenology of the Human Person* (Cambridge, MA: Cambridge University Press, 2008), 48–67.

7. Tomasello, *Constructing a Language: A Usage-Based Theory of Language Acquisition* (Cambridge, MA: Harvard University Press, 2003), 328. The remark occurs while discussing Chomsky's Universal Grammar.

8. Augustine, *Confessions*, trans. Henry Chadwick (Oxford: Oxford University Press, 1991), 1.6.8.

9. Ibid., 1.8.13.

10. Wittgenstein, *Philosophical Investigations*, §6.

11. See, e.g., John Locke, *An Essay Concerning Human Understanding* (New York: Dover, 1959), Bk. III, chap. 9, sec. 6. I briefly discuss Locke's views at the beginning of chapter 1.

12. See Bloom, *How Children Learn the Meanings of Words* (Cambridge, MA: MIT Press, 2000), "Mindreading, Communication, and the Learning of the Names for Things," *Mind and Language* 17 (2002): 37–54, and "Word Learning, Intentions, and Discourse," *Journal of the Learning Sciences,* 14 (2005): 311–314, and Tomasello, *Constructing a Language* and *Origins of Human Communication* (Cambridge, MA: MIT Press, 2008).

13. Johnson, *Logic*, vol. 1 (Cambridge: Cambridge University Press, 1921), 94.

14. Russell, *Human Knowledge: Its Scope and Limits* (London: Allen & Unwin, 1948), 78.

15. Kripke, *Naming and Necessity* (Oxford: Blackwell, 1980); Putnam, "The Meaning of 'Meaning,'" in *Mind, Language, and Reality* (Cambridge: Cambridge University Press, 1975), 215–271.

16. Kuhn, *The Essential Tension* (Chicago: University of Chicago Press, 1977); Hull, *Science as a Process: An Evolutionary Account of the Social and Conceptual Development of Science* (Chicago: University of Chicago Press, 1988), 496–508.

17. Some justification for this is that a fortunate philosopher might follow and participate in the profession for more than half a century. The living memory of my oldest readers will reach back to the days they first began their graduate studies about seventy years ago. So the number, though arbitrary, does have roots in a feature of human nature.

18. Wittgenstein, *On Certainty*, ed. G. E. M. Anscombe and G. H. von Wright, trans. Denis Paul and G. E. M. Anscombe (New York: Harper & Row, 1969), §§369–370; cf. §456.

19. Anita Avramides similarly argues for the primacy of the conceptual over the epistemological problem of other minds. She does not include phenomenological authors in her study, however, and consequently neglects the problem of how minds are experienced, a consideration that would aid her exploration of the conceptual problem. See Avramides, *Other Minds* (London: Routledge, 2001). I will return to her views at the beginning of chapter 8.

20. Searle, "Animal Minds," *Midwest Studies in Philosophy* 19 (1994): 218.

21. Robert Sokolowski, *Introduction to Phenomenology* (Cambridge: Cambridge University Press, 1999), 37.

22. Wittgenstein, *Philosophical Investigations*, §66.

23. Ibid., §129.

24. Wittgenstein, *Culture and Value*, ed. G. H. von Wright, trans. Peter Winch (Chicago: University of Chicago Press, 1980), 63.

25. Merleau-Ponty, *Phenomenology of Perception*, trans. Colin Smith (London: Routledge Classics, 2002), 66.

26. Searle, "The Phenomenological Illusion," in *Erfahrung und Analyze*, ed. Maria E. Reicher and Johann Christian Marek (Vienna: ÖBV & HPT, 2005), 335.

27. Sokolowski, "Husserl's Discovery of Philosophical Discourse," *Husserl Studies* 24 (2008): 169.

28. Husserl, "Tobaccology," *New Yearbook for Phenomenology and Phenomenological Research* 4 (2004): 274–283, and Gretchen Gusich, "A Phenomenology of Emotional Trauma: Around and About the Things Themselves," *Human Studies* 35 (2012): 505–518.

29. Augustine, *The Free Choice of the Will*, trans. Robert Russell, OSA (Washington, DC: The Catholic University of America Press, 1968), 2.10.28.112.

30. Ibid., 2.7.19.77–78.

31. Augustine, *Confessions* 1.8.13. Translation modified.

32. Merleau-Ponty, "An Unpublished Text by Maurice Merleau-Ponty: A Prospectus of His Work," trans. Arleen B. Dallery, in *The Primacy of Perception*, ed. James M. Edie (Evanston, IL: Northwestern University Press, 1964), 8.

33. Sokolowski, *Introduction to Phenomenology*, 12.

1 The Philosophy of Action, Perception, and Play

1. Quine, "Epistemology Naturalized," in *Ontological Relativity and Other Essays* (New York: Columbia University Press, 1969), 81.

2. Locke, *An Essay Concerning Human Understanding* (New York: Dover, 1959), Bk. III, chap. 9, sec. 6.

3. Ibid., Bk. III, chap. 9, sec. 9.

4. Quine, "Ontological Relativity," in *Ontological Relativity and Other Essays*, 26.

5. Ibid., 30–31.

6. Ibid., 31.

7. Ibid.

8. According to Quine, two systems that accorded equally with all observable behavior could mean different things by the same expression, such as "is the same as" and "belongs with." "Then when in the native language we try to ask 'Is this *gavagai* the same as that?' we could as well be asking 'Does this *gavagai* belong with that?" Ibid., 33.

9. Ibid., 28.

10. Ibid., 39.

11. "Semantics is vitiated by a pernicious mentalism as long as we regard a man's semantics as somehow determinate in his mind beyond what might be implicit in his dispositions to overt behavior." Ibid., 27.

12. Quine, *The Roots of Reference* (La Salle, IL: Open Court, 1974), 44–45.

13. Davidson, "The Emergence of Thought," in *Subjective, Intersubjective, Objective* (Oxford: Clarendon Press, 2001), 128.

14. Ibid., 128.

15. Davidson, "The Third Man," in *Truth, Language, and History* (Oxford: Clarendon Press, 2005), 160, and "Seeing Through Language," in *Truth, Language, and History*, 141, respectively.

16. On this point, see also Davidson, "Rational Animals," in *Subjective, Intersubjective, Objective*, 105, "The Third Man," 160–161, and "Seeing Through Language," 140–141.

17. Quine, *Roots of Reference*, 50. Quine also says that "hidden neural mechanisms" are irrelevant for this process, in "Indeterminacy of Translation Again," *Journal of Philosophy* 84 (1987): 10.

18. Davidson, "Meaning, Truth, and Evidence," in *Truth, Language, and History*, 50.

19. "Proximal theories, no matter how decked out, are Cartesian in spirit and consequence." Davidson, "Meaning, Truth, and Evidence," 58.

20. Ibid., 59.

21. Ibid., 60.

22. Ibid.

23. Hume, *Enquiry Concerning Human Understanding*, in *Enquiries*, 3rd ed., ed. L. A. Selby-Bigge and P. H. Nidditch (Oxford: Clarendon Press, 1975), sec. XII, 152. Cf. Davidson, "The Third Man," 160.

24. Føllesdal, "Triangulation," in *The Philosophy of Donald Davidson*, ed. Lewis Edwin Hahn (Chicago: Open Court, 1999), 720.

25. Davidson, "The Second Person," in *Subjective, Intersubjective, Objective*, 119.

26. Davidson, "Reply to W. V. Quine," in *The Philosophy of Donald Davidson*, 84.

27. Grice, "Meaning," in *Studies in the Way of Words* (Cambridge, MA: Harvard University Press, 1989), 220.

28. Davidson, "The Second Person," 120 (my emphasis).

29. Davidson, "Seeing Through Language," 140.

30. Ibid.

31. Davidson speaks of three generalizations: "The child finds tables similar; we find tables similar; and we find the child's responses in the presence of tables similar. It now makes sense for us to call the responses of the child responses to tables." "The Second Person," 119.

32. Føllesdal points out that Davidson's appeal to mutual links in a causal change is infected with ambiguity. "Triangulation," 724.

33. Davidson, "Seeing Through Language," 141.

34. Searle, "Collective Intentions and Actions," in *Consciousness and Language* (Cambridge: Cambridge University Press, 2002), 105. His reasoning is as follows: "Ask yourself what you must take for granted in order that you can ever have or act on

collective intentions. What you must suppose is that *the others are agents like yourself, and that they have a similar awareness of you as an agent like themselves, and that these awarenesses coalesce into a sense of us as possible or actual collective agents.*" Ibid., 104 (my emphasis).

35. Searle, "Animal Minds," *Midwest Studies in Philosophy* 19 (1994): 206–219, at 218.

36. Searle uses the term "biologically primitive" in several senses: to designate an irreducible whole, a biological drive, or an intention without a background. See his *The Construction of Social Reality* (New York: Free Press, 1995), 24, *Mind, Language, Society: Philosophy in the Real World* (New York: Basic Books, 1998), 95, and *Intentionality* (Cambridge: Cambridge University Press, 1983), 141n1, respectively. In the conclusion to "Animal Minds," he writes that biology can identify the structures responsible for consciousness and thereby give grounds for finding it at work in other kinds of animals.

37. McDowell, *Mind and World* (Cambridge, MA: Harvard University Press, 1994), 90.

38. Ibid.

39. Ibid., 91.

40. Thompson, *Life and Action: Elementary Structures of Practice and Practical Thought* (Cambridge, MA: Harvard University Press, 2008), 10–11.

41. Juarrero, *Dynamics in Action: Intentional Behavior as a Complex System* (Cambridge, MA: MIT Press, 1999).

42. Anscombe, *Intention* (Ithaca, NY: Cornell University Press, 1969), sec. 4.

43. O'Regan and Noë, "A Sensorimotor Account of Vision and Visual Consciousness," *Behavioral and Brain Sciences* 24 (2001): 939–1031; Noë and Thompson, "Introduction," in *Vision and Mind: Selected Readings in the Philosophy of Perception* (Cambridge, MA: MIT Press, 2002), 1–14; and Noë, *Action in Perception* (Cambridge, MA: MIT Press, 2004).

44. Varela, Thompson, and Rosch, *The Embodied Mind: Cognitive Science and Human Experience* (Cambridge, MA: MIT Press, 1991); Humphrey, *Seeing Red: A Study in Consciousness* (Cambridge, MA: Harvard University Press, 2006); Rowlands, *Body Language: Representation in Action* (Cambridge, MA: MIT Press, 2006); Gallagher, *How the Body Shapes the Mind* (Oxford: Clarendon Press, 2005); and Gallagher and Zahavi, *The Phenomenological Mind: An Introduction to Philosophy of Mind and Cognitive Science* (London: Routledge, 2008).

45. Sheets-Johnstone, *The Primacy of Movement*, 2nd ed. (Amsterdam: John Benjamins, 2011); see also Gallagher, *How the Body Shapes the Mind*. In a related way, Mark Johnson argues that the embodied mind, which includes movement and

imagination, is the origin of meaning. See his *The Body in the Mind: The Bodily Basis of Meaning, Imagination, and Reason* (Chicago: University of Chicago Press, 1987) and *The Meaning of the Body: Aesthetics of Human Understanding* (Chicago: University of Chicago Press, 2007).

46. Thompson, *Mind in Life: Biology, Phenomenology, and the Sciences of Mind* (Cambridge, MA: Harvard University Press, 2007).

47. Ibid., 392–393.

48. Ibid., 398–401.

49. Ibid., 400–401.

50. Ibid., 411.

51. *The Art and Thought of Heraclitus: An Edition of the Fragments with Translation and Commentary*, ed. and trans. Charles Kahn (Cambridge: Cambridge University Press, 1979), 29.

52. This is the theme of the *Sixth Logical Investigation*. See Husserl, *Logical Investigations*, vol. 2, trans. J. N. Findlay (Amherst, NY: Humanity Books, 2000).

53. Heidegger, *Being and Time*, trans. John Macquarrie and Edward Robinson (New York: Harper & Row, 1962), 102–106.

54. Sokolowski, *Presence and Absence: A Philosophical Investigation of Language and Being* (Bloomington: Indiana University Press, 1978). See also his *Introduction to Phenomenology* (Cambridge: Cambridge University Press, 1999), 33–40.

55. Sokolowski, *Introduction to Phenomenology*, 37.

56. Noë, *Varieties of Presence* (Cambridge, MA: Harvard University Press, 2012), 5. For a similar view, see Frederick Olafson, *What Is a Human Being? A Heideggerian View* (Cambridge: Cambridge University Press, 1995), 46–131.

57. Gadamer, "Man and Language," in *Philosophical Hermeneutics*, trans. and ed. David E. Linge (Berkeley: University of California Press, 1976), 63.

58. Ibid.

59. Ibid., 66.

60. Gadamer, *Truth and Method*, rev. ed., trans. Joel Weinsheimer and Donald G. Marshall (New York: Continuum, 1998), 108.

61. Ibid., 109.

62. Ibid.

63. Gadamer, "The Relevance of the Beautiful," in *The Relevance of the Beautiful and Other Essays*, trans. Nicholas Walker, ed. Robert Bernasconi (Cambridge: Cambridge University Press, 1986), 23.

64. Gadamer, *Truth and Method*, 108.

65. Gadamer, "The Relevance of the Beautiful," 23.

66. Ibid.

67. Ibid.

68. Ibid., 24.

69. Ibid.

70. Gadamer, "The Play of Art," in *The Relevance of the Beautiful and Other Essays*, 128–129.

71. Ibid., 129.

72. Gadamer, "Image and Gesture," in *The Relevance of the Beautiful and Other Essays*, 79.

73. Ibid.

2   The Science of Prelinguistic Joint Attention

1. Keller, *The Story of My Life* (New York: Doubleday, 1903), 23.

2. Wittgenstein, *Philosophical Investigations*, 193.

3. See Marco Iacoboni, *Mirroring People: The New Science of How We Connect with Others* (New York: Farrar, Straus & Giroux, 2008), 16–18.

4. Ibid., 17.

5. On this point, see Naomi Eilan, Christoph Hoerl, Teresa McCormack, and Johannes Roessler, *Joint Attention: Communication and Other Minds: Issues in Philosophy and Psychology*, ed. N. Eilan et al. (Oxford: Clarendon Press, 2005), v.

6. Bickerton, *Language and Human Behavior* (Seattle: University of Washington Press, 1995), 51. For the difference between protolanguage and language, see Derek Bickerton, *Language and Species* (Chicago: University of Chicago, 1990), 105–129.

7. Sokolowski, *Phenomenology of the Human Person*, 65.

8. Chomsky, *Aspects of the Theory of Syntax* (Cambridge, MA: MIT Press, 1965); Pinker, *The Language Instinct: How the Mind Creates Language* (New York: HarperCollins, 1994).

9. Tomasello, *Constructing a Language*, 303.

10. Bloom, *How Children Learn the Meanings of Words*; "Mindreading, Communication, and the Learning of the Names for Things"; "Précis of *How Children Learn the Meanings of Words*," *Behavioral and Brain Sciences* 24 (2001): 1095–1103; and "Theo-

ries of Word Learning: Rationalist Alternatives to Associationism," in *Handbook of Child Language Acquisition*, ed. William C. Ritchie and Tej K. Bhatia (San Diego: Academic Press, 1999), 249–278.

11. Bloom, *How Children Learn the Meanings of Words*, 61. Indeed, he says that "much of [the book] is a defense of this Augustinian theory." "Précis," 1099.

12. See Bloom, *How Children Learn the Meanings of Words*, 62–65.

13. Ibid., 46.

14. Elena Lieven, "Crosslinguistic and Crosscultural Aspects of Language Addressed to Children," in *Input and Interaction in Language Acquisition*, ed. C. Gallaway and B. J. Richards (Cambridge: Cambridge University Press, 1994), 56–73.

15. Tomasello, "Could We Please Lose the Mapping Metaphor, Please?" *Behavioral and Brain Sciences* 24 (2001): 1119.

16. Bloom, *How Children Learn the Meanings of Words*, 8.

17. Tomasello, *Origins of Human Communication*, 59.

18. Hannes Rakoczy and Tomasello, "The Ontogeny of Social Ontology: Steps to Shared Intentionality and Status Functions," in *Intentional Acts and Institutional Facts: Essays on John Searle's Social Ontology*, ed. Savas L. Tsohatzidis (Dordrecht: Springer, 2007), 113–138.

19. Ibid., 123.

20. Bloom, "Mindreading, Communication, and the Learning of the Names for Things," and Tomasello, Malinda Carpenter, Josep Call, Tanya Behne, and Henrike Moll, "Understanding and Sharing Intentions: The Origins of Cultural Cognition," *Behavioral and Brain Sciences* 28 (2005): 1–17, respectively.

21. See Bloom, "Mindreading, Communication, and the Learning of the Names for Things," 41–42.

22. Barbara Landau and Lila R. Gleitman, *Language and Experience: Evidence from the Blind Child* (Cambridge, MA: Harvard University Press, 1985), 49–50.

23. Keller, *The Story of My Life*, 23. Her teacher, Ann Mansfield Sullivan, describes the process as follows: "When she wants to know the name of anything, she points to it and pats my hand." Ibid., 316.

24. Cathy Urwin, "Dialogue and Cognitive Functioning in the Early Language Development of Three Blind Children," in *Language Acquisition in the Blind Child: Normal and Deficient*, ed. Anne E. Mills (London: Croom Helm, 1983), 153.

25. In correspondence with the author, Paul Bloom raised the objections to the primacy of bodily movement addressed in this section.

26. Colwyn Trevarthen, "Communication and Cooperation in Early Infancy: A Description of Primary Intersubjectivity," in *Before Speech*, ed. M. Bullowa (Cambridge: Cambridge University Press, 1979); Trevarthen and P. Hubley, "Secondary Intersubjectivity: Confidence, Confiding, and Acts of Meaning in the First Year," in *Action, Gesture and Symbol: The Emergence of Language*, ed. A. Lock (London: Academic, 1978), 183–229; Stein Bråten, "Intersubjective Communion and Understanding: Development and Perturbation," in *Intersubjective Communication and Emotion in Early Ontogeny*, ed. Stein Bråten (Cambridge: Cambridge University Press, 1999), 372–382; Gallagher, *How the Body Shapes the Mind*, 225–230; and Gallagher and Zahavi, *The Phenomenological Mind*, 187–195. Tomasello follows the division of the stages but does not think the first stage can properly be regarded as "intersubjective" on the grounds that the child is not yet aware of intentionality and subjectivity. *The Cultural Origins of Human Cognition* (Cambridge, MA: Harvard University Press, 1999), 59.

27. Tomasello, *Cultural Origins*, 74, 179.

28. Ibid., 59.

29. See Meltzoff and Moore, "Infant Intersubjectivity: Imitation, Identity, and Intention," in *Intersubjective Communication and Emotion in Early Ontogeny*, ed. Stein Bråten (Cambridge: Cambridge University Press, 1999), 52.

30. Gallagher and Zahavi, *The Phenomenological Mind*, 189.

31. Tomasello, *Cultural Origins*, 61, 92, 179.

32. Ibid., 62, 81.

33. Ibid., 73.

34. Gallagher and Zahavi, *The Phenomenological Mind*, 189.

35. Bråten, "Intersubjective Communion and Understanding," 373.

36. Tomasello, *Cultural Origins*, 179.

37. Gallagher and Zahavi, *The Phenomenological Mind*, 191–195.

38. Tomasello, *Cultural Origins*, 87.

39. Ibid.

40. David F. Armstrong, William C. Stokoe, and Sherman E. Wilcox, *Gesture and the Nature of Language* (Cambridge: Cambridge University Press, 1995); David F. Armstrong and Sherman E. Wilcox, *The Gestural Origin of Language* (Oxford: Oxford University Press, 2007); Michael C. Corballis, *From Hand to Mouth: The Origins of Language* (Princeton, NJ: Princeton University Press, 2002); Michael C. Corballis, *The Recursive Mind: The Origins of Human Language, Thought, and Civilization* (Princeton,

NJ: Princeton University Press, 2011); and Tomasello, *Origins of Human Communication*.

41. Tomasello, *Origins of Human Communication*, 45–49. Daniel J. Povinelli, Jesse M. Bering, and Steve Giambrone take a more parsimonious view based on repeated experiments in their laboratory: "Chimpanzees do not, in fact, understand a key aspect of these gestures—namely, that the gestures must be seen by the recipients in order for the gesture to function." "Chimpanzees' 'Pointing': Another Error of the Argument by Analogy?" in *Pointing: Where Language, Culture, and Cognition Meet*, ed. Sotaro Kita (Mahwah, NJ: Erlbaum, 2003), 59. Human children understand this factor by age two. They conclude that the pointing behavior of chimps differs fundamentally from that of humans.

42. Rakoczy and Tomasello, "The Ontogeny of Social Ontology," 132.

43. Ibid., 119.

44. Tomasello, *Cultural Origins*, 105.

45. Giacomo Rizzolatti and Corrado Sinigaglia, *Mirrors in the Brain—How Our Minds Share Actions and Emotions*, trans. Frances Anderson (Oxford: Oxford University Press, 2008), 98.

46. Ibid., 130.

47. Ibid., 125, 131.

48. Ibid., 134–135.

49. Ibid., 117, 156.

50. Ibid., 117.

51. Ibid., 156. See also Erica A. Cartmill, Sian Beilock, and Susan Goldin-Meadow, "A Word in the Hand: Action, Gesture and Mental Representation in Humans and Non-human Primates," *Philosophical Transactions of the Royal Society of London, Series B: Biological Sciences* 367 (2012): 138.

52. Arbib, *How the Brain Got Language: The Mirror System Hypothesis* (Oxford: Oxford University Press, 2012), ix.

53. Goldman, *Simulating Minds: The Philosophy, Psychology, and Neuroscience of Mindreading* (Oxford: Oxford University Press, 2006), 132.

54. Gallese, "Before and Below 'Theory of Mind': Embodied Simulation and the Neural Correlates of Social Cognition," *Philosophical Transactions of the Royal Society of London, Series B: Biological Sciences* 362 (2007): 659–669.

55. Gallagher, "Neural Simulation and Social Cognition," in *Mirror Neuron Systems*, ed. J. A. Pineda (New York: Humana Press, 2009), 367.

56. Gallese, "Neuroscientific Approach to Intersubjectivity," in *The Embodied Self: Dimensions, Coherence and Disorders*, ed. T. Fuchs, H.C. Sattel, P. Henningsen (Stuttgart: Schattauer, 2010), 85–86.

57. See also Gallagher and Zahavi, *The Phenomenological Mind*, 171–181.

58. Iacomboni, *Mirroring People*, 262. Also see Gallese, "Mirror Neurons, Embodied Simulation, and the Neural Basis of Social Identification," *Psychoanalytic Dialogues* 19 (2009): 526, 529.

59. Among other things, it is not clear how a difference in the intensity of the neuronal firing accounts for the difference between the first-person and second-person perspective. I will say more about the brain in section 10.2. I borrow the terminology of correlation from Paul Ricoeur: "I therefore propose that we say that the brain is the substrate of thought (in the broadest sense of the term) and that thought is the indication of an underlying neuronal structure. Substrate and indication would thus constitute the two aspects of a dual relation, or correlation." Paul Ricoeur and Jean-Pierre Changeux, *What Makes Us Think? A Neuroscientist and a Philosopher Argue about Ethics, Human Nature, and the Brain*, trans. M. B. DeBevoise (Princeton, NJ: Princeton University Press, 2000), 47.

60. Sperber and Wilson, *Relevance: Communication and Cognition*, 2nd ed. (Malden, MA: Blackwell, 1995), 49.

61. Wilson and Sperber, *Meaning and Relevance* (Cambridge: Cambridge University Press, 2012), 151–152.

62. Ibid., 36.

63. David Wilkins, "Why Pointing With the Index Finger Is Not a Universal (in Sociocultural and Semiotic Terms)," in *Pointing: Where Language, Culture, and Cognition Meet*, ed. Sotaro Kita (Mahwah, NJ: Erlbaum, 2003), 171–215.

64. See Susan Goldin-Meadow, *Hearing Gesture: How Our Hands Help Us Think* (Cambridge, MA: Harvard University Press, 2003); Adam Kendon, *Gesture: Visible Action as Utterance* (Cambridge: Cambridge University Press, 2004); and David McNeill, *Gesture and Thought* (Chicago: University of Chicago Press, 2005).

65. Sperber and Wilson, *Relevance*, 50.

66. Ibid., 156–157.

67. "Charity prompts the interpreter to maximize the intelligibility of the speaker, not sameness of belief." Donald Davidson, *Inquiries into Truth and Interpretation* (Oxford: Oxford University Press, 1984), xix.

68. An outlier is biologist Rupert Sheldrake, who defends telepathy in *The Sense of Being Stared At and Other Aspects of the Extended Mind* (New York: Crown Publishers, 2003).

3 Wittgenstein: Ostension Makes Language Public

1. Wittgenstein, *Zettel*, ed. G. E. M. Anscombe and G. H. von Wright, trans. G. E. M. Anscombe (Berkeley: University of California Press, 1967), §605.

2. G. E. Moore, "Proof of an External World," in *Philosophy in the Twentieth Century: An Anthology*, vol. 2, ed. William Barrett and Henry D. Aiken (New York: Random House, 1962), 599.

3. Wittgenstein, *On Certainty*, §370; cf. §456. On this passage, see Marie McGinn, *Sense and Certainty: A Dissolution of Skepticism* (Oxford: Blackwell, 1989), esp. 142–146.

4. Wittgenstein, *Zettel*, §227.

5. See, e.g., Heraclitus, frag. 1, in *The Art and Thought of Heraclitus*, 29, and Luke 24:19.

6. Wittgenstein quotes Goethe's Faust, who was translating *logos* from the prologue to the Gospel of John not as "word" but as "deed." Wittgenstein, *Culture and Value*, 31; Goethe, *Faust*, I.

7. Wittgenstein, *Culture and Value*, 46; cf. Wittgenstein, *Philosophical Investigations*, §546.

8. Wittgenstein, *Philosophical Investigations*, §7.

9. Ibid., p. 200. See also §120.

10. Ibid., §355.

11. Wittgenstein, *On Certainty*, §475.

12. Wittgenstein, *Philosophical Investigations*, §25.

13. Wittgenstein, *Zettel*, §412.

14. Wittgenstein, *Philosophical Investigations*, preface.

15. Ibid., §83.

16. Ibid., §120.

17. Ibid.

18. Ibid., §133.

19. Ibid., §19.

20. Ibid., p. 226.

21. Ibid., §38.

22. Wittgenstein, *The Blue and Brown Books* (New York: Harper & Row, 1958), 45.

23. Stanley Cavell, *In Quest of the Ordinary: Lines of Skepticism and Romanticism* (Chicago: University of Chicago Press, 1988), 171.

24. Others who pursue a phenomenological reading include Stephen Mulhall, *On Being in the World: Wittgenstein and Heidegger on Seeing Aspects* (London: Routledge, 1990), and Søren Overgaard, *Wittgenstein and Other Minds: Rethinking Subjectivity and Intersubjectivity with Wittgenstein, Levinas, and Husserl* (New York: Routledge, 2007).

25. Wittgenstein, *Philosophical Investigations*, §126.

26. Ibid., §90 (emphases in original).

27. See Fergus Kerr, *"Work on Oneself": Wittgenstein's Philosophical Psychology* (Arlington, VA: The Institute for the Psychological Sciences Press, 2008), 104–111.

28. Wittgenstein, *Zettel*, §606.

29. Wittgenstein, *Philosophical Investigations*, §275.

30. Ibid., §293.

31. Wittgenstein, *The Big Typescript TS 213*, ed. and trans. C. Grant Luckhardt and Maximilian A. E. Aue (Malden, MA: Blackwell, 2005), 153.

32. Ibid., 151.

33. Wittgenstein, *On Certainty*, §455.

34. Wittgenstein, *Philosophical Investigations*, §380.

35. Ibid., §258.

36. Ibid., §269.

37. Ibid., §257.

38. See Wittgenstein, *Brown Book*, 77, *Philosophical Investigations*, and the *Big Typescript*.

39. Wittgenstein, *Philosophical Investigations*, §3.

40. Wittgenstein, *Big Typescript*, 23.

41. Wittgenstein, *Philosophical Investigations*, §49; cf. §26.

42. Wittgenstein, *Big Typescript*, 24.

43. Wittgenstein, *Philosophical Investigations*, §32.

44. Ibid., §§33–38.

45. Wittgenstein, *Philosophical Investigations*, §6; *Big Typescript*, 33–35.

46. Wittgenstein, *Philosophical Investigations*, §6.

47. Ibid., §31.

48. Ibid., §6 (my emphasis). About this difference, Meredith Williams writes, "Ostensive training, unlike ostensive definition classically conceived, does not impute *higher* cognitive competencies to the novice in order to explain low-level forms of behavior." *Wittgenstein, Mind, and Meaning: Toward a Social Conception of Mind* (London: Routledge, 1999), 193. More recently, she insightfully characterizes the posture of Wittgenstein's infant as beginning in a state of "blind obedience" in the sense that the infant does not come hardwired with mental machinery but is instead introduced to language by means of a normative habituation to a form of life: "The initiate learner is blind to cognitive alternatives. Yet that very blindness is necessary for becoming a participant, for acquiring the background understanding against which full semantic, cognitive and epistemic competence can be exercised." *Blind Obedience: Paradox and Learning in the Later Wittgenstein* (London: Routledge, 2010), 106.

49. Wittgenstein, *Philosophical Investigations*, §6.

50. Ibid., §5. "Language games are the forms of language with which a child begins to make use of words." *Blue Book*, 17. "Children are taught their native language by means of such games. ..." *Brown Book*, 81.

51. See, e.g., *Philosophical Investigations*, §31.

52. Ibid., §2.

53. Wittgenstein, *On Certainty*, §455.

54. Wittgenstein, *Philosophical Investigations*, §§19–20.

55. Wittgenstein, *Big Typescript*, 154.

56. Augustine, *Confessions* 1.8.13. Translation modified.

57. Wittgenstein, *Big Typescript*, 130.

58. "Ostensive teaching of words ... will form an important part of the training, because it is so with human beings; not because it could not be imagined otherwise." Wittgenstein, *Philosophical Investigations*, §6.

59. Wittgenstein, *Big Typescript*, 130; cf. 38–39, 46.

60. Wittgenstein, *Zettel*, §594.

61. Wittgenstein, *Philosophical Investigations*, §206. Translation modified. Kerr and Mulhall likewise think this passage echoes Augustine. See Kerr, *Theology after Wittgenstein* (Oxford: Blackwell, 1986), 41, and Mulhall, *Wittgenstein's Private Language: Grammar, Nonsense, and Imagination in* Philosophical Investigations, *§§243–315* (Oxford: Clarendon Press, 2007), 31.

62. Wittgenstein, *Big Typescript*, 46. "An animal cannot point to a thing that inter-ests it." Wittgenstein, *Last Writings on the Philosophy of Psychology*, vol. 2, *The Inner and the Outer 1949–1950*, ed. G. H. von Wright and Heikki Nyman, trans. C. G. Luck-hardt and Maximilian A. E. Aue (Oxford: Blackwell, 1992), 41.

63. Wittgenstein, *Zettel*, §219.

64. Wittgenstein, *Big Typescript*, 45.

65. Wittgenstein, *Philosophical Investigations*, §647.

66. Wittgenstein, *Zettel*, §220.

67. Ibid., §222.

68. Ibid., §223.

69. Ibid., §161.

70. Ibid., §494.

71. Ibid., §513.

72. Wittgenstein, *Big Typescript*, 29; cf. 37: "'Not' makes a rebuffing gesture. No, it *is* a rebuffing gesture."

73. Ibid., 29.

74. Wittgenstein, *Philosophical Investigations*, p. 219.

75. Wittgenstein, *Big Typescript*, 37. Cf. *Culture and Value*, 51–52.

76. Wittgenstein, *Big Typescript*, 153.

77. Wittgenstein, *Brown Book*, 77.

78. Wittgenstein, *Big Typescript*, 27.

79. Wittgenstein, *On Certainty*, §§535–538.

80. Ibid., §540; cf. §§547–548.

81. Wittgenstein, *Philosophical Investigations*, §6.

82. Ibid., p. 218.

83. Wittgenstein, *Last Writings on the Philosophy of Psychology*, vol. 2, 43.

84. Wittgenstein, *Philosophical Investigations*, §288.

85. Ibid., §43.

86. Wittgenstein, *Big Typescript*, 41–42.

87. Ibid., 31.

88. Wittgenstein, *Brown Book*, 103.

89. Wittgenstein, *Last Writings on the Philosophy of Psychology*, vol. 2, 62.

90. "Here is the picture: He sees it immediately, I only mediately. But that's not the way it is. He doesn't see something and describe it to us." Ibid., 92.

91. Ibid., 62.

92. Wittgenstein, *Zettel*, §225.

93. Wittgenstein, *Remarks on the Philosophy of Psychology*, vol. 2, ed. G. H. Von Wright and Heikki Nyman, trans. C. G. Luckhardt and M. A. E. Aue (Chicago: University of Chicago Press, 1980), §170.

94. Wittgenstein, *Philosophical Investigations*, p. 223; cf. §284.

95. On avowals, see P. M. S. Hacker, *Wittgenstein, Meaning, and Mind* (Oxford: Blackwell, 1993), 83–96.

96. Wittgenstein, *Last Writings on the Philosophy of Psychology*, vol. 2, 62. On the inner and outer, Paul Johnston reads Wittgenstein conservatively according to the grammatical method and Stephen Mulhall approaches Wittgenstein's analysis in a somewhat more phenomenological manner. I incline toward the latter kind of reading. See Johnston, *Wittgenstein: Rethinking the Inner* (London: Routledge, 1993), ix, and Mulhall, *On Being in the World*, chap. 3.

97. Wittgenstein, *Philosophical Investigations*, §281.

98. Wittgenstein, *Last Writings on the Philosophy of Psychology*, vol. 2, 66.

99. Wittgenstein, *Philosophical Investigations*, p. 178. "I can be as *certain* of someone else's sensations as of any fact." Though the certainty differs from mathematics, the difference is logical, not psychological. Ibid., p. 224.

100. Ibid., §420.

101. Ibid., §284.

102. Wittgenstein, *Last Writings on the Philosophy of Psychology*, vol. 2, 65.

103. Ibid., vol. II, 66.

104. Russell, *Human Knowledge*, 78.

105. Ibid., 80.

106. Ibid., 85.

107. Ibid., 78.

108. Ibid., 84.

109. Ibid., 209.

110. "I give the name 'animal inference' to the process of spontaneous interpretation of sensations." Ibid., 182.

111. Ibid., 202.

112. Ibid., 504.

113. Ibid., 208.

114. Ibid., 503.

115. Wittgenstein, *Last Writings on the Philosophy of Psychology*, vol. 2, 36.

116. Wittgenstein, *Philosophical Investigations*, p. 224.

117. Ibid., p. 222. Cf. p. 221.

118. Ibid., §288.

119. Ibid., §246.

120. Wittgenstein, *Zettel*, §540.

121. Wittgenstein, *Last Writings on the Philosophy of Psychology*, vol. 2, 63.

122. Ibid., 59.

123. Wittgenstein, *Zettel*, §541.

124. Ibid., §545.

4   Merleau-Ponty: Gestural Meaning and the Living Body

1. Merleau-Ponty, "An Unpublished Text," 5.

2. Husserl, *Ideas Pertaining to a Pure Phenomenology and to a Phenomenological Philosophy, Second Book: Studies in the Phenomenology of Constitution*, trans. Richard Rojcewicz and André Schuwer (Dordrecht: Kluwer Academic, 1989).

3. Heidegger, *History of the Concept of Time: Prolegomena*, trans. Theodore Kisiel (Bloomington: Indiana University Press, 1985), 122.

4. Merleau-Ponty, *Phenomenology of Perception*, viii.

5. I sketch the relation of *Being and Time* to Husserl in "Disentangling Heidegger's Transcendental Questions," *Continental Philosophy Review* 45 (2012): 77–100.

6. Merleau-Ponty, *Phenomenology of Perception*, 105n1. See Ted Toadvine, "Merleau-Ponty's Reading of Husserl: A Chronological Overview," in *Merleau-Ponty's Reading of Husserl*, ed. Ted Toadvine and Lester Embree (Dordrecht: Springer, 2002), 227–286.

7. Merleau-Ponty, *Phenomenology of Perception*, xxiii.

8. Talia Welsh, *The Child as Natural Phenomenologist: Primal and Primary Experience in Merleau-Ponty's Psychology* (Evanston, IL: Northwestern University Press, 2013), 108.

9. Merleau-Ponty, *Phenomenology of Perception*, xix.

10. "The real has to be described, not constructed or formed." Ibid., xi.

11. Ibid.

12. Ibid., xiv.

13. Ibid., xxii.

14. Shaun Gallagher, Dan Zahavi, and Evan Thompson are just some of the phenomenologically minded authors who, following Merleau-Ponty, engage trends in contemporary science. On Merleau-Ponty's relation to psychology, see Welsh, *The Child as Natural Phenomenologist*, 22–44.

15. Merleau-Ponty, *Consciousness and the Acquisition of Language*, 97; *Phenomenology of Perception*, 217.

16. Merleau-Ponty, *Consciousness and the Acquisition of Language*, 14. Translation modified.

17. Ibid., 13.

18. Ibid., 17–18; cf. Merleau-Ponty, "The Child's Relations with Others," in *The Primacy of Perception*, ed. James M. Edie (Evanston, IL: Northwestern University Press, 1964), 149.

19. Merleau-Ponty, "The Child's Relations with Others," 99. The emphasis on habituation was foreshadowed by his earlier characterization of a word as a tool. *Consciousness and the Acquisition of Language*, 95. On habituation, see Hubert Dreyfus, "The Current Relevance of Merleau-Ponty's Phenomenology of Embodiment," *Electronic Journal of Analytic Philosophy* 4 (1996).

20. Merleau-Ponty, "The Child's Relations with Others," 109.

21. Ibid., 113.

22. Merleau-Ponty, "An Unpublished Text," 7.

23. Merleau-Ponty, *Phenomenology of Perception*, 215. Translation modified.

24. Ibid., 225.

25. Ibid., 225, 227.

26. Ibid., 226.

27. Ibid., 220.

28. Ibid., 225.

29. Ibid., 215. Translation modified.

30. Merleau-Ponty, *The Structure of Behavior*, trans. Alden L. Fisher (Boston: Beacon Press, 1963), 182.

31. Ibid., 209.

32. Merleau-Ponty, *Phenomenology of Perception*, 229–230 (my emphasis).

33. Merleau-Ponty, "An Unpublished Text," 5.

34. Merleau-Ponty, *Consciousness and the Acquisition of Language*, 44.

35. Merleau-Ponty, *Themes from the Lectures at the Collège de France 1952–1960*, trans. John O'Neill (Evanston, IL: Northwestern University Press, 1970), 6.

36. Merleau-Ponty, *Phenomenology of Perception*, 409.

37. In fact, in his lecture courses he takes Descartes as his point of departure rather than "the pre-Cartesian conceptions of nature as a destiny or total dynamic of which man is a part." Merleau-Ponty, *Themes from the Lectures*, 67. His history of nature culminates in the Husserlian return of the lifeworld and recent developments of physics (quantum and relativity theory) away from classical determinism.

38. Merleau-Ponty, *Phenomenology of Perception*, 409. In this way, idealism and realism equally miss the interrelationship of within and without, because they each take a stand on a distorted moment of a fundamental unity. Ibid., 423–424.

39. Merleau-Ponty, *Consciousness and the Acquisition of Language*, 32.

40. Paul Guillaume, *Imitation in Children*, trans. Elaine P. Halperin (Chicago: University of Chicago Press), 1973.

41. Merleau-Ponty, *Consciousness and the Acquisition of Language*, 33. This is a position that Tomasello advocates today; see Tomasello, *The Cultural Origins of Human Cognition*, 82–83.

42. Merleau-Ponty, *Consciousness and the Acquisition of Language*, 36.

43. Ibid.

44. Ibid., 36–37, 40.

45. Ibid., 47. See Scheler, *The Nature of Sympathy*, trans. Peter Heath (New Brunswick, NJ: Transaction Publishers, 2008), 213–264.

46. See Husserl, *Cartesian Meditations: An Introduction to Phenomenology*, trans. Dorion Cairns (The Hague: Martinus Nijhoff, 1977), 89–151.

47. Merleau-Ponty, *Consciousness and the Acquisition of Language*, 48.

48. Ibid., 49.

49. Ibid., 50.

50. Merleau-Ponty, "The Child's Relations with Others," 113–121.

51. Shaun Gallagher and Andrew Meltzoff argue, in contrast to Merleau-Ponty, that newborns have a primitive sense of self and other which makes possible the repertoire of imitating acts we now know newborns to be capable of. Their conception modifies but does not replace the primary stage. Gallagher and Meltzoff, "The Earliest Sense of Self and Others: Merleau-Ponty and Recent Developmental Studies," *Philosophical Psychology* 9 (1996): 211–233.

52. Merleau-Ponty, "The Child's Relations with Others," 119.

53. Ibid., 136. The child learns *"there can be a viewpoint taken on him,"* which is to say he is *"visible*, for himself and others." Ibid.

54. Ibid., 121.

55. Ibid., 118.

56. Ibid., 119, 153–155; cf. *Phenomenology of Perception*, 414.

57. Merleau-Ponty, "The Child's Relations with Others," 121.

58. "From the start to the finish of the development, the living relation with others is the support, the vehicle, or the stimulus for what we abstractly call the 'intelligence.'" Ibid., 140.

59. Ibid., 137–138.

60. Merleau-Ponty, *The Visible and the Invisible*, ed. Claude Lefort, trans. Alphonso Lingis (Evanston, IL: Northwestern University Press, 1968), 189, 255. "What we are calling flesh ... has no name in any philosophy." Ibid., 147.

61. Ibid., 155.

62. Ibid., 214–215, 220–221.

63. "The other ... is caught up in a circuit that connects him to the world, as we ourselves are, and consequently also in a circuit that connects him to us—and this world is *common* to us, is intermundane space—..." Ibid., 269.

64. Ibid., 142; cf. "Dialogue and the Perception of the Other," in *The Prose of the World*, ed. Claude Lefort, trans. John O'Neill (Evanston, IL: Northwestern University Press, 1973), 138.

65. He writes that "through other eyes we are for ourselves fully visible." Merleau-Ponty, *The Visible and the Invisible*, 143.

66. Ibid., 263. Translation modified.

67. Ibid., 271.

68. Merleau-Ponty, "Eye and Mind," in *The Primacy of Perception*, ed. James M. Edie (Evanston, IL: Northwestern University Press, 1964), 163.

69. Ibid., 162.

70. Merleau-Ponty, *The Visible and the Invisible*, 138.

71. Merleau-Ponty, *Themes from the Lectures*, 131.

72. Merleau-Ponty, "An Unpublished Text," 7.

73. Heidegger, *Fundamental Concepts*, 309.

74. Ibid., 205.

75. Ibid., 208.

76. Ibid., 205.

77. Heidegger, *Being and Time*, 178.

78. Heidegger, *Fundamental Concepts*, 66.

79. Ibid., 104; Ryle, *The Concept of Mind* (New York: Barnes & Noble, 1949), 104.

80. Heidegger, *Fundamental Concepts*, 67.

81. Ibid.

82. Heidegger later remedies this neglect by emphasizing the constitutive role of the animate body for human comportment. "Within philosophy we must not limit the word 'gesture' merely to 'expression.' Instead, we must characterize all comportment of the human being as *being-in-the-world*, determined by the bodying forth of the body. Each movement of my body as a 'gesture' … is always already in a certain region which is open through the thing to which I am in a relationship, for instance, when I take something into my hand." *Zollikon Seminars*, ed. Medard Boss, trans. Franz Mayr and Richard Askay (Evanston, IL: Northwestern University Press, 2001), 90–91.

83. He calls it "a paradox of Being, not a paradox of man." Merleau-Ponty, *The Visible and the Invisible*, 136; cf. 264, 274.

84. Merleau-Ponty, "The Child's Relations with Others," 140.

85. Merleau-Ponty, *The Visible and the Invisible*, 266.

86. Ibid., 264.

87. On the key term "reversibility," see Martin Dillon, *Merleau-Ponty's Ontology*, 2nd ed. (Evanston, IL: Northwestern University Press, 1997), 153–176, and Renaud Barbaras, *The Being of the Phenomenon: Merleau-Ponty's Ontology*, trans. Ted Toadvine and Leonard Lawlor (Bloomington: Indiana University Press, 2004), 153–173, 244–256.

88. Merleau-Ponty, "Dialogue and the Perception of the Other," 142. Translation modified. Cf. *The Visible and the Invisible*, 264–265.

89. Similarly, Tomasello observes that the child must not only learn the meaning of a word heard but understand it as a possibility for speaking. *The Cultural Origins of Human Cognition*, 99–100, 105.

90. Plato, *Sophist*, trans. Nicholas P. White, in *Complete Works*, 254c–257a.

91. Merleau-Ponty, *The Visible and the Invisible*, 263.

92. Merleau-Ponty, *Themes from the Lectures*, 9. "In a sense, if we were to make completely explicit the architectonics of the human body, its ontological framework, and how it sees itself and hears itself, we would see that the structure of its mute world is such that all the possibilities of language are already given in it." *The Visible and the Invisible*, 155.

93. Merleau-Ponty, *Husserl and the Limits of Phenomenology: Including Texts by Edmund Husserl* (Evanston, IL: Northwestern University Press, 2002), 18.

5 Augustine: Word Learning by Understanding the Movements of Life

1. Augustine, *The Trinity*, trans. Stephen McKenna (Washington, DC: The Catholic University of America Press, 1963), 10.1.2.

2. Wittgenstein thinks Augustine misinterprets the essence of language (as resting on ostensive definition), not the dynamics of word acquisition (which requires in part ostensive teaching). See *Philosophical Investigations*, especially §§5–6.

3. Myles Burnyeat, "Wittgenstein and Augustine *De magistro*," *Proceedings of the Aristotelian Society, Supplementary Volumes* 61 (1987): 1–24.

4. Christopher Kirwan, "Augustine on the Nature of Speech," in *Language: Companions to Ancient Thought 3*, ed. Stephen Everson (Cambridge: Cambridge University Press, 1994), 188–211, and "Augustine's Philosophy of Language," in *The Cambridge Companion to Augustine*, ed. Eleonore Stump and Norman Kretzmann (Cambridge: Cambridge University Press, 2001), 186–204.

5. Aquinas, *On Truth (De veritate)*, trans. Robert W. Mulligan, SJ, James V. McGlynn, SJ, and Robert W. Schmidt, SJ (Indianapolis: Hackett, 1994), q. 11, a. 1, ad. 8.

6. Wittgenstein, *Philosophical Investigations*, §1.

7. Ibid., §2.

8. Ibid., §7.

9. Compare this to what Wittgenstein says elsewhere: "Suppose a man described a game of chess, without mentioning the existence and operations of the pawns. His

description of the game as a natural phenomenon will be incomplete. On the other hand we may say that he has completely described a simpler game. In this sense we can say that Augustine's description of learning the language was correct for a simpler language than ours." Wittgenstein, *The Blue and Brown Books*, 77.

10. Quintilian, *Institutio oratoria*, trans. H. E. Butler (London: William Heinemann, 1922), 11.3.87.

11. Ambrose, "On the Duties of the Clergy," trans. H. de Romestin, E. de Romestin and H. T. F. Duckworth, in *Nicene and Post-Nicene Fathers, Second Series*, vol. 10, ed. Philip Schaff and Henry Wace (Buffalo, NY: Christian Literature Publishing, 1896), 1.18.

12. In a related way, Gadamer maintains that Christian reflection on the Incarnation of the Word led to an increased appreciation for the being of language. Gadamer, *Truth and Method*, 418–428. For commentary, see John Arthos, *The Inner Word in Gadamer's Hermeneutics* (Notre Dame, IN: University of Notre Dame Press, 2009).

13. Augustine, *Confessions* 6.5.7.

14. Ibid., 7.9.13–7.21.27.

15. Antoine Arnauld notes the parallel in the "Fourth Set of Objections," in *The Philosophical Writings of Descartes*, vol. 2, trans. John Cottingham, Robert Stoothoff, and Dugald Murdoch (Cambridge: Cambridge University Press, 1984), hereafter CSM II, 139. Two contemporary interpreters who take this approach are Gareth Matthews, *Thought's Ego in Augustine and Descartes* (Ithaca, NY: Cornell University Press, 1992), and Stephen Menn, *Descartes and Augustine* (Cambridge: Cambridge University Press, 1998). Matthews for his part does underscore one important difference: Augustine, unlike Descartes, recognizes that animals have sense awareness and that correspondingly we have animal powers of awareness. Matthews does not seem to realize that the implications of this difference are so profound as to negate the value of the Augustine–Descartes analogy altogether. See Matthews, "Augustine and Descartes on the Souls of Animals," in *From Soul to Self*, ed. M. James C. Crabbe (London: Routledge, 1999), 102–106.

16. In this way, Hubert Dreyfus misunderstands the episode in which Augustine marvels that Saint Ambrose is reading the scriptures silently, a relatively rare practice in the ancient world. Augustine is not trying to convince people they have private inner selves. Rather, as Thomas Prufer argues, he is inviting people to discover a new kind of dialogue between self and the divine Other, a dialogue in principle available to all. Note that Augustine's conversion coincides with his discovery of this unvoiced dialogue. At the invitation of the children saying, "Take and read," he picks up the scriptural text and thinks he is being addressed by God directly. He comes then to enjoy the same position that Ambrose did in the earlier episode. See *Confessions* 6.3.3, 8.12.29; Dreyfus, *On the Internet*, 2nd ed. (London: Routledge,

2009), 51; and Prufer, *Recapitulations: Essays in Philosophy* (Washington, DC: The Catholic University of America Press, 1993), 27–34.

17. See Kerr, *Theology after Wittgenstein*, 38–42. Kerr favors Gareth Matthews's reading of Augustine as Cartesian, but he notes that the claim is controversial. Kerr, "Augustine and Aquinas in the Light of Postmodern Thought: Other Minds Skepticism," in *Augustine and Postmodern Thought: A New Alliance Against Modernity?*, ed. L. Boeve, M. Lamberigts, and M. Wisse (Leuven: Uitgeverij Peeters, 2009), 109n19.

18. Norman Malcolm, *Ludwig Wittgenstein: A Memoir*, 2nd ed. (Oxford: Oxford University Press, 2001), 59–60.

19. Ibid., 19.

20. Husserl, *On the Phenomenology of the Consciousness of Internal Time* (1893–1917), ed. and trans. John Brough (Dordrecht: Kluwer, 1991), 3.

21. Heidegger, *Being and Time*, 492.

22. Arendt, *Love and Saint Augustine*, ed. and trans. Joanna Vecchiarelli Scott and Judith Chelius Stark (Chicago: University of Chicago Press, 1996); on Gadamer, see Jean Grondin, *Introduction to Philosophical Hermeneutics* (New Haven, CT: Yale University Press, 1994), xi, xiv.

23. Jean-Luc Marion develops a phenomenological reading of the *Confessions*. Against the Cartesian analysis, he rightly argues that Augustine decenters the self. However, his approach differs from mine in several respects. First, he thinks phenomenology is opposed to what he calls metaphysics and would no doubt reject my attempt to marry Augustine and Aristotle. Second, he focuses on the decentering of self in the act of confessing, in the weak will, and in time; I do so by means of the flesh and the communal character of speech. See Jean-Luc Marion, *In the Self's Place: The Approach of Saint Augustine*, trans. Jeffrey L. Kosky (Palo Alto, CA: Stanford University Press, 2012), especially 9–10.

24. Augustine, *Confessions* 1.6.10.

25. Ibid., 1.6.8. Translation modified.

26. Ibid.

27. Kirwan calls Augustine's view "certainly false," because the later Augustine is able to sense the frustration of the infant ("Nature of Speech," 206). However, we must distinguish between being able to perceive frustration over something and being able to perceive exactly what it is that is the source of frustration. For a young infant who lacks controlled voluntary movement, we can certainly see the former but not the latter.

28. Augustine, *De doctrina Christiana*, trans. R. P. H. Green (Oxford: Oxford University Press, 1995), 2.1.1. Translation modified.

29. Ibid., 2.2.3. Translation modified.

30. Ibid.

31. Augustine, *Free Choice of the Will* 2.10.28.112. See also 2.7.15.58–78. Augustine does make the exception of sensed things altered by our sensing; we cannot both taste the exact same morsel of cake, though we can both see it.

32. On these distinctions, see B. Darrell Jackson, "The Theory of Signs in St. Augustine's *De doctrina Christiana*," in *Augustine: A Collection of Critical Essays*," ed. R. A. Markus (Garden City, NY: Doubleday, 1972), 96–98.

33. Augustine, *De doctrina Christiana* 2.1.2.

34. Ibid. Translation modified.

35. The question of animal communication is left open by Augustine. He thinks many animals, such as chickens and doves, appear to give signs to each other in order to signify. "Whether (as with a facial expression or a shout of pain) they accompany emotion without any desire to signify, or whether they are really given in order to signify something, is another question, and irrelevant to the matter at hand." Ibid., 2.2.3.

36. Ibid., 2.3.4.

37. Ibid.

38. Ibid., 2.24.37. Cf. Wittgenstein, *Philosophical Investigations*, §355: "And this language like any other is founded on convention."

39. Augustine, *De doctrina Christiana* 2.24.37. Translation modified.

40. Augustine, *The Teacher*, in *Against the Academicians; The Teacher*, trans. Peter King (Indianapolis, IN: Hackett, 1995), 10.34. "Before I made this discovery, the word was a mere sound to me; but I learned that it was a sign, when I found out of what thing it is the sign—and, as I said, I learned this not by anything that signifies but by its appearance." Ibid., 10.33.

41. Ibid., 13.43.

42. Ibid., 8.22.

43. Augustine, *Confessions* 1.8.13 (my emphasis).

44. Mulhall, *Inheritance and Originality: Wittgenstein, Heidegger, Kierkegaard* (Oxford: Clarendon Press, 2001), 48.

45. Augustine, *Confessions* 1.14.23.

46. Ibid., 4.8.13 (my emphasis). Translation modified.

47. "Prensabam memoria, cum ipsi appellabant rem aliquam et cum secundum eam uocem corpus ad aliquid mouebant, uidebam, et tenebam hoc ab eis uocari rem

illam, quod sonabant, cum eam uellent ostendere." Ibid., 1.8.13. Translation modified.

48. "Hoc autem eos uelle ex motu corporis aperiebatur tamquam uerbis naturalibus omnium gentium, quae fiunt uultu et nutu oculorum ceteroque membrorum actu et sonitu uocis indicante affectionem animi in petendis, habendis, reiciendis fugiendisue rebus." Ibid. Translation modified. On the role of human eye movement for shared attention and thus word acquisition, see Tomasello, *Why We Cooperate* (Cambridge, MA: MIT Press, 2009), 75–76.

49. Augustine, *The Teacher* 3.6.

50. Ibid., 10.34.

51. Augustine, *Confessions* 1.8.13.

52. Augustine, *The Teacher* 3.6.

53. Ibid., 10.29.

54. Ibid., 10.32.

55. Burnyeat, "Wittgenstein and Augustine *De magistro*," 22.

56. Wittgenstein, *On Certainty*, §467.

57. Augustine, *Confessions* 1.14.23.

58. In addition to Burnyeat's essay, cited above, see Matthews's claim: "For language learning one must rely, he thinks, on the teacher within." *Thought's Ego in Augustine and Descartes*, 157.

59. "Just as an especially violent emotion is reflected in the countenance so that inward meditations are to some extent recognized outwardly by men, so it should not be incredible if even milder thoughts afford some indications through the medium of the body. These cannot be recognized by the dull sense of men, but can be through the keen perception of demons." Augustine, *The Divination of Demons*, trans. Ruth Wentworth Brown, in *Treatises on Marriage and Other Subjects*, ed. Roy J. Deferrari (New York: The Fathers of the Church, 1955), 5.9.

60. See Bloom, "Précis," 1096.

61. Bloom counts as one of the merits of the theory that Augustine thinks children learn words "in the context of sentences" rather than the "usual assumption" that children hear words "in isolation." Bloom, "Theories of Word Learning," 249. He regards this as important, because syntactical cues can help disambiguate intentions of language-speakers (263–264).

62. Wittgenstein, *Philosophical Investigations*, §32.

63. Ibid., §6, §§31–32.

64. Augustine, *The Trinity* 15.10.19.

65. Gadamer, quoted in Grondin, *Introduction to Philosophical Hermeneutics*, xiv. Kirwan recognizes the first but not the second point. He misconstrues Augustine as suggesting a mental "rehearsal" when all that is needed is a nonverbal anticipation. Augustine does not think we say to ourselves what we are going to say before we say it, which, after all, would invite an infinite regress. Moreover, it must be remembered that discourse in the heart is not private but occurs before and with God. See Kirwan, "Nature of Speech," 200–201, 209–210.

66. Matthews, *Augustine* (Malden, MA: Blackwell, 2005), 23–24. By "fully developed" he means the baby is like a foreign visitor who "can talk and reason with himself in his native language (in the case of baby Augustine the language must have been 'Mentalese'), but he is utterly bewildered by what people in the society around him are saying." Matthews, *Thought's Ego in Augustine and Descartes*, 152.

67. "For at that time I knew nothing more than how to suck and to be quieted by bodily delights, and to weep when I was physically uncomfortable" (Augustine, *Confessions* 1.6.7).

68. Ibid., 1.14.23.

69. Augustine, *The Teacher* 10.35. He thinks that "words do no more than prompt man to learn" (14.46). Cf. 11.36–38 and *Confessions* 10.10.17.

70. Augustine, *The Trinity* 10.1.2.

71. Augustine, *On Merit and the Forgiveness of Sins, and the Baptism of Infants*, trans. Peter Holmes and Robert Ernest Wallis, rev. Benjamin B. Warfield, in *Nicene and Post-Nicene Fathers, First Series*, vol. 5, ed. Philip Schaff (Buffalo, NY: Christian Literature Publishing, 1887), 1.35.66. See also the discussion of infancy's deep ignorance in *The Trinity* 14.5.7.

72. "Wittgenstein apparently takes it that such a view is transparently absurd. But the argument that I just sketched suggests, on the contrary, that Augustine was precisely and demonstrably right and that seeing that he was is prerequisite to any serious attempts to understand how first languages are learned." Jerry Fodor, *Language of Thought* (Cambridge, MA: Harvard University Press, 1979), 64.

73. Matthews, *Augustine*, 54.

74. On other minds, though not on word acquisition, Matthews recognizes that Augustine is not asking an epistemological question. What I am calling "phenomenological" is the question he formulates: "Augustine wants to explain how it ever occurs to us (or to beasts, for that matter) to attribute minds, or souls, to other beings." Matthews, *Thought's Ego in Augustine and Descartes*, 121.

75. I will introduce the Cartesian approach in 6.5.

76. Augustine, *The Trinity* 8.6.9 (my emphasis). Translation modified. On this passage, see Charles Brittain, "Non-Rational Perception in the Stoics and Augustine," *Oxford Studies in Ancient Philosophy*, vol. 22, ed. David Sedley (Oxford: Oxford University Press, 2002), 296–301, and Matthews, "Augustine and Descartes on Minds and Bodies," in *The Augustinian Tradition*, ed. Matthews (Berkley: University of California Press, 1998), 224–225.

77. Augustine, *The Trinity* 13.1.3 (my emphasis). Translation modified. On this passage, see Matthews, *Thought's Ego*, 122.

78. Augustine, *Greatness of Soul*, trans. Joseph M. Colleran, C.SS.R. (New York: The Newman Press, 1950), 24.45: "And, while this awareness is not called sensation, because the body is not affected by the fire, it is nevertheless termed recognition through sensation [*cognitio per sensum*], because the fire is conjectured [*coniectatum*] and established from an experience of the body."

79. "Sed sicut homines, inter quos uiuentes motusque uitales exerentes uiuimus, mox ut aspicimus, non credimus uiuere, sed uidemus, cum eorum uitam sine corporibus uidere nequeamus, quam tamen in eis per corpora remota omni ambiguitate conspicimus." Augustine, *The City of God*, trans. Henry Bettenson (New York: Penguin Books, 1984), 22.29. Translation modified. Augustine, in order to account for the resurrection of the dead and the beatific vision, argues on philosophical grounds against metaphysical dualism. A good statement of Augustine's non-dualism can be found in Peter Burnell, *The Augustinian Person* (Washington, DC: The Catholic University of America Press, 2005), 18–44.

80. "Neque quasi humanae prudentiae rationisque proprium est. Et bestiae quippe sentiunt uiuere non tantum se ipsas sed etiam inuicem atque alterutrum et nos ipsos, nec animas nostras uident sed ex motibus corporis idque statim et facillime quadam conspiratione naturali." Augustine, *The Trinity* 8.6.9. Translation modified.

81. Augustine, *City of God* 22.29; *Free Choice of the Will* 2.5.12.44.

82. By contrast, Matthews—perhaps under the influence of Russell—thinks of awareness of others as existing in one way in philosophers and in an analogous way in other animals. The text rather suggests an identity, not an analogy, since awareness of others is handled by inner sense, common to all. Matthews, *Augustine*, 56.

83. Augustine, *Free Choice of the Will* 2.4.10.38.

84. Ibid., 2.3.8.27–28.

85. In addition to the *Confessions* text, cited above, Augustine's view of infant psychology can be gleaned from the following: "An infant child has only the impulse to get something or get rid of it fully developed, whereas its muscles are untractable because of their recent formation and imperfect co-ordination." Augustine, *The Greatness of Soul* 22.39.

86. Augustine, *Literal Commentary on Genesis* 8.21.42, as quoted by Burnell, *The Augustinian Person*, 28.

87. This may solve a problem in Bloom, who wonders why word learning starts at around twelve months of age. One developmental milestone is motor control, but he notes that "appealing to motor control can't address the emergence of language comprehension, only production." Bloom, *How Children Learn the Meanings of Words*, 45. For Augustine, motor control enables the infant to understand ostensive acts and thereby referential intent.

88. Augustine, *Greatness of Soul* 33.72; cf. *Confessions* 10.17.26.

89. Indeed, experts on great apes say that "while you can train them to point to direct their trainers to food, they never quite get the hang of it; when they see someone else point, they are mystified." See Bloom, *How Children Learn the Meanings of Words*, 85.

90. Burnyeat, "Wittgenstein and Augustine *De magistro*," 23. In a similar vein, see Bloom, *How Children Learn the Meanings of Words*, 84.

91. Augustine, *The Trinity* 11.2.2–5.

92. Augustine, *Confessions* 1.14.23.

93. Augustine, *The Trinity* 10.9.12.

94. Wittgenstein, *Philosophical Investigations*, §241.

95. Augustine, *Confessions* 4.14.22. Translation modified.

96. In the context of *The Teacher*, which argues that Christ is the only absolute teacher, Augustine emphasizes the difficulty of knowing the intentions of a speaker by means of his words. For instance, he may merely be reporting a view that he does not know, he could be lying, he could be saying one thing while thinking of another, and he could mean one thing and say another (13.42). In the end, however, Augustine thinks these marginal situations do not undermine communication entirely: "I now give in and concede that when words are heard by someone who knows them, he can know that the speaker had been thinking about the things they signify" (13.45).

97. Augustine, *In Psalmos* (41.13), as cited in *An Augustine Synthesis*, ed. Erich Przywara, SJ (New York: Sheed & Ward, 1936), 421. On the limitation of signs, see John Rist, *Augustine: Ancient Thought Baptized* (Cambridge: Cambridge University Press, 1994), 33–34.

6 Aristotle: Natural Movement and the Problem of Shared Understanding

1. Aristotle, *Politics*, trans. B. Jowett, in *The Complete Works of Aristotle: The Revised Oxford Translation*, ed. Jonathan Barnes (Princeton, NJ: Princeton University Press, 1984), 1.2, 1252a24–25.

2. Aristotle, *Metaphysics*, trans. W. D. Ross, in *The Complete Works of Aristotle*, 1.6, 987a31–987b1.

3. Consider, for instance, the famous treatment of insight in Plato's *Seventh Letter*, 341c, 344b.

4. Plato, *Cratylus*, trans. C. D. C. Reeve, in *Complete Works*, 423a—b. Plato makes this point as part of his overall argument against the view that words imitate the natures of things. I do not think we should construe the quoted statement as somehow constituting Plato's theory of the expressive body. In my view, that account is simply undeveloped, perhaps owing to his lifelong allegiance to Cratylus's doctrine of universal flux.

5. Searle, "What Is an Institution?" *Journal of Institutional Economics* 1 (2005): 12.

6. For example, Deborah Modrak's excellent book handles the conceptual dimension of language acquisition but not its social dimension. See *Aristotle's Theory of Language and Meaning* (Cambridge: Cambridge University Press, 2000).

7. Aristotle, *Metaphysics* 1.6, 987a29–987b13.

8. For this last claim, see Wolfgang-Rainer Mann, *The Discovery of Things: Aristotle's Categories and Their Context* (Princeton, NJ: Princeton University Press, 2000).

9. Aristotle, *Physics*, trans. R. P. Hardie and R. K. Gaye, in *The Complete Works of Aristotle*, 1.1, 184a12.

10. Aristotle, *Posterior Analytics*, trans. Jonathan Barnes, in *The Complete Works of Aristotle*, 2.19.

11. Galileo Galilei, "Letters on Sunspots," in *Discoveries and Opinions of Galileo*, trans. Stillman Drake (New York: Doubleday, 1957), 126–127, and Descartes, *Discourse on Method*, CSM II, 147.

12. Galileo wrote of Aristotle that "he not only admitted manifest experience was among the most powerful ways for forming conclusions about the problems of natural philosophy, but even considered it the most important. So while he argued the immutability of the heavens from the fact that no alteration had been seen in them at any time, it is credible that if his senses had shown him what is now clear to us, he would have followed the [contrary] opinion to which these wonderful discoveries have now led us." Quoted by Ian Glass, *Revolutionaries of the Cosmos: The Astro-Physicists* (Oxford: Oxford University Press, 2006), 22.

13. Thompson, *Life and Action*, 10.

14. Aristotle, *Metaphysics* 4.6, 1011a6–13 (my emphasis).

15. Aristotle, *Physics* 1.1, 184a19–21.

16. Ibid., 1.8, 191a25–27.

17. Aristotle, *Posterior Analytics* 2.19, *Metaphysics* 1.1, 9.10, and *On the Soul*, trans. J. A. Smith, in *The Complete Works of Aristotle*, 3.6.

18. See Gadamer, *Truth and Method*, 351.

19. Plato provides the backdrop to Aristotle's program: "Do you think that without rest anything would be the same, in the same state in the same respects? Not at all. Well then, do you see any case in which intelligence is or comes-to-be anywhere without these things? Not in the least. And we need to use every argument we can to fight against anyone who does away with knowledge, understanding, and intelligence but at the same time asserts anything at all about anything. Definitely." *Sophist*, in *Complete Works*, 249b–c.

20. Aristotle, *Metaphysics* 4.10, 1006a19–27. Translation modified.

21. *De interpretatione*, trans. J. L. Ackrill, in *The Complete Works of Aristotle*, 3, 16b19–21.

22. Aquinas considers the objection that simply saying "dog" does not invite rest in the listener, who is wondering what it is the speaker will say about the thing named. He distinguishes the first and second operation of the intellect, simple apprehension and judgment, and he says that there is a rest in regard to the first operation but not in regard to the second. *Aristotle: On Interpretation*, trans. Jean T. Oesterle (Milwaukee: Marquette University Press, 1962), 50.

23. Commenting on this passage, Terence Irwin takes the point to be that even equivocation presupposes an identical subject: "When O says 'Man is F and not F', his thesis can be expanded into 'Man is F and man is not F'; and if O is to present the thesis he intends to, he must signify the same subject in both occurrences of 'man.'" Irwin, *Aristotle's First Principles* (Oxford: Oxford University Press, 1988), 182. That seems to be Aristotle's point later (*Metaphysics* 4.4, 1006b11–18), but not in the passage under consideration, for Aristotle does not have the interlocutor assert "Man is F and not F" but only "Man," which implicitly involves "is F."

24. Aristotle, *Metaphysics* 4.4, 1006b7–10. Translation modified. The first emphasis is mine. "And at the same time our discussion with him is evidently about nothing at all; for he says nothing. For he says neither 'yes' nor 'no,' but both 'yes' and 'no'; and again he denies both of these and says 'neither yes nor no'; for otherwise there would already be something definite" (1008a29–33).

25. Ibid., 4.7, 1012a21–25: "And the starting-point in dealing with all such people is definition. Now the definition rests on the necessity of their meaning something; for the formula [*logos*], of which the word is a sign, becomes its definition [*horismos*]." Cf. 7.10–12, in which Aristotle says the logos has parts. On definition, see Modrak, *Aristotle's Theory of Language and Meaning*, 163–179.

26. Cf. Aristotle, *Metaphysics* 4.4, 1008a30–34.

27. Plato, *Theaetetus*, trans. M. J. Levett and Myles Burnyeat, in *Complete Works*, 263e4–5.

28. Aristotle, *Metaphysics* 4.4, 1006b19–22. Translation modified. Cf. *Categories*, trans. J. L. Ackrill, in *The Complete Works of Aristotle*, 1, 1a1–5.

29. Aristotle, *De interpretatione* 2, 16a27–29, *On the Soul* 2.8, 420b30–421a2, 3.6, 429a5–8. Michael Tomasello concurs: "For all mammals, including nonhuman primates, vocal displays are mostly unlearned, genetically fixed, emotionally urgent, involuntary, inflexible responses to evolutionarily important events that benefit the vocalizer in some more or less direct way." *Origins of Human Communication*, 53–54. He underscores that ape gestures, rather than vocalizations, are the precursor to human speech, because they display great flexibility.

30. Aristotle, *Politics* 1.2, 1253a9–18.

31. "Every sentence is significant (not as a tool [*organon*] but, as we said, by convention" (Aristotle, *De interpretatione* 4, 17a1). Cf. *On the Soul*, 2.1. Aquinas distinguishes the natural organs used in speaking, such as the lungs, vocal cords, tongue, and dentition with the artificial or conventional words these natural organs are used to speak. *Aristotle: On Interpretation*, 58.

32. Aristotle, *De interpretatione* 2, 16a26–29.

33. Ibid., 1, 16a3–7. Modrak offers her book, *Aristotle's Theory of Language and Meaning*, as a commentary on this passage.

34. In a famous text, Aristotle discusses the cognitive apprehension of a thing as canceling ignorance. Whereas propositions are either true or false, the essence of a thing is either grasped as true or simply unknown. Regarding simples, "contact [*thigein*] and expression [*phanai*] are truth (expression [*phasis*] not being the same as affirmation [*kataphasis*]), and ignorance is non-contact." *Metaphysics* 9.10, 1051b24–25. Translation modified. On this passage, see Kurt Pritzl, "Aristotle's Door," in *Truth: Studies of a Robust Presence*, ed. K. Pritzl (Washington, DC: The Catholic University of America Press, 2010), 27.

35. Indeed, not only are sensible and intellective affections inward, even the objects of understanding "are in a sense within the soul itself," in contrast to the objects of sensation which are "outside." Aristotle, *On the Soul* 2.5, 417b20–24.

36. Modrak characterizes the dynamic as follows: "Meanings for Aristotle are in the head because they are in the world. The structure of our psychological states are like those found in the world because the latter cause the former." *Aristotle's Theory of Language and Meaning*, 273. Her emphasis, however, remains cognitive rather than intersubjective.

37. Aristotle, *Metaphysics* 1.1, 980a27.

38. Aristotle, *Sense and Sensibilia*, trans. J. I. Beare, in *The Complete Works of Aristotle*, 1, 437a1–4.

39. Aristotle, *Metaphysics* 4.5, 1010a11–14.

40. Ibid., 4.4, 1008b10–12.

41. Aristotle, *Movement of Animals*, trans. A. S. L. Farquharson, in *The Complete Works of Aristotle*, 7, 701a34–37.

42. Ibid., 6, 700b14–16.

43. Aristotle, *Physics* 2.1, 193a4–7.

44. Ibid., 192b21–23.

45. Aristotle does not discuss pointing per se, but he does highlight the interplay of movement and rest in every bodily movement. See *Movement of Animals* 1, 698a17–20.

46. *Progression of Animals*, trans. A. S. L. Farquharson, in *The Complete Works of Aristotle*, 4, 705b9–14.

47. Aristotle, *Metaphysics* 9. Aryeh Kosman and Jonathan Beere argue that it is more accurate to translate *energeia* with the causal term "activity" than the modal term "actuality." In analyzing the being of living things, Aristotle is talking about the exercise of capacities to act; he is not making points of logic. See Kosman, *The Activity of Being: An Essay on Aristotle's Ontology* (Cambridge, MA: Harvard University Press, 2013), vii—xi, and Beere, *Doing and Being: An Interpretation of Aristotle's* Metaphysics Theta (Oxford: Oxford University Press, 2009), 167.

48. Kosman, *Activity of Being*, 74–75.

49. Ibid., 254.

50. Gerard Manley Hopkins, "As Kingfishers Catch Fire," in *Poems of Gerard Manley Hopkins*, ed. Robert Bridges (London: Humphrey Milford, 1918), 54.

51. Beere, *Doing and Being*, 21.

52. Descartes, "Letter to Mersenne, 28 January 1641," in *The Philosophical Writings of Descartes*, vol. 3, trans. John Cottingham, Robert Stoothoff, Dugald Murdoch, and Anthony Kenny (Cambridge: Cambridge University Press, 1991), hereafter CSM III, 173.

53. Descartes, *Principles of Philosophy*, CSM I, 233.

54. Ibid., 233. For the criticism of Aristotle, see Descartes, *The World*, CSM I, 94.

55. Descartes, *Principles of Philosophy*, 220–221.

56. Ibid., 221.

57. Descartes, *Discourse on Method*, 136, 141.

58. Descartes, "Optics," CSM I, 153.

59. On this point, see Sokolowski, *Phenomenology of the Human Person*, 201n9.

60. Descartes, "Optics," 166.

61. One of Descartes's interlocutors, Arnauld, raises this very example, expressing incredulity that a sheep should flee a wolf owing only to the mechanics of light and the sheep's nervous system without recourse to felt experience. Descartes, as we will see, points to our own experience of mindless reflexes, such as bracing ourselves when tripping, to show that we can handle animal movements purely mechanically. For the objection and response, see "Fourth Set of Objections" and "Fourth Set of Replies," CSM II, 144, 161, respectively.

62. Descartes, "Fourth Set of Replies," 161.

63. Descartes, "Letter to More, 5 February 1649," CSM III, 365.

64. Ibid., 365. Cf. "Fourth Set of Replies," 162, and "Sixth Set of Replies," CSM II, 288.

65. Descartes, "Letter to More, 5 February 1649," 366 (my emphasis).

66. Descartes, "Letter to More, 15 April 1649," CSM III, 374 (my emphasis).

67. Descartes says that he is a thinking thing and denies that he is in any way identifiable with "that structure of limbs which is called a human body." *Meditations on First Philosophy*, CSM II, 18.

68. "In fact I expressly supposed that this matter lacked all those forms or qualities about which they dispute in the Schools." Descartes, *Discourse on Method*, 132.

69. Ibid., 140.

70. Descartes, *Principles of Philosophy*, 218. See also the "Letter to Hyperaspistes, August 1641," CSM III, 189–190.

71. Descartes, *Principles of Philosophy*, 219.

72. Aristotle, *Movement of Animals* 7, 701b10–17.

73. Aristotle, *Poetics*, trans. I. Bywater, in *The Complete Works of Aristotle*, 4, 1448b6–9.

74. By contrast, the Megarians absurdly denied that an actuality reveals a concomitant potentiality that transcends its realization. See Aristotle, *Metaphysics* 9.3.

75. Aristotle, *On the Soul* 2.5, 417b22–23.

76. In this vein, George Butterworth suggests that one reason chimpanzees in the wild do not point is that "whole-body orienting" is precise enough for what they have to communicate. "Pointing as the Royal Road to Language," in *Pointing: Where Language, Culture, and Cognition Meet*, ed. Sotaro Kita (Mahwah, NJ: Erlbaum, 2003), 15.

77. Rakoczy and Tomasello, "The Ontogeny of Social Ontology," 119.

78. Aristotle, *Nicomachean Ethics*, trans. W. D. Ross and J. O. Urmson, in *The Complete Works of Aristotle*, 9.9, 1170a31–2. See also *On the Soul* 3.2 and 3.4.

79. Aristotle, *Nicomachean Ethics* 9.9, 1170b10–13.

80. Aristotle, *On the Soul* 3.4, 429a27–28.

81. Aristotle saw our hands, senses, and thought as three foci of meaning: "It follows that the soul is analogous to the hand; for as the hand is a tool of tools, so thought is the form of forms and sense the form of sensible things." *On the Soul* 3.8, 432a1–3.

82. Aristotle, *Posterior Analytics* 2.19, 100a17–100b1.

83. Aristotle, *Physics* 1.1, 184a24–184b13. See also *Topics*, trans. W. A. Pickard-Cambridge, in *The Complete Works of Aristotle*, 6.4, 141b9–14: "For a solid falls under perception most of all, and a plane more than a line, and a line more than a point; for most people learn such things earlier; for any ordinary intelligence can grasp them whereas the others require a precise and exceptional understanding."

84. Aristotle, *Metaphysics* 4.4, 1007a22–1007b18.

85. *Categories* 5, 3b10–13. Translation modified.

86. See Bloom, *How Children Learn the Meanings of Words*, 10–12.

87. Searle, "Collective Intentions and Actions," 105.

7 Phenomenology: Discovering Ostension

1. J. L. Austin, "Other Minds," in *Philosophical Papers*, 3rd ed., ed. J. O. Urmson and G. J. Warnock (Oxford: Oxford University Press, 1979), 108.

2. Sellars, "Philosophy and the Scientific Image of Man," in *Science, Perception, and Reality* (New York: The Humanities Press, 1963), 7–8, 15.

3. Augustine, *City of God*, 22.29. Translation modified.

4. Russell, *Human Knowledge*, 209.

5. Wittgenstein, *Philosophical Investigations*, p. 223; cf. §284.

6. Austin, "Other Minds," 107 (my emphases).

7. Ibid., 109.

8. "Now if words, which signify nothing except by human convention, suffice to make us think of things to which they bear no resemblance, then why could nature not also have established some sign which would make us have the sensation of light,

even if the sign contained nothing in itself which is similar to this sensation? Is it not thus that nature has established laughter and tears, to make us read joy and sadness on the faces of men?" Descartes, *The World*, 81, repeated at "Optics," part 4, 165.

9. T. S. Eliot, "The Dry Salvages," in *Four Quartets* (San Diego, CA: Harcourt Brace & Co., 1943), lines 211–212.

10. Wittgenstein, *Big Typescript*, 29.

11. For historical and conceptual justification for this claim, see Avramides's *Other Minds*.

12. Descartes, *Meditations*, 22.

13. Ibid., 21.

14. "Letter to More, 15 April 1649," CSM III, 374. Cf. "Letter to More, 5 February 1649," CSM III, 366.

15. Descartes, "Letter to More, 5 February 1649," 365. Cf. "Fourth Set of Replies," 162, and "Sixth Set of Replies," 288, both in CSM II.

16. Ryle, *The Concept of Mind*, 13.

17. Ibid., 14–15.

18. MacIntyre, *Dependent Rational Animals: Why Human Beings Need the Virtues* (Chicago: Open Court, 1999), 14.

19. Alva Noë and Evan Thompson call this the "orthodox view" before detailing various "heterodox views," including their own enactive approach. See their introduction to *Vision and Mind*.

20. Noë, *Action in Perception*, 85.

21. For a defense of this claim, see Stephen Mulhall, *On Being in the World*.

22. J. L. Austin, *Sense and Sensibilia*, ed. G. J. Warnock (Oxford: Clarendon Press, 1962), 52. He says that even things "generically different" might be "qualitatively alike." Ibid., 54. On deception in emotions, also see his essay, "Other Minds," 111–113.

23. See Sokolowski, *Introduction to Phenomenology*, 14–15, and Heidegger, *The Basic Problems of Phenomenology*, rev. ed., trans. Albert Hofstadter (Bloomington: Indiana University Press, 1982), 60: "Perceiving must be the perception-of something in order for me to be able to be deceived *about* something." Both Sokolowski and Heidegger point out that radical mistakes, such as hallucinations, are cases in which we think we are perceiving but really are imagining.

24. For a thought experiment concerning robots with misleading behavior, see John Searle, *The Rediscovery of Mind* (Cambridge, MA: MIT Press, 1992), 70–71.

25. Gadamer, "The Play of Art," 129.

26. Searle, "Animal Minds," 217.

27. Aristotle, *Eudemian Ethics*, trans. J. Solomon, in *The Complete Works of Aristotle*, 7.12, 1245b20–24.

28. Davidson, "The Third Man," 161. Quine develops this point in the first chapter of *Word and Object* (Cambridge, MA: MIT Press, 1960).

29. Clark, *First Language Acquisition*, 2nd ed. (Cambridge: Cambridge University Press, 2009), 28.

30. Davidson, "Gadamer and Plato's *Philebus*," in *Truth, Language, and History*, 275 (my emphasis).

31. "If I am unable to produce an appropriate symbolic interpretive response to an unfamiliar foreign word, I can only use physical co-occurrence to guess at what objects or events might be relevant to what is being said." Deacon, *The Symbolic Species: The Co-evolution of Language and the Brain* (New York: W. W. Norton, 1997), 63. Cf. Hume, *Enquiry Concerning Human Understanding*, sec. III, 24.

32. Heidegger observes, in a somewhat different context: "If nearness and neighborliness could be conceived parametrically, then a distance of the magnitude of one millionth of a second, and of one millimeter, would have to mean the nearest possible neighboring nearness, compared with which even the distance of a yard and a minute represents extreme remoteness." *On the Way to Language*, trans. Peter D. Hertz (New York: Harper & Row, 1971), 103.

33. This is a central thesis in Noë's *Varieties of Presence*.

34. Hume, *Enquiry Concerning Human Understanding*, sec. XII, 153.

35. Sokolowski provides a clear overview. See *Introduction to Phenomenology*, 19–20.

36. Noë, *Action in Perception*, 84–86.

37. Hume, *Enquiry Concerning Human Understanding*, sec. XII, 152.

38. Ibid., 151–152.

8   Mind: The Logic of Ostension

1. Adolf Portmann, *Animal Forms and Patterns: A Study of the Appearances of Animals*, trans. Hella Czech (New York: Schocken Books, 1967), 197.

2. Roald Dahl, *Charlie and the Chocolate Factory*, illustrated by Quentin Blake (New York: Alfred A. Knopf, 2001), 107.

3. I discuss this duality in "Unmasking the Person," *International Philosophical Quarterly* 50 (2010): 447–460.

4. Avramides notes that Augustine was not only the first to pose the epistemological problem; he was also the first to pose the conceptual problem. On her view, the analytic tradition, following the Cartesian mold, poses the epistemological problem without the conceptual problem, which is a major oversight she intends to rectify with her book. As I noted in chapter 5, Augustine was also the first to pose the phenomenological problem. His appeal to animate minds, apparently unknown to Avramides, goes a long way to countering the kind of worry she expresses about the conceptual problem of other minds. See Avramides, *Other Minds*, 46–50.

5. Ibid., 253.

6. Wittgenstein, *Last Writings on the Philosophy of Psychology*, vol. 2, 66.

7. Edith Stein, *The Problem of Empathy*, 3rd ed., trans. Waltraut Stein (Washington, DC: ICS Publications, 1989), 87; Hans Jonas, *Phenomenon of Life: Toward a Philosophical Biology* (New York: Harper & Row, 1966), 91; and Thompson, *Mind in Life*, 162–165.

8. Descartes, *Meditations*, 19.

9. Ibid., 18.

10. Bloom, *How Children Learn the Meanings of Words*, 62.

11. Meltzoff and Moore, "Infant Intersubjectivity," 52.

12. Ibid., 52, 61.

13. See *The Oxford English Dictionary*, ed. John Simpson, s.v. "Manifest." The origin of the second part is more obscure, although it is of the same root as *infestus* or "hostile."

14. Augustine, *Confessions* 6.9.14–15. Chadwick translates *manifestum* here as "red-handed," but the crowd did have the false belief that it had caught him in the act of committing the crime.

15. Wittgenstein, *Remarks on the Philosophy of Psychology*, vol. 2, §356.

16. On aspect perception, see Mulhall, *On Being in the World*.

17. He writes, "Spontaneous—this word stresses the fact that the appearance of an animal may change from one moment to the next with a change in internal conditions; and that this alternation takes place involuntarily, so that the animal does not simulate moods, but its actual moods are infallibly reproduced in its appearance." Portmann, *Animal Forms and Patterns*, 197.

18. Ibid., 187.

19. Henry, *Material Phenomenology*, trans. Scott Davidson (New York: Fordham University Press, 2008), 132–133.

20. Noë, *Action in Perception*, 164. For the inseparability of motility and perception, see also Drew Leder, *The Absent Body* (Chicago: University of Chicago Press, 1990), 17–20.

21. Noë, *Action in Perception*, 29.

22. Austin, "Other Minds," 108–109.

23. Nietzsche, *The Will to Power*, trans. Walter Kaufmann and R. J. Hollingdale (New York: Random House, 1967), §492.

24. See 4.5 of this volume and Heidegger, *Fundamental Concepts*, 205.

25. Wittgenstein, *Philosophical Investigations*, §285.

26. Nietzsche, *Human, All Too Human: A Book for Free Spirits*, trans. Marion Faber and Stephen Lehmann (Lincoln: University of Nebraska Press, 1984), no. 216.

27. Andrew N. Meltzoff and M. Keith Moore, "Imitation in Newborn Infants: Exploring the Range of Gestures Imitated and the Underlying Mechanisms," *Developmental Psychology* 25 (1989): 954–962.

28. Sellars writes, "Yet the essentially social character of conceptual thinking comes clearly to mind when we recognize that there is no thinking apart from common standards of correctness and relevance, which relate what *I do* think to what *anyone ought to* think. The contrast between '*I*' and 'anyone' is essential to rational thought." "Philosophy and the Scientific Image of Man," 16–17.

29. Williams, *Blind Obedience*, 106–107, and *Wittgenstein, Mind, and Meaning*, 193.

30. Augustine, *Confessions* 6.8.13. Translation modified.

31. On hylomorphism, see Aristotle, *On the Soul* 2.1 and *Metaphysics* 8.6. For instructive commentary, see Kosman, *Activity of Being*, 87–121.

32. Nietzsche, *The Antichrist*, no. 14, in *Portable Nietzsche*, ed. and trans. Walter Kaufmann (New York: Viking Penguin, 1954), 580. As this quotation suggests, Nietzsche's mechanism reflects the trends of his age. See Christian Emden, *Nietzsche on Language, Consciousness, and the Body* (Urbana, IL: University of Illinois Press, 2005), 82–87.

33. Nietzsche, *Beyond Good and Evil: Prelude to a Philosophy of the Future*, trans. Walter Kaufmann (New York: Vintage Books, 1989), §192.

34. Chalmers, *The Conscious Mind: In Search of a Fundamental Theory* (New York: Oxford University Press, 1996), 96.

35. Chalmers, *Philosophy of Mind: Classical and Contemporary Readings*, ed. David Chalmers (Oxford: Oxford University Press, 2002), 653. For the problem of other minds, he includes only a reading from Russell with the following comments: "Bertrand Russell ... argues that our belief in other minds is grounded in an *analogy* with our own case: roughly, that others are broadly similar to ourselves, that we have minds, so that others have minds. This raises many questions (should one accept an analogy based only on a single case?), but it is far from obvious what the alternatives are." See also Chalmers, *The Conscious Mind*, 246.

36. See Thompson, *Mind in Life*, 230–234.

37. Searle, "Collective Intentions," 97.

38. Searle, *Intentionality*, 230.

39. Davidson, "Meaning, Truth, and Evidence," 58.

40. On this point, see my article, "Unmasking the Person," *International Philosophical Quarterly* 50 (2010): 447–460, at 453–459.

41. Sokolowski, *Introduction to Phenomenology*, 14.

42. Noë, *Action in Perception*, 164.

43. Evan Thompson notes that Aristotle, unlike Descartes, does not develop first-person accounts for things; although he has a more robust sense of life, it is not complemented with a phenomenology of personal experience. *Mind in Life*, 228–229. I think the phenomenology is implicit in the Aristotelian understanding, and thinkers like Augustine draw it out in a way that avoids the Cartesian egocentric predicament.

44. For a summary of Augustine's speculation on this question, see Gerard O'Daly, *Augustine's Philosophy of Mind* (Berkley, CA: University of California Press, 1987), 80–84.

9 Epistemology: Disambiguating Ostension

1. Descartes, "Letter to Mersenne, 21 January 1641," CSM III, 168–169.

2. Devitt and Sterelny, *Language and Reality: An Introduction to the Philosophy of Language*, 2nd ed. (Cambridge, MA: MIT Press, 1999), 90–93.

3. Wittgenstein, *Philosophical Investigations*, p. 223.

4. Quine recognizes, though exaggerates, the phenomenon: "Vagueness is of the essence of the first phase of word learning." *Word and Object*, 85. He treats vagueness principally in terms of a term's extension (125–129). Sokolowski discusses vagueness in terms of thinking as a deficiency in clarity and distinctness. *Introduction to Phenomenology*, 105–108.

5. See Aristotle, *Nicomachean Ethics* 2.1.

6. McDowell, *Mind and World*, 91.

7. Mill, *On Liberty* (Upper Saddle River, NJ: Prentice-Hall, 1997), 72.

8. Aquinas, *Summa theologiae*, English Dominicans translation (New York: Benzinger Brothers, 1947), I–II, q. 94, a. 2. On the importance of inclinations for human nature, see Kenneth L. Schmitz, *Person and Psyche* (Arlington, VA: The Institute for Psychological Sciences Press, 2009), 17–32.

9. Thompson, *Life and Action*, 68–76.

10. *Intention*, section 4.

11. Ralph Waldo Emerson, "The Over-Soul," in *The Selected Writings*, ed. Brooks Atkinson (New York: Modern Library, 1940), 267. To be sure, he has in mind some kind of impersonal world soul, which he terms God or Jove. Against this idealism, I agree with Aristotle that there's no need to suggest that the third thing, our common nature, is a separately existing thing. Our common nature exists only in our individual realizations of it.

12. Quine, "Ontological Relativity," 34.

13. Ibid.

14. Aristotle, *Physics* 2.8, 198b33–34.

15. Quine, "Ontological Relativity," 31.

16. Husserl, *Logical Investigations*, vol. 2, 784–786.

17. Nietzsche, *The Gay Science*, trans. Walter Kaufmann (New York: Vintage Books, 1974), 218.

18. Wittgenstein, *The Blue and Brown Books*, 175 (my emphasis). See also P. M. S. Hacker, *Insight and Illusion: Themes in the Philosophy of Wittgenstein*, rev. ed. (Oxford: Clarendon Press, 1986), 186.

19. Kuhn, *The Essential Tension*, 310.

20. Burnyeat, "Wittgenstein and Augustine *De magistro*," 23. In a similar vein, see Bloom, *How Children Learn the Meanings of Words*, 84.

21. Wittgenstein, *Philosophical Investigations*, §6.

22. Aristotle, *Physics* 2.1, 193a30.

23. On shape as the principal property at work in identification, see Sokolowski, *Phenomenology of the Human Person*, 108–112.

24. Descartes, *Meditations*, 20.

25. Ibid., 22.

26. Gassendi, "Fifth Set of Objections," CSM II, 191.

27. Descartes, "Fifth Set of Replies," CSM II, 248. Gassendi had addressed Descartes as "O Mind," and Descartes addresses him in kind.

28. Kripke, *Naming and Necessity*, 119.

29. Plato, *Cratylus*, 439b.

30. Putnam, "The Meaning of 'Meaning,'" 227–229.

31. Plato, *Phaedrus*, trans. Alexander Nehemas and Paul Woodruff, in *Complete Works*, 263a.

10 Metaphysics: Movement, Manifestation, and Language

1. Alexander Pope, "Essay on Man," in *The Poetical Works of Alexander Pope* (New York: Thomas Y. Crowell, 1896), II.35–36.

2. *Annie Hall* (dir. Woody Allen, 1977).

3. Plato, *Sophist*, 254c–257a.

4. Quine, *The Roots of Reference*, 44–45.

5. Perhaps this is what Plato had in mind when he spoke of the great and the small as underlying the five great kinds.

6. Hume, *Enquiry Concerning Human Understanding*, sec. III, 24.

7. Plato, *Sophist*, 249b.

8. Ibid., 249c.

9. Ibid., 248e–249a.

10. Leibniz, *Monadology*, in *Philosophical Essays*, trans. Roger Ariew and Daniel Garber (Indianapolis: Hackett, 1989), sec. 17. Searle's famous Chinese room argument against strong artificial intelligence employs a similar thought experiment. Searle, "Minds, Brains, and Programs," *Behavioral and Brain Sciences* 3 (1980): 417–424.

11. Leibniz, *Monadology*, sec. 7.

12. Wittgenstein, *Philosophical Investigations*, §284.

13. Nietzsche, *The Gay Science*, 38.

14. Husserl, *Logical Investigations*, vol. 1, 90–211.

15. Ibid., vol. 2, 665–851.

16. Heidegger, *Plato's "Sophist,"* trans. Richard Rojcewicz and André Schuwer (Bloomington: Indiana University Press, 1997), 338.

17. Ibid., 401.

18. See Heidegger, *Zollikon Seminars*, 155.

19. Ricoeur and Changeux, *What Makes Us Think?*, 202.

20. Ibid., 47.

21. Noë, *Action in Perception*, 222. Further support for the Searle–Noë thesis concerning consciousness correlation can be found in the work of biophysicist Robert Shulman, whose research on brain metabolism shows that the entire brain is active independent of "sensory and cognitive input." *Brain Imaging: What It Can (and Cannot) Tell Us about Consciousness* (Oxford: Oxford University Press, 2013), 94, 75–113.

22. Sokolowski, *Phenomenology of the Human Person*, 225–237.

23. Ibid., 198–202. His analysis is rooted in the investigations of James J. Gibson, *The Ecological Approach to Visual Perception* (Hillsdale, NJ: Erlbaum, 1986).

24. Hawking and Mlodinow, *The Grand Design* (New York: Bantam Books, 2010), 46.

25. Ibid., 46–47.

26. Noë, *Action in Perception*, 229.

27. Thompson, *Life and Action*, esp. chapters 2–4.

28. Fitch, "Nano-intentionality: A Defense of Intrinsic Intentionality," *Biology and Philosophy* 23 (2008): 157–177.

29. For Aristotle and Augustine, too, there is an even higher way of being an animal: the life of the divinity.

30. Augustine, *Free Choice of the Will* 1.7.14.59.

31. About metabolism, Hans Jonas notes that the organism maintains itself by maintaining a dynamic relation to what is other: "In this remarkable mode of being, the material parts of which the organism consists at a given instant are ... only temporary, passing contents whose joint material identity does not coincide with the identity of the whole which they enter and leave, and which sustains its own identity by the very act of foreign matter passing through its spatial system, the living form." *The Phenomenon of Life*, 75–76. See Terrence Deacon, *Incomplete Nature: How Mind Emerged from Matter* (New York: W. W. Norton, 2011), 468–474.

32. Schrödinger, *What Is Life? The Physical Aspect of the Living Cell* (Cambridge: Cambridge University Press, 1967), 73.

33. Jonas, *The Phenomenon of Life*, 104–107; Deacon, 474–480.

34. Portmann, *Animal Forms and Patterns*, 197.

35. Robert Sokolowski writes, "The ability to deal with the absent is a constitutive element in rationality." *Phenomenology of the Human Person*, 136. Coming to a similar insight from a different angle, Terrence Deacon says that relatedness to absence is a defining feature of life in general and mind in particular: "This paradoxical intrinsic quality of existing with respect to something missing, separate, and possibly nonexistent is irrelevant when it comes to inanimate things, but *it is a defining property of life and mind.*" *Incomplete Nature*, 3.

36. Davidson, "Seeing Through Language," 135.

37. Heidegger, *On the Way to Language*, 122.

38. Aristotle, "Melissus, Xenophanes, and Gorgias," trans. T. Loveday and E. S. Forster, in *The Complete Works of Aristotle*, 980b4–8. Gorgias' own texts do not survive; this is a summary written by a later Aristotelian and included in the Aristotelian corpus.

39. Brontë, *Jane Eyre* (New York: Carleton Publisher, 1864), 153.

40. Aristotle, "Melissus, Xenophanes, and Gorgias," 980b10–15.

41. Wittgenstein, *Big Typescript*, 45.

42. Borg, "Intention-Based Semantics," in *The Oxford Handbook of the Philosophy of Language*, ed. Ernest Lepore and Barry C. Smith (Oxford: Clarendon Press, 2006), 261.

43. Wittgenstein, *Big Typescript*, 40.

44. Nietzsche, "Truth and Lies in an Extra-Moral Sense," in *Philosophy and Truth: Selections from Nietzsche's Notebooks of the Early 1870s*, ed. and trans. Daniel Breazeale (New York: Humanity Books, 1990). Maudemarie Clark provides an influential analysis of this essay in *Nietzsche on Truth and Philosophy* (Cambridge: Cambridge University Press, 1990), 63–93. I would add that the central ideas of this unpublished text appear in condensed form in Nietzsche's *Human, All Too Human*, §11.

45. For this example, see Paul Bloom, "Children Think before They Speak," *Nature* 430 (2004): 410–411.

46. Aristotle, *Physics* 2.1, 193a3–9.

47. Hegel, *Science of Logic*, trans. A. V. Miller (Atlantic Highlands, NJ: Humanities Press International, 1989), 67–78.

48. See Clarke, "The 'We Are' of Interpersonal Dialogue as the Starting Point for Metaphysics," in *Explorations in Metaphysics: Being, God, Person* (Notre Dame, IN: University of Notre Dame Press, 1994), 31–44.

49. Damasio, *Descartes' Error: Emotion, Reason, and the Human Brain* (New York: A Grosset/Putnam Book, 1994), 248.

50. Lewontin, *The Triple Helix: Gene, Organism, and Environment* (Cambridge, MA: Harvard University Press, 2000), 3.

51. Sellars, "Philosophy and the Scientific Image of Man," 7–8, 15.

52. Ibid., 7.

53. Ibid., 20.

54. Ibid.

55. Kuhn, *The Essential Tension*, 313.

56. Cf. Sellars, "Philosophy and the Scientific Image of Man," 8, 40.

Conclusion: The Origin of the Human Conversation

1. Wittgenstein, *Culture and Value*, 48.

2. Quine, *Theories and Things* (Cambridge, MA: Harvard University Press, 1981), 192.

3. See *The Oxford English Dictionary*, ed. John Simpson, s.v. "Converse."

4. Plato, *Theaetetus*, 174b. Translation modified.

5. Descartes, "Third Set of Objections with Replies," CSM II, 126. Descartes had little patience for Hobbes, as his reply to this point reveals. He writes to Mersenne, April 21, 1641, "I did not think I should have made my Replies to the Englishman [i.e., Hobbes] any longer, since his objections seemed so implausible to me that to answer them at greater length would have been giving them too much importance" (CSM III, p. 180).

6. I take the phrase "human conversation" from Michael Oakeshott. See "The Voice of Poetry in the Conversation of Mankind," in *Rationalism in Politics and Other Essays*, new ed. (Indianapolis, IN: Liberty Press, 1991), 488–541.

7. Wittgenstein, *The Blue and Brown Books*, 81.

Bibliography

Ambrose. "On the Duties of the Clergy." Trans. H. de Romestin, E. de Romestin, and H. T. F. Duckworth. In *Nicene and Post-Nicene Fathers, Second Series*, vol. 10, ed. Philip Schaff and Henry Wace. Buffalo, NY: Christian Literature Publishing, 1896.

Anscombe, G. E. M. *Intention*. Ithaca, NY: Cornell University Press, 1969.

Aquinas, Thomas. *Aristotle: On Interpretation*. Trans. Jean T. Oesterle. Milwaukee: Marquette University Press, 1962.

Aquinas, Thomas. *On Truth (De veritate)*. Trans. Robert W. Mulligan, SJ, James V. McGlynn, SJ, and Robert W. Schmidt, SJ. Indianapolis: Hackett, 1994.

Aquinas, Thomas. *Summa theologiae*. English Dominicans translation. New York: Benzinger Brothers, 1947.

Arbib, Michael. *How the Brain Got Language: The Mirror System Hypothesis*. Oxford: Oxford University Press, 2012.

Arendt, Hannah. *Love and Saint Augustine*. Ed. and trans. Joanna Vecchiarelli Scott and Judith Chelius Stark. Chicago: University of Chicago Press, 1996.

Aristotle. *Categories*. Trans. J. L. Ackrill. In *The Complete Works of Aristotle: The Revised Oxford Translation*. Ed. Jonathan Barnes. Princeton, NJ: Princeton University Press, 1984. *Categoriae et Liber De Interpretatione*. Ed. L. Minio-Paluello. Oxford: E Typographeo Clarendoniano, 1949.

Aristotle. *De interpretatione*. Trans. J. L. Ackrill. In *The Complete Works of Aristotle: The Revised Oxford Translation*. Ed. Jonathan Barnes. Princeton, NJ: Princeton University Press, 1984. *Categoriae et Liber De Interpretatione*. Ed. L. Minio-Paluello. Oxford: E Typographeo Clarendoniano, 1949.

Aristotle. *Eudemian Ethics*. Trans. J. Solomon. In *The Complete Works of Aristotle: The Revised Oxford Translation*. Ed. Jonathan Barnes. Princeton, NJ: Princeton University Press, 1984. *Ethica Eudemia*. Ed. Franciscus Susemihl. Lipsiae: In aedibus B. G. Teubneri, 1884.

Aristotle. "Melissus, Xenophanes, and Gorgias." Trans. T. Loveday and E. S. Forster. In *The Complete Works of Aristotle: The Revised Oxford Translation*. Ed. Jonathan Barnes. Princeton, NJ: Princeton University Press, 1984.

Aristotle. *Metaphysics*. Trans. W. D. Ross. In *The Complete Works of Aristotle: The Revised Oxford Translation*. Ed. Jonathan Barnes. Princeton, NJ: Princeton University Press, 1984. *Aristotle's Metaphysics*. Ed. W. D. Ross. Oxford: Clarendon Press, 1958.

Aristotle. *Movement of Animals*. Trans. A. S. L. Farquharson. In *The Complete Works of Aristotle: The Revised Oxford Translation*. Ed. Jonathan Barnes. Princeton, NJ: Princeton University Press, 1984. *Aristotle's* De Motu Animalium. Ed. Martha Craven Nussbaum. Princeton: Princeton University Press, 1978.

Aristotle. *Nicomachean Ethics*. Trans. W. D. Ross and J. O. Urmson. In *The Complete Works of Aristotle: The Revised Oxford Translation*. Ed. Jonathan Barnes. Princeton, NJ: Princeton University Press, 1984. *Ethica Nicomachea*. Ed. I. Bywater. Oxford: E Typographeo Clarendoniano, 1894.

Aristotle. *On the Soul*. Trans. J. A. Smith. In *The Complete Works of Aristotle: The Revised Oxford Translation*. Ed. Jonathan Barnes. Princeton, NJ: Princeton University Press, 1984. *De Anima*. Ed. W. D. Ross. Oxford: E Typographeo Clarendoniano, 1956.

Aristotle. *Physics*. Trans. R. P. Hardie and R. K. Gaye. In *The Complete Works of Aristotle: The Revised Oxford Translation*. Ed. Jonathan Barnes. Princeton, NJ: Princeton University Press, 1984. *Physica*. Ed. W. D. Ross. Oxford: E Typographeo Clarendoniano, 1950.

Aristotle. *Poetics*. Trans. I. Bywater. In *The Complete Works of Aristotle: The Revised Oxford Translation*. Ed. Jonathan Barnes. Princeton, NJ: Princeton University Press, 1984. *De Arte Poetica Liber*. Ed. Rudolfus Kassel. Oxford: E Typographeo Clarendoniano, 1965.

Aristotle. *Politics*. Trans. B. Jowett. In *The Complete Works of Aristotle: The Revised Oxford Translation*. Ed. Jonathan Barnes. Princeton, NJ: Princeton University Press, 1984. *Aristoteles' Politik*. Ed. Alois Dreizehnter. München: Wilhelm Fink Verlag, 1970.

Aristotle. *Posterior Analytics*. Trans. Jonathan Barnes. In *The Complete Works of Aristotle: The Revised Oxford Translation*. Ed. Jonathan Barnes. Princeton, NJ: Princeton University Press, 1984. *Prior and Posterior Analytics*. Ed. W. D. Ross. Oxford: Clarendon Press, 1965.

Aristotle. *Progression of Animals*. Trans. A. S. L. Farquharson. In *The Complete Works of Aristotle: The Revised Oxford Translation*. Ed. Jonathan Barnes. Princeton, NJ: Princeton University Press, 1984. *De animalium incessu*. Ed. W. Jaeger. Leipzig: Teubner, 1913.

Aristotle. *Sense and Sensibilia*. Trans. J. I. Beare. In *The Complete Works of Aristotle: The Revised Oxford Translation*. Ed. Jonathan Barnes. Princeton, NJ: Princeton University Press, 1984. *Parva Naturalia*. Ed. David Ross. Oxford: Clarendon Press, 1955.

Aristotle. *Topics*. Trans. W. A. Pickard-Cambridge. In *The Complete Works of Aristotle: The Revised Oxford Translation*. Ed. Jonathan Barnes. Princeton, NJ: Princeton University Press, 1984. *Topica et Sophistici Elenchi*. Ed. W. D. Ross. Oxford: E Typographeo Clarendoniano, 1963.

Armstrong, David F., William C. Stokoe, and Sherman E. Wilcox. *Gesture and the Nature of Language*. Cambridge: Cambridge University Press, 1995.

Armstrong, David F., and Sherman E. Wilcox. *The Gestural Origin of Language*. Oxford: Oxford University Press, 2007.

Arnauld, Antoine. "Fourth Set of Objections." In *The Philosophical Writings of Descartes*, vol. 2, trans. John Cottingham, Robert Stoothoff, and Dugald Murdoch, 139–153. Cambridge: Cambridge University Press, 1984.

Arthos, John. *The Inner Word in Gadamer's Hermeneutics*. Notre Dame, IN: University of Notre Dame Press, 2009.

Augustine. *The City of God*. Trans. Henry Bettenson. New York: Penguin, 1984. *De civitate Dei*. Turnholti: Typographi Brepols, 1955.

Augustine. *Confessions*. Trans. Henry Chadwick. Oxford: Oxford University Press, 1991. *Confessionum libri XIII*. Ed. Lucas Verheijen, O.S.A. Turnholti: Typographi Brepoli, 1981.

Augustine. *The Divination of Demons*. Trans. Ruth Wentworth Brown. In *Treatises on Marriage and Other Subjects*. Ed. Roy J. Deferrari. New York: The Fathers of the Church, 1955. *De divinatione daemonvm*. Ed. Joseph Zycha. Vindobonae: F. Tempsky, 1900.

Augustine. *De doctrina Christiana*. Trans. R. P. H. Green. Oxford: Oxford University Press, 1995. *De doctrina Christiana libri IV*. Ed. Joseph Martin. Turnholti: Typographi Brepols, 1962.

Augustine. *Free Choice of the Will*. Trans. Robert Russell, OSA. Washington, DC: The Catholic University of America Press, 1968. *De libero arbitrio libri tres*. Ed. W. M. Green. Turnholti: Typographi Brepols, 1970.

Augustine. *Greatness of Soul*. Trans. Joseph M. Colleran, C.SS.R. New York: The Newman Press, 1950. *De quantitate animae liber unus*. Ed. Wolfangus Hörmann. Vindobonae: Hoelder-Pickler-Tempsky, 1986.

Augustine. *In Psalmos* (XLI.13). In *An Augustine Synthesis*. Ed. Erich Przywara, SJ. New York: Sheed & Ward, 1936.

Augustine. *On Merit and the Forgiveness of Sins, and the Baptism of Infants*. Trans. Peter Holmes and Robert Ernest Wallis, and revised by Benjamin B. Warfield. In *Nicene and Post-Nicene Fathers, First Series*, vol. 5, ed. Philip Schaff. Buffalo, NY: Christian Literature Publishing, 1887. *De peccatorum meritis et remissione et de baptismo parvulorum ad Marcellinum libri tres*. Ed. Carl Urba and Jospeh Zycha. Vindobonae: F. Tempsky, 1913.

Augustine. *The Teacher*. In *Against the Academicians; The Teacher*. Trans. Peter King. Indianapolis, IN: Hackett, 1995. *De Magistro liber unus*. Ed. K.-D. Daur. Turnholti: Typographi Brepols, 1970.

Augustine. *The Trinity*. Trans. Stephen McKenna. Washington, DC: The Catholic University of America Press, 1963. *De trinitate libri XV*. Ed. W. J. Mountain. Turnholti: Typographi Brepols, 1968.

Austin, J. L. "Other Minds." In *Philosophical Papers*, 3rd ed. Ed. J. O. Urmson and G. J. Warnock. Oxford: Oxford University Press, 1979.

Austin, J. L. *Sense and Sensibilia*. Ed. G. J. Warnock. Oxford: Clarendon Press, 1962.

Avramides, Anita. *Other Minds*. London: Routledge, 2001.

Barbaras, Renaud. *The Being of the Phenomenon: Merleau-Ponty's Ontology*. Trans. Ted Toadvine and Leonard Lawlor. Bloomington: Indiana University Press, 2004.

Beere, Jonathan. *Doing and Being: An Interpretation of Aristotle's* Metaphysics Theta. Oxford: Oxford University Press, 2009.

Bickerton, Derek. *Language and Human Behavior*. Seattle: University of Washington Press, 1995.

Bickerton, Derek. *Language and Species*. Chicago: University of Chicago, 1990.

Bloom, Paul. "Children Think before They Speak." *Nature* 430 (2004): 410–411.

Bloom, Paul. *How Children Learn the Meanings of Words*. Cambridge, MA: MIT Press, 2000.

Bloom, Paul. "Mindreading, Communication, and the Learning of the Names for Things." *Mind and Language* 17 (2002): 37–54.

Bloom, Paul. "Précis of *How Children Learn the Meanings of Words*." *Behavioral and Brain Sciences* 24 (2001): 1095–1103.

Bloom, Paul. "Theories of Word Learning: Rationalist Alternatives to Associationism." In *Handbook of Child Language Acquisition*, ed. William C. Ritchie and Tej K. Bhatia, 249–278. San Diego: Academic Press, 1999.

Bloom, Paul. "Word Learning, Intentions, and Discourse." *Journal of the Learning Sciences* 14 (2005): 311–314.

Borg, Emma. "Intention-Based Semantics." In *The Oxford Handbook of the Philosophy of Language*, ed. Ernest Lepore and Barry C. Smith, 250–266. Oxford: Clarendon Press, 2006.

Bråten, Stein. "Intersubjective Communion and Understanding: Development and Perturbation." In *Intersubjective Communication and Emotion in Early Ontogeny*, ed. Stein Bråten, 372–382. Cambridge: Cambridge University Press, 1999.

Brittain, Charles. "Non-Rational Perception in the Stoics and Augustine." In *Oxford Studies in Ancient Philosophy*, vol. 22, ed. David Sedley, 253–307. Oxford: Oxford University Press, 2002.

Brontë, Charlotte. *Jane Eyre*. New York: Carleton Publisher, 1864.

Burnell, Peter. *The Augustinian Person*. Washington, DC: The Catholic University of America Press, 2005.

Burnyeat, Myles. "Wittgenstein and Augustine *De magistro*." *Proceedings of the Aristotelian Society, Supplementary Volumes* 61 (1987): 1–24.

Butterworth, George. "Pointing as the Royal Road to Language." In *Pointing: Where Language, Culture, and Cognition Meet*, ed. Sotaro Kita, 9–33. Mahwah, NJ: Erlbaum, 2003.

Cartmill, Erica A., Sian Beilock, and Susan Goldin-Meadow. "A Word in the Hand: Action, Gesture, and Mental Representation in Humans and Non-human Primates." *Philosophical Transactions of the Royal Society of London, Series B: Biological Sciences* 367 (2012): 129–143.

Cavell, Stanley. *The Claim of Reason: Wittgenstein, Skepticism, Morality, and Tragedy*. New York: Oxford University Press, 1979.

Cavell, Stanley. *In Quest of the Ordinary: Lines of Skepticism and Romanticism*. Chicago: University of Chicago Press, 1988.

Chalmers, David. *The Conscious Mind: In Search of a Fundamental Theory*. New York: Oxford University Press, 1996.

Chalmers, David. *Philosophy of Mind: Classical and Contemporary Readings*. Oxford: Oxford University Press, 2002.

Chomsky, Noam. *Aspects of the Theory of Syntax*. Cambridge, MA: MIT Press, 1965.

Clark, Eve V. *First Language Acquisition*, 2nd ed. Cambridge: Cambridge University Press, 2009.

Clark, Maudemarie. *Nietzsche on Truth and Philosophy*. Cambridge: Cambridge University Press, 1990.

Clarke, W. Norris, SJ. "The 'We Are' of Interpersonal Dialogue as the Starting Point for Metaphysics." In *Explorations in Metaphysics: Being, God, Person*. Notre Dame, IN: University of Notre Dame Press, 1994.

Corballis, Michael C. *From Hand to Mouth: The Origins of Language*. Princeton, NJ: Princeton University Press, 2002.

Corballis, Michael C. *The Recursive Mind: The Origins of Human Language, Thought, and Civilization*. Princeton, NJ: Princeton University Press, 2011.

Dahl, Roald. *Charlie and the Chocolate Factory*. Illustrated by Quentin Blake. New York: Alfred A. Knopf, 2001.

Damasio, Antonio. *Descartes' Error: Emotion, Reason, and the Human Brain*. New York: A Grosset/Putnam Book, 1994.

Davidson, Donald. "Dialectic and Dialogue." In *Truth, Language, and History*. Oxford: Clarendon Press, 2005.

Davidson, Donald. "The Emergence of Thought." In *Subjective, Intersubjective, Objective*. Oxford: Clarendon Press, 2001.

Davidson, Donald. "Gadamer and Plato's *Philebus*." In *The Philosophy of Hans-Georg Gadamer*, ed. Lewis Edwin Hahn, 421–432. Chicago: Open Court, 1997.

Davidson, Donald. *Inquiries into Truth and Interpretation*. Oxford: Oxford University Press, 1984.

Davidson, Donald. "Meaning, Truth, and Evidence." In *Truth, Language, and History*. Oxford: Clarendon Press, 2005.

Davidson, Donald. *Plato's Philebus*. New York: Garland, 1990.

Davidson, Donald. "Rational Animals." In *Subjective, Intersubjective, Objective*. Oxford: Clarendon Press, 2001.

Davidson, Donald. "Reply to W. V. Quine." In *The Philosophy of Donald Davidson*, ed. Lewis Edwin Hahn, 80–86. Chicago: Open Court, 1999.

Davidson, Donald. "The Second Person." In *Subjective, Intersubjective, Objective*. Oxford: Clarendon Press, 2001.

Davidson, Donald. "Seeing Through Language." In *Truth, Language, and History*. Oxford: Clarendon Press, 2005.

Davidson, Donald. "The Third Man." In *Truth, Language, and History*. Oxford: Clarendon Press, 2005.

Deacon, Terrence. *Incomplete Nature: How Mind Emerged from Matter*. New York: W. W. Norton, 2011.

Deacon, Terrence. *The Symbolic Species: The Co-evolution of Language and the Brain*. New York: W. W. Norton, 1997.

Descartes, René. *Discourse on Method*. In *The Philosophical Writings of Descartes*, vol. 1. Trans. John Cottingham, Robert Stoothoff, and Dugald Murdoch. Cambridge: Cambridge University Press, 1984.

Descartes, René. "Fifth Set of Replies." In *The Philosophical Writings of Descartes*, vol. 2. Trans. John Cottingham, Robert Stoothoff, and Dugald Murdoch. Cambridge: Cambridge University Press, 1984.

Descartes, René. "Fourth Set of Replies." In *The Philosophical Writings of Descartes*, vol. 2. Trans. John Cottingham, Robert Stoothoff, and Dugald Murdoch. Cambridge: Cambridge University Press, 1984.

Descartes, René. "Letter to Hyperaspistes, August 1641." In *The Philosophical Writings of Descartes*, vol. 3. Trans. John Cottingham, Robert Stoothoff, Dugald Murdoch, and Anthony Kenny. Cambridge: Cambridge University Press, 1991.

Descartes, René. "Letter to Mersenne, 21 January 1641." In *The Philosophical Writings of Descartes*, vol. 3. Trans. John Cottingham, Robert Stoothoff, Dugald Murdoch, and Anthony Kenny. Cambridge: Cambridge University Press, 1991.

Descartes, René. "Letter to Mersenne, 28 January 1641." In *The Philosophical Writings of Descartes*, vol. 3. Trans. John Cottingham, Robert Stoothoff, Dugald Murdoch, and Anthony Kenny. Cambridge: Cambridge University Press, 1991.

Descartes, René. "Letter to Mersenne, 21 April 1641." In *The Philosophical Writings of Descartes*, vol. 3. Trans. John Cottingham, Robert Stoothoff, Dugald Murdoch, and Anthony Kenny. Cambridge: Cambridge University Press, 1991.

Descartes, René. "Letter to More, 5 February 1649." In *The Philosophical Writings of Descartes*, vol. 3. Trans. John Cottingham, Robert Stoothoff, Dugald Murdoch, and Anthony Kenny. Cambridge: Cambridge University Press, 1991.

Descartes, René. "Letter to More, 15 April 1649." In *The Philosophical Writings of Descartes*, vol. 3. Trans. John Cottingham, Robert Stoothoff, Dugald Murdoch, and Anthony Kenny. Cambridge: Cambridge University Press, 1991.

Descartes, René. *Meditations on First Philosophy.* In *The Philosophical Writings of Descartes*, vol. 2. Trans. John Cottingham, Robert Stoothoff, and Dugald Murdoch. Cambridge: Cambridge University Press, 1984.

Descartes, René. "Optics." In *The Philosophical Writings of Descartes*, vol. 1. Trans. John Cottingham, Robert Stoothoff, and Dugald Murdoch. Cambridge: Cambridge University Press, 1984.

Descartes, René. *Principles of Philosophy.* In *The Philosophical Writings of Descartes*, vol. 1. Trans. John Cottingham, Robert Stoothoff, and Dugald Murdoch. Cambridge: Cambridge University Press, 1984.

Descartes, René. "Sixth Set of Replies." In *The Philosophical Writings of Descartes*, vol. 2. Trans. John Cottingham, Robert Stoothoff, and Dugald Murdoch. Cambridge: Cambridge University Press, 1984.

Descartes, René. "Third Set of Objections with Replies." In *The Philosophical Writings of Descartes*, vol. 2. Trans. John Cottingham, Robert Stoothoff, and Dugald Murdoch. Cambridge: Cambridge University Press, 1984.

Descartes, René. *The World*. In *The Philosophical Writings of Descartes*, vol. 1. Trans. John Cottingham, Robert Stoothoff, and Dugald Murdoch. Cambridge: Cambridge University Press, 1984.

Devitt, Michael, and Kim Sterelny. *Language and Reality: An Introduction to the Philosophy of Language*, 2nd ed. Cambridge, MA: MIT Press, 1999.

Dillon, Martin C. *Merleau-Ponty's Ontology*, 2nd ed. Evanston, IL: Northwestern University Press, 1997.

Dreyfus, Hubert L. "The Current Relevance of Merleau-Ponty's Phenomenology of Embodiment." *Electronic Journal of Analytic Philosophy* 4 (1996).

Dreyfus, Hubert L. *On the Internet*, 2nd ed. London: Routledge, 2009.

Eilan, Naomi, Christoph Hoerl, Teresa McCormack, and Johannes Roessler. "Preface." In *Joint Attention: Communication and Other Minds: Issues in Philosophy and Psychology*, ed. N. Eilan, et al. Oxford: Clarendon Press, 2005.

Eliot, T. S. "The Dry Salvages." In *Four Quartets*. San Diego, CA: Harcourt Brace & Co, 1943.

Emden, Christian. *Nietzsche on Language, Consciousness, and the Body*. Urbana, IL: University of Illinois Press, 2005.

Emerson, Ralph Waldo. *The Works of Ralph Waldo Emerson*, vol. 3: *Essays*. Boston: Fireside Edition, 1907.

Engelland, Chad. "Disentangling Heidegger's Transcendental Questions." *Continental Philosophy Review* 45 (2012): 77–100.

Engelland, Chad. "Unmasking the Person." *International Philosophical Quarterly* 50 (2010): 447–460.

Fitch, W. Tecumseh. "Nano-intentionality: A Defense of Intrinsic Intentionality." *Biology and Philosophy* 23 (2008): 157–177.

Fodor, Jerry. *Language of Thought*. Cambridge, MA: Harvard University Press, 1979.

Føllesdal, Dagfinn. "Triangulation." In *The Philosophy of Donald Davidson*, ed. Lewis Edwin Hahn, 719–728. Chicago: Open Court, 1999.

Gadamer, Hans-Georg. "Image and Gesture." In *The Relevance of the Beautiful and Other Essays*. Ed. Robert Bernasconi. Trans. Nicholas Walker. Cambridge: Cambridge University Press, 1986.

Gadamer, Hans-Georg. "Man and Language." In *Philosophical Hermeneutics*. Ed. and trans. David E. Linge. Berkeley: University of California Press, 1976.

Gadamer, Hans-Georg. *Plato's Dialectical Ethics: Phenomenological Interpretations Relating to the Philebus*. Trans. Robert M. Wallace. New Haven, CT: Yale University Press, 1991.

Gadamer, Hans-Georg. "The Play of Art." In *The Relevance of the Beautiful and Other Essays*. Ed. Robert Bernasconi. Trans. Nicholas Walker. Cambridge: Cambridge University Press, 1986.

Gadamer, Hans-Georg. "The Relevance of the Beautiful." In *The Relevance of the Beautiful and Other Essays*. Ed. Robert Bernasconi. Trans. Nicholas Walker. Cambridge: Cambridge University Press, 1986.

Gadamer, Hans-Georg. "Reply to Donald Davidson." In *The Philosophy of Hans-Georg Gadamer*, ed. Lewis Edwin Hahn, 434–435. Chicago: Open Court, 1997.

Gadamer, Hans-Georg. *Truth and Method*, rev. ed. Trans. Joel Weinsheimer and Donald G. Marshall. New York: Continuum, 1998.

Galilei, Galileo. "Letters on Sunspots." In *Discoveries and Opinions of Galileo*. Trans Stillman Drake. New York: Doubleday, 1957.

Gallagher, Shaun. *How the Body Shapes the Mind*. Oxford: Clarendon Press, 2005.

Gallagher, Shaun. "Neural Simulation and Social Cognition." In *Mirror Neuron Systems*, ed. J. A. Pineda, 355–371. New York: Humana Press, 2009.

Gallagher, Shaun, and Andrew N. Meltzoff. "The Earliest Sense of Self and Others: Merleau-Ponty and Recent Developmental Studies." *Philosophical Psychology* 9 (1996): 211–233.

Gallagher, Shaun, and Dan Zahavi. *The Phenomenological Mind: An Introduction to Philosophy of Mind and Cognitive Science*. London: Routledge, 2008.

Gallese, Vittorio. "Before and Below 'Theory of Mind': Embodied Simulation and the Neural Correlates of Social Cognition." *Philosophical Transactions of the Royal Society of London, Series B: Biological Sciences* 362 (2007): 659–669.

Gallese, Vittorio. "Mirror Neurons, Embodied Simulation, and the Neural Basis of Social Identification." *Psychoanalytic Dialogues* 19 (2009): 519–536.

Gallese, Vittorio. "Neuroscientific Approach to Intersubjectivity." In *The Embodied Self: Dimensions, Coherence, and Disorders*, ed. T. Fuchs, H. C. Sattel, and P. Henningsen, 77–92. Stuttgart: Schattauer, 2010.

Gassendi, Pierre. "Fifth Set of Objections." In *The Philosophical Writings of Descartes*, vol. 2. Trans. John Cottingham, Robert Stoothoff, and Dugald Murdoch. Cambridge: Cambridge University Press, 1984.

Gibson, James J. *The Ecological Approach to Visual Perception*. Hillsdale, NJ: Erlbaum, 1986.

Glass, Ian. *Revolutionaries of the Cosmos: The Astro-Physicists*. Oxford: Oxford University Press, 2006.

Goldin-Meadow, Susan. *Hearing Gesture: How Our Hands Help Us Think*. Cambridge, MA: Harvard University Press, 2003.

Goldman, Alvin I. *Simulating Minds: The Philosophy, Psychology, and Neuroscience of Mindreading*. Oxford: Oxford University Press, 2006.

Grice, H. P. *Studies in the Way of Words*. Cambridge, MA: Harvard University Press, 1989.

Grondin, Jean. *Introduction to Philosophical Hermeneutics*. New Haven, CT: Yale University Press, 1994.

Guillaume, Paul. *Imitation in Children*. Trans. Elaine P. Halperin. Chicago: University of Chicago Press, 1973.

Gusich, Gretchen. "A Phenomenology of Emotional Trauma: Around and About the Things Themselves." *Human Studies* 35 (2012): 505–518.

Habermas, Jürgen. *The Theory of Communicative Action*, vol. 2: *Lifeworld and System: A Critique of Functionalist Reason*. Trans. Thomas McCarthy. Boston: Beacon Press, 1987.

Hacker, P. M. S. *Insight and Illusion: Themes in the Philosophy of Wittgenstein*, rev. ed. Oxford: Clarendon Press, 1986.

Hacker, P. M. S. *Wittgenstein, Meaning, and Mind*. Oxford: Blackwell, 1993.

Hawking, Stephen, and Leonard Mlodinow. *The Grand Design*. New York: Bantam Books, 2010.

Hegel, Georg Wilhelm Friedrich. *Science of Logic*. Trans. A. V. Miller. Atlantic Highlands, NJ: The Humanities Press International, 1989.

Heidegger, Martin. *The Basic Problems of Phenomenology*, rev. ed. Trans. Albert Hofstadter. Bloomington: Indiana University Press, 1982.

Heidegger, Martin. *Being and Time*. Trans. John Macquarrie and Edward Robinson. New York: Harper & Row, 1962.

Heidegger, Martin. *The Fundamental Concepts of Metaphysics*. Trans. William McNeill and Nicholas Walker. Bloomington: Indiana University Press, 1995.

Heidegger, Martin. *History of the Concept of Time: Prolegomena*. Trans. Theodore Kisiel. Bloomington: Indiana University Press, 1985.

Heidegger, Martin. *Plato's "Sophist."* Trans. Richard Rojcewicz and André Schuwer. Bloomington: Indiana University Press, 1997.

Heidegger, Martin. *On the Way to Language*. Trans. Peter D. Hertz. New York: Harper & Row, 1971.

Heidegger, Martin. *Zollikon Seminars*. Ed. Medard Boss. Trans. Franz Mayr and Richard Askay. Evanston, IL: Northwestern University Press, 2001.

Henry, Michel. *Material Phenomenology*. Trans. Scott Davidson. New York: Fordham University Press, 2008.

Heraclitus. *The Art and Thought of Heraclitus: An Edition of the Fragments with Translation and Commentary*. Ed. and trans. Charles Kahn. Cambridge: Cambridge University Press, 1979.

Hopkins, Gerard Manley, SJ. "As Kingfishers Catch Fire." In *Poems of Gerard Manley Hopkins*, Ed. Robert Bridges. London: Humphrey Milford, 1918.

Hull, David. *Science as a Process: An Evolutionary Account of the Social and Conceptual Development of Science*. Chicago: University of Chicago Press, 1988.

Hume, David. *Enquiry Concerning Human Understanding*. In *Enquiries*, 3rd ed. Ed. L. A. Selby-Bigge and P. H. Nidditch. Oxford: Clarendon Press, 1975.

Humphrey, Nicholas. *Seeing Red: A Study in Consciousness*. Cambridge, MA: Harvard University Press, 2006.

Husserl, Edmund. *Cartesian Meditations: An Introduction to Phenomenology*. Trans. Dorion Cairns. The Hague: Martinus Nijhoff, 1977.

Husserl, Edmund. *Ideas Pertaining to a Pure Phenomenology and to a Phenomenological Philosophy, Second Book: Studies in the Phenomenology of Constitution*. Trans. Richard Rojcewicz and André Schuwer. Dordrecht: Kluwer Academic, 1989.

Husserl, Edmund. *Logical Investigations*, vols. 1 and 2. Trans. J. N. Findlay. Amherst, NY: Humanity Books, 2000.

Husserl, Edmund. *On the Phenomenology of the Consciousness of Internal Time (1893–1917)*. Ed. and trans. John Brough. Dordrecht: Kluwer, 1991.

Husserl, Edmund. "Tobaccology." *New Yearbook for Phenomenology and Phenomenological Research* 4 (2004): 274–283.

Iacoboni, Marco. *Mirroring People: The New Science of How We Connect with Others*. New York: Farrar, Straus & Giroux, 2008.

Irwin, Terence. *Aristotle's First Principles*. Oxford: Oxford University Press, 1988.

Jackson, B. Darrell. "The Theory of Signs in St. Augustine's *De Doctrina Christiana*." In *Augustine: A Collection of Critical Essays*, ed. R. A. Markus, 92–137. Garden City, NY: Doubleday, 1972.

Johnson, Mark. *The Body in the Mind: The Bodily Basis of Meaning, Imagination, and Reason*. Chicago: University of Chicago Press, 1987.

Johnson, Mark. *The Meaning of the Body: Aesthetics of Human Understanding*. Chicago: University of Chicago Press, 2007.

Johnson, W. E. *Logic*, vol. 1. Cambridge: Cambridge University Press, 1921.

Johnston, Paul. *Wittgenstein: Rethinking the Inner*. London: Routledge, 1993.

Jonas, Hans. *The Phenomenon of Life: Toward a Philosophical Biology*. New York: Harper & Row, 1966.

Juarrero, Alicia. *Dynamics in Action: Intentional Behavior as a Complex System*. Cambridge, MA: MIT Press, 1999.

Keller, Helen. *The Story of My Life*. New York: Doubleday, 1903.

Kendon, Adam. *Gesture: Visible Action as Utterance*. Cambridge: Cambridge University Press, 2004.

Kerr, Fergus. "Augustine and Aquinas in the Light of Postmodern Thought: Other Minds Skepticism." In *Augustine and Postmodern Thought: A New Alliance against Modernity?* ed. L. Boeve, M. Lamberigts, and M. Wisse, 103–121. Leuven: Uitgeverij Peeters, 2009.

Kerr, Fergus. *Theology after Wittgenstein*. Oxford: Blackwell, 1986.

Kerr, Fergus. *"Work on Oneself": Wittgenstein's Philosophical Psychology*. Arlington, VA: The Institute for the Psychological Sciences Press, 2008.

Kirwan, Christopher. "Augustine on the Nature of Speech." In *Language: Companions to Ancient Thought 3*, ed. Stephen Everson, 188–211. Cambridge: Cambridge University Press, 1994.

Kirwan, Christopher. "Augustine's Philosophy of Language." In *The Cambridge Companion to Augustine*, ed. Eleonore Stump and Norman Kretzmann, 186–204. Cambridge: Cambridge University Press, 2001.

Kosman, Aryeh. *The Activity of Being: An Essay on Aristotle's Ontology*. Cambridge, MA: Harvard University Press, 2013.

Kripke, Saul. *Naming and Necessity*. Oxford: Blackwell, 1980.

Kuhn, Thomas. *The Essential Tension*. Chicago: University of Chicago Press, 1977.

Landau, Barbara, and Lila R. Gleitman. *Language and Experience: Evidence from the Blind Child*. Cambridge, MA: Harvard University Press, 1985.

Leder, Drew. *The Absent Body*. Chicago: University of Chicago Press, 1990.

Leibniz, Gottfried Wilhelm. *Monadology*. In *Philosophical Essays*. Trans. Roger Ariew and Daniel Garber. Indianapolis: Hackett, 1989.

Lewontin, Richard. *The Triple Helix: Gene, Organism, and Environment*. Cambridge, MA: Harvard University Press, 2000.

Lieven, Elena. "Crosslinguistic and Crosscultural Aspects of Language Addressed to Children." In *Input and Interaction in Language Acquisition*, ed. C. Gallaway and B. J. Richards, 56–73. Cambridge: Cambridge University Press, 1994.

Locke, John. *An Essay Concerning Human Understanding*. New York: Dover, 1959.

MacIntyre, Alisdair. *Dependent Rational Animals: Why Human Beings Need the Virtues*. Chicago: Open Court, 1999.

Malcolm, Norman. *Ludwig Wittgenstein: A Memoir*, 2nd ed. Oxford: Oxford University Press, 2001.

Malpas, Jeff. "Gadamer, Davidson, and the Ground of Understanding." In *Gadamer's Century: Essays in Honor of Hans-Georg Gadamer*, ed. Jeff Malpas, Ulrich Arnswald, and Jens Kertscher, 195–215. Cambridge, MA: MIT Press, 2002.

Mann, Wolfgang-Rainer. *The Discovery of Things: Aristotle's Categories and Their Context*. Princeton, NJ: Princeton University Press, 2000.

Marion, Jean-Luc. *In the Self's Place: The Approach of Saint Augustine*. Trans. Jeffrey L. Kosky. Palo Alto, CA: Stanford University Press, 2012.

Matthews, Gareth B. *Augustine*. Malden, MA: Blackwell, 2005.

Matthews, Gareth B. "Augustine and Descartes on Minds and Bodies." In *The Augustinian Tradition*, ed. Matthews, 222–232. Berkley: University of California Press, 1998.

Matthews, Gareth B. "Augustine and Descartes on the Souls of Animals." In *From Soul to Self*, ed. M. James C. Crabbe. London: Routledge, 1999.

Matthews, Gareth B. *Thought's Ego in Augustine and Descartes*. Ithaca, NY: Cornell University Press, 1992.

McDowell, John. "Gadamer and Davidson on Understanding and Relativism." In *Gadamer's Century: Essays in Honor of Hans-Georg Gadamer*, ed. Jeff Malpas, Ulrich Arnswald, and Jens Kertscher, 173–193. Cambridge, MA: MIT Press, 2002.

McDowell, John. *Mind and World*. Cambridge, MA: Harvard University Press, 1994.

McGinn, Marie. *Sense and Certainty: A Dissolution of Skepticism*. Oxford: Basil Blackwell, 1989.

McNeill, David. *Gesture and Thought*. Chicago: University of Chicago Press, 2005.

Meltzoff, Andrew N., and M. Keith Moore. "Imitation in Newborn Infants: Exploring the Range of Gestures Imitated and the Underlying Mechanisms." *Developmental Psychology* 25 (1989): 954–962.

Meltzoff, Andrew N., and M. Keith Moore. "Infant Intersubjectivity: Imitation, Identity, and Intention." In *Intersubjective Communication and Emotion in Early Ontogeny*, ed. Stein Bråten, 47–62. Cambridge: Cambridge University Press, 1999.

Menn, Stephen. *Descartes and Augustine*. Cambridge: Cambridge University Press, 1998.

Merleau-Ponty, Maurice. "The Child's Relations with Others." In *The Primacy of Perception*, ed. James M. Edie, 96–155. Evanston, IL: Northwestern University Press, 1964; *Les Relations avec autrui chez l'enfant*. Paris: Centre de Documentation Universitaire, 1975.

Merleau-Ponty, Maurice. *Consciousness and the Acquisition of Language*. Trans. Hugh J. Silverman. Evanston, IL: Northwestern University Press, 1973; "La Conscience et l'acquisition du langage," in *Psychologie et pédagogie de l'enfant: Cours de Sorbonne 1949–1952*, ed. Jacques Prunair. Lagrasse: Verdier, 2001.

Merleau-Ponty, Maurice. "Dialogue and the Perception of the Other." In *The Prose of the World*, ed. Claude Lefort, 131–146. Trans. John O'Neill. Evanston, IL: Northwestern University Press, 1973. "La Perception d'autrui et le dialogue." In *La Prose du Monde*, ed. Claude Lefort, 182–203. Paris: Gallimard, 1969.

Merleau-Ponty, Maurice. "Eye and Mind." In *The Primacy of Perception*, ed. James M. Edie, 159–190, 1964. Evanston, IL: Northwestern University Press; *L'Oeil et L'Esprit*. Paris: Gallimard, 1964.

Merleau-Ponty, Maurice. *Husserl and the Limits of Phenomenology: Including Texts by Edmund Husserl*. Trans. Leonard Lawlor and Bettina Bergo. Evanston, IL: Northwestern University Press, 2002. *Merleau-Ponty: Notes de cours sur* L'Origine de la géométrie *de Husserl suivi de Recherches sur la phénoménologie de Merleau-Ponty*, ed. Renaud Barbaras. Paris: Presses Universitaires de France, 1998.

Merleau-Ponty, Maurice. *Phenomenology of Perception*. Trans. Colin Smith. London: Routledge Classics, 2002. *Phénoménologie de la perception*. Paris: Gallimard, 1945.

Merleau-Ponty, Maurice. *The Structure of Behavior*. Trans. Alden L. Fisher. Boston: Beacon Press, 1963; *La Structure du Comportement*, 3rd ed. Paris: Presses Universitaires de France, 1953.

Merleau-Ponty, Maurice. *Themes from the Lectures at the Collège de France 1952–1960*. Trans. John O'Neill. Evanston, IL: Northwestern University Press, 1970; *Résumés de cours, Collège de France 1952–1960*. Paris: Gallimard, 1968.

Merleau-Ponty, Maurice. "An Unpublished Text by Maurice Merleau-Ponty: A Prospectus of His Work." Trans. Arleen B. Dallery. In *The Primacy of Perception*, ed. James M. Edie, 3–11. Evanston, IL: Northwestern University Press, 1964; "Un inédit de Maurice Merleau-Ponty." In *Parcours deux: 1951–1961*, ed. Jacques Prunair. Lagrasse: Verdier, 2000.

Merleau-Ponty, Maurice. *The Visible and the Invisible*, ed. Claude Lefort. Trans. Alphonso Lingis. Evanston, IL: Northwestern University Press, 1968; *Le Visible et l'invisible*, ed. Claude Lefort. Paris: Gallimard, 1964.

Mill, John Stuart. *On Liberty*. Upper Saddle River, NJ: Prentice-Hall, 1997.

Modrak, Deborah. *Aristotle's Theory of Language and Meaning*. Cambridge: Cambridge University Press, 2000.

Moore, G. E. "Proof of an External World." In *Philosophy in the Twentieth Century: An Anthology*, vol. 2, ed. William Barrett and Henry D. Aiken, 584–603. New York: Random House, 1962.

Mulhall, Stephen. *Inheritance and Originality: Wittgenstein, Heidegger, Kierkegaard*. Oxford: Clarendon Press, 2001.

Mulhall, Stephen. *On Being in the World: Wittgenstein and Heidegger on Seeing Aspects*. London: Routledge, 1990.

Mulhall, Stephen. *Wittgenstein's Private Language: Grammar, Nonsense, and Imagination in* Philosophical Investigations, *§§243–315*. Oxford: Clarendon Press, 2007.

Nietzsche, Friedrich. *The Antichrist*. In *Portable Nietzsche*. Ed. and trans. Walter Kaufmann. New York: Viking Penguin, 1954.

Nietzsche, Friedrich. *Beyond Good and Evil: Prelude to a Philosophy of the Future*. Trans. Walter Kaufmann. New York: Vintage Books, 1989.

Nietzsche, Friedrich. *The Gay Science*. Trans. Walter Kaufmann. New York: Vintage Books, 1974.

Nietzsche, Friedrich. *Human, All Too Human: A Book for Free Spirits*. Trans. Marion Faber and Stephen Lehmann. Lincoln: University of Nebraska Press, 1984.

Nietzsche, Friedrich. *Thus Spoke Zarathustra: A Book for All and None*. Ed. Adrian del Caro and Robert B. Pippin. Trans. Adrian del Caro. Cambridge: Cambridge University Press, 2006.

Nietzsche, Friedrich. "Truth and Lies in an Extra-Moral Sense." In *Philosophy and Truth: Selections from Nietzsche's Notebooks of the Early 1870s*. Ed. and trans. Daniel Breazeale. New York: Humanity Books, 1990.

Nietzsche, Friedrich. *The Will to Power*. Trans. Walter Kaufmann and R. J. Hollingdale. New York: Random House, 1967.

Noë, Alva. *Action in Perception*. Cambridge, MA: MIT Press, 2004.

Noë, Alva. *Varieties of Presence*. Cambridge, MA: Harvard University Press, 2012.

Noë, Alva, and Evan Thompson. "Introduction." In *Vision and Mind: Selected Readings in the Philosophy of Perception*, 1–14. Cambridge, MA: MIT Press, 2002.

Oakeshott, Michael. "The Voice of Poetry in the Conversation of Mankind." In *Rationalism in Politics and Other Essays*, new ed. Indianapolis, IN: Liberty Press, 1991.

O'Daly, Gerard. *Augustine's Philosophy of Mind*. Berkley, CA: University of California Press, 1987.

Olafson, Frederick. *What Is a Human Being? A Heideggerian View*. Cambridge: Cambridge University Press, 1995.

O'Regan, J. Kevin and Alva Noë. "A sensorimotor account of vision and visual consciousness." *Behavioral and Brain Sciences* 24 (2001): 939–1031.

Overgaard, Søren. *Wittgenstein and Other Minds: Rethinking Subjectivity and Intersubjectivity with Wittgenstein, Levinas, and Husserl*. New York: Routledge, 2007.

Pinker, Steven. *The Language Instinct: How the Mind Creates Language*. New York: HarperCollins, 1994.

Plato. *Cratylus*. Trans. C. D. C. Reeve. In *Complete Works*. Ed. John Cooper. Indianapolis, IN: Hackett , 1997.

Plato. *Phaedrus*. Trans. Alexander Nehemas and Paul Woodruff. In *Complete Works*, ed. John Cooper Indianapolis, IN: Hackett, 1997.

Plato. *Seventh Letter*. Trans. Glenn R. Morrow. In *Complete Works*. Ed. John Cooper. Indianapolis, IN: Hackett, 1997.

Plato. *Sophist*. Trans. Nicholas P. White. In *Complete Works*. Ed. John Cooper. Indianapolis, IN: Hackett, 1997.

Plato. *Theaetetus*. Trans. M. J. Levett and Myles Burnyeat. In *Complete Works*. Ed. John Cooper. Indianapolis, IN: Hackett, 1997.

Pope, Alexander. "Essay on Man." In *The Poetical Works of Alexander Pope*. New York: Thomas Y. Crowell, 1896.

Portmann, Adolf. *Animal Forms and Patterns: A Study of the Appearances of Animals*. Trans. Hella Czech. New York: Schocken Books, 1967.

Povinelli, Daniel J., Jesse M. Bering, and Steve Giambrone. "Chimpanzees' 'Pointing': Another Error of the Argument by Analogy?" In *Pointing: Where Language, Culture, and Cognition Meet*, ed. Sotaro Kita, 35–68. Mahwah, New Jersey: Erlbaum, 2003.

Pritzl, Kurt. "Aristotle's Door." In *Truth: Studies of a Robust Presence*, ed. K. Pritzl, 15–39. Washington, DC: The Catholic University of America Press, 2010.

Prufer, Thomas. *Recapitulations: Essays in Philosophy*. Washington, DC: The Catholic University of America Press, 1993.

Putnam, Hilary. "The Meaning of 'Meaning.'" In *Mind, Language, and Reality*. Cambridge: Cambridge University Press, 1975.

Quine, Willard Van Orman. "Epistemology Naturalized." In *Ontological Relativity and Other Essays*. New York: Columbia University Press, 1969.

Quine, Willard Van Orman. "Indeterminacy of Translation Again." *Journal of Philosophy* 84 (1987): 5–10.

Quine, Willard Van Orman. "Ontological Relativity." In *Ontological Relativity and Other Essays*. New York: Columbia University Press, 1969.

Quine, Willard Van Orman. *The Roots of Reference*. La Salle, IL: Open Court, 1974.

Quine, Willard Van Orman. *Theories and Things*. Cambridge, MA: Harvard University Press, 1981.

Quine, Willard Van Orman. *Word and Object*. Cambridge, MA: MIT Press, 1960.

Quintilian. *Institutio oratoria*. Trans. H. E. Butler. London: William Heinemann, 1922.

Rakoczy, Hannes, and Michael Tomasello. "The Ontogeny of Social Ontology: Steps to Shared Intentionality and Status Functions." In *Intentional Acts and Institutional Facts: Essays on John Searle's Social Ontology*, ed. Savas L. Tsohatzidis, 113–138. Dordrecht: Springer, 2007.

Ricoeur, Paul, and Jean-Pierre Changeux. *What Makes Us Think? A Neuroscientist and a Philosopher Argue about Ethics, Human Nature, and the Brain*. Trans. M. B. DeBevoise. Princeton, NJ: Princeton University Press, 2000.

Rist, John. *Augustine: Ancient Thought Baptized*. Cambridge: Cambridge University Press, 1994.

Rizzolatti, Giacomo, and Corrado Sinigaglia. *Mirrors in the Brain—How Our Minds Share Actions and Emotions*. Trans. Frances Anderson. Oxford: Oxford University Press, 2008.

Rowlands, Mark. *Body Language: Representation in Action*. Cambridge, MA: MIT Press, 2006.

Russell, Bertrand. *Human Knowledge: Its Scope and Limits*. London: Allen & Unwin, 1948.

Ryle, Gilbert. *The Concept of Mind*. New York: Barnes & Noble, 1949.

Scheler, Max. *The Nature of Sympathy*. Trans. Peter Heath. New Brunswick, NJ: Transaction Publishers, 2008.

Schrödinger, Erwin. *What is Life? The Physical Aspect of the Living Cell*. Cambridge: Cambridge University Press, 1967.

Schmitz, Kenneth L. *Person and Psyche*. Arlington, VA: The Institute for Psychological Sciences Press, 2009.

Searle, John. "Animal Minds." *Midwest Studies in Philosophy* 19 (1994): 206–219.

Searle, John. "Collective Intentions and Actions." In *Consciousness and Language*, 90–105. Cambridge: Cambridge University Press, 2002.

Searle, John. *The Construction of Social Reality*. New York: Free Press, 1995.

Searle, John. *Intentionality*. Cambridge: Cambridge University Press, 1983.

Searle, John. *Mind, Language, Society: Philosophy in the Real World*. New York: Basic Books, 1998.

Searle, John. "Minds, Brains, and Programs." *Behavioral and Brain Sciences* 3 (1980): 417–424.

Searle, John. "The Phenomenological Illusion." In *Erfahrung und Analyse*, ed. Maria E. Reicher and Johann Christian Marek, 317–336. Vienna: ÖBV & HPT, 2005.

Searle, John. *The Rediscovery of Mind*. Cambridge, MA: MIT Press, 1992.

Searle, John. "What Is an Institution?" *Journal of Institutional Economics* 1 (2005): 1–22.

Sellars, Wilfrid. "Language as Thought and as Communication." In *In the Space of Reasons: Selected Essays of Wilfrid Sellars*. Ed. Kevin Scharp and Robert B. Brandom. Cambridge, MA: Harvard University Press, 2007.

Sellars, Wilfrid. "Philosophy and the Scientific Image of Man." In *Science, Perception, and Reality*. New York: The Humanities Press, 1963.

Sellars, Wilfrid. "Some Reflections on Language Games." In *In the Space of Reasons: Selected Essays of Wilfrid Sellars*. Cambridge, MA: Harvard University Press, 2007.

Sheets-Johnstone, Maxine. *The Primacy of Movement*, 2nd ed. Amsterdam: John Benjamins, 2011.

Sheldrake, Rupert. *The Sense of Being Stared At and Other Aspects of the Extended Mind*. New York: Crown Publishers, 2003.

Shulman, Robert. *Brain Imaging: What It Can (and Cannot) Tell Us about Consciousness*. Oxford: Oxford University Press, 2013.

Sokolowski, Robert. "Husserl's Discovery of Philosophical Discourse." *Husserl Studies* 24 (2008): 167–175.

Sokolowski, Robert. *Introduction to Phenomenology*. Cambridge: Cambridge University Press, 1999.

Sokolowski, Robert. *Phenomenology of the Human Person*. New York: Cambridge University Press, 2008.

Sokolowski, Robert. *Presence and Absence: A Philosophical Investigation of Language and Being.* Bloomington: Indiana University Press, 1978.

Sperber, Dan, and Deirdre Wilson. *Relevance: Communication and Cognition,* 2nd ed. Malden, MA: Blackwell, 1995.

Stein, Edith. *The Problem of Empathy,* 3rd ed. Trans. Waltraut Stein, Waltraut. Washington, DC: ICS Publications, 1989.

Thompson, Evan. *Mind in Life: Biology, Phenomenology, and the Sciences of Mind.* Cambridge, MA: Harvard University Press, 2007.

Thompson, Michael. *Life and Action: Elementary Structures of Practice and Practical Thought.* Cambridge, MA: Harvard University Press, 2008.

Toadvine, Ted. "Merleau-Ponty's Reading of Husserl: A Chronological Overview." In *Merleau-Ponty's Reading of Husserl,* ed. Ted Toadvine and Lester Embree, 227–286. Dordrecht: Springer, 2002.

Tomasello, Michael. *Constructing a Language: A Usage-Based Theory of Language Acquisition.* Cambridge, MA: Harvard University Press, 2003.

Tomasello, Michael. "Could We Please Lose the Mapping Metaphor, Please?" *Behavioral and Brain Sciences* 24 (2001): 1119–1120.

Tomasello, Michael. *The Cultural Origins of Human Cognition.* Cambridge, MA: Harvard University Press, 1999.

Tomasello, Michael. *Origins of Human Communication.* Cambridge, MA: MIT Press, 2008.

Tomasello, Michael. *Why We Cooperate.* Cambridge, MA: MIT Press, 2009.

Tomasello, Michael, Malinda Carpenter, Josep Call, Tanya Behne, and Henrike Moll. "Understanding and Sharing Intentions: The Origins of Cultural Cognition." *Behavioral and Brain Sciences* 28 (2005): 1–17.

Trevarthen, Colwyn. "Communication and Cooperation in Early Infancy: A Description of Primary Intersubjectivity." In *Before Speech,* ed. M. Bullowa. Cambridge: Cambridge University Press, 1979.

Trevarthen, Colwyn, and P. Hubley. "Secondary Intersubjectivity: Confidence, Confiding, and Acts of Meaning in the First Year." In *Action, Gesture and Symbol: The Emergence of Language,* ed. A. Lock, 183–229. London: Academic, 1978.

Urwin, Cathy. "Dialogue and Cognitive Functioning in the Early Language Development of Three Blind Children." In *Language Acquisition in the Blind Child: Normal and Deficient,* ed. Anne E. Mill, 142–161. London: Croom Helm, 1983.

Varela, Francisco J., Evan T. Thompson, and Eleanor Rosch. *The Embodied Mind: Cognitive Science and Human Experience.* Cambridge, MA: MIT Press, 1991.

Welsh, Talia. *The Child as Natural Phenomenologist: Primal and Primary Experience in Merleau-Ponty's Psychology*. Evanston, IL: Northwestern University Press, 2013.

Wilkins, David. "Why Pointing With the Index Finger Is Not a Universal (in Sociocultural and Semiotic Terms)." In *Pointing: Where Language, Culture, and Cognition Meet*, ed. Sotaro Kita, 171–215. Mahwah, NJ: Erlbaum, 2003.

Williams, Meredith. *Blind Obedience: Paradox and Learning in the Later Wittgenstein*. London: Routledge, 2010.

Williams, Meredith. *Wittgenstein, Mind, and Meaning: Toward a Social Conception of Mind*. London: Routledge, 1999.

Wilson, Deirdre, and Dan Sperber. *Meaning and Relevance*. Cambridge: Cambridge University Press, 2012.

Wittgenstein, Ludwig. *The Big Typescript TS 213*. Ed. and trans. C. Grant Luckhardt and Maximilian A. E. Aue. Malden, MA: Blackwell, 2005.

Wittgenstein, Ludwig. *The Blue and Brown Books*. New York: Harper & Row, 1958.

Wittgenstein, Ludwig. *Culture and Value*. Ed. G. H. von Wright. Trans. Peter Winch. Chicago: University of Chicago Press, 1980.

Wittgenstein, Ludwig. *Last Writings on the Philosophy of Psychology*, vol. 2: *The Inner and the Outer 1949–1950*. Ed. G. H. von Wright and Heikki Nyman. Trans. C. G. Luckhardt and Maximilian A. E. Aue. Oxford: Blackwell, 1992.

Wittgenstein, Ludwig. *On Certainty*. Ed. G. E. M. Anscombe and G. H. von Wright. Trans. Denis Paul and G. E. M. Anscombe. New York: Harper & Row, 1969.

Wittgenstein, Ludwig. *Philosophical Investigations*, 2nd ed. Trans. G. E. M. Anscombe. Oxford: Blackwell, 1958.

Wittgenstein, Ludwig. *Remarks on the Philosophy of Psychology*, vol. 2. Ed. G. H. von Wright and Heikki Nyman. Trans. C. G. Luckhardt and M. A. E. Aue. Chicago: University of Chicago Press, 1980.

Wittgenstein, Ludwig. *Zettel*. Ed. G. E. M. Anscombe and G. H. von Wright. Trans. G. E. M. Anscombe. Berkeley: University of California Press, 1967.

Index